1st edition

40.⁰⁰

labor hist

D1535076

"Rights, Not Roses"

THE WORKING CLASS IN AMERICAN HISTORY

A list of books in the series appears at the end of this book.

"Rights, Not Roses"

Unions and the Rise of Working-Class Feminism, 1945–80

Dennis A. Deslippe

University of Illinois Press
Urbana and Chicago

Library of Congress Cataloging-in-Publication Data
Deslippe, Dennis A. (Dennis Arthur), 1961–
Rights, not roses : unions and the rise of working-class feminism,
1945–80 / Dennis A. Deslippe.
p.   cm. — (The working class in American history)
Includes bibliographical references and index.
ISBN 0-252-02519-9 (acid-free paper)
ISBN 0-252-06834-3 (pbk. : acid-free paper)
1. Women in trade-unions—United States. 2. Equal pay for equal
work—United States. 3. Sex discrimination against women—United
States. 4. Sex discrimination in employment—United States. I. Title.
II. Series.
HD6079.2.U5D47   2000
331.4′78′0973—dc21   99-6426
CIP

1 2 3 4 5 C P 5 4 3 2 1

To Alison

Contents

ACKNOWLEDGMENTS

Over the course of this project I have benefited from valuable financial, institutional, and individual support. I was fortunate to have been the recipient of the University of Iowa Graduate College's Ada Louisa Ballard Dissertation Fellowship and the Department of History's Louis Pelzer Fellowship. I am also honored to have received a Schlesinger Library of Radcliffe College's Dissertation Research Grant, the American Historical Association's Littleton-Griswold Research Grant, a Henry J. Kaiser Family Foundation Travel Research Grant from the Walter P. Reuther Archives of Labor and Urban Affairs at Wayne State University, and an American Philosophical Society Research Grant. I wish to acknowledge the assistance of Mary Bennett of the State Historical Society of Iowa, Lee Sayrs and Bob Reynolds of the George Meany Memorial Archives, Jim Quigel of Rutgers University Library, and Margaret Raucher and Thomas Featherstone of the Reuther Archives, as well as the knowledgable staff at the State Historical Society of Wisconsin, the University of Maryland Library, the Lyndon B. Johnson Presidential Library, and the Schlesinger Library at Radcliffe College.

There are many other people without whose help and encouragement this project could never have been completed. My dissertation committee at the University of Iowa, Shelton Stromquist, Linda Kerber, Ellis Hawley, Kenneth Cmiel, and Sally Kenney, offered thorough readings of draft chapters. Long after my graduate study was completed, Linda Kerber continued to take an interest in my work; she encouraged me to move beyond the details of my research and look for the larger significance of the struggle for equality. Shel Stromquist has been a model adviser: through his teaching, research, and commitment to labor history he has been a source of inspiration. He offered reassurance as I sought academic employment, encouraging me to continue to research and to publish. As I finished my graduate school years those I worked with in the Campaign to

Organize Graduate Students (now, COGS-UE Local 896) reminded me in a profound way that higher education is not shielded from the larger world, and the "real, lived experiences" of the working people I study share common ground with graduate employees who eke out a living on campuses today.

My thanks as well to those who read, offered suggestions, and encouraged me at the various stages of research and writing: Karen Beckwith, Marvin Bergman, Eileen Boris, Bob Buchanan, Dave Cohen, Patricia Cooper, Merle Davis, Elizabeth Faue, Sonia Pressman Fuentes, Christopher Johnson, Eric Karolak, Harvey Kaye, Doug Loranger, Ruth Neddleman, Joan Sangster, and Dan Swinarski. As I began the process of revising my dissertation, Nancy Gabin and Susan Hartmann generously read my manuscript and suggested revisions. Melvyn Dubofsky and the participants in his 1996 NEH Summer Seminar provided good cheer and fierce debate in equal measure; for six energetic weeks we grappled with the vexing issues surrounding labor history and, in the process, they helped to improve this manuscript. My former colleagues at Shippensburg University of Pennsylvania and my current colleagues at the Australian National University have created a collegial environment in which to teach and do research. At the University of Illinois Press, Richard Wentworth, Emily Rogers, and Carol Betts shepherded my manuscript to completion with expertise. I am enormously grateful to Dorothy Sue Cobble for her insistence that I clarify my arguments for the final revision. I owe special thanks to Alice Kessler-Harris, whose exhaustive comments, constant encouragement, and pathbreaking work have shaped my own efforts.

I imposed on others over the years more times than I care to admit, whether it was by sleeping on spare couches, getting rides to archives, or eating good meals they prepared. For all their hospitality I thank them with deep gratitude: my in-laws, Austin and Pat Kibler; my cousin, David Bruno; and friends Nick Lessins and Lydia Esparza Lessins, Bob Odenkirk, Christina Chen, and Vince Wisser. My parents, Henry and Phyllis Deslippe; my brother, Mark; and my sisters, Susan, Mary, and Anne, and their spouses and children, have all offered endearing support and love.

As I put these acknowledgments to paper on a beautiful Australian summer day I think back to that cold winter afternoon in the State Historical Society of Iowa ten years ago when I began this project as a seminar paper in women's history and Alison Kibler sat down across the table from me to work on her own research. She has never stopped doing her own work but, with boundless energy, has served as a constructive critic of this book, moved across the world with me, and, with our daughter, Therese, has been a constant, loving presence in my life.

"Rights, Not Roses"

Introduction

This is a study of how unionists embraced and fought for gender equality in the decades following World War II. Rather than view this process merely as the result of impersonal economic, social, and legal developments beyond working women's control, I focus on how women—and men—shaped gender relations in contract negotiations, politics, and the fight for equal rights legislation. By gender equality I mean the notion that traditional gender roles, those ordering men and women into social categories on the basis of their biological differences, be replaced with a new focus on an individual's talents, abilities, and ambitions irrespective of his or her sex. Such a belief has bound together mainstream, or liberal, feminists since the 1960s.

Recently historians have shaken loose the depiction of union women as invisible in the emergence of second-wave feminism. Whether considering a single union or broad national patterns of change, scholars have pointed to unionists' contributions to the campaign for equality. The changes women brought about with this new understanding of their rights have had a dramatic effect on contemporary women. Where once they were assigned to work in sex-segregated jobs under seniority and wage schemes separate from and unequal to those of men, they now expect to be able to vie with men for positions on an equal basis. The most important issues relating to women in the paid work force today, such as sexual harassment, pay equity, and pregnancy and family leave, were central concerns to unionists who first openly challenged the old system.[1]

My own treatment of the rise of working-class feminism ventures beyond the existing literature in several ways. It calls for an expanded consideration of how a newly formed consciousness took shape in the two decades following World War II. While, as scholars point out, women workers' experiences in war plants in the 1940s and their increased labor force participation in the 1950s and 1960s prompted them to challenge employment practices, the technological transformation of industrial jobs that resulted in a breakdown of established notions of appropriate women's employment played an equally important role. The law was most crucial to this process, especially Title VII of the Civil Rights Act of 1964, which banned sex discrimination in employment. Title VII proved to be the catalyst to women's expressing open support for gender equality. Unionists seized on this new legal tool to force their unions and employers to enact workplace changes.

By providing a comparative analysis of unions, I explain why organized labor's response to demands for gender equality varied so widely across unions. Women's rejection of the stratified world of men and women's work was a painful process that divided the labor movement. Men especially resisted the threat of losing their privileged positions. Depending on the industrial sector, region, and union to which they belonged, men succeeded often in thwarting implementation of federal equal employment opportunity law. Many women themselves rejected calls for equality, especially those comfortable in secure positions. Even activists demanding change exhibited varying degrees of apprehension as they left behind practices they had hitherto defended. Ultimately, however, opponents failed to stem the tide toward equality. When union women found sympathetic male leaders they were able to push their efforts for change with considerable success; where they faced fierce male opposition they persevered, drawing inspiration from a growing feminist movement within organized labor's ranks. If recalcitrant male unionists did not exactly cause female workers to become feminists, their behavior led many women to think carefully about their status and the need for change. This they did in the belief that they were acting in the best interests of the whole working class. "We were working for men and women," Betty Talkington, a unionist and early National Organization for Women member, observed in 1983. "Whenever you better conditions for one sex, especially if you're working for women, you automatically get it for men too."[2]

The significance of union women's efforts was felt beyond the confines of organized labor. Scholars have acknowledged the visibility of unionists in second-wave feminism but not their centrality in multilayered negotiations with middle-class feminists and government officials over the form and character of changes taking place. The history of union women's "consumption" of Title VII demonstrates that rank-and-file women were at the forefront of feminism's resurgence. Their legal protests against workplace inequality legitimized middle-class, professional feminists' calls for stronger federal antidiscrimination guidelines. These two feminist contingents came together to work on issues of common interests in the 1970s. It was an uneasy alliance, however, one fraught with a historic mistrust of motives and differing priorities. Union women were not cowed in the face of the seemingly more powerful feminists, nor did they abandon the cause of gender equality because of resistance to change within labor's ranks.

This book is part of the larger story of working-class women's struggle to define their place in society over the course of the last 150 years. In supporting gender equality, women came to reject the protective laws that eased their working conditions but limited their pay and the kinds of work in which they could engage. These laws taken together—what I call "protectionism"—had served women wage earners for some seventy-five years as a defense against the highly exploitive industrial world of work. This protectionism originated with the labor advocates of the nineteenth century who sought to defend all workers by minimizing health hazards, gaining compensation for job-related accidents, and winning a shorter work week. They believed that, once freed from the dangers and drudgery of industrialization, free labor could thrive in the American republic. Time and again they were disheartened as judicial decisions invalidated existing measures and rendered nearly hopeless the case for future legislation.[3]

Into this breach came a new set of measures, ones aimed at protecting women and children from the worst excesses of the industrial order. Forged at the turn of the century by reform-minded legislators and approved, at least in part, by a cautious judiciary, these laws did not seek to preserve workers' independence as earlier attempts had; rather, they offered restrictions and prohibitive regulations. They acknowledged women workers' tenuous and marginal place in the work force but did so by accepting at face value the belief that women were at a disadvantage compared to men because of their natural biological differences.[4] Supporters of protective laws were steadfastly practical about their efforts, seeing in them the best possible reform obtainable at the time. "We must help the women workers to overcome the handicap under which they are asked to work," Margaret Drier Robins of the Women's Trade Union League (WTUL) explained simply in 1920.[5] The fruits of these Progressive-era reformers' efforts were significant. By midcentury there were state laws for women mandating minimum wage, working hours, and meal and rest periods. Legislation limited nightwork, industrial work, and the weight women were required to lift. Employers were made to provide women workers with seats. While not all states had enacted laws on all these measures, nearly all states had some protective laws for women workers on the books.[6]

To those women toiling in cotton mills and food processing plants, in garment shops and laundries, and at other work sites, these laws provided welcome relief. Women made up only about 20 percent of the labor force and found themselves crowded into a remarkably small number of occupations. Even when they worked in the same factories as men they were segregated and received unequal pay; where seniority practices existed, women and men were kept on separate lists. Unlike men, women workers had little access to trade unions. Protective laws, reformers held, would prevent women workers from dragging down industrial standards and, as one pamphlet put it at the time, "permit efficient motherhood and healthy children."[7] Male labor leaders backed these efforts, claiming, in the words of Adolph Strasser of the Cigar Makers International Union and founding member of the American Federation of Labor (AFL), "it is the duty of government to protect the weak, and females are considered the weak in society."[8] Strasser's interest in preserving working women's health was self-serving: men believed that protective laws would stem the flow of women into the work force in general and prohibit their entry into the highly skilled jobs that male unionists dominated. To this end, union officers went as far as fining and even expelling members who instructed women in certain job skills.[9]

While protectionism brought immediate relief to working women, it had inherent flaws that would crystallize only decades later. By considering females as a special category of worker, defined by their physical stamina and moral character and not by their rights or as participants in the "freedom of contract" doctrine that informed male workers' struggles, reformers transformed the domestic code of the nineteenth century into the labor law of the twentieth. In the long run, Alice Kessler-Harris argues, "the price was steep."[10] The law constructed women as anomalies in the workplace and it defined them primarily as mothers, not providers. As Kessler-Harris and others have pointed out, this foreclosed consideration of providing support for women so they might defend their positions. In effect, women could not argue for such things as nurseries for their children while they worked or police patrols for dangerous streets around factories and shops that employed them at night.[11]

Women union activists, preferring to focus on bringing more women into the labor movement, treated protectionism as a "last resort."[12] They grumbled little, however, and came to view these new laws as part of an arsenal that labor could deploy against powerful employers. Moreover, as the scores of letters written by women to Franklin and Eleanor Roosevelt in the 1930s attest, most working-class women were in accord with male unionists and middle-class reformers about the need to defend the "provider's wage" against the less-deserving women, especially those who were married. Rose Schneiderman, a longtime union activist, noted that women who wanted to make claims to the same jobs, hours, and wages as male workers "might be putting their own brothers or sweethearts, or husbands out of a job."[13] The issue was more complex than Schneiderman's comment suggests, for single and divorced women and widows argued that they too were providers and deserving of employment. Their voices, however, were largely muted in an industrial relations system predicated on gender inequality.[14]

Women unionists rejected the only other viable option to protective laws at the time, the Equal Rights Amendment (ERA). Having succeeded in getting protective legislation passed and overseeing the creation of the U.S. Women's Bureau in the Department of Labor, activists viewed the ERA when it was introduced in the 1920 as a direct threat to their hard-won gains. Few wished to abandon these for what they saw as a nebulous, untested statement of equality. Legal experts aligned with this perspective claimed that the amendment, as one of them put it, "would operate like a blind man with a shot gun. No lawyer can confidently predict what it would hit."[15]

The fault lines between the pro-ERA forces and the unionists ran deep by the mid-1920s and continued through the 1960s. Opponents attacked the ERA's language of liberal individualism. Its chief supporters, the small but vocal contingent of upper-class, mainly professional women in the National Woman's Party (NWP), argued that a formal constitutional guarantee of equality would improve women's economic status. Unionists responded that such a prediction amounted to naivete at best, calculated cruelty to working women at worst. Deep personal animosity developed between the two groups as a result of their differences about gender politics. Alice Hamilton, a reformer and Harvard professor of industrial medicine, wrote privately to NWP member Edith Houghton Hooker, accusing her of leading "a sheltered, safe, [and] beautifully guarded" life that left her ignorant of the "weary toilers who hold desperately to their jobs."[16] *The Nation* publicly characterized the NWP's position as "always logically sound and theoretically progressive. Humanly, however, it is impractical."[17]

The debate over the ERA unsettled women unionists: they would not reject protectionism but were unwilling to cede to the NWP the mantle of women's rights entirely, casting themselves as realistic defenders of women's rights. "I consider myself a good feminist, but I believe I am a practical one," stated Mary Anderson, a former shoe worker and head of the U.S. Women's Bureau.[18] The bold organizing drives undertaken by women earlier in the century and the vital role they played in the emergence of the Congress of Industrial Organizations (CIO) in the 1930s and early 1940s kept alive in women activists a belief that their objectives were grander than the piecemeal improvements protective laws brought. Still, these activists could not bring themselves to endorse the ERA nor would they formulate demands for gender equality while their numbers remained relatively small and the needs of organizing workers great. Defenders of sex-based protective legislation, Nancy Cott writes in her history of feminism in the 1920s, "were grappling with problems so difficult they would still be present more than a half century later."[19] What would come to be rejected by women in the 1960s had been embraced by their predecessors in the early 1900s.

My study begins in the mid-1940s when the war's effect and the ensuing vast changes in the workplace and the home brought to the fore long unresolved issues. The events leading up to the appearance of Title VII twenty years later did not follow a linear progression to equality. Rather they represented a convergence of disparate factors that changed the gender consciousness of women unionists. Despite the absence of a mass women's movement, a corps of women union activists and women in organizations identified with the liberal wing of the Democratic Party came together to advocate passage of equal pay legislation. Equal pay, they held, delivered on the promise of individual rights and affirmed the trend toward higher consumption by families. The drive for legislation opened up a new dialogue on women's roles in the labor movement and society at large that would gather force in the 1960s. Once begun, the transformation was rapid. In the mid-1960s the American Federation of Labor–Congress of Industrial Organizations (AFL-CIO) attempted to ignore Title VII's proscription on sex discrimination; by the early 1970s the federation publicly spoke out for gender equality and backed the formerly dreaded ERA.

In mapping the changing relationships between men and women workers, I treat unions as, in Nancy Gabin's phrase, the "social space" where workers addressed most visibly and forcefully the transformations that occurred after 1945. Until recently, historians have dismissed the history of unionism in the United States in this period as an uninspiring chapter in the slow decline and loss of militant fortitude. They noted, as the activist and journalist Sidney Lens characterized it at the time, that the movement had undergone a "corrosion of idealism and dedication."[20] Certainly the roots of organized labor's decline, so painfully visible in the 1980s, lay in the lethargic response to organizing drives and in the political losses and compromises of the postwar period. Nevertheless, for women union activists as for men during this period, unionism still served as the most visible sign of a working-class presence in a country dominated by corporations. In the 1950s and early 1960s, unions could point with pride to a membership of some 18 million workers. In the mid-1950s, when union membership was at its highest level, 35 percent of the total nonagricultural work force was unionized. Improved wages accompanied this bolstered membership. In this same period the wages of unionists in the primary labor market jumped by 50 percent over prewar levels, and they leaped another 50 percent by the late 1960s. Unionists received life, sickness, and accident insurance; survivor's benefits; improved pensions; and supplemental unemployment benefits. Despite their disappointment with such crippling legislation as the Taft-Hartley Act (1947) and the

Landrum-Griffin Act (1959), unionists could be reassured that the longtime AFL-CIO president George Meany was a powerful figure in Washington, D.C., political circles. If the labor movement had a more circumscribed vision than in previous decades, it still counted for something in the Democratic Party.[21]

Working-class feminists drew on these common beliefs and experiences, but some women encountered a more favorable environment for change than did others. While all unions were subjected to sex discrimination complaints, there were marked differences in their support for Title VII. The case studies of the United Packinghouse Workers of America (UPWA) and the International Union of Electrical Workers (IUE) serve to explain the varying support for the emergence of gender equality. The choice of these two unions as examples of labor's response to demands for gender equality may strike some as curious given the larger and more visible role in social movements and U.S. politics played, for example, by the United Automobile Workers (UAW). In fact, while they were not the largest of unions during this period, the UPWA and IUE were hardly inconsequential. With some 304,000 members, the IUE was a powerful political force in the AFL-CIO as well as the halls of Congress. The UPWA's membership of 80,000 was relatively small. Still, as a regional union the UPWA had an impact on state and local politics in Illinois, Iowa, and other midwestern states. Both labor organizations were industrial unions that originated during the tumultuous early years of the CIO. Each could claim a significant role in advancing the cause of unionism, and each supported such demands as civil rights, minimum wage, and improved public housing.

Their similarities end there for they had quite divergent histories of gender relations. It is because of the stark differences in women's experiences with the enforcement of Title VII in these two unions that I have used them as case studies. They are not meant to represent all labor unions in statistical terms but they do provide a vivid contrast of responses to working-class feminism. The UPWA displayed a "confrontationist" approach to its women members' demands for enactment of equal employment opportunity law while the IUE exhibited an "accommodationist" approach. The explanation for each union's stance lies with several key factors, including the proportion of women to total members, the sexual division of labor under which its members worked, the union's political structure, and its political and leadership history.

The membership composition of each organization helped to determine conditions under which women unionists' demands for change might be successful. In the IUE, women made up around 35 percent of the union's total membership and constituted what Elizabeth Faue calls a "strategic plurality": male leaders depended at least in part on their support for reelection and other crucial approval and thus were attentive to women's demands.[22] The IUE leadership could boast of having a model Title VII compliance program because of this numerical power. By contrast, women made up only 20 percent of the total UPWA membership. Most of the union's sex discrimination complaints came from Iowa locals and these units had around 12 percent female members. Accordingly, women had little voice in determining union policy. The strongly independent UPWA locals—celebrated by several scholars as an example of democratic rank-and-file unionism—failed to deliver justice to their women members in the 1960s and 1970s. The union's decentralized organizational structure actually empowered male unionists to resist the enforcement of Title VII. The IUE women succeeded not only because of their numbers but also because their union, though it lacked the dynamic and heroic history of the UPWA, had a large, centralized institutional structure with headquarters in Washington, D.C., and responded effectively to equal employment opportunity laws. Moreover, IUE women worked in staff positions and had a long history of participating in interunion and liberal interest groups working on "women's issues."

There were contingent factors that contributed to these histories as well. In the UPWA, women faced massive layoffs due to technological displacement and packinghouse reorganization by management after 1955, which resulted in pitched battles between men and women for a dwindling number of jobs. Male unionists viewed Title VII as a sharp challenge to their already beleaguered job security. In the IUE, union leaders responded to its women members' needs more readily because it competed for members with the United Electrical Workers in the 1950s. Yet even with a "predisposition" to embracing gender equality, the IUE incurred sex discrimination complaints. Faced with the federal government's strengthened resolve in the late 1960s to enforce Title VII and with pressure from rank-and-file women, the union's legal counsel instituted an aggressive compliance program. The scheme absolved the union of future charges, satisfied the demands of women workers, and fended off attacks on collective bargaining practices by incorporating government antidiscrimination guidelines into existing industrial relations practices. IUE women expressed their determination to continue advocating for equality by joining with other union women to establish the Coalition of Labor Union Women (CLUW) in 1974. While UPWA women could not claim such an active role in union feminism due to the obstacles placed before them by men, they too asserted their belief in gender equality. Working-class feminism came into existence as much from rank-and-file women protesting discrimination and forcing their own unions to change as from top-down changes in union policy.

Differently situated women—especially African-American unionists—responded to the momentum toward gender equality in a variety of ways. Far from viewing feminism with "a mixture of disdain, distrust, and fear," as one historian characterized it, black women unionists were present in the ranks of second-wave feminism from its inception.[23] The fact that black women supported the civil rights movement did not divert their keen interest in fighting for gender equality as well. Indeed, the successes of the civil rights movement helped to clear the way for a budding working-class feminism in several ways: by bringing black women into jobs and labor unions in greater numbers; by crafting a language of rights common to social protest movements; and by providing legal tools through equal employment opportunity measures that encouraged black and white women to join forces.

In those labor organizations with a relatively good, or at least improving, civil rights record, black women engaged in activism with white workers on behalf of gender equality. Conversely, less racially progressive unions lacked a strong, multiracial feminist contingent. In these unions, black women tended to maintain ties exclusively with the civil rights movement. As demonstrated by the history of the Tobacco Workers International Union (TWIU), which I discuss throughout this book, however, even when black women lacked the immediate institutional and emotional support available to union feminists elsewhere, they often included sex discrimination grievances in their formal race discrimination complaints. In the process they made government officials and white women unionists aware of the racialized context of feminism, just as white and black union women modified the approach of middle-class feminists to take into account the world of wage-earning women.

The experiences of the women and men analyzed in this book prompt us to consider the range of racial and gender identities that have bedeviled working-class egalitarians. Each union had an "ecology," and that ecology informed the decisions workers made about how best to attain their objectives and even helped define those objectives. As much as this study is an account of working-class fragmentation, however, it is also a story of rank-and-file determination to overcome division and to form coalitions for change. In the fifteen years following Title VII's passage, women unionists succeeded in overturning protectionist barriers to equality. Often placing themselves at physical and economic risk, they pushed their labor organizations to promote feminist issues and increased their leadership roles. Because of working-class feminism, Marjorie Albert of the Allied Distributive Workers noted in 1979, "no union leader stands up today without tipping his hat to women's rights. That's a big change."[24] By 1980, gender equality was the goal of union women and hence that of labor as well.

1

Beyond the Doldrums:
Postwar Organized Labor and "Women's Issues," 1945–63

When she sat down before a tape recorder in 1976 to recount her half-century of experiences in the labor movement, the activist and educator Pauline Newman noted with some dismay the passing of support for women's protective laws. Newman's career began at the height of support for protectionism and ended as the labor movement endorsed the law of equality embodied in the Equal Rights Amendment (ERA). Newman could not bring herself to back this measure. "If the amendment had passed[,] what would have happened to the legislation we worked for?" she asked. "We worked so hard for it, for what it meant for the organized and the unorganized, especially for the unorganized women." Despite her opposition to the ERA, Newman acknowledged the historical shift in support to gender equality, a change that came about, she said, "because of the general demand on the part of women to do everything and be everywhere." "It's a different world today," the veteran unionist admitted. "There is a younger generation . . . who is not only better informed but more courageous to demand what they think is their due."[1]

The "different world" of which Newman spoke was already in the making in the 1940s. Working-class women's support for gender equality evolved over several decades, often indirectly challenging prevailing practices rather than confronting them wholesale. In the immediate postwar period, women began to think differently about their status in the workplace and at home. Their ideas developed further as demographic, economic, and technological transformations began to affect workers in the 1950s and early 1960s. This chapter examines what Alice Kessler-Harris calls the "radical consequences of incremental change" in the twenty years leading up to the emergence of working-class feminism in the early sixties.[2] During this important period, ground was cleared for a new understanding of gender relations. "As the gap between norms and behavior grew ever wider," writes William Chafe, "there developed a basis in reality for a collective effort to challenge traditional views."[3]

Of all the social institutions affecting working women, organized labor addressed these changes most visibly. Unions were not naturally sympathetic to the demands of women workers. The resistance women activists encountered from men in changing their own labor organizations' practices is a sobering reminder of the uphill battle to build support for gender equality. Gladys Dickason, a vice-president and research director of the Amalgamated Clothing Workers (ACWA), observed in 1947 that the labor movement had "played an important part in the progress women have made toward full participation in the country's political, economic, and social life."[4] Nonetheless, the benefits that traditionally accrued to women workers were incidental to efforts at organizing the basic industries. There, women made up a sizable minority of the work force but rarely constituted a majority. Female membership in unions jumped from 265,000 early in the 1930s to 800,000 at the end of the decade and the proportion of the female labor force that was unionized increased from 2.4 percent to 6 percent for the same period.[5] Before World War II, however, labor leaders paid little attention to working women's specific needs. "Women had an awfully tough time in the union because the men brought their prejudices there," one Chicago packinghouse woman organizer recalled. "Some of my brothers, who believed in equality and that woman should have rights, didn't crank the mimeograph, didn't type. . . . And when the union came around giving out jobs with pay, the guys got them."[6] This pattern of behavior continued into the postwar period.

As women activists pointed out on numerous occasions, however, unions were resistant to change but they were not immutable. Industrial unions, in particular, offered their women members the greatest opportunity to grapple with the problems affecting them. Committed, at least formally, to the notion of democracy and fairness to all their members, the unions founded in the turbulent 1930s sought social reform in the legislatures as much as at the bargaining table. This suited the small but growing cadre of women union activists as they struggled to find their place in their respective unions. They saw their efforts not as separate from those of organized labor but as central to its ongoing goal of shaping and defining the liberal state. As Nancy Gabin points out in her history of women in the United Automobile Workers (UAW), labor organizations served "not only as a constraint on but also as a resource for female collective action."[7] The women unionists who came together to address their concerns drew strength from labor's principles and organizational power. Given the dearth of institutional support, they established coalitions with women in political and religious groups identified with the liberal wing of the Democratic Party. Together, they formed the core of what would become mainstream feminism in the 1970s.

In a labor movement divided along lines of skill, geographical region, race, and gender, women activists had their work before them; they also had reason to believe that, if their demands were accepted by their union leaders, they could significantly change the lives of millions of women across the country. The years following World War II were ones of large union memberships, significant union influence in national politics, improved race relations among workers, and the unification in the mid-1950s of the two large labor federations, the American Federation of Labor and the Congress of Industrial Organizations, into the AFL-CIO. As countless scholars have pointed out, this was an optimistic period in United States history; it was also one marked by uncertainty and restlessness. Union women lived out this uneasy tension in their work lives, in their unions, and at home with their families.

The Legacy of World War II and Reconversion

The story of union women's support for gender equality begins at the end of World War II with the cessation of women's wartime employment. As dramatically as they had come into the war plants, they left or, in most cases, were fired. In the early months of 1945 the war wound down in Europe, prompting employers to dismiss their female employees as they reconverted production for a peacetime economy. "The war was over on August 14 and we went in on the 15th. They lined us up and had our paychecks ready for us," said one woman punch-press operator from St. Louis.[8] By the spring, over 300,000 women had been laid off; that figure climbed to over 3,000,000 by the next year. In Detroit, the proportion of women in the automobile industry work force fell to 7.5 percent from 25 percent; in Los Angeles only 14 percent of the women who had worked in aircraft plants during the war still held their jobs in mid-1946. Nationally, women's share of employment in durable goods industries plummeted 50 percent. Many of these workers had considerable difficulty securing new jobs.[9] A survey of 20,000 women workers in Detroit revealed that 72 percent of them had not yet found new jobs weeks after being released, despite their efforts. A note of desperation marked their search for work. "I was looking around madly for something to do, because I didn't have that much money to last very long," one divorced woman with children reported.[10] Those fortunate to secure employment took severe pay cuts: women who had earned an average of 85 to 90 cents an hour were now accepting jobs that paid only 45 to 50 cents an hour.[11]

African Americans were hit especially hard by these employment practices. The war had brought black women into higher-paying, unionized jobs but reconversion layoffs had made these gains ephemeral. Writing in the pages of the *Atlantic Monthly* at the close of World War II, one observer of the economic dislocation sweeping the nation noted that "Negro women . . . find it hard to get a job in anything but the service positions . . . [and] are rarely rehired into the kinds of high-paying jobs they held during the war."[12] From the vantage point of the last half of the 1940s there was scant evidence of improvement in African-American women workers' status. Sixty percent of all African-American women workers in the postwar period were concentrated in institutional and private household service jobs while only 16 percent of white women toiled in such positions. Not only had black women been forced to return to these jobs at rates nearly those of the prewar years, but the anti-labor backlash embodied in the Taft-Hartley Act of 1947 scuttled much of the progress made in organizing minority workers, especially in the South. African-American women found unions unwilling to help them retain their jobs: even the Brotherhood of Sleeping Car Porters, a union whose leadership and membership was overwhelmingly African American, ignored women workers' requests that it fight their furloughing.[13] "A year after the war's end," notes Jacqueline Jones, "the disadvantaged position of black workers in a peacetime economy had become obvious once again."[14]

When factories resumed production, men returned to higher-paying positions while women scrambled for the much-smaller number of "women's" jobs available. Many women had to accept the low-paying service industry jobs they held before the war. This was a situation for which employers, union leaders, and government officials did not apologize. Women, they noted, had entered the war plants only to spell the men drafted into the armed forces. Veterans retained their full seniority rights. Women, having performed their civic duty, were to return these jobs to their rightful holders. And so, as Sara Evans puts it, "as men were mustered out of the army, women were mustered out of the factories."[15]

Many women were willing to comply. "I was happy to stay at home and be a housewife. . . . It was delightful to not be working," one West Coast woman told an interviewer in the early 1980s.[16] Not all women workers shared this vision of postwar life, however, especially when they saw nonveteran men take jobs in violation of seniority agreements. Those who surveyed war workers reported that as many as four out of five women in industrial manufacturing positions preferred to keep their jobs.[17] When the layoffs came, young women and women who had not worked before the war tended to leave quietly; older, more experienced women were not as accepting. Many women of all ages, regardless of marital status, were desperate to keep the jobs on which they had come to rely in order to support themselves and their families, and they balked at leaving the factories. A few fought back. Women workers at several Detroit-area automobile plants threw up picket lines and carried signs reading "How Come No Work for Women?" "Ford Hires New Help. We Walk the Street," and "Stop Discrimination Because of Sex."[18]

With most of the nation unsympathetic to the concept of expanding women workers' rights, however, these protesting women found few allies. Writers and editors of mass-circulation magazines led the way in pressuring women to stay at home. Taking a page from the nineteenth century, they asserted that women were to be the emotional center of the family and home. "Being a good wife, a good mother, in short a good homemaker is the most important of all the occupations in the world," wrote one man in the *Saturday Review.* "I put it down as an axiom that no woman with a husband and small children can hold a full-time job and be a good homemaker at the same time."[19] Whether it was in *McCall's,* the *Ladies Home Journal,* or in books such as *Modern Woman: The Lost Sex,* by Ferdinand Lundberg and Marynia Farnham, the message was clear: women, especially married women with children, had no "right" to be in the work force, at least not in traditionally male-dominated fields. Women "would do well to recapture those functions in which they have demonstrated superior capacity. Those are, in general, the nurturing functions around the home," asserted Lundberg and Farnham.[20] "One day I realized that my office job was only a substitution for the real job I'd been hired for: that of being purely a wife and mother," wrote one woman in the pages of *Good Housekeeping* in 1951.[21] The public tended to agree: a poll by *Fortune* magazine in 1946 revealed that less than 22 percent of men and 29 percent of women interviewed thought that women "should have an equal chance with men" for any job. Women who had to support themselves fared only marginally better. Of those polled, 46 percent of the men and less than 50 percent of the women believed these women should have an "equal chance."[22]

Given this context it is not surprising that male unionists had little regard for those women who sought to stay in their jobs. As Ruth Milkman, Nancy Gabin, Amy Kesselman, and other scholars have demonstrated, union leaders ignored established seniority procedures in order to rid their ranks of women. Much of the ground for this discriminatory behavior had been cleared during World War II when, despite the entry of women into "male" jobs and notwithstanding their bolstered earnings, a sexual division of labor, unequal pay, and unequal seniority lists persisted. A Princeton University assessment of 72 companies completed late in the war found that 22 percent of the firms studied still maintained separate seniority lists according to sex and that 40 percent of employers admitted that they took a woman's marital status into consideration in determining layoffs. Annie Stein of the Women's Trade Union League (WTUL) reminded union women that single seniority lists offered few guarantees to women workers. Even in those cases "women's jobs may be endangered as in the case of one auto parts plant where by agreement of the employer and the union all men were retained and women with greater seniority fired."[23] The war may have temporarily enabled women to move into better positions but it had not fundamentally altered men's view of their secondary status. "The men do not easily give up their prejudices," observed one journalist at the war's end. "Men are ganging up on women in industry, and it is up to women to go into action to stop that old-fashioned attitude from denying them jobs and opportunity."[24]

Union leaders seemed not to notice their own inconsistent observance of seniority rules. "I was furious," a Minnesota woman wartime worker recalled. "I went to the union about it, too. Didn't do a bit of good. They said, 'Boys from the service, you know.'"[25] After the work of ousting women was complete, Frieda Miller, director of the U.S. Women's Bureau, suggested that labor officers and employers could help women recoup these losses with supplementary training, job upgrading, and supervisory work. Joseph A. Beirne, president of the Communications Workers of America (CWA), bristled at the suggestion, however, declaring that "it has never been a practice of this union to destroy its own seniority agreement or countenance a violation of it just because the person who might be affected would be a woman."[26]

Women union leaders were stymied as to how to "go into action" against these men, or even on what basis. As Sara Evans notes, "women lacked collective, public spaces within which to redefine themselves as a group in relation to society or to critique a social order that simultaneously called on them and restricted their possibilities."[27] Activists and sympathetic policy makers worried about the fate of these women but their response was wholly inadequate. "The women of America formed a hidden army upon which Hitler in his madness failed to count," Margaret Hickey of the Women's Advisory Committee of the War Manpower Commission observed in December 1944. "That once hidden army of women is now in the open. We must face it realistically and guard against the creation of another 'hidden' army of the unemployed."[28] Hickey was frustratingly vague on how this could be done. She called for the overall maintenance of high wages and full employment but little else. Others echoed her narrow range of remedies with varying degrees of specificity. Noting that women's massive job layoffs "came so suddenly it left us almost breathless," the WTUL recommended an increased minimum wage, equal pay guarantees, and full employment as ways to stave off a further deterioration in women's status.[29] Offering little in the way of a substantial program to bring this about, Frieda Miller acknowledged that women "would like to retain, some if not all, of the gains" made during the war.[30] Mostly, the U.S. Women's Bureau and government policy makers focused their energies on the modest goals of retraining and directing women into jobs men did not generally seek.

This was not exactly a case of emerging feminism cut down by postwar labor policies. For the most part scholars are correct in arguing that the 1940s did not mark a definitive step toward gender equality; they point instead to what Nancy Gabin terms the "ambiguous legacy" of that decade. During those years women experienced short-term frustration as they attempted to parlay wartime gains into permanent practices. At the same time, the period had a profound effect on the development of women's consciousness, particularly in the years immediately following the war. Alice Kessler-Harris argues that "Rosie the Riveter" was less a harbinger of contemporary feminism and more a symbol of the patriotic American and "represented a response to emergency rather than a shift in attitude."[31] Kessler-Harris points out that the numbers of women entering paid employment in the first half of the 1940s, while impressive, actually continued a pattern of women's increased participation in the labor force that had begun in the preceding two decades. If one takes account of those women who had worked for pay before World War II and the sizable number of women who would have come into the labor force despite the war, she notes, only about 25 percent of women war workers were new to paid labor during this period.[32]

Still, gender relations had been altered significantly by the war, albeit in ways that would crystallize only two decades later in a different social and economic context. Management and union leaders may have successfully restructured the postwar world along prewar lines, but an extensive disruption to workplace practices had taken place and assured that what they erected following 1944 would prove a shaky edifice indeed. The practice of assigning specific jobs to men and women by gender was undermined most significantly by the wholesale recruitment of women as war plant workers, which revealed the artificiality of job-typing by sex. During the war, the U.S. Department of Labor broke down industrial tasks into 1,500 jobs, 1,050 of which the government claimed women could perform on an equal footing with men. Another 300 were labeled as "partly suitable" for women. This prompted one observer at the time to note that "the easy assumption of masculine excellence hangs by the slender thread of 100 job types."[33]

In peacetime this reconfigured sexual division of labor did not revert to the more customary alignment of job categories in every case. In auto, steel, packinghouse, electrical, and other industries, some women simply held on to their positions, formally classified as "male." Alice Peurala, a Chicago steel worker, remembered that the manager hiring her in the 1950s told her that "in that particular occupation in the steel mills they had hired women during the war and there were a number of women still left on that occupation. It seemed to be one that one stuck with."[34] Such cases, however, appear rarely in the historical record. The overwhelming majority of women could only look on with bitterness as the wave of layoffs left them with a new understanding of the arbitrary and discriminatory boundaries dividing "men's" and "women's" work. "We began to look a little differently at the whole question of equal rights for women . . . when the . . . layoffs and recalls came and these were all sorts of innuendoes about not calling back women because allegedly there weren't any jobs open that they could perform," Lillian Hatcher of the UAW recalled. Women realized that "to say that she wanted to be classified forever as a female worker was hurting the working woman . . . because there were many jobs that were tagged male occupations that women could perform as well as any other person."[35] At the time, this awareness did not translate into open protest against employment policy. Mary Callahan of the International Union of Electrical Workers (IUE) noted that "the postings on the board would say female or male. And we never questioned it; either as a union or I, as a person, never questioned it. Every once in a great while, I'd say, 'You know that doesn't seem fair, that we could do that during the war, and now we're back where we started from.'"[36] Callahan's observation illustrates the absence of a full-scale collective effort in the 1940s to challenge the prevailing notions of what constitutes "men's" and "women's" work. Women unionists sought to retain their positions but did not offer a public critique of what their work meant or who was able to perform industrial jobs.

The achievements of these wartime workers, though limited, had a lasting impact on the changing consciousness of women in the 1960s and 1970s. Years after the war, women recalled how they had worked successfully in "male" jobs. One Los Angeles woman remembered the transforming effect the war had on her friends' mothers who headed off to the war plants: "For the first time in their lives, they worked outside the home. They realized that they were capable of doing something more than cook a meal. I remember going to Sunday dinner one of the older women invited me to. She and her sister at the dinner table were talking about the best way to keep their drill sharp in the factory. I had never heard anything like this in my life. It was marvelous."[37] Countless women across the country spoke of a deep sense of pride in the work they had accomplished. "It was a special thing," a Brooklyn women recalled of her welding job. "At the end of the day I always felt I'd accomplished something. It was good—there was a product, there was something to be seen."[38]

The other significant advance of women workers in this period fared only slightly better in the postwar years. The campaign to improve women's wages through equal pay for equal work, after gathering strength during the war, limped along into the 1950s. Men had long supported the measure, especially in industries where the replacement of men with women loomed large. To say that equal pay mattered to union men, however, does not mean that it mattered greatly. The indifference of union leaders and the general public was largely responsible for such slow progress. Except in electrical manufacturing, most unions dropped the matter at war's end, when it became clear that management was not interested in substituting female for male workers. "Though hundreds of contracts today pay lip service to equal pay for equal work, the brutal truth is that it does not exist except in the beginners' jobs," one journalist noted in 1945.[39] If efforts at the bargaining table and in the grievance process failed to bring about equal pay, male union officers were unwilling to consider stepped-up protests. "It is the kind of thing that bothers us a great deal and yet it is not something we would want to call a strike about," Joseph Beirne admitted.[40] Equal pay demands were not central to contract demands. "In a good many instances it has been the last thing that labor was asking for and has been abandoned as they get toward a settlement," Secretary of Labor Lewis Schwellenbach noted in 1948.[41]

As the discussion in the next chapter will make clear, male unionists did not neglect the drive for equal pay completely. In the context of reconversion and massive employer and conservative political offensives—capped by passage of the Taft-Hartley Act in 1947—women workers' demands were subordinated to other goals. Employers and male unionists worked to return women to a marginal status in the workplace. Believing they had done so, they treated women's concerns with casual indifference. Women had little reason to expect that a dramatic change in their working lives was imminent.[42]

The Not-So-Quiescent 1950s

The massive layoffs and demotions of women workers in the immediate postwar years gave way to an equally significant, although less studied, phenomenon in the late 1940s: the steady rise in proportion and number of women in the paid labor force. With their new responsibilities came changes in the workplace, family life, and social norms. Historians have only recently come to think of the two decades after the close of World War II as a period of progressively destabilizing gender relations. If the 1950s did not exactly usher in a new age of feminism, neither was it a decade of women's conformity to traditional gender roles. Overlaying the conservatism of the period were, as Joanne Meyerowitz writes, "subtle expressions of ambivalence, contradiction, and self-parody in postwar gender ideals."[43] As more women went on the payroll at factories, offices, retail stores, and schools, they began to find a way to assert their dual roles as housewife and wage earner. In the process, they conveyed the idea that working women's rights were a legitimate issue for public debate.

Many women never actually left the work force in 1944–46: 3.25 million quit or were fired between September 1945 and November 1946 but this reduction was partially offset by the nearly 2.75 million women who assumed new jobs, thus making the net decline only 600,000 positions. While younger women starting families after World War II tended to stay at home, the percentage of mothers in the work force with children between the ages of six and seventeen shot up to 41.5 percent in 1963 from 30.3 percent in 1950, a 37 percent increase. In 1940 women made up 25 percent of the total labor force; the Department of Labor reported in 1961 that 34 percent of all workers—24 million—were women. That figure would climb to 40 percent by 1970.[44]

While necessity continued to propel most women into the labor force, their growing presence in the ranks of paid employment in the decades following the war brought a new set of expectations. This came in large measure from the trend of increased consumption. The hallmarks of the postwar economic system— business expansion, increased military spending, government deficit spending, and increased wages—shaped the decisions individuals and married couples made about their work lives. Improved household conveniences, smaller families, and husbands at school under the GI bill led married women with children to return to work. Their reasons varied according to the economic status of their families and the aspirations they shared with their husbands. For some, the attainment of paid work was a selfless act of spousal support, often done so that husbands could advance their education and careers. "My husband wanted his master's degree so . . . I went to work in the same restaurant that I'd worked in years before," the wife of a University of Southern California graduate recalled. Others hoped to help achieve their families' upwardly mobility. Referring to her reentry into the paid labor force after she and her husband purchased a house in the 1950s, a Los Angeles resident commented, "When you bite off such a large bill, you need a little help." Many national leaders came to view these new workers in a favorable light. This was especially true of leaders of unions with a large number of women members. The IUE's James Carey explained how the new workers' wages were crucial to the nation's economic well-being: "The extra pay-check has raised an increasing number of families into middle and upper income brackets. This means then that a family with this extra check has a greater demand on the market. . . . This increase in demand means more production to meet this demand and to produce, more jobs are made available."[45] In the context of the U.S. cold war struggle for dominance, a woman's contribution to the family's purchasing power redounded to the nation's advantage. One scholar asserted in 1960 that "the potential contributions of women in the labor force are of particular importance if the United States is to be successful in its struggle to maintain its economic and political position vis-à-vis the Soviet Union and Communist China."[46]

As nonthreatening as these developments seemed at the time, women's increased work force participation brought with it implications for a long-term transformation in gender relations. At first the changes were barely perceptible, affecting women's attitudes toward work but not increasing their dissatisfaction with their wages or their places within unions. Women found that they drew personal satisfaction from employment. Almost 90 percent of the women interviewed in Greensboro, North Carolina, and the Champaign-Urbana area in Illinois stated that they liked their jobs, especially the opportunity to be with their peers and receive recognition for their efforts. Women began to expect that they would stay in the labor force and became concerned with job rights and their personal investment in the policies of employers and unions. They worked, one scholar noted in 1960, "because the jobs are available, they have the time, and paid employment is not frowned upon. . . . In recent years the labor force rate of wives has been rising most rapidly in families where the husband's income is relatively high."[47] Research revealed that women sought work for many reasons. In a 1955 University of Michigan study, 48 percent of women workers cited financial necessity as the reason for seeking employment; 21 percent said that a sense of accomplishment kept them in the work force. A "sense of independence" led many of the study's subjects to hold their jobs. This was true even for those who cited finances as their primary reason for working outside the home.[48]

Most government data from this period did not distinguish between white women and black women in assessing general employment patterns. Evidence that did focus on black women indicates that by the early 1950s it was clear that, like white women, they would not revert to the old work force structure. The fifteen years preceding the arrival of federal equal employment opportunity measures in the mid-1960s marked a slow but definitive advance for African-American workers. Healthy economic growth coupled with civil rights activism in the North opened up new positions for African-American men and women. In particular, women moved out of low-paying employment sectors such as agricultural labor, where their participation decreased from 16 percent to 8 percent of their total work force involvement; they increasingly occupied higher-paying jobs like machine operator, where their participation jumped from 4 percent to 16 percent.[49] By 1960 a labor economist could report to Congress that African-American women had "made some headway in moving into higher level and higher status occupations, particularly in Northern States," although he quickly reminded lawmakers that "a very large majority are still in low-status and generally low-paid occupations."[50]

A core group of black women and white women in industrial unions in the 1950s seized on this modest but steady increase in women's work force participation as an opportunity to improve women workers' status. They served as a kind of vanguard for "women's issues," forming alliances across unions and ultimately coming to advocate gender equality. These women unionists were few in number, elected to a handful of leadership positions, and they tended to be on staff at international union offices (see tables 1 and 2). Most came from large industrial unions affiliated with the CIO where women filled anywhere from 20 to 60 percent of the membership ranks (women made up about 13 percent of the CIO's total membership). Women in these unions did not achieve many elected positions but did justify male leaders' developing programs for women workers. They were from the ranks of the college-educated middle class and the working class with shop-floor backgrounds, in equal proportion. Despite their varying backgrounds, however, they differed little in their social policy perspective. Katherine Ellickson, for example, was raised in a secular Jewish home, attended Vassar College, taught and wrote on labor issues, and moved between union positions and government jobs before settling in as associate director of the CIO Research Department in the 1940s. Caroline Davis came up from the rank and file. Davis worked at the Excel Corporation plant in Elkhart, Indiana, and became active in UAW Local 764 in the early 1940s. She was an effective negotiator and held several positions, including bargaining committee member, local president, and international staff member. In 1947 Walter Reuther appointed her director of the union's Women's Bureau, a position she held until her retirement in the early 1970s. Both Davis and Ellickson served on John F. Kennedy's President's Commission on the Status of Women (PCSW) in the early 1960s, a group that, in addressing many of the legal and extralegal inequities women faced, helped spark the emergence of modern feminism.[51]

The activists strove to increase their influence in a labor movement generally hostile to sharing power with women. Unionism was part of a "man's world," characterized by two industrial relations experts in the early 1950s as "violent, aggressive, and very masculine." It took considerable fortitude to attend meetings that were usually held at night in deserted areas of towns, let alone remain active. As the authors of this particular study described unions, "They are not the kind of organization a respectable girl joins—certainly not the kind of organization in which a respectable girl should become active." And yet, women's "interest and devotion" to the cause of organized labor came "close to equaling that of men" when union leaders "made the needs of women members a prior-

Table 1. Percentage of AFL and CIO Leaders by Sex and Union Type, 1946

Union Type	Men		Women	
	AFL	CIO	AFL	CIO
Professional	2.5	7.1	13.2	9.1
White collar	5.1	7.1	22.6	25.0
Craft	48.5	0.6	18.9	4.5
Transportation	11.2	3.2	1.9	4.5
Service	2.0	3.9	9.4	2.3
Government service	13.3	1.3	15.1	9.1
Industrial	9.7	74.0	—	31.8
Needle trades	7.7	2.6	18.9	13.6

Source: Gary M. Fink, ed., *Biographical Dictionary of American Labor* (Westport, Conn.: Greenwood Press, 1984), 41. Used with permission of Greenwood Publishing Group, Inc., Westport, Conn.

Table 2. Percentage of Men and Women AFL and CIO Leaders by Union Position, 1946

Union Position	Men		Women	
	AFL	CIO	AFL	CIO
National federal official	1.0	1.9	—	—
State/regional federal official	6.0	7.1	1.9	2.3
Local federal official	8.5	7.8	5.7	6.8
National union official	17.6	13.0	17.0	4.5
State/regional union official	16.1	20.1	11.3	15.9
Local union official	45.2	44.2	54.7	36.4
National staff official	1.5	1.9	5.7	20.5
State/regional staff official	0.5	—	—	9.1
Local staff official	—	1.3	1.9	4.5
Editor/educator	3.5	2.6	1.9	—

Source: Gary M. Fink, ed., *Biographical Dictionary of American Labor* (Westport, Conn.: Greenwood Press, 1984), 41. Used with permission of Greenwood Publishing Group, Inc., Westport, Conn.

ity."[52] Most of the women who entered the ranks of activists were either single or had no children; the few who had children often had parents who shared the burden of childcare so that they could go to meetings, run for office, and serve as convention delegates. Catherine Conroy was typical in this regard: "I had no responsibility. I lived with my parents. . . . They charged me a little room and board but it wasn't too bad, and I wasn't involved in any emotional way with anyone."[53] Conroy worked as a telephone operator in Milwaukee and held several appointed positions with the CWA. Like Caroline Davis, she served on the President's Commission on the Status of Women; later, she participated in the founding of the National Organization for Women and the Coalition of Labor Union Women.

Activists like Conroy found that they had few resources or opportunities to hold meetings and formulate strategy within the confines of the CIO. The sole exception was in the UAW where, as compensation for their painfully unfair treatment by automobile unionists in the mid-1940s, the union's executive board members created the UAW Women's Bureau. As a result, despite the growing antipathy for "women's issues," the bureau's staff was able to draw considerable attention to their concerns.[54] There was little organizational support elsewhere for such efforts, either at the constituent union level or in the upper echelons of the CIO. Some women tried to make male unionists more attentive to women workers' needs but with little success. Writing to her supervisor, Victor Reuther, in 1954, Katherine Ellickson proposed the formation of a CIO women's committee and the appointment of federation employees to initiate contact with women's organizations and government agencies. Ellickson suggested that the new group collect and disseminate information on women workers as well as sponsor workshops for representatives from constituent unions. Careful not to appear to be advocating a radical measure, she assured Reuther that "the committee and staff would have to lean over backwards to avoid any interference in the internal affairs of CIO affiliates."[55] Nothing came of Ellickson's proposal; not until the early 1960s would the labor organization—by then the AFL-CIO—sponsor a meeting to discuss women's concerns.

Overt discrimination frequently accompanied such blatant neglect. Even in unions with relatively good support of programs for women workers, such as the UAW, the behavior of male unionists had a sobering effect on women. The UAW's Dorothy Haener "believed all these things they said to me about non-discrimination and fair employment and so forth"; yet, in Haener's own experience, when "reality hit me" the union did not treat women members fairly. "It was difficult for me to accept that."[56] Florence Peterson, one of the union's handful of female international representatives, confirmed Haener's statement: "I learned about sex discrimination at [the UAW's] Solidarity House. Any woman who had worked for the union has to fight to avoid being tied to the desk because, at least in those years, that was the appropriate place [for women]."[57] Katherine Ellickson had the same frustration at the CIO headquarters. "As a woman it was certainly more difficult for me to function in the labor movement," she lamented in a 1976 interview. "I was not one of the boys. . . . We made some effort to get together with other union women . . . but there was no formal machinery within the CIO or later within the AFL-CIO for doing this."[58]

If women found their treatment at the hands of male unionists objectionable, they remained part of a loyal opposition within the labor movement, refusing to break ranks publicly with union leaders. Given that they first came into the labor movement in the heady days of the 1930s, believed fervently in the cause of organized labor, and made careers of advancing their union membership, it should come as no surprise that they viewed themselves as advocates of industrial unionism, first and foremost. Many were attracted to organizing on the basis of social unionism, the very principle upon which the CIO had been founded. Social unionist advocates promised fair treatment and inclusion of all of its members in the formation of labor union policy. Women unionists found this appealing, as they did the notion that unions should engage in social reform. Social unionism was not so much a constant political philosophy as a loosely formed belief about the important role unionism should play in the polity. Its advocates maintained that the labor movement had social rights and responsibilities beyond simple wage and benefit issues. Social unionists considered themselves the catalyst for broad social change that valued human rights over property rights. CIO activists supported social unionism in its many forms, including embracing corporatism, flirting with the formation of a labor party, and fighting racial discrimination. At a basic level the approach was practical, inextricably linked to the CIO's origins as a network of labor organizers reaching out to industrial workers, many of them semiskilled white women and minority men and women. This outlook contrasted sharply with the AFL leadership's support for narrow business unionism. In the CIO's early years the embryonic collectivism of social unionism had its socialist, progressive, and Catholic variants in the ideas and actions of such leaders as Sidney Hillman, Walter Reuther, Philip Murray, and a multitude of middle-level officers who came up from the shop floor and moved into regional and national positions. Although social unionism receded in the face of modern business unionism in the 1950s, its rhetorical strength continued to embolden activists, including women unionists.[59]

Union women worked through the labor movement as best they could, accepting the limitations and lack of institutional support. They embraced a strategy of pushing for increased interest within their respective unions in "women's issues" and, concurrently, of seeking allies outside organized labor to advance their causes. Most of their national efforts rested on a loosely formed coalition sponsored by the Women's Bureau of the U.S. Department of Labor. The so-called "Women's Bureau coalition" had as its members unionists and those representing liberal interest groups, some of whom had their roots in the progressive movement. These groups included the Women's Trade Union League, the National Consumers League, and the League of Women Voters. Religion-based organizations and business and professional organizations participated as well, although in a less concerted fashion. Notwithstanding Cynthia Harrison's contentions that the coalition was made up of "primarily educated, middle-class white women" and that it lacked "major labor organizations and political clubs," unionists spearheaded most of the coalition's efforts.[60] Besides Esther Peterson, an ACWA staff member and later a director in the U.S. Women's Bureau in the Kennedy administration, the coalition files are replete with unionists' names on its committees: Gladys Dickason, also of the ACWA; Mary Callahan and Gloria Johnson of the IUE; Sylvia Gottlieb of the CWA; Mildred Jeffrey, Caroline Davis, and Dorothy Haener of the UAW; and Katherine Ellickson of the CIO Washington office staff. These women formed alliances and friendships that endured through the emergence of working-class feminism in the 1970s.[61]

Not all unionists enjoyed even these limited opportunities for activism. Women in the other large labor federation, the AFL, found their male leaders less interested than the CIO leaders in promoting "women's issues." With women filling only 10 percent of its ranks, AFL officers' advocacy on behalf of women workers was virtually nonexistent. Unlike CIO unionists, who held an ideological commitment to seeking equal treatment for all workers regardless of race, creed, or sex, AFL unionists occupied the exclusionary skilled trades whose histories were marked by discriminatory practices. If CIO men fell short of living up to their espoused principles, AFL men rarely offered even a pretense of promising nondiscriminatory treatment. Labor leaders in both federations helped oversee continued job segregation by sex during World War II as well as women's exclusion from key sectors of the postwar labor force, but a Women's Bureau study cited only the AFL-affiliated International Brotherhood of Electrical Workers (IBEW) and the International Association of Machinists (IAM) for denying African-American women the right to join their organizations. In her study of women workers in the wartime shipyards of Portland and Vancouver, based on oral history, Amy Kesselman reports that the International Brotherhood of Boilermakers, an old-line AFL trade union, did not admit women until 1942, and then only reluctantly and on a segregated basis. The IBEW and the IAM were nearly as hostile to their women members. At the war's end most unions in the shipyards terminated the women's union membership outright without even pretending to follow seniority guidelines.[62]

The paucity of women in the upper echelons of the AFL illustrates the restricted place of women in the federation. Few AFL women held staff positions at the international level although a greater percentage of AFL women leaders than CIO women held elected posts as heads of local and international unions (see tables 1 and 2). Whereas large, male-dominated industrial unions often provided few elective opportunities for CIO women, specialized unions in the AFL facilitated greater female involvement, especially in such employment sectors as the needle trades, government service, craft, and white collar unions. Only a handful of these women, however, appear to have engaged in serious activism. These included Myra Wolfgang of the Hotel and Restaurant Workers (HERE) and Evelyn Dubrow of the International Ladies' Garment Workers (ILGWU). In all, relatively few women appeared in the ranks of labor leadership; none sat on the AFL's executive board.[63]

This pattern of gender relations in the AFL continued until the federation's merger with the CIO in the mid-1950s. "You could pretty much say that the issue of women and labor was not upper-most in the American Federation of Labor's mind," Nancy Pratt recalled. "In fact, it was pretty much bottom-most." Pratt, an Antioch College graduate, came to work at the labor organization's Washington, D.C., headquarters from the government's Wage Stabilization Board in 1952. Hired as a research department assistant by research director Boris Shiskin, who "just wanted someone to talk to about opera, ballet, and literature," Pratt found that she was the sole woman staff member in an organization dominated by white men. While federation officers "gave lip service to 'women's issues,'" as Pratt put it, AFL leaders devoted few resources to addressing such concerns.[64] Activists in the U.S. Women's Bureau coalition certainly seemed to expect little from the labor federation: for several years they were not even represented at meetings of the bureau's Trade Union Advisory Committee. The bureau's director, Frieda Miller, wrote to AFL president William Green in 1950 to apologize for not inviting him to appoint a permanent representative of the federation at group meetings, mentioning that she had simply overlooked his organization. Green accepted Miller's cryptic explanation without complaint.[65]

The AFL's lack of concern for addressing women's needs manifested itself most publicly in its dealings with its African-American members. Black women workers were not averse to working on behalf of "women's issues." Those women in unions with a relatively good, or at least improving, record of civil rights supported the U.S. Women's Bureau coalition. Addie Wyatt (United Packinghouse Workers of America), Gloria Johnson (IUE), and Lillian Hatcher (UAW), among others, joined middle-class women in the National Council of Negro Women to participate in the coalition's activities. These women helped bring about racial equality as well, both as activists in the labor movement and in civil rights organizations. Most of these union women came from CIO, whose labor organizations "generally contended for racial equality . . . sometimes over the opposition of white CIO members."[66] African Americans had found in the CIO an ally in their campaign to pressure Franklin D. Roosevelt to create the Fair Employment Practices Commission (FEPC) during World War II. The FEPC was charged with investigating discrimination against workers in the war industries. FEPC officers denounced discrimination against African-American women on the basis of their race. African-American women themselves were determined to fight on their own behalf. In the commission's first report, covering the last half of 1943 and all of 1944, it noted that women filed more than one-quarter of all cases the FEPC received for investigation.[67] As their numbers in union ranks increased in the 1950s, these women seized opportunities to keep labor leaders focused on the goal of racial equality. Women played an active role in the short history of the National Negro Labor Council (NNLC), a group formed by labor leaders committed to organizing black workers and countering the wave of red-baiting sweeping the country. At the NNLC's founding meeting in 1951, African-American women constituted one-third of the delegates; they proved to be a reliable source of leadership for the organization until its voluntary disbanding in 1956 in the face of government threats to list it as a "Communist-front organization."[68]

The ties between African-American women and white women workers were weakest in AFL and southern-based unions, where minority women's access to high-paying jobs lagged far behind that of white women. For African-American waitresses, for example, discrimination by white women in the HERE came in the form of utilizing unfair practices in hiring halls, and in their failure to organize saloon and nightclub workers, a work force that African-American women populated in disproportionate numbers. The history of race and gender relations in the Tobacco Workers International Union (TWIU) illustrates the complex factors mitigating cross-racial cooperation as well. Formed at the turn of the century as an AFL union, the TWIU had nearly 34,000 members in its seventy local unions, most of them in the South.[69] TWIU leaders organized black workers into the union in a reluctant acknowledgment of their numerical significance in many plants. E. Lewis Evans, a longtime TWIU president, wrote privately to one labor activist that the "Nigs" must be brought into the union or the "BOSSES will use him to defeat our general purpose."[70] Social equality was out of the question, however. Through the 1930s the TWIU's leaders had, as one historian put it, "attempted to forget the Negro question" until made to remember it by the threat of CIO unionism and the civil rights movement. Subsequently, tobacco unionists strove to improve the TWIU's record but they did not eliminate race-segregated locals until the early 1960s.[71]

African-American women experienced the full force of inequality in the tobacco work force in the areas of hiring, job assignment, and technological displacement. They were often excluded from plants; when hired, they were almost always underrepresented in the better-paying positions. One TWIU international officer, R. J. Petree, reported to a Lorillard and Company representative in 1961 that the ratio of African-American to white employees at the company's Greensboro, North Carolina, facility reflected the racial composition of the community at large. Unfortunately, he noted, "equal opportunities were not available to colored females . . . largely due to our adherence to local customs which we had been advised existed."[72] African-American women at Lorillard in Greensboro opposed these "local customs" in a complaint submitted to the President's Committee on Equal Employment Opportunity (PCEEO). The resulting PCEEO investigation revealed, among other things, that Lorillard had begun to integrate black women in the processing plants and cafeteria but a state segregation law required that rest rooms remain segregated.[73]

While racial inequality did not disappear in the decades following World War II, white and African-American women unionists worked together in an unprecedented manner on a wide range of issues, including civil rights legislation, labor law reform, and equal pay. Given a social space, freed from the worst excesses of racism, union women began to collaborate on issues of common concern. White women activists increasingly strove to connect the issues important to the Women's Bureau coalition to those of the civil rights movement. In the process they hoped to strengthen the case for increased attention to "women's issues." Katherine Ellickson, for example, wrote in a draft commentary for President Kennedy's Commission on the Status of Women Report released in 1963 that "just as the president has done in the field of race discrimination, so he must carry over into the field of women."[74] While the relationship between those advocating for racial equality and those seeking gender equality would not develop fully until the late 1960s, activists in both camps were laying the groundwork for promoting such equal employment opportunity measures as affirmative action by sharing ideas and providing support for key demands.

One relationship that did not improve in the postwar period was that between women unionists and supporters of the Equal Rights Amendment (ERA) led by the National Woman's Party (NWP). The divisions between union women and NWP activists were rooted in the two groups' fundamentally different understanding of how best to improve women's status. The NWP was a small organization whose relatively affluent, well-educated members came together in the 1920s in the wake of the woman suffrage campaign. Under the long-term guidance of Alice Paul, the NWP called for legal and political equality through the passage of the ERA. It denounced sex-based protective legislation, writes Nancy Cott, as "an anachronism, an artifact of women's long history of economic dependence, keeping alive in women the self-deprecating 'psychology of the unpaid worker' long inculcated by domestic servitude."[75] Unionists viewed the NWP position as elitist and out of touch with the daily difficulties wage-earning women faced. The specific problem with the ERA, as one opponent of the amendment wrote in the mid-1940s, was that it failed "to take into account that there are physical and functional differences between men and women. These differences require special consideration, such as laws prohibiting the employment of women in mines."[76] Unionists explained that NWP advocates underplayed the role of economic and social imperatives facing working-class women unionists, a sign of the membership's upper-class support. The NWP not only refused to endorse equal pay measures but attacked the very existence of the U.S. Women's Bureau as antithetical to women's progress. "We do not want women to have any more legislation setting them apart from other workers, and certainly do not want it given more power over the lives of women," Nora Stanton Barney of the NWP's National Advisory Council commented.[77]

By the 1940s the two factions were irreconcilable in their mutual distrust and varying political and economic world views, often lodging exaggerated charges against each other. ERA backers claimed that CIO members opposed the amendment, as one Arizona NWP member put it, because of the "fierce male desire to keep women in a subservient position."[78] Alice Paul even suspected the CIO of sending spies to the party's Washington, D.C., headquarters in order to make trouble. Most ERA supporters probably would have agreed with the head of the Connecticut Committee for the ERA, who charged in 1950 that "our big enemy is organized labor."[79] Women in unions and liberal groups were equally vociferous in their denunciations of the NWP. Representing the ILGWU and the WTUL before a Senate subcommittee hearing on the ERA in 1938, Pauline Newman charged the amendment's supporters with being "numerically insignificant, industrially ignorant, politically theoretical, and socially muddled."[80] Years later the same sentiments prevailed among unionists. "All these women who were working for the equal rights amendment would never help us on the equal pay bill and on the things that would really give substance to some of the women's rights questions," Esther Peterson complained in 1968. "I've always felt they were a bit superficial and unrealistic in their approach."[81] The long-simmering personal animosities and ideological differences dividing these two social movements would never really be eradicated. It would take the rise of second-wave feminism to bring about a rapprochement, and only then in a vastly different social and legal context.

During the long period separating the introduction of the ERA in the 1920s and its passage through the U.S. Congress some fifty years later, unionists and others thwarted its legislative advance. This was not difficult given the lack of firm public support for the ERA. On occasion, however, opponents faced charges by the NWP that, in their refusal to back the ERA, they engaged in unfair treat-

ment to women. Their response—to offer crippling amendments to the measure—was a transparent effort to weaken the ERA, but it was effective nevertheless. Republican Congressmen Robert Taft and James Wordsworth submitted the
first such proposal, known as the Status Bill, in 1947; it declared that "in law and
its administrations no distinctions on the basis of sex shall be made except such
as are reasonably justified by differences in physical structure, biological, or social function."[82] The bill failed miserably. Even in the congressional anti-ERA
camp many found its wording confusing and a threat to women's very employment. The second measure, sponsored by Democrat Carl Hayden in 1950, offered
a more nuanced and conciliatory proposal, but it too diluted the ERA's objective: "The provisions of this article shall not be construed to impair any rights,
benefits, or exemptions conferred by law upon persons of the female sex."[83]
Hayden attached his rider to the ERA in the Senate, stymieing NWP members.
With its appearance legislators could claim to support both the pro- and anti-
ERA forces. "If forced to vote on the measure, members of Congress could now
have it both ways: equality and special privileges for women," notes Cynthia
Harrison.[84] NWP leaders refused to abandon their long-standing commitment
to an unequivocal amendment and so rejected the Hayden rider and, in the process, stalled the ERA's approval. With such maneuvering, opponents had not only
stopped the ERA's advance but checked the NWP's claim to speak for the best
interest of women.

The fierce opposition of the Women's Bureau coalition to the ERA underscores
the need to distinguish between advocacy on behalf of what traditionally was
known as "women's issues" and support for gender equality. Notwithstanding their
growing doubts about the value of protectionism, industrial unionists forged
ahead in defending protective measures for women, arguing that such laws were
necessary to conserve the health of the nation's mothers and daughters. The CIO's
Political Action Committee, for example, backed a Social Security Act amendment that would permit women to retire earlier than men. They did so on the
grounds that, as Katherine Ellickson put it, "women in practice have a harder
time than men in obtaining and maintaining jobs as they get older and many
wives are younger than their husbands, so that both would benefit if the age is
lowered to 62 or 60."[85] Ellickson's reasoning on this particular matter illustrates
the multiple objectives embedded in protectionist measures: they accrued benefits
to women but even more to men, who, in this case, would no longer compete
with older women for jobs. In retirement men would not be left at home alone
while their younger wives were at work.

The distinction between "women's issues" and issues relating to gender equality was fluid: demands in the 1970s that fell under the banner of equality had

been understood several years earlier in the context of protectionism. This was certainly the case with maternity policy. Unions such as the UAW, ACWA, ILGWU, TWUA, and USW decried the lack of federal and state benefits for pregnant women and sponsored their own health insurance plans to provide for their female members. They were moved to do so, not by the notion of the comparable nature of pregnancy to other disabilities, which was covered in the Pregnancy Discrimination Act of 1978, but rather by the 1908 Supreme Court decision in *Muller v. Oregon* that women were primarily mothers in need of protection in the workplace. Even when union activists defended the right of married women to paid employment—a seemingly unambiguous matter—that right was usually cast more in terms of working women's ability to augment the family purchasing power and, hence, bolster the national economy than as a matter of individual rights.[86]

While there was no definitive break with protectionism in the 1950s, there were signs that the new roles of women were already changing the goals and strategies of those who were union activists. Quietly, the Women's Bureau coalition moved away from advocating time and weight limitations and toward expanding job opportunities for women, especially in newly created occupations that were as yet sex-neutral. The coalition did not exactly abandon protective measures as much as subordinate their importance to a new set of priorities, addressing a group of women who were younger and who identified less with the legislation first passed during the Progressive age. These included women in aircraft, electronics, and plastics technologies. Also, coalition members put a new emphasis on securing benefits that would permit women to remain in the work force, unencumbered by domestic responsibilities. In the early 1950s the CIO supported tax exemptions for child-care expenses; by mid-decade, women unionists had expanded their efforts to include legislation allowing the deduction of costs for hiring household workers and nursery school expenses. They pushed as well for housekeeping services, after-school programs, low-cost nurseries, community restaurants, and convenient shopping facilities for working women.[87]

Searching for ways to expand job opportunities for women, however, was not synonymous with demanding equality. Coalition members took a circuitous route in addressing the long-term implications of women's greater labor force participation. This should remind us not to assign too much significance to the effect a single change in industrial relations might have had on gender relations before the 1960s. The mere influx of women into the work force did little by itself to destabilize prevailing practices. Union women would suggest potentially bold policies only to justify their implementation by appealing to the basic tenets of protectionism. During the Korean War, for example, members of the Labor

Advisory Committee of the U.S. Women's Bureau sought to improve women workers' status by bringing them into "men's" jobs, much as had occurred in World War II. They did not make a case for opening these jobs to women on the grounds of equality, however, for that would have challenged too many of the underlying assumptions of the sexual division of labor. "The idea which is sometimes prevalent, that women cannot do the same kinds of jobs as men, is fallacious," committee members asserted in late 1950. They went on to restate the old view of women's suitability for certain kinds of jobs, thus undercutting a suggestion of equality: "If a sound engineering program is carried out in a plant, there are few jobs which women cannot handle. Women's skills are particularly good in jobs where manual dexterity is required."[88] Women activists seemed to be forming a new understanding of workplace relations but were doing so in a halting manner. At the midpoint between World War II and the emergence of second-wave feminism, the growing inadequacies of protectionism were beginning to manifest themselves in indirect and inchoate ways.

Given the reserve with which women broached the subject of inequality, the continuing push for equal pay proved to be the most suitable means for expressing their dissatisfaction. The equal pay campaign neither confronted masculine-privileged employment practices nor directly challenged women's marginalization in unions. Rather, in a period characterized by economic expansion, it promised to confirm the centrality of the family as an economic unit by delivering enhanced consumer power through women's increased wages. It did this even while implicitly acknowledging the rights of wage-earning women as individuals and not on account of their sex. Equal pay was a confirmation of the superiority of the postwar free enterprise system and the notion that American-style democracy protected one's rights. As the next chapter's discussion of equal pay legislation suggests, national leaders enlisted the equal pay issue in the struggle against Soviet communism. "Khrushchev has predicted that by 1970 Russia will overtake this country economically," Democratic legislator Claude Pepper said in defense of equal pay. "We need all the incentive that we can provide to the labor force of this nation to keep America superior in economic power and progress in the free world today."[89] Equal pay advocates also attempted to embarrass reticent legislators by reminding them that the International Labor Organization backed equal pay and that Canadian provinces and Great Britain had equal pay measures on their books a full ten years before the United States.[90]

No national leaders were more vocal in advocating equal pay than male union officers. Their rhetorical zeal for equal pay, however, usually outstripped the equal pay guarantees they obtained in collective bargaining agreements. The author of one union journal article noted in 1950 that fighting for equal pay was "the democratic thing to do. It was also the smart thing to do—smart for male workers, who will be protecting their own wage levels; smart for employers, who will be protecting themselves against unfair tactics of competitors who try to produce cheap products with cheap labor; and smart for consumers, who will be protecting themselves and the economy from unscrupulous schemers who have no regard for the quality of products."[91] Most contracts did not reflect a commitment to equal pay: a Bureau of Labor Statistics study completed in the early 1950s found that only one-fifth of the 2,644 bargaining agreements analyzed contained equal pay clauses. The apathy with which labor negotiators viewed the matter in the immediate aftermath of World War II continued in most unions throughout the 1950s.[92] In light of the slow and uneven progress made at the bargaining table, union women placed most of their energies in bringing the matter to national attention by lobbying for federal legislation. As the next chapter illustrates, that struggle would take on a life of its own in the legislative realm, informing the growing debate over gender equality but operating beyond the reach of most women workers in local unions.

Automation and the Reconsideration of Protectionism, 1955–63

The rapid introduction of automation into the workplace by employers was crucial in stimulating support for gender equality. By the mid-1950s, changes like this gave force to growing doubts about the benefits of the sex-segregation and protective laws that limited women's working hours and employment options. Technological change affected workers adversely through de-skilling and displacement. The pace of automation varied widely across industrial sectors and unions, but as mechanization was adopted, stunned employees found themselves vying with each other over progressively fewer stable, high-paying positions. Opinion Research Corporation surveyors found that two-thirds of the labor leaders they questioned believed automation to be unionism's most serious problem. Several unionists testified at a government hearing on the matter in 1961, noting that both production and unemployment had jumped dramatically over the previous decade. The UAW representative told the gathering that 160,000 workers had been displaced by automation between 1947 and 1960; United Steel Workers (USW) officers claimed to have lost 95,000 workers between 1937 and 1959.[93] Fearful of being labeled obstructionists, federation officers welcomed the new technology formally; but George Meany cautioned that automation was "rapidly becoming a curse to this society . . . in a mad race to produce more and more with less and less labor and without any feeling [as to] what it may mean to the whole economy."[94] The author of a government report on unemployment warned that "if a city the size of Detroit can be shaken by automation, no community in the country can be complacent about its effects."[95]

Significantly, the effects of technological innovation were not gender neutral. Researchers found in 1957 that, of the laid-off workers at a closed automobile parts supplier firm, all of the women had exhausted their unemployment compensation benefits while just one-third of white males and three-fourths of African Americans (presumably males) had done so. Most of the women over forty claimed they faced both sex and age discrimination. According to one forty-eight-year-old woman, "At . . . [X company] I'm sure they were hiring new women but they didn't hire me because of my age."[96] Authors of the U.S. Department of Labor's 1964 study of workers in petroleum refineries and in the automotive equipment, glass jar, and floor covering industries reported that women's unemployment rate due to automation was almost three times that of men. In addition, those analyzing the study's data indicated that age discrimination affected women at a younger age than it affected men.[97] Two industrial relations scholars observed the negative effects automation had on women: "Automation has tended to increase shift work, and, on occasion, female workers have consequently been affected adversely by state laws restricting hours of work for women. Moreover, when women are displaced, they will rarely relocate, and almost all are too young to be eligible for early retirement. In the main, when faced with displacement, they accept severance pay and thus terminate permanently their current employment. Some seek alternative employment, but others withdraw from the labor market."[98]

African-American women workers were particularly susceptible to job losses due to automation. In the absence of data on minority women's displacement, specific examples from certain industries must suffice to illustrate this. Beginning in the late 1940s, for example, when the American Tobacco Company introduced the mechanized removal of tobacco stems, more than a thousand African-American women were laid off and most of them were never called back to work. The overall employment figures of the tobacco work-force are telling: in 1930 African Americans made up nearly 66 percent of the female work force; mechanization helped to lower that figure to 36.8 percent in 1950, and to 25 percent in 1960. African-American women in other industrial sectors suffered similar fates. The number of African-American women in the packinghouse industry increased more than fivefold between 1940 and 1950; the introduction of new machines and job combinations, however, caused a sharp decline in the proportion of all women in the industry, from 23 percent in the early 1950s to 14 percent in 1955. The greatest losses came in the Midwest. In Chicago, Armour and Company dismissed five thousand African American women when it closed its flagship plant in the early 1960s. These women found that, even as they made slow but definitive advances in moving into higher-paying unionized jobs, their progress was checked by cruel and frequent layoffs.[99]

Labor leaders seemed paralyzed by the limitations inherent in collective bargaining agreements. They were unable to respond forcefully to automation and similar changes. In an attempt to assert some control over technological developments, several union leaders pushed to set up joint automation committees with management, but these efforts had limited success. The problem of technology, in fact, was part of the larger issue of management's claim to determine the means and ends of production. In this area, government as a rule sided with employers. As James Atleson argues in his *Values and Assumptions in American Labor Law,* courts and administrative agencies since the nineteenth century had almost always backed business owners in their assertion that production decisions inherently were a managerial prerogative. Workers on the shop floor chafed under employers' mandates as union leadership often remained quiescent. The battle over control, begun at the onset of industrialization and continued into the twentieth century, shifted decidedly in favor of management following World War II. By embracing the New Deal collective bargaining framework, which depended heavily on state intervention, union leaders committed their members to an increasingly circumscribed system of labor relations.[100] While pockets of shop-floor militancy continued to exist, and collective bargaining allowed for a slowing-down of automation's effects, employers effectively wrested from unions the basic "right to manage" in the postwar reconfiguration of industrial relations. Employers after 1945, reports Howell John Harris, "had altered [their] . . . aims from fighting off unionism to attempting to confine the scope of bargaining, limit it to local levels, and turn the union machinery into a force for stability within the plant."[101]

Automation removed job elements previously used to justify sex segregation, thus challenging the notion that certain kinds of work were best suited for either men or women. As innovations whittled away at long-standing workplace designs, the argument that working women needed protective policies increasingly came under fire. "Automation promises to relieve more and more workers from dangerous, dirty, heavy, and backbreaking jobs," predicted one labor specialist in the mid-1950s. "Industrial hygienists foresee the elimination of a large percentage of traumatic injuries from lifting, handling, and unloading of stock and contact with fumes and dangerous materials. Illustrative is the 85 percent reduction in hernia cases where automation machinery was installed in a Ford plant." As a result, he concluded, protective laws "may have a smaller role in the future than in the past."[102] Marjorie Turner, a labor economist at San Diego State College, was even bolder in her assessment. The effect of job-typing on women workers was decidedly negative: "Sex labeling takes its toll. Women remain unprepared for promotion, believing such opportunities are not available."[103] Turner regarded job-typing by sex as a product of "cultural factors" that were "hardly reliable" in predicting individual performance. She noted that, although job labels were "often viewed as permanent, substitution of females for males may take place without difficulty, especially in periods of manpower shortage."[104]

This reconsideration of job-typing was not simply a discussion carried on in policy circles. Sex discrimination charges flooding the U.S. Women's Bureau from rank-and-file workers indicated their dissatisfaction with job-typing schemes. A letter from Mrs. W. B. McPherson of Jacksonville, Florida, was typical. "Women are not being assigned work . . . they could do," she told the bureau. Laws, responded a bureau representative, "do not usually prohibit discrimination on a sex basis in hiring or promotion of workers. . . . Moreover the Federal regulation applicable to Government contractors does not prohibit discrimination in employment on the basis of sex."[105] People in national unions began questioning sex segregation in the face of automation's reordering of job contents as well. "The great majority of occupations and industrial processes of today are not by their nature exclusively 'men's work' or 'women's work,'" Esther Peterson observed in 1962. "Heavy lifting and arduous work are more and more frequently being done by mechanical means and machine power. Given necessary training and opportunities for employment, women are capable of performing nearly any kind of job."[106] Jacob Clayman of the AFL-CIO's Industrial Union Department concurred, arguing that "we have to start to think a wee bit differently than we have in the past as we have separated men and women exclusively in terms of muscular power." Clayman continued, "If anybody . . . can read the signs on the horizon automation will invite women . . . to do as well as any other man no matter how muscular and even though he conforms to the Mr. Atlas type."[107]

Unionists came to doubt the validity of protective laws through their experiences with economic, technological, and ideological changes. Transforming their assumptions about gender relations, however, was a longer and more uneven process. Working women in the mid-1940s had been angered by their demotions and layoffs from the "men's" positions in which they had worked successfully during the war, but they lacked the popular support necessary to fight these perceived injustices. By the late 1950s a fifteen-year campaign for equal pay had provided women activists with, as Alice Kessler-Harris terms it, "expanded notions of justice, encouraging perceptions of male/female equality that had previously been invisible."[108] Armed with this powerful new sense of equality and a growing share of the total work force that increased from 29 percent in 1950 to 33 percent in 1960, women activists attacked the old argument that the small number of working women necessitated protective policies.[109] Such measures, Nancy

Pratt observed in 1957, were "more often based on social tradition rather than physical aptitudes." True equality, Pratt asserted, meant "an integrated plant with equal opportunity for job promotion and transfer to any job for which an individual is trained."[110]

Beyond stray expressions of discontent, more organized efforts by unionists helped inch women toward demanding gender equality. As shown in the case studies of the International Union of Electrical Workers and the United Packinghouse Workers of America, industrial unionists endorsed equal treatment for women and de-emphasized protective measures at least a decade before the Civil Rights Act of 1964. At the UAW Women's Bureau and at the local level, automobile union women expressed their frustration with obstacles to gender equality they encountered. The bureau introduced and lobbied for the abolition of separate seniority lists for women and men as early as the mid-1940s. Protectionist practices gave way slowly, however, even in this supposedly progressive labor organization. During negotiations in September 1961, activists in UAW Local 663 in Anderson, Indiana, forced General Motors and the UAW's International Executive Board to accept a single seniority list as the local's principle demand after a prolonged struggle.[111] At the federation level Boris Shishkin gently raised the issue of the AFL-CIO's reconsideration of gender equality with George Meany in 1957. Without directly embracing the ERA, Shishkin noted that many AFL-CIO affiliates already called for nondiscrimination clauses in collective bargaining agreements. He suggested that Meany give sex discrimination "a full-dress treatment," including calling for an executive council statement on equal rights for women, development of programs designed to eliminate discrimination against working women, and the appointment of a qualified woman unionist as a special assistant to the federation chief, to be in charge of "women's affairs."[112] Meany was not interested in enacting such recommendations. There is no indication that he responded to Shishkin's communique, and federation leaders did not carry out any of his proposals. There is no archival record of Shishkin's further consideration of the matter.

Despite hints of a changing attitude toward gender relations at the national level between 1945 and 1963, both men and women unionists were deeply ambivalent about embracing equality fully. Male unionists, in particular, were skeptical about rejecting a system that had benefited them by keeping women from high-paying jobs. And yet, many found the paychecks their wives brought home essential to the family budget. Some union leaders began to acknowledge this increasingly complex understanding of women workers' place. Federation officer William Schnitzler, for example, said, "There is simply no way to turn the clock back [on gender relations], even if it were desirable." In calling for change, however, his rhetoric indicates that he was more concerned with strengthening the family-wage ideal than with empowering women: "The work of women has become essential to the operation of the economy, to the maintenance of consumer purchasing power and to the economic stability of millions of families." Ideally, Schnitzler continued, wage and employment levels should be kept high enough "to afford the family a genuine choice with respect to a wife's work."[113]

Women workers themselves sometimes held contradictory positions for gender difference and equality. "I believe justice demands that we receive the same rights, privileges and protections as male workers," wrote a woman unionist from Missouri. While she supported the inclusion of the category "sex" in antidiscrimination codes, this same woman decried "so-called equal rights legislation" and did not believe mothers of small children should work.[114] Some women expressed outright opposition to equality measures for fear that women workers would lose the modest gains afforded by state laws and union contracts. Women in UAW Local 602 with considerable seniority in their departments were surprised to find that the labor organization's Women's Bureau—not hostile males trying to oust them from the industry—advocated single seniority lists. "These women feared, not without reason," Nancy Gabin notes, "that management would assign them to harder or dirtier jobs if they had to compete with men for status."[115] As in other industrial unions, however, UAW women and some sympathetic men were moving toward the conclusion that women, as Gabin puts it, "had a right to sex-blind treatment" based on "an understanding of their rights as union members."[116] Generally, however, women were "confused" as to their place in the work world, the economist Elizabeth Faulkner Baker noted at the time. "Some women want the old ways, while others welcome the new, but most women are between."[117]

Women voiced both their unhappiness with inequality and their reluctance to discard protection measures entirely at a meeting organized by staff members of the AFL-CIO's Industrial Union Department (IUD) in June 1961. The IUD functioned as an official organization in which unionists planned strategies for contract negotiations. More important, it was a loose grouping of labor leaders from industrial unions who "considered [the IUD] an adequate continuation of the CIO" within the merged federation.[118] Headed by the UAW's Walter Reuther and the IUE's James Carey, the IUD provided the lone forum in the AFL-CIO bureaucracy for those espousing social unionism; fifteen of the eighteen AFL-CIO unions with the largest female memberships were affiliated with the IUD (see table 3). This "exceptional conference," as Katherine Ellickson characterized it, brought together women from such unions as the UAW, IUE, ILGWU, CWA, USW, and ACWA and other labor representatives.[119] Veteran activists made up the conference's planning committee; these unionists included Caroline

Davis (UAW), Sylvia Gottlieb (CWA), Gloria Johnson (IUE), Evelyn Dubrow (ILGWU), and Connie Kopelov (ACWA). In his foreword to the meeting's published proceedings, Jacob Clayman of the IUD credited Esther Peterson, who had by then moved to her position in the Kennedy administration, for her "encouragement and assistance" in the conference's development.[120] Many of these women sat together on the National Committee on Equal Pay or attended U.S. Women's Bureau meetings but they had never participated in an interunion gathering designed to consider working-class "women's issues" solely from a labor movement perspective.

Table 3. Women Members in Unions with 50,000 or More Women Members, 1958 and 1968

	1958		1968	
	No.	%	No.	%
AFL-CIO				
Bakery[a]	—[b]	—	52,300	32
Clothing	282,000	75	—	—
Communications	153,200	60	178,800	50
Electrical (IUE)	111,300	40	113,500	35
Electrical (IBEW)	225,000	30	269,100	30
Garment, ladies	332,200	75	364,000	80
Government (AFGE)	24,000	40	97,300	33
Hotel	174,500	40	146,900	32
Machinists	99,300	10	—	—
Meat Cutters[c]	77,200	14	75,000	15
Railway Clerks	41,200	11	56,000	20
Retail Clerks	176,900	58	—	—
Retail, Wholesale	56,000	35	70,000	40
Service Employees	52,000	20	128,400	33
State, County	—	—	—	—
Steel	—	—	—	—
Teachers	33,000	65	99,000	60
Textile Workers	78,800	40	73,200	40
Unaffiliated				
Automobile Workers	102,700	10	176,700	12
Teamsters	156,000	11	—	—
Telephone	54,000	60	51,500	97
Totals				
Selected unions	2,408,000	26.0	2,964,000	26.3
All unions	3,274,000	18.2	3,940,000	19.5

Source: Lucretia M. Dewey, "Women in Labor Unions," *Monthly Labor Review* 94 (Feb. 1971): 43.
    a. Includes the Bakery and Confectionary Workers Union of America (Ind.) and the American Bakery and Confectionary Workers International Union, AFL-CIO.
    b. A dash (—) indicates that the data were not reported. Estimates made by the Bureau are included in the totals. Figures include members in areas outside the United States, primarily Canada.
    c. Includes the Packinghouse Workers of America in 1958 and 1968.

Walter Reuther sounded themes familiar to unionists in his keynote address to conference participants, such as the need for a guaranteed annual wage, support for civil rights, and support for equal pay. The most far-reaching efforts at analyzing workplace discrimination, however, occurred in the "discussion groups" held over the two-day conference period. There is no verbatim record of the proceedings but IUD staff members included a telling summary of each group's recommendations in the conference report. In these small gatherings, women considered single seniority lists, questioned the continued validity of protective laws, and demanded congressional action banning sex discrimination in employment. Many of their conversations focused on automation. While their recommendations anticipated elements of the post-1964 period, participants kept one foot in the protectionist camp. Those in the "Economic Problems: Job Opportunities" group, for example, demanded that a ban on "sex, age, and marital status" discrimination be included in fair employment practice laws. They urged union leaders at the same time to "promote stronger and more protective contract provisions for women workers."[121] In another meeting, the "Legislative Problems: Protective Legislation" assembly reported that "the need was stressed . . . for revising outdated laws where this can be done without sacrificing basic protections."[122]

More than anything, this event was a catalyst for women activists attempting to come to terms with the cumulative effects of economic and technological changes affecting their status as workers. In the end, conference participants pulled back from advocating startling departures in working-class gender relations. Instead, they endorsed equal pay legislation, condemned the ERA, and called for continued study of the issues raised at the meeting. Having met as a group and raised these inchoate demands for equality, they were not yet certain as to how to proceed. The women nevertheless understood their marginalization on the shop floor and in the union hall as a source of their frustration. "I have a great bone to pick with the organized labor movement in this country," said Bessie Hillman of the Clothing Workers to the IUD assembly. "In my opinion they are the greatest offenders as far as discrimination against women is concerned. . . . There isn't a woman on the AFL-CIO council—only 31 men."[123] In the absence of equal rights legislation and a mass movement of feminists, however, Hillman could offer little in the way of a concrete agenda for change.

"To work was one thing; to call into question traditional attitudes toward sex roles was another," William Chafe notes in his study of U.S. women and equality. "For the latter to happen, new perceptions had to evolve and a new frame of reference had to develop."[124] These new possibilities had begun to emerge by the mid-1960s, but they moved against the forces of tradition, industrial policy, and the law. Women unionists sought to make sense of the economic and social changes affecting their lives. They were working in ever greater numbers and under new conditions, but increasingly outdated laws regulated their working lives. They looked to their labor organizations to respond in a meaningful manner to these changes but found union leaders either hesitant or unwilling to reconsider the value of protectionism. The women experienced these transformations but felt the pull of accepted industrial relations practices too strong to break decisively. The growing gap between ideology and reality would result in a new consciousness of working-class feminism over the course of the next decade. During the years 1945–64 union women began to lay the groundwork for this feminism with their sometimes isolated, scattered, and unorganized expressions of discontent. To this they added a focused and organized nationwide call for equal pay legislation in what would become the first step in a drive for gender equality.

2

Prospects for Equality:
Union Women, Equal Pay Legislation,
and National Politics, 1945–63

Shortly before the American Federation of Labor's (AFL) merger with the Congress of Industrial Organizations (CIO) in 1955, federation president George Meany wrote a significant article in *Fortune* outlining organized labor's agenda for the next quarter-century. Meany's observations were noteworthy both in his support for a continuation of the hardheaded pragmatism Samuel Gompers brought the AFL and for his acknowledgment that labor's goals and means were changing to reflect the social and economic transformations affecting the postwar United States. Summarizing the AFL's traditional position, Meany wrote: "We do not seek to recast American society in any particular doctrinaire or ideological image. We seek an ever rising standard of living. Sam Gompers put the matter succinctly. When asked what the labor movement wanted, he answered, 'More.'"[1] Antiunion employers and conservative politicians' success in passing the Taft-Hartley Act in 1947, however, had forced the AFL to modify its nonpartisan policy of pursuing private collective bargaining exclusively and to join the CIO in advocating social and political change through state action. The AFL, Meany noted, had established the organization's League for Political Education in 1948 in response to attacks on its survival. He added that, beyond "bread-and-butter" issues, the labor movement was now interested in automation, shorter hours, and racial equality as a way of protecting its members and buttressing the nation's "world moral leadership" role in the midst of the cold war.[2]

Meany did not mention in his article the ever-growing number of women in union ranks or their concerns. Nevertheless, his comments reveal the context in which activists campaigned for equal pay legislation in the postwar period, culminating in the passage of the Equal Pay Act of 1963. He celebrated the "American profit system" brought to prosperity by a male-defined labor force whose higher wages would fortify family life: "the workers' wives and families have greater comforts and opportunities for social and cultural development than families of workers in any other land." Meany destabilized this understanding of the family-wage ideology, however, by incorporating individual rights into his patriotic vision. In particular, he denounced racial inequality as detrimental to the strength of the labor movement. "Where there is no individual liberty," Meany asserted that "there is no free trade-union movement."[3] These competing notions of wage justice smoldered in a near combustible state during these years as unionists negotiated the shifting contours of race and gender relations in the family and workplace.

In pushing for an equal pay law, women activists echoed many of Meany's sentiments. Social unionism's clarion call for labor to lead in the legislative battle for justice informed their efforts. Where once the labor and liberal group activists, joined together in the U.S. Women's Bureau coalition, promoted the scores of protective laws for women passed over the previous half-century, after 1945 their focus shifted to lobbying legislators to secure job opportunities and higher wages for women workers. The turnaround in the coalition's priorities was notable: no new protective measures appeared on the lawbooks, while the number of states with equal pay laws jumped from two in 1940 to 22 in 1963.[4] The long campaign for a federal measure reached fruition in the early 1960s as the Kennedy Administration's Esther Peterson, formerly of the AFL-CIO Industrial Union Department, brought the bill to a vote with the help of like-minded legislators.

The importance of the political and legislative history of "women's issues" in the two decades preceding the appearance of the Civil Rights Act of 1964 lies in the key role union women played in growing political support for gender equality. The shifting political winds and unevenness of male unionists' support should dissuade scholars from viewing the Equal Pay Act of 1963 as inevitable. Several mitigating factors emerged between 1945—the year an equal pay bill first appeared in Congress—and the early 1960s that threatened to thwart its passage. The AFL resisted the measure until the federation merged with the CIO in the mid-1950s; public interest in improving women's economic status waned in the late 1950s; and, in the face of constant resistance from conservative lawmakers, equal pay proponents encountered an atmosphere of intransigence. When it came to supporting gender equality beyond that of equal pay, union women displayed their own ambiguity. They could back equal pay but not the Equal Rights Amendment (ERA), which proved too threatening both in its identification with traditional backers who were unfriendly to organized labor and in its promise of equality in unknown forms. In the end, the ERA would receive union women's support only with the arrival of second-wave feminism in the 1960s and 70s.

The politics of "women's issues" in the years immediately preceding this period of mass support for gender equality provides a lens by which to view the shift in consciousness of union women's support, from protectionism to equality. While the technological, economic, and social changes affecting women workers at the local union level helped to feed the growing sense of dissatisfaction with inequality, at the national level the efforts of the small corps of women activists battling for equality legislation built the case for gender equality as well.

A False Start: The Early Campaign for a Federal Equal Pay Law, 1945–54

Mary Anderson, the U.S. Women's Bureau director, crafted the first federal equal pay bill in 1945, confident that the widespread support for equal pay during World War II would carry over into the postwar period. She called for nondiscrimination in wages paid for "comparable work" rather than "equal work." It would take nearly twenty years, however, for Anderson's proposal to become law, and another decade for her call for "equal pay for comparable worth" to gain significant support. Far from being a fanciful design with little basis in current practices, however, her proposal at war's end reflected the mood of a period steeped in the language of corporativism. Her legislative plan provided for an "advisory committee" that would establish wage differentials among different types of work; employers in violation of the law were to be blacklisted. Anderson's bill forbade management from discharging women without cause, a provision intended to prevent women's replacement with men during postwar reconversion. Borrowing from language in the National War Labor Board's General Order no. 16, promulgated in 1942, Anderson tried not only to eliminate unequal pay for those doing identical work but also to remedy the injustice of differential pay for jobs assigned according to sex. Frieda Miller, Anderson's successor in the bureau, continued to work for equal pay into the 1950s.[5]

The Women's Bureau explored the possibility of what is now called "comparable worth" in a series of hearings and investigations held in 1945 and 1947. The bureau scuttled its incipient campaign in the face of contention over how best to develop evaluation schemes and job point weights. Moreover, as Alice Kessler-Harris argues, equal pay, rather than comparable worth, best reflected the dominant mood of the postwar United States. Equal pay promised individual justice, helped increase economic growth by putting more money in some women's pockets, and reduced potential workplace friction by maintaining occupational sex-segregation. This buttressed the male-defined family wage ideology while comparable worth's "gender justice . . . seemed to negate the possibility of an appropriate family standard of living."[6] While bills before Congress continued to use comparable worth terminology, most supporters quietly abandoned pushing for an application beyond that meaning work of an identical or nearly identical nature.

Public opinion favored equal pay legislation, but significant forces balked at it, viewing the measure as a prolabor initiative. Reflecting the mood of many in the business community, conservative Democratic and Republican legislators defeated equal pay proposals in successive legislative sessions. Some groups rejected the measure outright, claiming it would "involve undue interference in the work relationship . . . interfere with efficient management, and prove disruptive to good relations between employer and employees," as one National Association of Manufacturers representative told a House hearing in 1950. Most critics proved cagier in their opposition. They agreed, for example, that a need for legislation existed but called for more studies on the matter.[7] Ohio Republican Frances P. Bolton proposed reducing the proposal's mandate from that modeled after the National Labor Relations Act, covering all employers engaged in businesses affecting "commerce," to the Fair Labor Standard Act's narrower application to those companies that participated only in interstate commerce. In the face of opposition from conservatives who rejected even these diluted terms, Bolton revised her bill, calling this time merely for a study of the equal pay problem, which alienated the Women's Bureau. Several factors account for the Anderson-style bill's undoing by the late 1940s, according to Cynthia Harrison: congressional apathy, conservative opposition, and a withering of public interest in rewarding women workers for their wartime contribution, an effort that was "beginning to fade from memory" as the country moved into the 1950s.[8]

Strong male support for equal pay legislation came from CIO leaders who testified before congressional committees in 1945, 1948, and 1950 that its enactment was a matter of justice to women workers, beneficial to men, and necessary to the nation's economic well-being. These leaders echoed sentiments coming out of the Women's Bureau during the same period. "The Federal Government must, if it wishes to maintain purchasing power and a decent standard of living for all workers, make it an unfair wage practice to permit wage differentials based on sex," Rubber Workers representative T. R. Owen told a group of senators in October 1945.[9] Arguing to that same gathering that proposed legislation was "indispensable" to women workers "because it will eliminate, once and for all, the low and discriminatory rates paid to women and protect their place in industry," United Electrical Workers spokesman Clifford McAvoy also championed its value to men, "because the existence of low women's rates in the plant serves to pull down their own wage standard."[10] CIO representatives giving testimony or submitting statements to Congress on the bill's behalf during these three sets of hearings included those from the automobile, textile, and pack-inghouse unions. Communications Workers president Joseph A. Beirne admonished House members in 1950 for having not yet passed an equal pay bill. "Even if the members of this committee are not tired of hearing the same favorable comments in support of this bill, I frankly am weary of repeating them," an exasperated Beirne told the lawmakers.[11] Helen Blanchard followed Beirne at the hearing, delivering a statement on behalf of the CIO and one of its constituent unions, the Clothing Workers. She spoke in stark terms: "The cornerstone of our democracy is equality. Too long have we permitted that concept of equality to be abused when applied to half of our population—the Women of our Nation." In attempting to navigate between support for gender equality and the retention of protectionism, Blanchard pulled back from endorsing an unmitigated equality that would have pleased ERA backers: "If any group in society has reason to be given a privileged position, it is certainly our mothers and sisters who are working. But they are not asking for a privileged position. They simply want to be accepted as equals. The very best Congress can do is to abolish the horrible practice of discrimination purely on the basis of sex."[12] No other public comment by an industrial unionist before the late 1960s would come as close as Blanchard's statement had to embracing the law of equality over the law of difference.

   That CIO male leaders remained committed formally to strong equal pay legislation in the early 1950s, even though opponents had halted its progress in Congress, served at least to keep the issue alive. They joined other liberal groups in rejecting the Bolton bill's narrow coverage, supporting instead Congresswoman Edith Green's proposal, modeled on Mary Anderson's original bill, which provided for blacklisting guilty employers and giving strong enforcement powers to the secretary of labor.[13] Legislative representative Thomas Burke and Walter Reuther's assistant Robert Oliver argued with Eisenhower's secretary of labor, James P. Mitchell, that reliance on judicial enforcement would be costly and time-consuming to workers; "administrative action enforced by courts of equity with provisions for expedited appeals" was more efficient, they contended.[14] Their preference for administrative, rather than judicial, enforcement reflected more than an advocacy of speedy justice; CIO officers were concerned that reliance on courts would impinge on normal collective bargaining. They were comfortable with the usually pro-union Labor Department's intervention in industrial relations but were wary of the fickleness of judicial rulings, especially when unions might be the target of equal pay suits, as they already had been in a few cases. This anxiety over federal courts' ordering extensive changes in job practices codified in collective bargaining agreements would develop in the 1960s and 1970s into open warfare between labor leaders and activists who challenged the root causes of race and gender inequality in the employment and wage structure.[15]

Notwithstanding support from CIO men, equal pay advocates had little to cheer about in the early 1950s. With the arrival of Republican rule in 1953, the executive branch's support for equal pay cooled considerably. So too did the measure's chance for passage. The Eisenhower administration ousted the U.S. Women's Bureau director, Frieda Miller, in 1953 and replaced her with the conservative Alice Leopold. Leopold endorsed equal pay legislation, as Anderson and Miller had done, but her primary connection to professional women and her threat to soften the bureau's anti-ERA stance soured her relationship with labor and progressive women. For the first time, the center of support for equal pay shifted outside the government and onto the National Committee on Equal Pay (NCEP), a successor organization to Mary Anderson's National Equal Pay Commission formed in the mid-1940s. CIO women participated fully in the group's activities; after the CIO's merger with the AFL in 1955, activists in the newly formed federation would take on an even greater role, dominating meetings and electing their representatives to the NCEP's executive board. The organization included the Women's Bureau coalition members as well as enemies of congressionally mandated equal pay, who attended meetings in order to monitor the group's activities. The NCEP—a weakly structured group whose officers had no formal authority over member organizations' positions—served as an conduit for legislative news and performed many of the bureau's old functions until the ascent of the Kennedy administration in 1961 and the appointment of CIO staff member Esther Peterson to head the U.S. Women's Bureau. Facing formidable conservative opposition, congressional indifference, and an administration indifferent to equal pay proposals, NCEP members had many obstacles to overcome.[16]

Advocates could expect little support for pending legislation from the other large labor federation of the period, the American Federation of Labor (AFL). The organization's leaders claimed that their objection to equal pay bills before Congress was based on their long-standing hostility to schemes involving the state in job evaluations and setting wage rates.[17] Samuel Gompers had forged the federation's voluntarism strategy at the turn of the century, and his successor, William Green, perfected it following the death of Gompers in 1924. AFL leaders had not always held this dim view of state intervention. Although economic protest had been a key emphasis of the AFL challenge to employers, members still viewed political action as part of the federation program through the late nineteenth century. "Our movement stands for the wage-earners doing for themselves what they can toward working out their own salvation. But those things they can not do for themselves the Government should do," Gompers observed

in 1898.[18] Faced with an onslaught of unfriendly court decisions, failed legislative programs, and mixed results in electoral battles, however, federationists moved
toward a rigid antistatist liberalism that emphasized a freedom-of-contract rhetoric
designed to elevate voluntarism to a matter of principle.[19] "One need but read
the history of the toilers," Gompers said in 1915 in sloughing off political phi-
losophies predicated on state action, "to learn how potent has been the power
vested in the constituted authorities of the time to twist laws intended to be of
interest to the workers to their very undoing even to the verge of tyranny."[20]

The AFL campaign against regulatory intervention took on new meaning with
the passage of the National Labor Relations Act (Wagner Act) in 1935. While
federation leaders appreciated the measure's guarantees of freedom to organize
and bargain collectively, they were alarmed, but could do little, about the newly
created National Labor Relation Board's ability to transform collective bargaining from an area of private concern to one of public interest.[21] "There never was,
nor will there ever be, a time that labor organizations will not prefer to settle their
disputes and differences by direct negotiations with the employer without resorting to outside agencies," the AFL general counsel told the Senate in 1939.[22] They
watched with consternation in 1935 as representatives of the newly formed CIO
split from AFL ranks and built competing institutions with ex-federationists and
previously unorganized mass production workers. Led by AFL president William
Green, the beleaguered unionists preempted further CIO gains by signing "sweet-
heart" contracts with employers, purging the CIO from local labor bodies, engaging in bloody guerrilla warfare, and, in larger AFL unions like the Machinists, Carpenters, Meatcutters, and Teamsters, launching intensive organizing
campaigns. These tactics "gave old-fashioned business unionism a new aggres-
siveness . . . without changing one atom of its social and political conservatism,"
contends one sociologist, Mike Davis.[23] By late 1937 the federation had recouped
its losses; the CIO had 3,700,000 members and the AFL had 3,400,000 members, more than double its 1932–33 memberships. By the start of World War II,
federation members had accepted the regulatory scope of the New Deal state but
continued to foil attempts at direct intervention in labor contract issues such as
equal pay mandates.

Trade unionists in the AFL, in fact, were neither consistent nor unified in their
approach to "women's issues" and legislation. Their relation to the state was both
reactive and fluid, subject to change if circumstances warranted. Despite their
denunciation of state intervention in labor matters, for example, federation leaders
had supported legislation for working women dating from its early voluntarism
days. Labor officers such as Samuel Gompers supported hours and wages laws
for women and children, claiming that these mostly unorganized workers were

a "dependent" class, in need of state "paternalism" such as minimum wage and other protections. These measures were necessary, claimed AFL legislative representative Walter J. Mason in 1948, "to safeguard mothers—actual and potential."[24] Positioning women and children as wards of the state helped circumvent employer attempts at heightening wage competition among all workers. Such measures, characterized by the legal historian William Forbath as the "visible hand of voluntarism," benefited higher-paid skilled men who made up the AFL's core membership and were able to pursue privatized collective bargaining.[25]

The federation's seesaw position on equal pay legislation illustrates the malleable nature of the AFL voluntarism ideology. Prior to 1951, convention delegates and leaders had endorsed equal pay proposals before Congress. They abandoned such support in the 1950s in the hopes of returning to a pre–Wagner Act industrial relations system. Testifying for the measure before a Senate subcommittee in 1945, AFL legislative representative Lewis Hines claimed proudly that his organization had supported equal pay contract provisions since 1882. Hines went on to say that the AFL was "wholeheartedly behind this bill and the purposes of the bill," claiming that "there is no justification—moral or economic—for a differential in wages between one worker and another who makes an equal contribution to the industry."[26] Federation leaders reversed their policy on equal pay legislation in 1951 with George Meany insisting that the labor federation had supported such a proposal only during periods of general wage control under the National War Labor Board and the Wage Stabilization Board. The AFL membership had never fully embraced such intervention in collective bargaining matter, Meany said, and it looked forward to a return to unfettered union-employer dealings. "When free collective bargaining is in effect," he noted in defending voluntarism, "we believe that more and better progress can be made by voluntary negotiation than by a law necessarily reaching deeply into the whole private system of wage determination."[27]

The AFL's opposition to equal pay legislation contributed to the measure's stall in Congress in the early 1950s. While it is difficult to gauge the federation's precise influence over the fate of legislation, it is clear that the public influence of Meany and the organization's intensive lobbying efforts was considerable. U.S. Women's Bureau chief Frieda Miller's attempt to woo the trade unionists to her position is likewise an indication of AFL strength. Equal pay advocates could no longer afford to overlook the federation's absence at meetings as they had in the late 1940s, when it appeared that the bill's passage was assured. Miller went so far in her efforts to welcome the AFL as to shift the tone of presentations at a 1952 bureau conference on equal pay away from stressing the necessity for legislation to emphasizing the need for women's wage improvements at the bargaining table. Although AFL representatives participated in the meeting, they held firm to their stance that collective bargaining was the only appropriate means for ensuring equal pay.[28] Delegates to the AFL's 1951 convention decried measures that increased federal authority in their privatized negotiations, "a [practice] we are finding most troublesome and constrictive under Taft-Hartley."[29] Persuading women to join unions, instead of "perpetuat[ing] a principle based upon the assumption that women are wards of the state," one officer argued elsewhere, would effectively eliminate inequality. Taking the long view of the matter, this particular unionist argued that inequality was "deeply rooted in our civilization"; what inequality unions and employers could not write out of work contracts, he asserted, would disappear only through "evolutionary processes" of change.[30] Federation president George Meany summarized the business unionist position neatly in 1953: "We feel that in a free competitive economy, the task of establishing and safeguarding the principle as well as practice of equal pay to women workers is properly within the province of collective bargaining and not of police action by the government."[31]

While union officers did not change their policy toward equal pay legislation by the time of the AFL's merger with the CIO in 1955, federationists did display growing support for legislative action in general. In response to the debilitating effects of the Taft-Hartley Act, AFL leaders established the League for Political Education paralleling the CIO's Political Action Committee in 1947. In 1952, the federation broke with the nonpartisan policy of Gompers and endorsed Democratic presidential candidate Adlai Stevenson. They lobbied for a further expansion of the Social Security program and an increased minimum wage, and they joined in enthusiastically supporting cold war politics.[32]

This embrace of a flexible voluntarism could be seen in their backing of state equal pay laws. Without offering much in the way of explanation, AFL officers approved state equal pay laws that existed in New York, Massachusetts, Rhode Island, Michigan, Illinois, Montana, and Washington, all while holding out on an endorsement of a federal law on the matter. In addition, at least three AFL-affiliated unions—the Teachers, Hotel and Restaurant Workers, and Garment Workers unions—supported federal action for equal pay. These organizations had a sizable percentage of women in their ranks who stood to benefit directly from such legislation.[33] Federation leaders were able to do little to control those who strayed from the Washington office's position, except to try to appoint representatives to public meetings on equal pay who, as legislative director Andrew Biemiller put it, "have a clear understanding of our position."[34] Although these detractors were a minority in the AFL, they would add their weight to the internal pressure put on Meany and the executive board members in the newly merged AFL-CIO in 1955 for approval of equal pay legislation.

"Ask the average businessman, the laboring man, and the public servant whether he believes in equal pay and you will get virtually unanimous agreement," Secretary of Labor Maurice J. Tobin told a conference on the subject in 1952. "They are for it just as they are against sin."[35] Convictions for such an ideal did not easily translate into action, however. Equal pay became an even more elusive goal by the late 1950s. One 1956 study of union contracts found that 195 (or 38 percent) included equal pay clauses; by 1961 that figure had dropped to 18 percent. The wage gap between full-time working men and women also widened during these years; women earned an average of 63.6 percent of men's wages in 1957, a figure that decreased to 60.6 percent in 1960.[36]

The eradication of unequal pay standards was not on the immediate horizon. Alice Kessler-Harris's claim, therefore, that "ultimate passage of [equal pay] legislation seemed certain" by the mid-1950s is undercut by the political and strategic blockades unionists and others faced at the time.[37] They could only look with discouragement to the measure's uncertain future. During the Truman and Eisenhower years, Cynthia Harrison reports, "women received from Congress virtually no recognition of their contribution to the war effort, or their new place in the American economy, or their importance within the electorate."[38] The efforts of advocates in the period 1945–54 served some good toward the campaign for equality. In the highly visible, surface world of national politics, union women managed to keep equal pay legislation alive; in the process, they sharpened their political skills and educated themselves in coalition-building in order to attain a goal central to improving their working lives.

The AFL-CIO Merger and "Women's Issues," 1955–60

On the surface, supporters of equal pay legislation had every reason to view with trepidation the widely publicized picture of a smiling George Meany clasping hands with CIO president Walter Reuther at the federation's merger convention in December 1955. Unlike the CIO, the AFL firmly rejected equal pay proposals before Congress, holding that such measures violated its voluntaristic notion of industrial relations. Given the AFL's domination of the newly merged federation, prospects appeared slim for an endorsement of equal pay by the AFL-CIO leadership. While the AFL's share of national union membership had increased from 62 percent to 64 percent since 1953, the CIO's had fallen from 23 percent to 20 percent. This superior numerical force translated into organizational power for

AFL unionists. The merger agreement gave ex-AFL officers seventeen seats on the unified executive council, leaving only ten seats to ex-CIO members. More important, it placed George Meany at the helm, a position he held until his retirement twenty-four years later, in 1979. Walter Reuther, the CIO's most vocal proponent of social unionism, served in a lesser capacity as vice-president in charge of the Industrial Union Department. Overseeing the council, as well as key units for political action, lobbying, and foreign policy, "Meany ran the Federation and Reuther occasionally complained," as Kim Moody, a labor journalist, observes.[39] Although celebrated as a merger of two equally powerful labor federations, their joining, in fact, was more a grafting of industrial unionism onto the AFL giant. "This is not a merger of honor. We are going *into* the AFL" said Mike Quill of the Transport Workers Union at the time.[40] "The AFofL continued in its own momentum," observed CIO staff member Katherine Ellickson, "and the CIO people were gradually worked into an existing framework."[41]

Yet, the AFL-CIO executive council did endorse equal pay legislation shortly after the merger. Several factors account for this policy change, foremost among them the abandonment of voluntarism by Meany and other AFL officers. The passage of Taft-Hartley, the resignation of Martin Durkin of the Plumbers Union as President Eisenhower's secretary of labor, and the Republican administration's appointment of probusiness representatives to the National Labor Relations Board (NLRB) all awakened the resolve of labor leaders to join CIO unionists in the politicization of labor relations. Meany's growing willingness to play the role of "conservative reformer" within the Democratic Party helped clear the ground for approval of equal pay legislation. With the CIO leadership's abandonment of more far-reaching social unionists goals such as industry councils, tying price increases into wage scales, and talk of forming a labor party, the disparate set of CIO and AFL labor ideologies converged by the mid-1950s into cautious liberalism.[42] Mike Davis explains Meany's goal:

> By making the new social movements dependent on the Federation's financial resources and legislative skills, Meany hoped to amplify the role of the trade-union bureaucracy in national politics. Although Reuther was willing, where Meany was not, directly to patronize the 1960s protest movements, their strategic aims were not dissimilar. Both thought the AFL-CIO's institutional political role could be powerfully expanded through skilled brokerage between the civil rights movement and national bourgeois politics.[43]

Tensions within the AFL-CIO over the character of the federation's program remained, but Meany was succeeding in balancing the demands by some unionists for social measures while resisting government encroachments on the position of white men who formed the organization's core membership.

AFL leaders may have also grown receptive to equal pay in the face of pressure from AFL-based unions backing congressional action. These unions included the International Ladies' Garment Workers (ILGWU), the American Federation of Teachers, the International Association of Machinists, and the Retail Clerks. They participated in the National Committee on Equal Pay (NCEP), the loosely formed coalition of labor, liberal, and professional groups working for such legislation. Representatives from the Automobile, Electrical, Clothing, and other CIO unions made up the largest contingent of the NCEP membership; they supported the equal pay bill originally introduced by Mary Anderson in 1945, which provided for National Labor Relations Act–based coverage for all employees engaged in businesses affecting commerce. Anderson's successor at the U.S. Women's Bureau, Frieda Miller, and, after her, House member Edith Green continued to favor the bill through the early 1960s. While evidence of the effect these AFL-affiliated unions had on the federation is mostly impressionistic in nature, the public embarrassment of having large unions with sizable female memberships diverge from official policy must have influenced executive board members' positions.[44]

Ellickson and research staff member Nancy Pratt's careful and persuasive work in advocating the organization's support of equal pay legislation softened the federationists' opposition further. Acting on an AFL-CIO convention resolution to study possible ways of bridging the two groups' positions on equal pay, the executive council ordered a committee formed in February 1956 to study the matter. The group, consisting of two representatives each from the research, social security, and legislation departments, in turn charged Ellickson and Pratt with examining and developing recommendations. The two women launched their campaign for the AFL-CIO's equal pay legislation endorsement from within the Research Department. Stanley Ruttenberg, one of the few ex-CIO department directors brought into the new federation, headed the department. Ruttenberg, according to Pratt, "believed women should be treated equally with men, which was actually part of CIO policy but not always carried out," and he proved to be an able ally in this endeavor.[45] He supervised the women's writing of an important memorandum to the committee outlining the history of equal pay. Pratt and Ellickson's document, more a brief in support of the legislation than a simple recounting of labor's past stand of the issue, highlighted how an equal pay law would benefit women workers' economic position. In addition, since the public already accepted the righteousness of the measure, labor's backing would reflect positively on the AFL-CIO. Many unions, Pratt and Ellickson maintained, already supported equal pay; a law endorsed by the federation would enhance union bargaining positions with management. Labor negotiators, they reasoned, would obtain contract gains without having to sacrifice other items under contention with employers.[46]

Ellickson and Pratt understood that they needed Meany's approval in order to sway reluctant board members, a move they successfully engineered by spring 1956. "We wrote to the state federations to see what they thought and we found that the New York State Federation of Labor, from which Meany had come, was for equal pay legislation," Ellickson recalled. "So we went to Meany with this, and the position of the merged organization became in favor of equal pay."[47] At its meeting in June 1956, the federation's executive council formally endorsed equal pay legislation.[48] Federation approval for Edith Green's bill, supported by the NCEP, came only with an amendment providing for primarily administrative rather than judicial enforcement of equal pay. This demand grew out of labor's long-standing distrust of judicial workplace conflicts, rooted in the multitude of strike injunctions and other orders handed down by judges in the late nineteenth and early twentieth centuries. Raising the specter that courts would jeopardize union security, committee members and union leaders noted with satisfaction the modification along these lines in the legislation's wording. AFL-CIO secretary-treasurer William F. Schnitzler privately observed that "the compromise would minimize the danger that collective bargaining agreements would suddenly be placed in danger through civil suits."[49]

Several Pittsburgh-area women cannery workers confirmed AFL-CIO officers' fears that courts would upset labor contracts when the workers sued their employer and union in 1960 on the basis of a state equal pay law. The women charged that their labor organization, the Glass Bottle Blowers Association (a supporter of federal equal pay legislation since 1945), had entered into an agreement for wage rates that paid men anywhere from 19 cents to 22 cents an hour more than women doing identical work, thus violating Pennsylvania's equal pay law passed in 1947. The lower court judge rejected the women's complaint. He did this not based on their evidence of unequal pay but because ruling in their favor would conflict directly with an approved and ratified contract. To permit the court to set aside this admittedly unequal wage scale, the judge argued, "would destroy the stability that such agreements must have and would result in making a mockery and a farce of labor-management negotiations and bargaining. We refuse to strike down and destroy what has taken labor so many years to attain."[50]

The tug-of-war between administrative relief and judicial rule continued. Union leaders could not have been pleased when, following the state's superior court affirmation of this judgment a year later, Pennsylvania's supreme court members reversed the decision in 1962. Citing a superior court judge's dissent, officers on the state's high court asserted that membership in a union engaged in

an unfair labor contract did not constitute a waiver of claims for equal pay. Denouncing the previous ruling as an "absurd construction" that "violate[d] the
fundamental rules of statutory interpretation," the superior court judge concluded
that "to hold otherwise would render the entire Act ineffectual in that the employer and the employee or his representative could bargain away statutory prohibition because of sex."[51]

By supporting administrative over judicial enforcement, federation officers
attempted to ensure the stability of bargaining relationships that had been created largely by administrative rulings and contract negotiations. Unionists of all
ideological stripes viewed judicial rulings as fickle at best and unfriendly to labor in general, but administrative regulation was another matter entirely; most
union members accepted the NLRB's stabilizing industrial relations system in
the 1945–65 period of rising wages and low unemployment. The price labor paid
for ceding to corporate leaders the right to contain and constrain union demands
appeared almost as soon as the ink was dry on "Treaty of Detroit." The discontent and stagnation that were prevalent after 1965 in the face of economic slow-
down and social unrest—in women unionists' protests, civil rights demands made
by African-American workers, and rank-and-file shop-floor revolts against harsh
working conditions and complacent union leaders—were rooted in this con-
stricted system of dispute resolution. That system severely curtailed alternative
protest forms and provided ever-tighter guarantees of incumbency to "stable"
unions against rival factions or other labor groups.

The achievement of relatively quiescent postwar capital-labor-state relations,
characterized by routinized grievance arbitration, no-strike pledges, and high
wages and benefits, came increasingly at the expense of activists who attempted
to challenge race and gender inequality. At the national level, executive council
members tried to protect unions against liability and concurrently to promote
justice for the council's dissatisfied members. To this end, they urged strong civil
rights legislation, but they constantly fought measures that would by-pass the
usually accommodating NLRB for the courtroom. Their defense of the principle
of noninterference in constituent affairs was baldly hypocritical; Meany and other
labor leaders exhibited a pattern of moving vigorously against supposed Com-
munists in the labor movement but often practiced nonconfrontation with unionists promoting inequality. While federation leaders threatened and cajoled unionists practicing race discrimination in the construction trades and southern union
locals, they chose not to use whatever formal powers they had to bring guilty
constituent unions into compliance with AFL-CIO policy.[52]

The campaign for an equal pay law was an example of the unevenness of the
federation leadership's backing of social legislation. The leaders paid more than

lip service to the demand for the measure but extended less than wholehearted support for its enactment. Nevertheless, their backing proved crucial to its eventual success. In coordinating the federation's legislation department, its director, Andrew Biemiller, played a key role in coordinating the labor organization's efforts to this end. "Andy had quite a following on the Hill. He had his own little constituency and he was quite a power," Nancy Pratt recalled in a 1992 interview. "While I don't think Andrew Biemiller gave much of a damn about women one way or another . . . he did his job because he was ordered to by George Meany."[53] Biemiller's assistant, George Riley, did most of the legwork for equal pay legislation, speaking at several NCEP meetings and communicating regularly with committee leaders on planning strategy. In June 1960, for example, Riley persuaded NCEP head Lorraine Hedberg not to add yet another equal pay proposal to the "multiplicity of bills" already crowding Congress's docket until after the fall election. Riley assured Hedberg that one agreed-upon bill could be introduced into the legislature at that time. Women federation staff members stayed in close contact with the NCEP's activities as well. Nancy Pratt obtained most of the NCEP members' approval for the AFL-CIO's amendment to the bill providing for administrative enforcement. Her successor in the AFL-CIO research department, Anne Draper, chaired the NCEP in the 1960s.[54]

Far from forming a phalanx with the NCEP, federation officers only selectively joined the group's efforts before the Kennedy administration's arrival in 1961. The labor organization's legislation department did not establish a standing subcommittee on equal pay as it did for other pressing issues;[55] George Riley justified its inaction on the grounds that "inasmuch as the Congress has not moved into this area in recent years . . . we have not formalized our stand through testimony."[56] Even after 1960 the male leadership kept an official distance from the committee: it turned down an NCEP request in 1962 to join as a signatory on a letter sent to Congress, claiming cryptically, "we already have made plans at our level for contacting members. . . . We should continue to proceed in that direction."[57]

Riley did attempt to generate congressional interest in equal pay legislation in early 1957, with negligible results. He had House members James Roosevelt and Martha Griffiths and Senator Wayne Morse introduce an equal pay proposal to legislative committees, but without success.[58] Even the usually accommodating NCEP members frustrated Riley's attempts when they informed him at a February 1957 strategy meeting that "not all groups were free to back a particular piece of legislation." They were presumably referring to those in professional women's groups that preferred only token legislation or no bill at all—a clear minority of committee members after the mid-1950s.[59] The NCEP was hobbled with a divided membership: unionists and most liberal group representatives were in accord on the legislation's necessity and the form it should take; professional women's organizations were split badly, with many backing equal pay in principle but holding back from formal approval for pending legislation. Proponents of equal pay, Cynthia Harrison concludes, were "fragmented by diverse goals and political beliefs and lacking effective and appropriate leadership."[60] By December the AFL-CIO legislation department members abandoned their efforts, reporting that, "due in large measure to the press of legislation which the Labor Committee deemed to have priority, the Congress this year failed to turn its attention to this important matter."[61]

As with the period 1945–54, immediate prospects for passage of an equal pay bill between 1955 and 1961 were dim indeed. In addition to the AFL-CIO's lukewarm support for legislation, the Eisenhower administration's only contribution to the measure's promotion was a hollow request to Congress to enact an equal pay law. U.S. Women's Bureau head Alice Leopold moved the agency away from its traditional cooperative relationship with labor activists by cementing firmer ties with professional women's groups and business associations. Leopold had alienated many of the bureau's advisory groups for several reasons. She considered softening the bureau's anti-ERA stance, leaving union women and others on tenterhooks by occasionally stating that her office took no position against the amendment. She did not realize NCEP members' fear that she would abandon federal equal pay legislation; she did, however, fail to provide data on the prevalence of unequal pay scales, information many in Congress requested before backing the bill. More important, Leopold rejected federation overtures to back their proposal; she endorsed instead the conservative bill introduced into the House by Frances P. Bolton. Bolton's bill gave enforcement power to administrators in the Wage and Hour Division of the Department of Labor to mediate disputes; they could not issue "cease and desist" orders as Edith Green authorized the Women's Bureau's head to do in her bill. Also, while the Bolton bill provided for the secretary of labor to file suit on the complainants' behalf, it did not include a blacklist provision for guilty employers, as did the Green measure.[62]

Industrial union activists kept the labor movement and the NCEP focused on the equal pay campaign during these years. "Of all the groups in our society . . . [unions] have probably worked the hardest for equality and this has been helped, of course, by the increasing participation of women in the trade union movement," Esther Peterson told a House hearing on equal pay in 1962.[63] Labor activists such as Peterson, Anne Draper, Gloria Johnson, Caroline Davis, and Dorothy Haener continued to advocate for legislation within their own unions while at the same time backing the NCEP as the primary national vehicle for promoting equal pay. Although the federation played a key role, it was not a dominant force. "My own feeling was that most of the activity was being done through coalitions . . . and the AFL-CIO was a part of it," the Electrical Workers' (IUE) Gloria Johnson recalled in a 1993 interview.[64] Even the estranged U.S. Women's Bureau director, Alice Leopold, acknowledged in 1956 that the committee was "sparking effort towards obtaining equal pay legislation."[65] Unionists dominated the loosely formed NCEP; they pushed for other members' support of an equal pay law that contained strong administrative enforcement. Male activists participated in, but did not control, NCEP meetings. The International Union of Electrical Workers' David Lasser, for example, denounced the Bolton bill, recommended that the group hold conferences to publicize its cause, and served by appointment as chairman of the NCEP committee on conferences.[66]

On the other major gender equality measure before Congress, the ERA, there was no discernible change in the AFL-CIO leaders' opposition. There was little pressure within their ranks to reverse the organizations' hostility to the amendment. Calling the ERA "dangerous legislation," federation legislative representative Hyman Bookbinder announced that the AFL-CIO would continue to support the Hayden rider to the amendment. The rider, which Bookbinder acknowledged "in effect wipes out the very foundation of the constitutional amendment itself," provided for a retention of protective measures for women workers.[67] Attempts by National Woman's Party (NWP) members to sway the labor organization's leaders on several fronts were not effective. Bookbinder reported to the federation's civil rights department head, Boris Shishkin, following a meeting with NWP officers in November 1957, that "their position was so completely adamant that I am convinced there is no point in 'negotiating' with Womans [*sic*] Party for an acceptable version of the amendment."[68] Nancy Pratt was more optimistic about such contacts but only as they helped shore up the federation's visibility with other lobbying groups. After meeting with NWP representatives, she told Stanley Ruttenberg of the AFL-CIO Research Department: "I am not sure these luncheons get us anywhere, but perhaps they are valuable as a demonstration of cooperation and good faith. . . . Kitty [Ellickson] and I generally manage to plug a couple of other legislative areas that labor's really interested in."[69] NWP members resorted unsuccessfully to redbaiting on at least one occasion. Nina Price, the NWP's New York City chairman, sent George Meany a *Daily Worker* clipping with this comment: "This is the article to which I called your attention because it shows the Communist opposition to the Equal Rights Amendment and the Communist support of the Hayden rider."[70] Meany remained unmoved by such pleas.

By the decade's end, unionists viewed compromise efforts on behalf of the ERA as, in the words of one male AFL-CIO staff member, "asinine." "If the [NWP] ladies who are now worrying about this did not have this to worry about they would have find something else. Vive le (sex) difference!" he wrote Andrew Biemiller in January 1960.[71] Women unionists were equally sharp in their denunciation of ERA supporters, if not as vitriolic in their descriptions of them. The ERA, Nancy Pratt observed years later, "was seen as being a creature of the Republican party and of . . . the right-to-work people to wipe out labor laws. And all the trade unions were against the Equal Rights Amendment."[72] Turbulent economic, social, and legal change—not a rapprochement between liberal and conservative women's groups—would eventually bring the AFL-CIO to embrace the ERA in 1973.

Piecemeal Equality: The Equal Pay Act of 1963

Prospects for the passage of an equal pay law increased significantly following John Kennedy's election in 1960. The new administration was not only more open to social legislation than the Republicans but included several unionists receptive to "women's issues." Key congressional figures marshaled support for the equal pay struggle as well. New York's Adam Clayton Powell, who replaced the intractable Graham Barden of North Carolina as chair of the important House Education and Labor Committee in 1960, favored equal pay legislation. Women legislators in particular played an important part in convincing colleagues to back equal pay proposals. Veterans from both parties such as Frances Bolton, Katherine St. George, and Edna Kelly introduced and supported various bills, eventually backing Oregon's Edith Green in her effort to pass a close version of the original Anderson equal pay measure. Green, who served in Congress from 1954 to 1975, worked as a prominent liberal on various committees, including serving as chair of the House Education and Labor's subcommittee on higher education. She also sat on John Kennedy's President's Commission on the Status of Women (PCSW).[73] "Few women served in Congress longer than Edith Green," notes Irwin Gertzog in his study of congressional women, "and fewer still were able to play so influential a role on their committees."[74] Representative William Ryan of New York claimed of Green in 1963 that "the gentlewoman from Oregon has worked with dedication and determination to see that women receive equal treatment with men in employment."[75]

Esther Peterson, more than anyone, revitalized interest in equal pay legislation from her post as Women's Bureau head and assistant secretary of labor for President Kennedy. First as a lobbyist for the Amalgamated Clothing Workers, then as IUD legislative representative, Peterson supported equal pay with vigor. Once Peterson was tapped for the labor department position to replace the Republican Alice Leopold, the administration gave her full responsibility for promoting equal pay legislation. She, in turn, hired United Rubber Workers lobbyist Morag Simchak in March 1961 to help in this daunting undertaking.

Peterson's ascent to a high government post, in fact, was only one of several signs to organized labor leaders that they enjoyed influence in national politics. Kennedy also named Arthur Goldberg, the country's most prominent labor lawyer and the AFL-CIO's special counsel, to be secretary of labor. In addition, the president enjoyed an almost father-son relationship with George Meany. The respect was mutual. "Washington is never going to be the same town again," the federation head lamented following Kennedy's assassination. "I don't know if I want to keep on working here."[76] Positive legislative and executive actions followed the Democrats' 1960 election victory. These included Executive Order 10988, released in 1962, which encouraged union representation among federal employees, and civil rights proposals introduced by the administration in the summer of 1963. For the most part, labor leaders supported the administration's foreign and domestic policies despite Kennedy's attempt to limit wage gains to the level of national productivity increases.[77]

Equal pay legislation, however, was not a priority for the incoming administration's liberal agenda in 1961. It fell to Peterson to push for its enactment. Responding to the chronic charge that little data existed to demonstrate the need for such legislation, Peterson undertook studies and urged hearings. She convened meetings with union and NCEP members in her office, agreeing with those present to back the Green bill.[78] With Secretary of Labor Arthur Goldberg's appointment to the U.S. Supreme Court in 1962, Peterson faced a new challenge in Under Secretary W. Willard Wirtz's promotion as Goldberg's replacement. Wirtz opposed equal pay legislation, believing it unnecessary. If Peterson did not convert the new secretary to her side, she at least convinced Wirtz not to obstruct the bill's movement to Capitol Hill, admonishing him in a forceful memorandum that "it does not seem unreasonable to spend approximately the same amount of money the government now spends on paper clips and stapling machines in order to protect the pay of 24 million women members of the labor force."[79]

Peterson had an ally in the federation's George Riley, who continued to oversee the federation's promotion of the bill. Federation officers threw their weight behind the bill after 1960, writing to and lobbying legislators. Writing to Goldberg in mid-1961 Riley noted with regret that "this legislation has had to yield to other activities in recent years. Somehow, it seems to me we have to drive our stakes and stand firmly for enactment in the foreseeable future if we are to have the legislation."[80] Riley expressed similar sentiments to Peterson, offering to work with her in "fending off weakening amendments" to the Green bill.[81] He advised NCEP members at the same time to encourage Goldberg to "use his further good influences in expediting the [bill's] movement."[82]

That the AFL-CIO did not in the end get the bill its leadership desired was a sobering reminder to federationists of their modest position in effecting change in national politics. Wrangling by conservatives in Congress over the bill's contents weakened the measure considerably; further stalling in the Senate led to the bill's demise for the 1962 session. Nevertheless, equal pay supporters rebounded the following year and succeeded in passing the Equal Pay Act of 1963. This came only with significant concessions to the business community. The act, now modeled on the Fair Labor Standards Act coverage, exempted employers with fewer than twenty-five employees and permitted a gradual elimination of wage differentials between men and women workers, all to the federationists' chagrin.[83]

Unionists were particularly troubled by conservatives' attempt to replace the language of "comparable worth" with that of "equal work." Since the bill's inception in the mid-1940s its advocates had insisted that "equal" would mean identical, and that slight differences might be used by employers to justify disparate wages. They had long ago scotched the notion that "comparable" should address the relative aspects of positions based on skill, effort, and responsibility, but they still clung to the belief that retaining such language would prevent employer chiseling. AFL-CIO secretary-treasurer William Schnitzler told senators that managers would make minor changes in job elements in order to evade the law. "The concept of equal should be broad enough to meet the varieties of practical circumstances," said Schnitzler.[84]

Labor representatives were in a weak position on this particular issue. Although they fought off the introduction of "equal" language into the bill, their fuzzy, narrowly construed notion of "comparable" said more about what they opposed than what they sought from legislators. They rejected job comparisons "literally restricted to the 'same kind of work,'" Anne Draper of the AFL-CIO research department and the NCEP chair wrote to Schnitzler. Citing the IUE's testimony on equal pay, Draper suggested that the revised bill with the "equal" clause would be "totally ineffective": "Some women required to perform highly skilled tasks may nonetheless receive rates approximating the pay of male janitors. Clearly the wage determination system has scrambled the job factors to produce this result." This was the crux of the problem, for in order to retain the "comparable" language unionists had to acknowledge that they would have to make job comparisons at individual work sites; they balked, however, at the establishment of a job evaluation system since it might strengthen management's already considerable control over employment matters. "We do not think the Secretary [of Labor] should get involved in making artificial comparisons of any kind and especially we would not wish the bill to seem to require employers to set up formal job evaluation systems," Draper reminded Schnitzler. "Many of our unions have very serious objections, based on their experience, to job evaluation systems as a general matter."[85] In the end, conservative lawmakers carried the day on the issue. Despite their misgivings in conceding to opponents on this matter, unionists and other NCEP members nevertheless honored Peterson's request to back the measure, claiming, as she put it, it was "better than nothing."[86]

Labor leaders were able to intervene at key points to ward off some of the debilitating changes being made to the pending legislation. Union representatives helped defeat an attempt by conservative members of Congress to include a provision in the bill postponing the effective date of the Equal Pay Act in the case of employees covered by current labor-management contracts until two years after enactment, or until contracts expired.[87] They asserted that such an allowance would be "inequitable in practice, unsound in principle," and—worried about how it would affect other legislation—"would serve as a dangerous precedent when we next attempt to examine the minimum wage or maximum hour provisions of the Fair Labor Standards Act."[88]

In the wake of victory, women unionists assessed with pride their important role in the struggle. This was not a frivolous exercise in self-approbation; rather, activists viewed the act's passage as a confirmation of their place within the labor movement and in the liberal wing of the Democratic Party. Women were in the forefront in bringing the measure to Congress. They had definitively moved beyond the role traditionally assigned them of providing auxiliary support to male unionists. Esther Peterson navigated treacherous political waters in convincing hesitant lawmakers that an equal pay law was necessary. Peterson's shepherding of the measure did not go unnoticed. House subcommittee chair Herbert Zelenko characterized the Women's Bureau chief as "a driving force in bringing this legislation to the front after so many years."[89] During a 1963 debate on the matter, another congressional member singled Peterson out for commendation: "Esther Peterson . . . has for many years worked so diligently and effectively to advance the cause of American working men and women."[90] Peterson's own colleagues acknowledged her leadership in the equal pay battle. "It could never have happened without the tremendous effort put forth on your part and the work of women in your U.S. Women's Bureau under your expert guidance," the UAW's Caroline Davis wrote in a congratulatory note. Union women had contributed greatly to the cause, Davis noted: "for 15 years that I have been on the staff of the UAW we have worked to secure passage of a law, and at a time had high expectations, only to have [them] dashed before we got very far."[91]

The struggle for a federal equal pay law was an undertaking union women would not let others forget during the height of second-wave feminism in the 1970s. Evaluating the growth of working-class feminism in 1977, Dorothy Haener summed up the legacy of women's activism during this period. "If there had not been a few people like us around doing the kinds of things that we have done," the automobile union activist noted, "much of what we have seen happen in the women's movement might not well have happened."[92]

Those gathered at the NCEP's White House celebration on June 11, 1964—the date the Equal Pay Act was put into effect—understood the law's limitations but hoped that it would serve as a symbolic victory for equality.[93] "This bill will *not* give most [working women] relief, since it does not give them equal opportunity," Peterson had acknowledged one year earlier. "It will, however, do some good, and will at least definitively point to the need for something to be done about equal opportunity in addition to equal pay."[94] Adam Clayton Powell argued that, "because of the dual discrimination they suffer," African-American women would benefit from the law. "This bill will relieve them at least of the down-grading wage discrimination based on sex."[95] The equal pay law, according to Cynthia Harrison, did offer "good results." In its first decade of enforcement, court decisions interpreted the meaning of "equal pay" broadly by refusing to limit the measure to identical jobs. As a result, the government awarded 171,000 employees $84 million in back pay.[96] While the act was, as the economist Claudia Goldin characterizes it, "a rather weak doctrine to combat discrimination"[97] in regard to occupational segregation and most differences in pay inequity, it marked the federal government's entrance into the effort of safeguarding working women's equal employment rights.[98]

Decisive and widespread calls for government action guaranteeing gender equality for men and women in the workplace would emerge, but not yet. Most legislators and union leaders in the first half of the 1960s remained fixed on the goal of race equality, not gender equality. When James Roosevelt, a California Democrat, proposed a fair employment practices bill in 1962 (a prototype of Title VII of the Civil Rights Act of 1964), making illegal, among other things, sex discrimination, Meany rejected the idea, claiming that the proscription on sex discrimination "would only be confusing."[99] Even so, the fact that Roosevelt toyed with the idea of including such a clause in the measure points to policy makers' acknowledging the appropriateness of battling sex discrimination in the workplace. There were other hints of a shift in thinking: in a 1960 Senate report on unemployment, legislators called on the U.S. Bureau of Employment Security to "expand its programs to reduce discrimination in employment against young people, older workers, nonwhites, women, the handicapped, and other groups."[100] Such a far-ranging challenge to tackle unfair treatment of these groups of workers would not be taken up for a few years.

The final act in this dress rehearsal for feminism's resurgence came not in the form of legislation, but in a report of a government commission, John Kennedy's President's Commission on the Status of Women. The Equal Pay Act of 1963 was an important but piecemeal legal step toward gender equality; Kennedy's PCSW, formed in the early 1960s, confronted the issue of protectionism in a wholesale manner, as its members brought to national scrutiny for the first time the unresolved question of whether protective laws for women workers should be retained in the face of growing support for equality. Their report, released in 1963, was a document fraught with paradoxes. In this sense it reflected uncertainty and resistance to change even among those who sensed that gender relations were already being transformed. It both affirmed the primacy of women's traditional roles and condemned discriminatory practices in government, and it offered proposals to reduce public gender inequalities without directly endorsing the ERA. The report's authors summoned academics, union leaders, government officers, and others to approach the matter in a cautious manner, noting that "experience is needed in determining what constitutes unjustified discrimination in the treatment of women workers."[101] As with the recommendations in the Industrial Union Department conference report two years earlier, PCSW members, including Peterson, Mary Callahan (IUE), Caroline Davis (UAW), Angela Bambace (ILGWU), Bessie Hillman (ACWA), and Addie Wyatt (UPWA), addressed this seeming conundrum by offering halfway recommendations. Unable to cross the Rubicon to equality themselves, commission members helped create a bridge for the advancement of the women's movement by releasing their widely publicized report and creating an ongoing institutional structure in which to discuss "women's issues."[102] Katherine Ellickson, PCSW executive secretary, later commented that it "furnished stimulus, institutional frameworks, and content for much of the subsequent growth of the women's movement."[103]

Over the course of the next decade, working-class women in dozens of unions and hundreds of locals across the country fashioned their demands for equality after the PCSW report and equal pay legislation that filtered down to them from Washington, D.C., as well as drawing upon their own varied experiences with automation, economic pressures, and the unfulfilled promise of equality. Hostile male workers, unwilling to embrace gender equality at the cost of their own economic status, left rank-and-file women impatient with the incremental change advocated by activists at the national level. As case studies of packinghouse and electrical workers will demonstrate, pressure from women unionists helped create a working-class feminist movement by the late 1960s. These workers had no tidy or uniform guides on this road to equality. It was the specific industrial structures in which the women worked, as well as the political and organizational histories of their individual local and international unions, that shaped the character of working-class feminism.

3

The Roots of Discontent:
Gender Relations in the United Packinghouse Workers,
1945–63

"I'll tell you the biggest trouble about the women was after the Civil Rights Law was signed," Virgil Bankson remarked in a 1978 interview. "That's when we had trouble with women."[1] Bankson was a retired officer of the United Packinghouse Workers of America (UPWA) and his observation was accurate. His Ottumwa, Iowa, union local was one of hundreds across the country charged with violating Title VII of the Civil Rights Act of 1964. The law banned sex discrimination in the work force and consequently challenged employment arrangements by which women were discriminated against in wages, layoffs, and seniority. Women's response to the law's passage was significant. By August 1967, 2,500 sex discrimination complaints had been filed by women workers against unions and employers.[2]

The packinghouse women's rejection of inequality and the UPWA's "confrontational" approach to federal mandates for equal employment opportunity were rooted in events that predate Title VII. Economic and social changes underway since women worked successfully in "men's" jobs during World War II helped erode the notion that women, as a group, were physiologically and psychologically unfit for certain positions. Beginning in the mid-1950s new automation blurred the line separating "men's" and "women's" jobs. In addition, a greater percentage of the paid work was undertaken by women, casting doubt on the argument that women were in the work force in modest numbers and only on a temporary basis and thus did not deserve to have their concerns addressed with the same thoroughness as men. Protective laws and job segregation by sex seemed increasingly at odds in a postwar world that emphasized individual rights.

The shape and character of the campaign for gender equality varied as differently situated women within differently positioned unions responded to the momentum toward equality. Over the course of the two decades preceding the passage of Title VII, packinghouse women gradually became receptive to the notion of gender equality. Ironically, as automation and reorganized production procedures made previously "heavy" work lighter, women were displaced at a higher rate than men in the packing industry. Younger men stepped in to take positions previously classified as "women's" jobs. Union leaders struggled to counter job losses among men but did little to assist women workers.

UPWA women responded to these changes as best they could, calling for greater representation in an attempt to stave off further employment losses. Convention delegates approved such measures only to run up against the strong tradition of local rank-and-file control. Marginalized within their union and competing with less-senior men for a diminishing pool of jobs, UPWA women became receptive to the growing desire for equality that would sweep through the labor movement after 1965 when Title VII of the Civil Rights Act went into effect. If their treatment at the hands of male unionists did not exactly cause them to embrace equality outright, it did make clear that prevailing practices and union leadership could not address their grievances.

Unionism, Gender Ideology, and Industrial Structures in the Packinghouse Work Force

Women may have become "trouble" for the UPWA only with their call for equality in the mid-1960s, but they had played a significant role in the packinghouse union since its inception. These experiences shaped their response to legislative and judicial mandates for gender equality. Notwithstanding Upton Sinclair's claim that a woman's labor in the packinghouse "was stupefying, brutalizing work; it left her no time to think, no strength for anything," women supported unionism in impressive ways.[3] They did so, however, in a gendered labor movement that they would challenge only after decades of working on jobs they were told they were unable to do, being shut out of union leadership circles, and finally, facing the onslaught of automation and job displacement that began to pit men against women workers in the 1950s.

The structure of the packinghouse work force illustrated the fundamental inequality between men and women. A 1953 report by the U.S. Department of Labor Women's Bureau identified the prevalent sexual division of labor in the industry. Most of the jobs open to women, the report claimed, were in the canning, casing, pork trimming, bacon slicing, sausage, and selected-meats departments. Few women were found in slaughtering, primary dressing, and cutting up of cattle, hogs, and sheep; women were nearly completely absent in departments such as hides, maintenance, shipping, and stockyards. Unequal wages accompanied sex-segregated worksites; male-dominated jobs occupied higher wage brackets while female-dominated positions brought lower pay. Among Cudahy packing workers in the 1950s, for example, 82 percent of "women's" jobs fell into the lowest three of twenty-two wage brackets; only 36.6 percent of "men's" jobs at Cudahy had similarly low remunerative rates. Frequent layoffs in "women's" departments, such as bacon slicing and sausage making, meant that female employees with significant amounts of seniority became unemployed while men with less seniority in more stable departments retained their jobs.[4]

Like other CIO unions, the early packinghouse union welcomed women into its ranks but did little to change gender inequality. The UPWA was born in a decade of severe economic crisis, a period marked by a reinforcement of the family-wage ideal, the continuation of sex-segregated jobs, male/female wage differentials, and the marginalization of women unionists from the centers of power. The UPWA began as the Packinghouse Workers Organizing Committee, or PWOC in 1937, formed out of a coalition of powerful, independent midwestern unions; it thrived in large packing plants in Chicago and in cities in Iowa, Nebraska, and Minnesota. Employers, four of whom—Armour, Swift, Cudahy, and Wilson—controlled 80 percent of the industry, offered formidable opposition to the UPWA, forcing women to struggle against both management and male unionists. If, according to an early CIO organizer in the packinghouses, Stella Nowicki, "the company didn't give a damn" about women workers, the union at times was equally hostile: "Women had an awfully tough time in the union because the men brought their prejudices there."[5]

Two distinctive features of the UPWA's organizational life emerged during the labor union's early years and would shape gender relations in the union throughout its existence. The first characteristic was the strongly independent nature of UPWA locals. Scholars have focused attention on the union's militancy in its formative period and on its sensitive efforts to reach African-American workers. In celebrating the rank and file, however, they have taken less notice of how the union stood in the way of efforts to bring about gender equality. The roots of this resistance ran deep, beginning with the fact that the PWOC did not convert into a fully chartered CIO union (i.e., the UPWA) until 1943. The UPWA's relative tardiness in entering the CIO fold is attributable, in part, to the packing oligopoly's resistance to unionism. At the same time, renegade unions were responsible for both encouraging the CIO to organize in packinghouses and frustrating the efforts of national leaders to institute centralized control. After leaving the Amalgamated Meatcutters and Butcher Workmen (AFL) in 1935, for example, Wilson workers in Cedar Rapids "went independent," forming the Mid-West Union of All Packinghouse Workers. The upstart union remained unaffiliated until members decided to organize a "live, wide awake union" within the

CIO in 1937, teaming up with another independent local in Austin, Minnesota, known as the Independent Union of All Workers.[6] Cedar Rapids packinghouse workers became part of the CIO's PWOC that same year as Local Industrial Union No. 51, later changed to Local 3.

Certification elections resulted in the establishment of an impressive number of new packinghouse locals by 1942. This was due to the efforts of CIO organizers, the National Labor Relations Board's (NLRB) favorable rulings for the PWOC, and the tight labor market created by World War II. Activists' strategy for organizing new locals, notes Roger Horowitz in his study of packinghouse unionism in Sioux City, Iowa, was "given shape by the workers themselves. . . . They built strong steward systems and used job actions to empower workers and break through the fear of managerial authority."[7] The international office, headed by Ralph Helstein, the UPWA's president since 1946, shared the rank and file's propensity for local autonomy. Unionists were fully aware that the impetus for CIO organizing had come from the local level. They prided themselves on their toughness and hostility to "outside meddlers," whether employers or—after Title VII's enactment—the law.

The other key aspect of UPWA life that influenced gender relations during the union's first decade was the codification of the union's organizational structure through the establishment of a "district" system. The UPWA did not differ from other CIO unions in forming districts; all large industrial labor organizations hoped to coordinate strategy by grouping their locals into regional districts. To this end, packinghouse unionists in the group's nine districts began holding annual conventions in 1946, publishing newsletters, and meeting with district directors who acted as intermediaries for locals and the international office. UPWA districts were more than mere mechanisms for accomplishing union business, however. Intentionally or not, charter members created them along lines that reflected regional commonalities, especially shared industrial structures. Away from the glare and formality of international conventions many workers saw district conventions as a middle ground of sorts where locals could join together in solidarity while discussing key issues.

Districts 1, 2, and 3 were the core of the UPWA. According to a 1966 study by the union's research department, almost 58 percent of the UPWA's members were located in Illinois, Iowa, Minnesota, Indiana, and Nebraska. District 1, which included the Chicago area, accounted for 18 percent, as did District 2, which included Minnesota. District 3 locals, covering Iowa and Nebraska, constituted 31 percent of the UPWA's total membership. These three midwestern districts dwarfed other districts, such as District 4, representing the Southwest and Pacific

Coast states, which made up only 4 percent of the packinghouse union's total ranks. Districts 1, 2, and 3 were similar in some ways. Many of the locals found within these district boundaries were among the first to be chartered into the UPWA. As such, their members took pride in viewing themselves as defenders of progressive industrial unionism.[8]

Equally telling, however, were the differences between the districts. As indicated in table 4, District 3 locals in cities such as Waterloo, Ottumwa, and Omaha were in large packing plants where the entire range of meatpacking procedures was carried out under one roof. Only District 2 depended as much as District 3 on large packing plants for its membership, but its total membership was much smaller. There were also large plants in District 1, but members there worked in a wider variety of specialized facilities, especially in food-processing jobs usually done by women. District 3, in fact, was distinct from the rest of the UPWA in having a smaller percentage of women members as part of the total membership: while women constituted 21 percent of the union's total membership, in District 3—the largest district in the union—they made up only 13 percent of the rank and file.[9]

In some cases, local community conditions or problems peculiar to one district resulted in struggles with issues not shared by the rest of the union, or shared to a lesser degree. For example, in District 1, where 60 to 70 percent of union members were African Americans—a considerably larger percentage than in other districts, including District 3—workers were in the vanguard of the UPWA's long-standing commitment to civil rights to African Americans. The union's support for racial equality—characterized by one scholar as "clearly superior" to that of other major industrial unions of the period—gave rise to the formation of strong civil rights committees, support for boycotts, large donations to civil rights groups, and the expulsion of union locals engaging in race discrimination in the South.[10] Women packinghouse workers in Chicago gained valuable experience from these efforts. Addie Wyatt, UPWA activist and, in the 1970s, cofounder of the Coalition of Labor Union Women, acknowledged that because of the union's civil rights efforts, African-American women "could flow into the civil rights struggle and be strong leaders within the movement."[11] District 1 women were among the first in the packinghouse union to raise their voices for women's rights. Most of the legal battles against sex discrimination occurred in District 3, however, where women were less numerous. These women were hit harder by the destructive technological displacement and work reorganization taken up by employers after 1955, and they lacked the skills held by their Chicago union sisters to secure their rights.[12]

Table 4. UPWA Membership in Districts 1, 2, and 3

Company	City/State	Per Capita Membership	Percentage of District Membership
District 1			
Hygrade	Indianapolis	1,929	15.5
Marhoefer	Muncie	845	6.8
Swift	Rochelle, Ill.	673	5.4
Emge	Ft. Branch, Ind.	520	4.2
Armour Soap	Chicago	514	4.2
Wilson	River Grove, Ill.	458	3.7
Swift	Chicago	423	3.4
Tee-Pak	Danville, Ill.	407	3.3
Libby	Chicago	358	2.9
Eckrich	Ft. Wayne	337	2.7
Swift	Evansville, Ind.	332	2.7
		6,796	54.8
District 2			
Hormel	Austin, Minn.	3,539	28.5
Armour	St. Paul	2,322	18.7
Swift	St. Paul	1,785	14.4
Wilson	Albert Lea, Minn.	1,033	8.3
Cudahy	Cudahy, Wis.	797	6.4
Tony Down	St. James, Minn.	597	4.8
		10,073	81.1
District 3			
Rath	Waterloo	3,119	14.6
Morrell	Ottumwa	2,273	10.7
Armour	Omaha	1,941	9.1
Wilson	Cedar Rapids	1,591	7.5
Swift	Omaha	1,232	5.8
Armour	St. Joseph, Mo.	1,023	4.0
Hormel	Ft. Dodge	852	4.0
Decker (Armour)	Mason City	813	3.8
Wilson	Omaha	795	3.7
Swift	Sioux City, Iowa	649	3.0
Cudahy	Omaha	611	2.9
Iowa Pak (Swift)	Des Moines	581	2.7
Swift	Denver	474	2.2
Wilson	Kansas City, Kans.	382	1.8
Morrell	Estherville, Iowa	379	1.8
IBP	Perry, Iowa	329	1.5
Cudahy	Denver	314	1.5
		17,358	81.3

Sources: Kerry to All Officers and District Directors, "Table 3.0: UPWA membership by district and by single plants with 300 or more members, per capita payments, March 1966," October 3, 1966, box 471, folder 3, United Packinghouse Workers of America Collection, State Historical Society of Wisconsin, Madison, Wis.

Note: These three districts made up 67.5 percent of the UPWA's total membership.

World War II and the Fluidity of Job Typing by Sex

The subjective and fluid nature of job classifications became apparent to women during World War II when large numbers found themselves in jobs previously held only by men. Many of the women involved in the legal battles of the 1960s had joined the UPWA in the 1940s and had witnessed firsthand the postwar reclassification of jobs as well as the reversion to more rigid segregation after 1945. Some had entered the packinghouse work force even before 1941 in "men's" or "heavy" jobs, as they were known. Armour and Company managers, for example, hired Mary Ashlock of Mason City, Iowa, in the late 1930s to work in the canned ham department. There, she recalled, she "used to have to sling those great big hams from one gondola to the next after I'd scaled them, weighed them." Most of these women desperately needed jobs. One woman at Armour worked while pregnant, up until the day she gave birth, without benefit of maternity leave, and returned to work two days later.[13]

Women entering the labor force during this period worked on both "men's" and "women's" jobs. Women from Ottumwa Local 1 were hired by John Morrell and Company for jobs that demanded "dexterity," such as packing livers, making wooden boxes, and working in sausage and bacon departments. When the war began, Morrell—Ottumwa's largest employer with over two thousand people on payroll—drafted women into higher-paying "men's" departments such as the "cut and kill" that had previously been considered too physically demanding for them. Ottumwa was a county seat with a population of thirty thousand and marked the division point for the Burlington and Milwaukee Railroad. It was also home to a John Deere factory. Morrell, however, was one of the town's few employers to offer relatively high-paying jobs to women. The war's onset helped to push these wages higher. Typical of the female workers was Elizabeth "Sue" Smith, hired by Morrell in 1942 to work on the "hog kill" at 72 cents an hour, an improvement over "women's" jobs that paid an average of 59 cents an hour. Smith worked "knife jobs" throughout the war, sometimes twelve-hour shifts, and earned the higher "men's" wages.[14]

The UPWA benefited greatly from the infusion of some twenty thousand new female hires entering the packinghouse gates during the war. Together with men, new women unionists quickly asserted their collective strength against management by staging wildcat strikes over production speedups, unfair employee discharges, and sexual harassment. In spite of the union's no-strike pledge during the war, rank-and-file members deemed job actions unavoidable in the face of employer aggression. "What could we do?" asked Stella Nowicki. "They [company contract violations] were so blatant. It was the only way. . . . There was this kind of solidarity. It was a tremendous experience."[15] Union officers acknowledged women members' presence, in turn, by working for pregnancy or maternity leave in contracts.

The other demand of women unionists, "equal pay for equal work," became part of the group's constitution in 1943. UPWA members hoped to discourage employers from hiring lower-paid women into men's positions and to give a limited margin of security and equality to those women working in "men's" jobs. A recruitment leaflet distributed to women workers in Des Moines in 1942 summarized union arguments for the measure, pleading for defense of the male wage as a family provider and for individual justice for women workers:

> Are you going to stand by and be forced against your will to accept your brother's, father's, or husband's job at a big reduction in pay or are you going to help obtain a contract that will give you equal pay for the job you are assigned to. The PWOC-CIO is the only organization in packing that has the strength to obtain this kind of contract and we urge you as women workers to do what they have done in other plants—get in and secure that protection. You need us and we need you. . . . More and more women are going to replace men, so let us protect your interests.[16]

Encouraged by union leaders, women filed countless equal pay grievances with the National War Labor Board (NWLB). Union lawyers also resorted to the NWLB in seeking justice, as in a 1943 complaint against the Armour, Wilson, Cudahy, and Morrell packing companies, charging that "the whole wage structure as it applies to women is obsolete and . . . needs complete overhauling."[17]

The union leadership's concern for equality did not extend beyond equal pay. At the war's close, packinghouse owners, in collusion with male unionists, helped oversee a massive layoff of women. In this regard, packinghouse employers and unionists mirrored other industries in their treatment of women workers.[18] Still, the lesson of their wartime work experiences was not lost on women. A woman delegate from Chicago attending the 1952 international convention, for example, fought against the assignment of men only to new packinghouse jobs by some employers. She recalled her own success in doing a "male" job during World War II.[19] "There are no such things as women's and men's jobs," a UPWA man asserted a decade later. "Women I know in the sugar refineries did everything a man did during the war. In the cities they drove buses and did everything a man did, and as soon as the war was over they couldn't do it anymore."[20] At the union's 1966 convention in Los Angeles another man rose to voice his support for full implementation of Title VII: "I can remember during the war years women carried torches and all this around the shipyards," he recounted in his remarks on why sex-based job classifications were flawed.[21] Indeed, in some cases women remained in "men's" departments after the war. UPWA president Helstein recalled visiting a packing plant in Grand Forks, North Dakota, in the late 1940s and finding a woman "about five-by-five" who could "throw those carcasses around better than most men."[22] Even at the strictly segregated Morrell plant in Ottumwa, sausage workers would be allowed to "pack hams"—a "man's" job—during labor shortages.[23]

Despite the success packinghouse women had in performing "men's" jobs, the rhetoric of special female "talents" persisted. The traditional notion that women, along with children, were in need of government and contract protection continued to dominate the labor movement's commitment to a sex-segregated workplace.[24] One male UPWA Local 46 member in Waterloo, Iowa, claimed that women "were a little more handy with their hands and dexterous," while Ralph Helstein informed a group of women unionists in the 1950s that meatpacking companies were "hiring you because of your dexterity, the way you do the kind of work they put you to. You're not doing heavy work."[25] These examples of sex-typing, "adopted to rationalize the specific boundaries between women's and men's work," as Ruth Milkman explains it in her study of automotive and electrical manufacturing, would not be seriously questioned by most UPWA members for another twenty years.[26]

"Women's Issues" in the Postwar UPWA

Most of the UPWA women's efforts were taken up in union skirmishes with management, but not with union men, following World War II. While the nation's conservative backlash against the Left and New Deal progressives did irreparable damage to labor's militant wing, varied and open-ended labor-management relations still occurred in several industrial sectors, including meatpacking. The institutionalization of collective bargaining often forced employers to be attentive to worker demands. Endlessly complex procedures for resolving workplace grievances resulted in compromises by employers hoping to avoid work stoppages. More important, shop-floor matters—the "stuff of rank-and-file militancy," as David Brody puts it—were the least tractable concerns within the formal framework of collective bargaining and were the focus of countless UPWA battles in the 1950s.[27] While leaders in unions such as the United Automobile Workers worked with management in attempting to eliminate disruptive wildcat walk-outs and slowdowns, the decentralized UPWA was unique not only in permitting such activity but in helping to organize it. For example, claiming Rath packing would not bargain in good faith, the chief steward in the Waterloo local coordinated wildcat work stoppages. UPWA leaders saw to it that wages lost due to these strikes were shared equally among all workers.[28]

A high level of worker solidarity characterized labor relations in the packing-house industry from its inception. Meatpacking-company managers worried that in their labor-intensive industry the chronically fluctuating price of livestock would impinge on their relatively tight profit margins. In a period of fairly high wages and union security for manufacturing workers such as those in the auto-mobile, steel, and rubber industries, one labor economist reported that packing-houses "still furnish[ed] some distasteful examples of labor relations at its most primitive level."[29] Management's modification of work processes, quickening of the production pace, and resistance to union demands all characterized the acri-monious nature of industrial relations.

The often-beleaguered UPWA membership seemed undaunted in the face of managerial offensives. "District Council 3 has never prostrated itself before the great god of fear," declared district director Russell Bull in 1953, "we have never yet given up our right to think for ourselves and to express our convictions openly."[30] Packinghouse workers drew strength for their battle against manage-ment through solidarity on the shop floor. The working-class communities in which they lived, characterized by the historian Wilson Warren in his discussion of 1940s Ottumwa as featuring a "closely knit neighborhood and a shared cul-tural identity," bolstered their resolve. Workers met in fraternal, religious, and entertainment venues to plan union strategy.[31] They defended the union in the form of massive strikes, first in 1946, then in 1948 when they lost a bitter ten-week strike that threatened the UPWA's very existence. Women members offered critically needed support to the packinghouse union. "They continued to fight militantly and all during the strike, they were there both night and day, and there were many times when you could see the women on the picket line and you couldn't see the men," a male delegate from Local 347 in District 1 reminded those attending the 1949 convention.[32] On the picket line "you saw women outnum-bering men three to one, and I don't say that with a boast," remarked a woman delegate modestly at a later convention, "but it is just to show you that women can do the job if given the chance."[33]

Women activists worked alongside men as department stewards in support of the union cause. Elected by the rank-and-file, stewards performed a wide range of duties including collecting dues, publicizing UPWA activities and news, and filing grievances. As the level of animosity in packinghouse industrial relations deepened following postwar reconversion, women stewards intensified their militant stance: "If we didn't get what we wanted, we said we gonna hit the bricks and we hit 'em," Ercell Allen, an African-American worker, recalled.[34] The women channeled their energies into a struggle for the UPWA's mere survival long after such matters had been secured by other unions.

Women's specific concerns were not absent from the packinghouse labor organization's agenda in the two decades preceding the passage of the Civil Rights Act of 1964. Women members drew on their wartime work histories and the limited role offered them during this period in formulating demands for equality that would only become clear in the mid-1960s. Following the crushing setback of the 1948 strike, leaders sought ways to unify their membership. In considering women's role in the UPWA, they reverted to a well-worn call for developing "women's activities" programs at the local and district level. Successive convention committees and officers' reports to the membership indicated what they had in mind. Women's auxiliary or activity groups were to support political candidates, educate members on consumer issues, and speak on any other problems "to which the women's activity committee may address itself." A front-page editorial cartoon in the July 1950 issue of the Waterloo Local 46 newsletter appealed to women workers in direct terms. In it, two women are discussing the value of union membership. The first woman claims, "It's our union as well as the men's— lets [*sic*] help them," and the second woman agrees: "Guess we should—the union has done alot for us, pregnancy leave pay, back pay—the union says we should get men's wage for [*sic*] same work—and now—new benefits coming up in contract negotiations!"[35]

By the early 1960s, UPWA women addressed increasingly diverse subjects, as outlined by one committee on women's activities: "housing; education segregation and discrimination; health and welfare; national and international affairs (economic, political and social); the role of women in international affairs; peace, politics and others."[36] Appeals to women's "special abilities" as a defense of familial and community needs lay buried in convention resolutions calling for women's participation in union matters. Often women workers were grouped with union wives and given a secondary, supporting role with little forethought. As UPWA vice-president Russell Lasley suggested in 1949, "women's committees within the confines of our local unions can do a great deal in educating housewives . . . on what the man of the family has to do in order to protect them and their children. . . . In sponsoring ladies' auxiliaries as an outgrowth of the women's committees within our local unions we can build strongly among our own local leadership among men who might be reluctant to do so because of a misunderstanding at home."[37] Discussions centering on women's activities usually attempted to relate UPWA women's status to that of middle-class women and not that of their working-class male counterparts. "There is no real reason why union women cannot be as effective in community affairs which have particular relevance to women as any other group or class of women," read District 3's "Report of Women's Activities Committee" in 1957.[38] Women were expected to build on their "social activism in both neighborhood and workplace" while men dominated the latter, "control[ling] the political skill, information, and means of communication necessary to consolidate power and stabilize the organization."[39]

The UPWA's union culture, however, retained a high degree of homosocial relations. For men this oftentimes entailed participating in the saloon culture and in fraternal organizations; "family" events at union functions and UPWA meetings included women. Union leaders sent out calls for women's representation on local executive boards and at conventions. "Take a look at this Convention. Are 25% of the delegates women? or 10%?" District 3's Russell Bull admonished his listeners in 1951. "What does it mean when women either do not seek or are not encouraged to seek an active place in the affairs of this union on every level? It means that we are divided."[40] How could women be brought into the centers of power? Union resolutions suggested that, beyond forming "women's activities" committees, locals should provide educational opportunities for training women as stewards, encourage women to run for office, and permit union local heads of women's groups to take places on executive boards and bargaining committees.

Equal pay was the single area in which UPWA leaders gave serious and sustained support for gender equality following World War II. They pursued two routes to bring about equal pay: legislation and collective bargaining negotiations. Unlike in large, Washington, D.C.–based industrial unions, packinghouse labor officers had neither the financial means nor political clout to occupy a prominent place in the battle for equal pay. They did, however, join other CIO unions in supporting equal pay legislation during this period by submitting statements backing the measure to congressional committees. Along with other industrial union leaders, UPWA officers backed such legislation on the grounds that American-style democracy protected individual rights (i.e., "equal pay for equal work") and that the increased consumption levels obtained by higher-paid women workers would invigorate an ever-expanding economy. Equal pay demands, in fact, cost male unionists little. They believed that an equal pay mandate would keep employers from hiring women to replace men. Male pay scales—not the lower women's rates—would be protected.[41]

Equal pay advocates found only limited success at the bargaining table. There, negotiators failed to eliminate separate job lists and wage scales, thwarting the reformers' attempts to improve women's status. Unionists were able to rid most contracts of the wage differentials that consistently paid women at rates lower than men even if they performed identical jobs. As they had numerous times previously, UPWA delegates at the 1954 convention proclaimed the removal of differentials as an important union goal. Negotiators' progress in honoring this pledge was slow and uneven. A 1952 government report found that local union efforts to this end were "relatively few and do not remove the basic differentials." The report's author noted that union representatives blamed the halting progress on women, who were "less inclined than men to bring their grievances to the attention of local and international representatives" and that "often women's problems get less attention than those of men."[42]

It was women themselves, however, who, as the same government report characterized it, "took their leaders to task for laxity in correcting unfair wage differences."[43] Chicago Swift Local 28 president John Lewis noted in 1950 that "the women of the Swift plant Local 28 have been holding a series of meetings discussing various problems that are confronting them, and found their major problem to be the wage differential."[44] Backed by the international's long-standing formal support for equal pay and prompted by UPWA women activists, union bargaining-committee members narrowed the wage differential in the early 1950s from 10 cents to 5 cents an hour; they also succeeded in incorporating an equal pay provision into contracts with major meatpacking companies in 1956.[45] The wage differential was gone for most workers by the decade's end, but not for all: at the UPWA's convention in 1960 delegates reported that "in some plants women are not receiving equal pay for equal work when they perform the same job as a man."[46]

There was no significant challenge to the privileging of male employment conditions following the victory for equal pay guarantees. The real obstacle to equality was not so much unequal pay for identical jobs, but rather the prevailing job classification system that placed "men's" jobs in the upper ranges of wage bracket schemes and "women's" jobs disproportionally near the bottom. Women were acutely aware of such inequity; however, they had neither a concrete plan to challenge such a system nor an ideological perspective from which to rethink job-typing by sex. "Women are still concentrated in the jobs in the lower 3 brackets. . . . In contrast, some of our men go up to bracket 22 in the powerhouse, in the floormen's jobs etc [sic]," a union research assistant wrote in 1959.[47] For the most part, men and women in the union continued to support protective legislation for working women and, thus, an industrial relations system predicated on the notion that women's work was secondary and could include only certain jobs. In needing protection from the harshest elements of paid labor, they could not make claims for equality. Following from this, UPWA members opposed the Equal Rights Amendment on the grounds that it "would have the end purpose of abolishing gains already won for women workers in the area of special labor legislation."[48]

If gender equality was not on the union's agenda in the period 1945–63, the UPWA's notable support for the civil rights movement indirectly helped lay the groundwork for working-class feminism. Just as the equal pay campaign introduced the notion of women's equal rights on the job, so the civil rights movement's emphasis on individual rights as opposed to group stereotyping could not help but call attention to the unique inequality women suffered. In the crucible of "rights talk" flowing out of the civil rights movement, gender relations in the packinghouse union were beginning to come under scrutiny. "The women's problem," Marion Simmons of UPWA District 4 staff suggested in 1956, "is very, very close to the big American problem, that of discrimination against Negro people."[49]

Minority women benefited most directly from the movement for equality in the 1950s and early 1960s. Segregated into the lowest-paid jobs, and shut out of packing plants completely in some cases, African-American women lobbied vigorously to have their employment concerns incorporated into the union's campaign for racial equality. Union leaders viewed the unfair treatment of African-American women in the workplace as a subset of race discrimination, and they established a program to eradicate such treatment. This effort included publicizing the problem in union literature and at conventions, bestowing awards to diligent locals, and using the collective bargaining process as a means of improving minority women's status. Their efforts bore fruit. By the early 1950s, Local 28 representing Swift workers in Chicago reported that, through arbitration, they had forced the company to hire thirteen African-American women who had been discriminated against when they applied for jobs. In Iowa, the Swift local in Sioux City was successful in securing African-American women's employment; Ottumwa Local 1 pressured management to hire African-American women for the first time since World War II.[50] Members of District 3's Human Relations Committee recommended in 1953 that "we set ourselves the task during the coming year of eliminating completely the discriminatory practices of companies insofar as Negro and Mexican women are concerned."[51] However, there were clear limits to how far minority women should advance. UPWA leaders judged their progress in battling this discrimination by assessing the improvement of minority women's status compared to that of white women—but not to that of white men or African-American men.

Notwithstanding such moves toward equality, women did not benefit overall from the vaunted UPWA progressivism. While African-American men and women workers' rights were promoted by unionists in the context of a burgeoning civil rights movement, women of both races had no such mass movement in which to fight for gender equality. Packinghouse women unionists may have "produced feminist challenges to male dominance in the union and industry" in this period, as one historian suggests, but the fruits of women's labor were meager.[52] At the international level no women ever held executive board positions nor was a permanent "women's bureau" established as in the United Automobile Workers. Women activists assigned much of the blame for their marginal status in the UPWA to male leaders. Most union leaders viewed the victory against differentials as the capstone to their efforts on behalf of women. Women, however, looked beyond equal pay to other issues, especially those of education and leadership opportunities. On these topics, successive convention resolutions called for new programs but male leaders offered only halfhearted support. Marian Davis of Local 42 was frank about the matter: "You men aren't kidding anybody. We women know that if you were really sincere in the women's program we would have a darn good program."[53] "Too often you have ignored us," delegate Huguette Plamondon told the UPWA convention audience in 1958. "Unfortunately, there is still a tendency for some men in our union to consider too often women members as constituting a special group, as a special or different membership."[54] Beyond such generally second-rate treatment lay more specific reasons for men's unwillingness to fight for women's gains. Chief among them was the reluctance of unionists to insist that the international office assert its power in enforcing long-standing resolutions on women workers. "We come here convention after convention and we sit here and hear these flowery speeches and the men agreeing and saying 'Yes, that is for us'; but we are tired of that. We want action," said one women at the 1952 convention.[55]

The propriety of the international office's overseeing the enactment of resolutions was debated nearly every year, with little consensus emerging. Many union members feared that giving a centralized power the responsibility to direct "women's" issues would negate the very foundation of UPWA strength. "Where is our old PWOC fight, where are the guts we had when we were trying to get our bellies off of our backbones?" asked one delegate in 1960. "We have to do it [that is, address women's concerns] on a local basis before we can bring it to the International and let them solve our problems."[56] Women delegates were frustrated with this argument, however: "the vast majority of our convention mandates on Women's Activities have yet to be fulfilled," reported the secretary of the Women's Action Committee at the 1954 convention in Sioux City, Iowa.[57] In an attempt to circumvent "this nebulous language, this loose language" that characterized previous resolutions, about which "in most instances nothing happened," they mandated in their proposals that year that "women *must* participate on all local union policy-making levels. . . . Women *must* be included as delegates to all schools, conferences, conventions, etc." [emphasis added].[58] Responding to criticism from male delegates that this resolution would strangle local autonomy, vice-president Russell Lasley hastened to assure those assembled that enforcement "must be left up to the discretion of the local union involved."[59]

The international increased its commitment to holding women's conferences and publicizing "women's" issues in the union press, but it did not force meatpacking locals that were negligent in this area, claiming it was preserving local autonomy. UPWA president Helstein took the edge off the 1954 resolution for action by underplaying its mandatory nature. "It seems to me that what is being sought by this resolution is an attempt to establish a policy that every local union will do everything that it can possible [sic] do to see to it that there is participation at all levels of the local union of workers in the activities and interests of the local."[60] Such an argument was disingenuous at best. The UPWA had justified strong intervention by the international in defense of civil rights according to race but would not duplicate such efforts to assist white and African-American women.[61]

Left to their own devices, UPWA local unions produced an uneven record of promoting "women's" concerns. Not surprisingly, Chicago locals, led by activists such as Addie Wyatt, headed the campaign for women's rights. Encouraged by older District 1 unionists, including Bessie McCauley, Rose Wright, and Sophie Koscrolowski, Wyatt formed alliances with like-minded women to work against discrimination across the country. In 1963 Esther Peterson appointed her to serve on the President's Commission on the Status of Women, a key group in the push to renew interest in women's political issues in the 1960s. To the west of District 1, in Iowa, "women's" activities were less developed. Few women were sent from District 3 locals to international meetings. District conferences for women workers began only in 1959, a full decade after similar meetings began in the Chicago area. Although women held 123 executive offices in District 3 locals (including five presidents and ten vice-presidents), men overwhelmingly occupied executive board positions in the large, dominating locals.[62] In District 1, for example, sixteen women held the important office of chief steward, while only seven women were chief stewards in District 3. Only one woman sat on bargaining boards in the Ottumwa and Cedar Rapids locals; no women were on the board in the district's largest local, in Waterloo.[63] Without the numbers enjoyed in Chicago locals, women found that their interests remained unaddressed. "The briefness of the report on women's activities indicates that not much work has been done in this field," wrote the author of District 3's Officers Report Committee for 1955.[64] The outlook for the advancement of vigorous programs in this area had not improved two years later, according to Local 1's Dave Hart: "I would venture at this time that there aren't two active women committees in this district. After the last convention, I went back to the locals and tried to organize women's activities and we got various excuses. . . . Men and women here are going to go back and start organizing women's activities or we are going to quit reporting on them."[65] Progress at the district level itself, however, was slow: on the eve of the passage of the Civil Rights Act, unionists in District 3 were still demanding that the standing Women's Activities Committee be activated.[66]

Attempts at the local level to build a viable women's program in District 3 foundered on the shoals of passivity and male hostility. In 1951, for example, a "Special Report of Committee from Local 1 [Ottumwa] on Problems" noted, "Although women constitute about 25% of the membership, there are no women in the local leadership and the women do not participate in local meetings, etc."[67] Committee members quickly pointed out that this was not the "fault" of anyone but rather "the result of the absence of forceful leadership of education programs, and of any real thinking and action to work out a program for the union."[68] They encouraged increased steward training and financial support of education for women workers but provided no blueprint for change. Similar halting steps were taken elsewhere in the district. A "women's affairs committee" was established by those at the women's conference of Waterloo Local 46 in 1953. The committee met infrequently, however, leaving a negligible record of activity. Only in the area of civil rights for minorities were women the beneficiaries of aggressive union efforts at all levels of the UPWA. This included District 3, where yearly "Anti-Discrimination Awards" were given to deserving locals that worked on securing employment for Hispanic and African-American women.[69]

It is difficult to measure precisely how much of the UPWA's lack of support for "women's" issues was a result of male antipathy or women's apathy. Overt hostility was rare in districts where women held a proportionately sizable share of the membership and made up an energetic civil rights contingent.[70] Not so in District 3, where men resisted proposals that the international executive board enforce convention mandates supporting women workers. Merle Thompson, Waterloo delegate, for example, declared at the UPWA's 1958 convention, "frankly, . . . the ladies are feeling a bit sorry for themselves."[71] Charging the resolutions committee with "creating an anti-women feeling amongst the men," Thompson bragged that Local 46 women were active but that "we haven't heard them get up here and grouse and blame it on them men."[72] Thompson, in fact, faced off against Dorothy Petersen, a local union colleague, five years later when he spoke out against a district proposal calling for the local union leadership to encourage women members to run for office. "I think this is improper and wrong to saddle the local union executive board when you say give full support in getting women elected. . . . We try to elect qualified people, whether they are women, part of the majority or minority groups," said Thompson.[73] While some men rose to defend the resolution, others supported Thompson. For example, Max Williams from Local 1 in Ottumwa laid the blame for the lack of women officers at the feet of women unionists: "Women do not attend the meetings. The ladies are going to have to help themselves."[74] Petersen, later a plaintiff in a sex-discrimination case, however, had the last word. "All we ask is that the executive board support the women. . . . We know that the rank-and-file elects you," she said. "But if the executive board would support the women, I am sure we would find more women here today."[75] The motion carried to adopt the resolution, but like most convention recommendations little support was forthcoming in bringing about its enactment.

Through the mid-1960s, women in the large District 3 packinghouse plants remained circumscribed in their union roles. In Ottumwa few women were elected to office. The outspoken Ethel Jerred complained that "the hardest part for women in the union, they would let us cook, and they would let us stand on the picket line, and they'd let us take these dirty heavy jobs, but when it came time for a woman to run for office . . . All you've got to do is look down through the history of the union and see how many women have served on the board as a steward, as a president, a vice-president. Especially in Local 1. And I know the same story has come to me from women in other plants."[76] Indeed, the record was equally poor elsewhere in Iowa. In Dubuque, Rachel Maerschalk was the sole woman on Local 31's executive board for many years.[77] Projects such as Easter Seals drives, political campaign support, and food collections for strikers' families were run by "women's activities" committees. Julia Naylor from Fort Dodge concluded that such activity groups "were just something to kind of get women off [union leaders'] backs."[78] As a result of unfulfilled convention promises and limitations at the local level, women keenly sensed their inequality within the UPWA. Slowly and haltingly they developed the networks they would use in their quest for equality in a diminishing job market.

Production Reorganization and Gender Inequality

UPWA women progressed from defending their "protected" second-class status to calling for equality as they lost economic ground. The roots of this tortuous advancement lay in the changes brought on by work reorganization and technological innovations affecting the packinghouse industry after 1955. Livestock supply dispersion, improved motorized transportation, and new marketing strategies increased the profitability of decentralized packinghouse operations across the United States. This hampered the growth of UPWA membership, which had thrived in large packinghouses found in District 3.[79]

By assigning work groups daily quotas and either paying them for work beyond those goals or permitting them to leave work early with full pay before completing their shifts, meatpacking companies set the stage for massive layoffs.

Under this system—known as "gaintime" or "sunshine bonus"—workers apparently enjoyed the generous benefits offered by management, but they also paid a price for them. "Before that [i.e., gaintime] everyone was happy, we'd sing at our work. We would visit," one woman remembered. "After we began to work incentive," she continued, "and got a few of those paychecks with the extra dollars in them, there was just no time for singing or for joke telling."[80] In order to finish quickly, Waterloo Rath worker Lucille Bremer recalled, workers "used their heads to find the best and fastest way to do things."[81] The result, noted Ethel Jerred, was fatal: "[Women] would go in and start doing all this gaintime and put out eight hours work in four or five or six. And so a job was chopped off here. They didn't care. They had seniority. It didn't bother them. It wasn't their job. And they were showing the company how people's jobs could be eliminated."[82] The effect on the union was devastating: at the time of the merger with the Amalgamated Meatcutters and Butcher Workmen in 1968 the UPWA had a membership of 68,000, down from its high of 104,000 in 1954.[83]

New automation, time studies, and work reorganization schemes contributed to this membership drop. "Such devices," Stephen Meyer maintains in his study of skilled automobile workers, "altered the workers' world—their shop traditions, their levels of skill, the patterns of control, and the social relations of the workplace."[84] Changes in the packinghouse industry, sometimes called the "B system" after Charles Bedaux's motion studies instituted in the early 1920s, were indeed unsettling. They even spawned a workplace ditty: "the B's they hum, the B's they buzz. We got one man where three men was."[85] This song certainly summarized the most obvious result of the changes affecting meatpacking production but it masked the fact that mechanization displaced mostly those working in "women's" departments such as bacon slicing and sausage processing. In Dubuque, work groups shrank from thirteen to eight workers as workloads became heavier. The mostly female department of "skinning wieners" in the Waterloo plant nearly disappeared, and management reduced workers in the sliced bacon area by approximately 80 percent. At the 1958 international convention, the women's activity committee reported that an average of three women to every man had been laid off. Facing unemployment, these workers' only recourse was to transfer to other "women's" departments or to accept jobs at company plants elsewhere. By 1964–65 even these options had been sharply reduced. Many women workers with fifteen or twenty years of seniority found themselves out of work.[86]

UPWA members unsuccessfully challenged these debilitating changes at the international, district, and local levels. Union president Helstein attempted to stem the tide of job displacement through joint management-labor "automation committees." He soon discovered that packinghouse owners had no intention of following union recommendations for extensive retraining programs, shorter work weeks, and various social welfare schemes. In a press statement sent to locals in 1963, Helstein reported that management had treated the committee from the outset as a "publicity gimmick." "The language of the agreement which established the Automation Committee," he charged, "has become a hypocritical and heart-less mockery."[87] International conference and convention delegates grappled with the issue as well. Participants in the 1955 Anti-Discrimination and Women's Activity Conference, for example, recognized the links between ongoing industry changes, dual seniority and job lists, and women's disproportionate job losses. They called for an immediate response to the problem: "The union cannot sit by and watch whole departments disappear. . . . It cannot sit by and watch long years of welding and forging a militant organization crumble as management pushes a button."[88] Appealing to cross-gender solidarity in their statement, they claimed that "men will be next unless a battle is put up for women. Men are already on their way: more job loads, faster speed ups every day. They have already felt the cold breath of the machine."[89] Unionists in many locals did little to address women's concerns. "The discussion is not so fresh and we are not talking so fast about us women as we were on issues that more or less concerned the men," a woman delegate noted at the 1958 convention.[90] The UPWA membership's ruling on the matter at that meeting was predictable in light of the organization's past record: while the union would encourage measures to protect women, a "local option" policy would be the rule on issues of seniority for workers.[91]

Packinghouse women workers were deeply ambivalent about embracing gender equality. Despite some misgivings, most women did not abandon protectionism before 1965, even in the face of economic setbacks. In his study of the UPWA, Bruce Fehn found that, while some locals negotiated for single seniority lists, most retained dual seniority in their contracts. Older women, satisfied with their high wages and troubled by the possibility that they might lose their positions to men and be forced to take unfamiliar jobs, opposed the fusing of seniority lists.[92] Following this reasoning, Women's Activities Committee members at District 3's 1959 meeting urged that separate seniority be continued. In an attempt to stave off further job losses through automation, they recommended that positions be "frozen. . . . That companies shall not combine female and male jobs. . . . That no portion of a female job be combined with a male job."[93] This last proposal had to do with the fact that automation displaced men as well, leading many of them to work at "women's" jobs. "Many women are losing jobs to men," a male delegate from Omaha noted at the district's 1963 gathering. "We want a local agreement stating a man can't take a woman's job or a woman can't take a man's job."[94] By moving into "women's" jobs, men helped call into question the inviolability of job-typing by sex. Women had begun to do this during World War II by succeeding at "men's" jobs; now, male workers unwittingly contributed to the growing belief in the artificiality of such job assignments.

Although there were few ardent supporters for doing away with protective laws wholesale and putting men and women on equal footing, a definite rumbling of support for pursuing such a new direction could be heard. This came in the form of modest suggestions that the union and employers revisit job classifications in light of changes brought by automation. At the international's 1954 convention the Women's Activities Committee members asked that locals "evaluate all jobs to determine whether they can be done by women . . . pay[ing] particular attention to all new jobs, especially those being created by increased mechanization, with a view toward greater bracket increases for women."[95] Women unionists often sent mixed messages, arguing for protectionism and equality, as they did at the UPWA's biennial meeting in 1960 when they called for leaders to guarantee that "women's" jobs continue to be done by women only and that collective bargaining agreements "include the no discrimination [clause] because of race, sex, or age."[96] Increasingly concerned by the threat of unemployment, and witness to the questionable value of separate job lists, distinguishable challenges to inequality surfaced in the years immediately preceding Title VII's passage.

"This International union is not going to stand idly by," announced Russell Lasley in 1966, "and see women eliminated from the plants with seniority and the right to have jobs within those plants . . . so have no fear."[97] Lasley's words, coming after a decade that saw the decimation of women's employment status in packinghouses, rang hollow. Union president Helstein had recognized the precarious state of workers' lives in the UPWA when he told convention delegates two years earlier, "We are in the process of dividing up scarcity, and have been for a long time."[98] The packinghouse union watched the process pit men and women workers against each other. "Remember it is not the men in the plants that are eliminating the jobs," Helstein continued, "it is the employer that is eliminating them."[99] Helstein was only half correct in his analysis. Although employer-initiated changes had not been supported by the union, male unionists had responded along gender lines, frustrating attempts by some women to make demands on the labor organization that would be costly to the men's economic position. Women unionists for the most part also had embraced a sex-segregated, separate seniority and a dual wage system, seeking to defend class solidarity and their own immediate interests.

In the face of their experiences with wartime work, marginalization in union life, and job displacement, however, packinghouse women began to back equality for all rather than protection for some. They came to reject protective measures, along with unequal wages, sex-segregated jobs, and seniority lists. "If we are going against discrimination we go together because this is not a man's union, this is our union," one woman unionist stated in 1956. "This is not a man's world, this is our world. We must unite ourselves together. Divided we fall, united we stand."[100] By the mid-1960s, women in the UPWA would look beyond their male coworkers and find their own legal tools to achieve this goal.

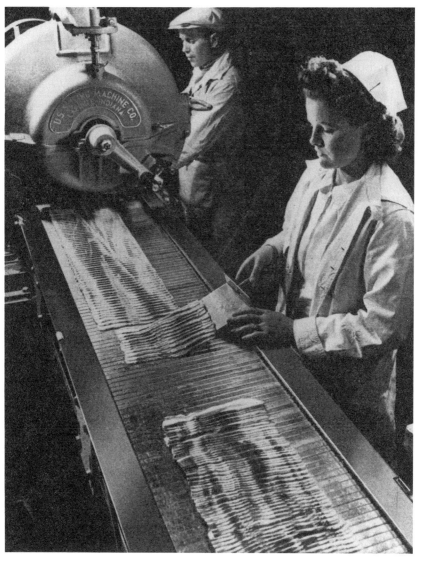

Rath packinghouse woman slicing bacon, 1941. By the early 1960s, automation displaced over half of individuals working in "female" jobs. (State Historical Society of Iowa, Iowa City)

Members of the IUE Research and Economics Department in 1958: (standing, left to right) Chuck Kimble and William Gary; (seated) David Lasser and Gloria Johnson. (International Union of Electrical Workers Photograph Archive, Special Collections and University Archives, Rutgers University Libraries)

Cover of program for the AFL-CIO Industrial Union Department's 1961 conference on working women. (Walter P. Reuther Library, Wayne State University)

problems of working women...

From The
ELLICKSON Collection

SUMMARY REPORT OF
A CONFERENCE
SPONSORED BY
INDUSTRIAL UNION DEPARTMENT
AFL-CIO
JUNE 12-14, 1961
MAYFLOWER HOTEL • WASHINGTON, D.C.

The IUE's Mary Callahan with the chair of the union's RCA Conference Board, Dan Arnold, in 1961. Callahan served the IUE for over thirty years in various staff positions, served on the President's Commission on the Status of Women in the early 1960s, and was a founding member of the CLUW. (International Union of Electrical Workers Photograph Archive, Special Collections and University Archives, Rutgers University Libraries)

President John F. Kennedy signs the Equal Pay Act of 1963 into law. Esther Peterson, former union staff member and director of the U.S. Women's Bureau, stands fifth from the right. (John F. Kennedy Library)

Ottumwa packinghouse worker Ethel Jerred chairs the women's delegates workshop at the 1967 UPWA District 3 conference. Jerred was an avid supporter of women's filing sex discrimination charges. (State Historical Society of Iowa, Iowa City)

First president of the CLUW, Olga Madar, stands at the podium at the 1974 founding conference in Chicago. (Walter P. Reuther Library, Wayne State University)

Some of the participants at the CLUW's founding convention. (Walter P. Reuther Library, Wayne State University)

IUE assistant general counsel Ruth Weyand testifies at congressional hearings on pregnancy disability legislation in 1978. (International Union of Electrical Workers Photograph Archive, Special Collections and University Archives, Rutgers University Libraries)

CLUW president Joyce Miller marches in support of striking workers in the late 1970s. (Photo by Images Unlimited; Walter P. Reuther Library, Wayne State University)

4

Accounting for Equality:
Gender Relations in the International Union of
Electrical Workers, 1945–63

"Among international unions and local unions, in and outside the AFL-CIO,"
wrote two officers of the Equal Employment Opportunity Commission a decade
after the passage of the 1964 federal law on equal employment opportunity, "there
is much variation in policy from enthusiastic support to outright hostility on the
part of a few, with relative indifference on the part of most." In particular, they
singled out the International Union of Electrical Workers (IUE) as having an
exemplary record of compliance with Title VII of the Civil Rights Act of 1964,
especially in fighting sex discrimination. The IUE's "alive and dynamic" program,
they reported, included naming full-time directors for social action and women's
activities and involved the substantial resources of the labor organization's legal
department, as mandated by the IUE's International Executive Board (IEB).[1] By
1981 IUE leaders had filed more than five hundred charges of sex and race discrimination with the Equal Employment Opportunity Commission (EEOC) and
over fifty lawsuits naming the IUE or its locals as plaintiffs against employers.[2]

At first glance the IUE's "accommodationist" record of resolving sex discrimination seems puzzling when compared to the records of other, more progressive
unions such as the United Packinghouse Workers (UPWA), which exhibited a
"confrontational" approach to Title VII mandates. Institutional and industrial
structures as well as political factors entrenched since the 1930s account for the
variance in the two unions' histories of gender relations. Unlike the rank-and-
file-led UPWA, the IUE was a large, centralized labor organization whose staff
at the Washington, D.C., headquarters maintained close contact with local
unions, making compliance with federal law much easier. More important, while
UPWA women made up anywhere from 12 to 20 percent of its membership, IUE
women filled 35 percent of their organization's ranks. This made IUE women's
positions in the work force and their demands more central to IUE policies. Also,

while the IUE did not have a visible and permanent "women's bureau" at the international level, as did the United Automobile Workers (UAW), women worked in IUE staff positions in the nation's capital; they participated in interunion and liberal interest groups that worked on "women's issues" in the 1950s and early 1960s through the U.S. Women's Bureau. In 1974 many of these activists helped establish the Coalition of Labor Union Women, a working-class feminist group.

The grounding of gender equality in the IUE, however, was not preordained. The IUE and the UPWA were alike in several ways: both had sizable female memberships and were committed to social unionist ideals. Like the packinghouse union, the IUE had contracts that promoted separate sex and seniority lists; both unions defended protective labor laws for women and opposed the Equal Rights Amendment (ERA). In the early years of industrial unionism, women electrical workers had to push for their inclusion in union leadership circles. They began to formulate demands for equal employment opportunity in the 1930s with nascent calls for wider job opportunities and participation in union affairs. In the United Electrical Workers (UE)—the IUE's parent organization—male unionists' receptivity to "women's issues" ebbed and flowed according to their own needs for wage security and defense against political enemies. During World War II, for example, the UE male leadership advocated equal pay. They abandoned women's concerns, however, when the pressing need to hold the labor organization together arose during the postwar anticommunist backlash. Conservative lawmakers, employers, and Congress of Industrial Organizations (CIO) leaders targeted specific locals and unions suspected of having Communist Party members in key positions. Through elections, union decertification, and expulsion from the CIO, they hoped to crush the power of so-called left-led unions. The UE was one such union; when efforts to dislodge its leftist leaders failed, dissident unionists left to form the IUE.

Competition in the 1950s between the IUE and the beleaguered UE forced labor leaders in both unions to become attentive once again to "women's issues." With the near-total collapse of the UE by the mid-1950s, women activists came into the IUE fold, further strengthening the organization's commitment to women's concerns. This came in the form of support for equal pay, pregnancy benefits, and the holding of conferences. The growing support for gender equality was checked, however, by the onslaught of employer-initiated changes in the electrical industry in the areas of contract negotiations, automation, and production relocation. In a scramble to respond effectively to changing industrial relations, unionists did not take up the cause of gender equality until after Title VII's passage forced them to address this demand.

Women Electrical Workers, Equal Pay, and Union Politics, 1936–49

Whatever changes the advent of industrial unionism brought electrical workers in the 1930s, the generations-old practices of sex-typing jobs and unequal pay continued when the IUE's predecessor, the UE, came into existence in 1936. The social unionist ideals that dominated the early CIO, however, gave women workers the tools with which to counter inequality. Although social unionism was eclipsed by business unionism in the 1950s, its rhetorical strength still emboldened activists. As in other unions, women electrical workers articulated their demands for equality using the lexicon of social justice.[3]

In the midst of the Depression, "women's issues" were not uppermost in the minds of either men or women electrical workers. Workers joined together to battle desperate economic conditions. Chartered as the first non-AFL union to be admitted to the CIO, the UE was formed out of a conjoining of members of independent locals representing workers in heavy electrical equipment plants, dissatisfied AFL local unionists in light electrical manufacturing plants, and several International Association of Machinists (IAM) workers in local bodies. According to longtime UE labor officer James Matles, the union's members, mostly centered in Massachusetts, New York, New Jersey, Pennsylvania, and the Ohio Valley region, were "hardly aware of one another's existence" initially. "All of them, however," Matles noted, "had a general sense of somehow starting on the road toward formation of an industrial organization."[4]

The composition of the early UE General Executive Board (GEB) reflected this diverse membership in its varying industrial sectors and in the political splits within its ranks, which would give way to full-blown internecine factionalism in the late 1940s. Unionists elected James Carey, a member of a Philco AFL local, as UE president. Known as the "boy wonder" president (he was twenty-five when he assumed office), Carey represented the UE's so-called "right wing," a loose coalition of Catholic activists, centrists, and socialists. Julius Emspak, secretary-treasurer from the tool-and-die section of the General Electric (GE) plant in Schenectady, New York, and James Matles, the director of organizing and a former IAM member, were part of the labor organization's "left wing," as Communist Party members, sympathizers, and independent militants were called.[5]

As several scholars have shown, women electrical workers during this period labored in factories in which there existed job segregation, separate seniority lists, and separate wage scales. Management, with male workers' approval, assigned women jobs based on the belief that they were better equipped physiologically to perform specific "light" tasks requiring "dexterity" and repetition. Conversely, male workers took higher-paying "heavy" jobs that union and management believed required more skill and physical exertion. As shown in table 5, women workers, for example, dominated in electric lamp and radio assembly jobs but held only a modest proportion of jobs in factories where workers built turbines, locomotives, and similar products. Working women did not oppose gender inequality. As Patricia Cooper found in her study of Philco Local 101 workers in Philadelphia, "women workers appear to have agreed with management and the union that men and women should do different things, that men's work is more valuable, and that this arrangement was natural and acceptable."[6] This acceptance of a codified occupational classification system benefiting male workers reflected a belief in the male-defined family-wage ideology, shared almost universally by workers during the Depression years.[7]

Many women needed and wanted employment, however, and they found it in the electrical industry. Unlike the capital-intensive, high-wage automobile industry, electrical manufacturing was labor intensive and employed large numbers of women. As such, the marginal skill and weight requirements blurred the boundaries between "men's" and "women's" jobs. In the wake of a lockout and subsequent reclassification of jobs at Philco in the 1930s, a few women began protesting the inequality and subjectivity of this scheme. "Reclassification made

Table 5. Female Workers in Electrical Factories by Industry Division, October 1939

Division	Number of Plants in Sample	Percentage of Female Workers
Automotive electrical equipment	19	30.1
Batteries, storage, and primary	46	17.9
Carbon products	8	13.8
Communications equipment	57	41.7
Electric lamps	20	77.3
Electrical appliances	55	27.9
Electrical measuring instruments	16	34.6
Electrical products not elsewhere classified	32	27.0
Generating, distribution and industrial apparatus	192	18.6
Insulated wire and cable	37	30.7
Radio, radio tubes, and phonographs	102	54.2
Wiring devices and supplies	63	30.8
X-ray and therapeutic apparatus and electronic tubes	16	7.2

Source: "Employment of Women in Wartime," *Monthly Labor Review* 55 (Sept. 1942): 44, cited in Ronald W. Schatz, *The Electrical Workers: A History of Labor at General Electric and Westinghouse, 1923–60* (Urbana: University of Illinois Press, 1983), 31.

sexual difference an explicit issue," Cooper reports, "and exposed different conceptions of gender among male and female workers and managers as each group pursued its class and gender issues."[8] In a period marked by a scarcity of employment for males, however, few challenged women's marginal status in the labor force.

Nevertheless, women who did not directly confront the issue of sex-segregation attempted at least some measure of participation in union affairs. Their assertiveness came not from past union experiences, as it had for some men. The example of family members—fathers, brothers, and husbands—inspired some women to become active. For most, it was their immediate work experiences that led them to activism. Ronald Schatz explains: "Because they worked in close proximity to one another, they often developed close friendships . . . [giving] women the solidarity needed to restrict their output under incentive wage [i.e., piecework] systems and to do battle with the boss when they felt aggrieved. . . . Workers who ordinarily manifested little interest in unions proved to be the most tenacious fighters in shop-floor disputes and strikes."[9]

Involvement in union affairs demanded time, and so most women activists were single or had limited familial duties. Longtime IUE officer Mary Callahan was typical. Widowed with a small son in 1935, Callahan maintained that she became involved because "I wasn't tied up too much with boyfriends. . . . I lived at home. My boy was taken care of so that I had more free time to go out. A lot of the women were engaged to be married, setting up houses, and they were going to quit."[10] Edith Hammer of IUE Local 463 in New York City helped organize a radio parts plant in the 1930s; from there she went on to become steward and shop chairman, and she served as international staff representative for twenty-five years. Hammer remained single. "In those days," she recalled, "what man would want to be married to a woman who travelled all the time and was out at meetings every night?"[11]

Male unionists needed to address women's concerns if they expected to recruit them into their ranks and, in the process, improve their own wages and working conditions. Although women made up only about 15 percent of the early UE membership, they comprised about 27 percent of the electrical industry work force.[12] Women electrical workers gave male union leaders mixed grades on their dealings with women members. "I always felt accepted," Local 601's recording-secretary Margaret Darin recalled. "I think I was respected by the officers of the union and, of course by the rank and file."[13] Women working in other locals and districts were not as fortunate. St. Louis UE staff member Mary Voltz, for example, claimed she was "not accepted by the other representatives of the UE. They were men. And they tried very hard to make me into an office clerk."[14] In this regard, the record of the electrical workers union was typical of most CIO organizations of the period. Men accepted women's contributions to building industrial unionism but refused to address women's growing aspirations to leadership positions.

While men at the highest level supported equal pay, women themselves led the long-term effort to improve their pay and job security. At the UE's 1939 convention, Local 475 women from New York were successful in passing an "Equal Rights for Married Women" resolution. In May 1941, Westinghouse Local 601 women in East Pittsburgh lobbied for, and received, an "extra raise" of five cents an hour to help decrease the wage differential between men and women. That same year, District 6 leaders sponsored a "women's conference" at which Ruth Young, District 4's executive secretary and the first woman member of the GEB, gave the keynote address. Despite their general encouragement, UE men did not always agree to the women's demands. Delegates to the 1939 convention, for example, failed to pass a resolution requiring the GEB to hire a woman organizer. Even the progressive international office refused to back activists' most far reaching proposal. The *UE News* editor ran a story on the 1941 women's meeting but failed to mention participants' call for equal employment opportunity for women in higher paid, skilled jobs and an end to job-typing by sex. The more acceptable equal pay resolution received a fair amount of coverage.[15]

The onset of World War II boosted efforts to integrate women into the union. During the war the *New York Times* credited the UE with "having done the best job among women" in securing equal pay contract provisions.[16] Their notable record came not from a long-standing policy of advocating for "women's issues" but from the need to accommodate the influx of new women members. By 1943 the labor organization's ranks had swelled with 298,000 new members, over 50 percent of them women; by mid-decade, women's share of total union membership shot up to 40 percent, from 33 percent in 1939. Greater leadership opportunities for women followed as the UE attempted to accommodate new members. As early as 1942, organizing director James Matles hired fourteen new women field representatives.[17]

The war did not fundamentally erase the boundaries separating women's and men's work. With the reclassification of male positions in order to fill wartime production quotas, women continued to express dissatisfaction with job-typing by sex. "A job is classified and then after it is classified by some superman complex a decision is reached by the masterminds of industry as to whether the job is to be a man's job or a woman's job," Margaret Darin complained in 1942. She derided the quasiscientific manner in which the classification occurred: "If it is designated as a women's job a 'W' is put next to the labor grade and 'presto change' the rate is reduced by 15 cents."[18] Although union leaders did renegotiate with employers over some job assignments and arranged for the transfer of women with significant seniority to higher paying "men's" jobs in order to placate unhappy women, they did not attempt to reconsider the basic assumptions underlying the occupational classification scheme.[19]

Even the UE's much-chronicled equal pay campaign ran out of steam at the war's close. As Ruth Milkman demonstrates in her study of gender relations in the electrical and automobile industries during World War II, the UE's male leaders—fearful of the influx of women workers into an industry already marked by low wages, piece work, and the threat of female substitution—demanded equal pay in contracts, government administration rulings, and the law. Equal pay had been a collective bargaining goal long before 1941 but UE officers stepped up their campaign by calling on the government to mandate equal pay through the War Labor Board (WLB). In a 1945 case that introduced the issue of comparable worth for the first time, the WLB ordered GE and Westinghouse to raise women workers' pay by four cents an hour and to set aside two cents per hour in a fund for upgrading jobs held by female employees. The war ended soon after the ruling and the electrical manufacturers ignored it for the most part.[20] By the late 1940s, a UE representative reported to the government that, since the WLB decision, only "certain partial adjustments have been made."[21]

Nevertheless, the UE leadership demonstrated sincere and long-term support for equal pay legislation, a policy also followed by the IUE. Union lobbyists argued that only a legal measure could bring employers to commit themselves to equal pay. The UE's Ruth Roemer told legislators at 1948 hearings that, despite the presence of equal pay contract clauses covering 585 plants and 354,000 workers, inequality existed due to the absence of an "equal pay for comparable worth" law. Unlike the secretary of labor and the UAW representative at the hearings, Roemer requested that the narrowly defined "equal work" clause not replace "comparable worth" language in the pending bill. While not directly confronting job-typing by sex, she attacked "historical differentials" that gave women who worked in a "comparable job, requiring comparable quality and quantity of production or comparable character of jobs, the performance of which require comparable skills," lower pay than that of their male counterparts. Roemer presented congressional members with evidence that the highest-paid woman usually drew a lower wage than the lowest-paid man. At GE's Cleveland plant, for example, women's highest job rate was $1.14 an hour while men's lowest rate was $1.18. Men hired in with at least $1.11 an hour at the Westinghouse plant in south Philadelphia but women at the highest wage level on their jobs could make only $1.06 an hour.[22] As other CIO union leaders had found, UE officers' pleas for an equal pay law fell on deaf ears as conservative lawmakers in the late 1940s saw little need to address the social concerns of working women.

UE women lost on several fronts in the half-decade following the war's end. Even before equal pay legislation fizzled in Congress, mass layoffs of women began in 1945, as employment in the industry as a whole dropped from 700,000 to 475,000 between September and December 1945. At GE, women's numbers fell by 21 percent; at Westinghouse they decreased by 29 percent. Overall, women workers as a proportion of the total electrical manufacturing work force went from a wartime high of 48.9 percent in April 1944 to 38 percent in 1950. Unlike the UAW and other unions, the UE's international officers defended women laid off without regard for seniority. UE educational director and executive secretary Ruth Young stated unequivocally in 1944, "It is the union's position that members, regardless of sex, have equal rights under the contracts and within the union. This applies to seniority as well as other questions."[23] UE leaders, however, did not protect women members against "downgrading" from higher-paying, more se- cure wartime positions to the traditional "women's" jobs.[24] Most women did not challenge this reversion to older, more-established sex segregation. "It was never tested really," Mary Callahan remembered. "Nobody complained. . . . It was the way of life. . . . Men just couldn't possibly do this intricate work, and women couldn't possibly do heavy work."[25] Those women who sought to retain their jobs found themselves at odds with each other as they argued over who was the most "deserving" of employment. Married and single women in particular faced off during this period, and local contract supplements appeared that provided for preferential layoffs for married women.[26]

Another significant blow to UE women came in the form of the anticommu- nist campaign as World War II ended and the cold war began. During this pe- riod the union disaffiliated from the CIO, the rival IUE came into existence in 1949, and the UE's ranks were decimated through the 1950s. While workers had joined together in the 1930s under the social unionist banner, political factional- ism had always threatened to undo their unity. The Communist Party's influence made little difference once the campaign against the Left and a backlash against labor began. Reacting to public pressure and the Taft-Hartley Act and sensing an opportunity to gain control of the union, the organization's right wing, led by James Carey, established the UE Committee for Democratic Action and Members for Democratic Action (MDA) in August 1946. When the MDA failed to dislodge left-wing officers, a CIO-sanctioned raiding of UE locals began. UE leaders boycotted the CIO's 1949 convention in protest and CIO convention delegates, in turn, retaliated by expelling the electrical workers' union, declaring that they would "no longer tolerate within the family of the CIO the Communist Party masquerading as a labor union."[27] Twenty-four hours later, CIO president Philip Murray issued a charter for the IUE.[28]

During the period leading up to the 1949 split, "women's issues" were neglected as GEB members struggled to fend off debilitating political attacks. In her history of UE gender relations, Lisa Kannenberg describes how resources available to women workers dried up as the union's legal and organizing demands increased: "The UE's attempt to continue its work toward the elimination of gender discrimination in the industry was thwarted in the postwar years. Within a year, the dizzying escalation of Cold War hysteria had forced the union to divert virtually all of its resources and energy to fight for sheer survival. Much of the UE's trade union program was, of necessity, shoved to the back burner as one challenge after another demanded response."[29] At the union's 1947 convention the officer's report neglected women's concerns entirely. On at least one occasion, union leaders heeded political expediency at the expense of women's seniority rights: when Springfield, Massachusetts, Local 202 (a right-wing stronghold) contract negotiators wrote a provision limiting married women's seniority, UE president Albert Fitzpatrick remained silent.[30] By 1950, the UE's Fair Practices Committee chairman noted "a serious weakness in the fight for women's rights. No districts reported any specific projects underway."[31]

Vying for Members: IUE, UE, and Women Workers, 1949–55

While scholars have pointed to the important role industrial structures play in shaping workplace gender relations, only recently have they begun to ascribe importance to other factors such as red-baiting, political affiliation, and interunion competition for members. These issues proved important to the history of gender equality in the IUE. Due to its competition with the UE for members, the labor organization bolstered its promotion of women workers' concerns by hiring women organizers, holding women's conferences, and advocating equal pay legislation. Women made up a sizable portion of the electrical industry's work force in 1950: they filled 51 percent of communication equipment positions, 36 percent of jobs in electrical appliance manufacturing, 31 percent of posts making electrical equipment for vehicles, and 29 percent of jobs in manufacturing electrical generators. The IUE's leadership could not dismiss the weakened UE's campaign for members for, even in the early 1950s, the UE could claim thousands of fiercely loyal workers who were not willing to abandon the rank-and-file-run union. In 1952, the IUE had 231,000 members; the UE still had 215,000 members, many of them in key locals such as the large GE plant in Schenectady, New York.[32]

The IUE competition for women members was not a one-dimensional, cynical, manipulative attempt on the part of organizers to sway workers to their ranks without a firm commitment to "women's issues." The relationship between union principles and practices was complex, one formed in the crucible of previous organizing efforts and industrial conflicts. Male unionists had understood for some time that they needed the alliance of women in order to keep their labor organization viable. That reality had long since become encoded into union principles. Besides being anticommunist, IUE leaders believed in liberal social unionism, whose principles were rooted in the need to organize all workers irrespective of race, ethnicity, sex, skill, or creed. Even in the increasingly quiescent 1950s this entailed demands for social justice, especially in the area of race and gender relations. Longtime activist and union officer Gloria Johnson thought the IUE "progressive, way out front"; from the union's founding, she said, the IUE had formulated "strong civil rights resolutions and strong women's resolutions."[33] Key IUE officers and staff members championed "women's issues," helping to bring them to prominence on the union's agenda. James Carey's assistant, David Lasser, undertook the grueling task of gathering data on pay inequity. A Massachusetts Institute of Technology graduate, science-fiction writer, and chairman of the Workers' Unemployed Unions in New York City during the Depression, Lasser came to the IUE after working in several New Deal agencies. By the early 1950s he had become head of the union's research department, where he spent the next decade working in support of equal pay.[34] "He was so sensitive to . . . the rights of workers and civil rights, human rights. He was way ahead of his time," Gloria Johnson recalled.[35] Lasser attended meetings of the National Committee on Equal Pay (NCEP), a loosely formed coalition of labor unions and liberal interest groups. In 1959 group members appointed him chairman of a permanent committee on conferences; at the IUE he helped prepare Carey's congressional testimonies on the matter.[36]

Not content to leave the matter to men, women played an active role in promoting gender issues in the IUE. Although no "women's bureau" existed as in the UAW, women served on international and district staffs and in elected capacities, mostly at the local level. U.S. Department of Labor researchers reported in 1953 that IUE women were candidates in ten of eighteen local union elections then underway. The entire Sandusky, Ohio, slate consisted of women, and ten of the eleven officers (including president and vice-president) of the IUE's Dover, New Hampshire, local were women. As in most CIO unions in the 1950s, the majority of women officers served as secretary or secretary-treasurer; none was head of an IUE district or on the IUE's International Executive Board. At the international level, women such as Gloria Johnson worked in staff positions.

An African American born and raised in a third-generation Washington, D.C., family, Johnson joined the ranks of middle-class labor activists such as Nancy Pratt and Katherine Ellickson. She received her B.A. and M.A. from Howard University, taught economics at Howard part-time, and worked at the Wage Stabilization Board until its dissolution in 1952. Subsequently, she joined the IUE and began a long career of activism in various positions, such as NCEP secretary-treasurer and Coalition of Labor Union Women president. Another formidable IUE national woman activist, Mary Callahan, had a markedly different background. Callahan, who left school in the tenth grade, became the first woman to sit on the IUE's IEB, in 1959. She had served for over two decades as a rank-and-file unionist, a local secretary-treasurer in Philadelphia, and on the War Labor Board's "women power" committee. In the early 1960s, John Kennedy appointed her to the President's Commission on the Status of Women.[37]

The IUE was one of the first industrial unions to hold regular "women's conferences." These national forums, characterized by longtime labor activist Katherine Ellickson as "very illuminating on the problems of local union women," provided women with an opportunity to gather to discuss issues of concern.[38] The union's IEB members heavily promoted the first such meeting, which was held in 1957 with over two hundred participants. President Carey and secretary-treasurer Al Hartnett, in particular, urged locals "where there is a substantial number of women workers to secure adequate representation," especially locals that the IUE was then organizing and that had a sizable proportion of women.[39] Conference coordinators asserted that women "do have particular problems which need and should have attention. . . . We call not only for those goals that we share with other members of our Union but also those particular aims to end inequalities that we as women suffer." While conference resolutions called for equal pay, increased participation for women in leadership positions, and the promotion of social legislation, those in attendance did not directly threaten male prerogatives on the shop floor or in the union hall. Nevertheless, by bringing women together, activists had carved out a space at the international level from which to address their concerns.[40]

Despite these promising signs the IUE was like most unions of the period in according women only limited decision-making power. Women were, for example, underrepresented at union conventions. The delegate composition at the 1962 convention was typical: women made up at least 35 percent of the union's membership, but only 8.5 percent of committee assignments went to women.[41] Mary Callahan, who came from a local that was 85 percent women, recalled the discouragement women experienced when it came time to choose delegates. "There seemed to be a taboo against it," Callahan said. "They were all male delegates and

the theory was that, 'Oh they are so tough!' and we believed it. . . . All these debates with men arguing! Well, we finally went to see one, and it was nothing. They
just wanted to go and get away from the eighty-five percent of us." As a delegate,
Callahan remembered the loneliness of being one of the few women at union
conventions. She ate many of her dinners alone in her hotel room because it was
thought inappropriate for women to socialize with men in restaurants.[42]

Gender relations at the local level in the IUE in the nearly fifteen years leading up to Title VII mirrored those throughout the general history of the labor
movement. IUE organizers' reports to the international office reveal not only the
prevalence of sex-segregation on the shop floor, but a sex-segregated unionism
as well. Most of the women assigned as field representatives worked exclusively
with other women. "I'm giving a shower for one of the girls married on Thurs-
day. And I'm making an evening gown for another so they are getting indebted
to me little by little," a New Jersey staff member, Kathleen McNee, wrote in 1956.[43]
Whether they took women bowling, gave a birthday party, or met in company
bathrooms with workers "because of noisy machines,"[44] these organizers implicitly understood their contacts would be women.[45] There were exceptions to this
practice, as when the IUE's Ruth Frank reported to Hartnett that she needed to
buy drinks for male workers at a Sylvania plant in West Virginia: "It is necessary
for me to ask your permission to spend some money on these guys at the plant.
They work two shifts and the only way to get them is to buy them a few 'brews'
at shift changes at the local 'clubs.' These workers are from out-lying Ohio and
West Virginia towns and are difficult to contact otherwise."[46] Such occurrences,
however, were rare.

Women organizers sometimes had difficulty making contact with other women.
Rosemary Mannie reported on her experiences from central Illinois: "I am making house calls every day and every evening[;] finding people home is a problem,
but even more so the problem is finding a woman who even has the time to talk
because of her household duties and children. This is not one of those open
hospitable small towns where one offers to help with the chores while selling a
union to the woman involved. These people are suspicious of outsiders and want
to see you only if they are not busy."[47] Women organizers occasionally doubted
their own effectiveness on account of their gender. For example, Mannie reported
on the IUE's loss to the UE in an election at a Minneapolis plant. She placed
much of the blame for the defeat on the absence of a male organizer. "Perhaps
an organizer of more years experience," she lamented, "and even though I hate
to admit it, a man instead of a woman would be able to either weld these factions or organize by ignoring them."[48] Another IUE woman, this one in Pennsylvania, echoed Mannie's sentiments, noting, "It's a real handicap to have to do

a double selling job—convincing people that a woman isn't so bad along with selling them on IUE-CIO."[49]

Clearly, IUE locals lagged behind the international in promoting women's rights. While IUE negotiators in Washington, D.C., pushed for better maternity provisions through improved health care coverage, the extension of pension provisions to widows and survivors, and equal pay contract clauses, union leaders at the local level signed supplemental labor agreements circumscribing women's rights.[50] In their contract with Philco, for example, Local 701 officers in Sandusky, Ohio, guaranteed "the rate for the job classification regardless of sex, color, or creed" but established lower rates for women operators, kept sex-segregated seniority lists, and allowed for discriminatory treatment of pregnant workers.[51] The Springfield, Massachusetts, Local 202 contract specified that "married women will not be considered for employment if their husbands are able to work"; the IUE Local 711 agreement in Mansfield, Ohio, mandated separate male and female seniority lists.[52]

In the battle for women members the UE's antidiscriminatory record outshone that of the IUE. Anything IUE leaders did on behalf of women workers, whether it be holding conferences or drafting contracts protecting women's seniority rights, the rival union did better. In early 1952, for example, the UE's Fair Practices Committee, District 11 in Chicago, and District 6 in Pittsburgh cosponsored the first postwar conference of any major union on "women's issues." Participants demanded that employers "regrade all jobs done by women up from common labor rate, under a single rate structure to eliminate discrimination as compared to jobs done by men."[53] The next spring, the international office held its first "National Conference on the Problems of Working Women" a full four years before the IUE did the same, and it published its widely distributed pamphlet *UE Fights for Women Workers*. In addition, the UE's executive board members recommended that all contracts include a model fair employment practices clause; an antidiscrimination clause "in regard to promotions, upgrading, apprenticeship, job training, layoffs, and discharges"; and a section denouncing discrimination against married women.[54]

Despite the nonbinding nature of these board recommendations, UE local leaders undertook an avid defense of their women members. As Lisa Kannenberg points out, faced with direct competition for members from the IUE, they linked their own insecurity with that of women and minorities and appealed to common themes of equality and nondiscrimination. While many IUE locals had separate seniority lists and seniority policies that discriminated against married women, the UE was unequivocal at the local and international level in its defense of single seniority lists. UE leaders continued to press for equal pay, as when

GE Local 429 officers pursued a test case of New Jersey's equal pay law.[55] UE activists and leaders believed the IUE to be reactionary in the area of women's rights. They explained in the pages of their 1950 GEB report:

> It was significant that in shop after shop where local leaders pursued this policy of discrimination against women workers, even to the point of undermining the right of women to work during layoff periods, those leaders and those shops turned up in the IUE camp. . . . These policies turned out to be the policies of those who became the enemies of our Union, [and] our Union, where it was able to defeat those policies, lost those locals and those members altogether. . . . In locals where women were encouraged to come forward in union leadership, such policies were defeated and our Union saved.[56]

Such observations, however, distorted the IUE's record on women's rights. In the areas of equal pay and holding conferences for women, the two unions had similar records. While it was true that some IUE locals discriminated against married women, single women—not hostile men—appear to have been at the forefront of such efforts. Moreover, unionists in the international office attempted to counter this unfair treatment. In 1947, the UE's GEB, its District 6 officers, and organized married women in Sharon, Pennsylvania, turned back a campaign by Local 617 single women to discriminate against married women in the area of layoffs.[57] The issue resurfaced in 1950 during UE-IUE elections. This time IUE field organizer Mary Lou Sauer defended married women's rights. "We held a meeting which I believed helped," she wrote at the time, "and also laid down the law to our [local] leaders on this basis: don't let your personal feeling interfere with principle, or with winning every available vote. We now have married women giving active support to IUE-CIO."[58]

Why did the IUE international allow pockets of discriminatory practice to exist while leading the fight for working women's rights? The answer, in part, lies in the organizational structure of the union. Locals were autonomous in making strike decisions, collecting dues, and signing supplemental agreements.[59] The IEB could suspend or revoke a local union's charter, but at the height of competition with the UE for members this was highly unlikely, especially over "women's issues," which held a low priority of concern for unions in the 1950s. Labor leaders laid important groundwork for the IEB's aggressive enforcement of Title VII mandates in the 1970s, however, by strengthening the president's control over errant locals. In 1959, new constitutional powers permitted James Carey to place an administrator in charge of a local when "a Local is involved in a controversy which adversely affects the welfare of its membership in a manner which threatens the Local's existence."[60] Carey used this authority on more than one occasion. He put RCA

Local 854 in Los Angeles in trusteeship, for example, in the face of multiple problems, including internal disarray and election corruption. Only when the legal threat of costly lawsuits arose in the late 1960s would IUE officers put this powerful weapon at the service of those fighting sex discrimination.[61]

The IUE's tolerance of discriminatory supplemental agreements can be explained by the fact that the two unions had different contract objectives. In his examination of the electrical union split, Ronald Schatz found that older UE leaders, as result of their experiences with the breakup of craft unionism following World War I and the devastating effects of the Great Depression on jobs and benefits, emphasized employment security. The younger generation of leaders that assumed power in the late 1940s, having come of age during a period of growing prosperity, gave priority to higher wages. Schatz is correct to note that this second type of union officer could be found in both labor organizations, but the majority of these leaders were in the vanguard of young, anticommunist activists who opposed the UE. These negotiators hammered out contracts establishing severance pay benefits, won the first guaranteed annual wage from a major electrical corporation, and secured improved pension, insurance, and health benefits. In pushing for enhanced national contracts, IUE officers overlooked instances where local memberships were threatened by layoffs that discriminated against married women. Meanwhile, the UE fought loss of control over job changes and defended seniority.[62]

"Women's issues," in fact, did not play a major role in determining UE-IUE election outcomes. No evidence exists to suggest that women as a group cast their lot with one particular union. Even anticommunism was not consistently a central factor in affiliation decisions. Instead, such issues as loyalty to the leadership from whence the local originated often influenced election results. The IUE proved strongest in consumer products plants, Carey's original base of support; the UE emerged victorious in old strongholds such as machine-building factories.[63]

Finding one determining issue in the history of UE-IUE elections is difficult, as the crazy-quilt affiliation map of electrical worker unionism suggests. In many cases workers voted on the basis of a "bread-and-butter" issue, such as the way the UE leadership had served members. IUE organizer Mary Lou Sauer reported to the international's secretary-treasurer Al Hartnett in 1950 that, in an upcoming election, it would be "difficult to estimate what effect the issue of Communism will have" on unionists; Sauer believed the UE would lose the showdown, not due to antileftist sentiment but because unionists "have been neglected by the UE for years."[64] Commenting on an election at Champion Motors in Minneapolis in 1954, Rosemary Mannie explained a UE victory in similar terms. "There is no question but what the UE Local 1139 has serviced this shop well, that the local treasury stands at more than $40,000, and that, to many in the shop local[,] issues were far more important than what was happening out East."[65] In that same vein, UE Local 524 in Peterborough, Ontario, turned back an IUE challenge in the early 1950s—two weeks after securing an increase of 17 cents an hour. Sometimes the UE did not satisfy the demands of local members, as when unionists "punished" the UE in Brockville, Ontario, for failing to get management to back off from its demand for a 4.5 percent wage reduction by voting in the IUE.[66]

By mid-decade the cumulative effects of McCarthyism and the diminished effectiveness of multiple unions negotiating with aggressive employers wore on the morale of UE members. Many voted to leave the union. In 1953, key UE officers in District 1, covering Philadelphia, Baltimore, and New Jersey, joined IUE and Machinists staff offices. The membership drain accelerated as news of a planned AFL-CIO merger spread. Many UE members viewed the planned federation as a positive development for the labor movement and became frustrated with their leadership's reluctance to consider seriously the possibility of joining the IUE after the merger. Membership figures told of the staggering loss of power. In March 1954, the 20,000-member Schenectady GE Local 301 quit the union for the IUE, thus robbing the UE of key influence in electrical-industry labor relations. In 1953 the union had 203,000 members; by 1960 that number had dropped to 59,000.[67]

The dramatic thinning of the UE's ranks had a damaging effect on women's activism. "The exodus from the UE was a near-fatal blow to the union," Lisa Kannenberg writes. "The UE's work toward women's equality was especially hard-hit. Districts 4 and 3 were decimated; Local 301 gone. Much of the energy and inspiration for the women's rights work of the UE had flowed from these sources."[68] By the late 1950s the vaunted UE Women's Conferences disappeared, to the dismay of the remaining rank-and-file women. "What happens after we go back to the plant? You find very little support from the men when it comes to women's wages and problems," Rose Garwachi of Local 190 told convention delegates in 1959. She continued, "Since we don't have any more women's conferences and since I see all you men here . . . I think it would be very nice for you . . . that you go back and see that the women are not discriminated against in your plants."[69] Local 421's Clara Fiering complained about the lack of time allocated for women's concerns at the next year's meeting. "We had a very short meeting of the women delegates. And frankly, although it really was valuable . . . it was most valuable in indicating how good it would have been if we could have time for a decent meeting. . . . We were in a hurry; we were wedged in during the lunch period, and I feel the women delegates have a lot to say, and a lot to contribute on the floor of the convention."[70] Many former UE activists, sorely missed by that union, eventually joined the IUE in its drive for women's rights.[71]

"Women's Issues" and Managerial Offensives against the IUE

IUE leaders forged ahead with their demands for equal pay following the union's de facto victory over the UE. Intensive managerial attacks on workers at the bargaining table and on the shop floor, however, crippled such efforts. While women's losses resulting from employers' actions were disproportionately more severe than men's, there was a noticeable lack of animosity on the part of women against male unionists. With women making up about 35 percent of the union's membership, IUE leaders sought to shore up women's support for the union. As one convention delegate saw it, it was "necessary for our Union to become concerned with the kinds of problems which . . . women face, particularly for the male members and especially for those in leadership positions, to aid in the development of a program that will result in a unified membership."[72] Unlike the packinghouse union's leadership, IEB members continued their advocacy for women, thus helping to maintain relatively peaceful gender relations in the IUE.

Union leaders would need the backing of the union's many women members for, beginning in the 1950s, IUE members encountered considerable obstacles from management in the form of "Boulwarism." Named after Lemuel R. Boulware, an advertising and marketing executive turned GE vice-president, this tactic emerged in the late 1940s as an attempt by employers to reassert their antiunion initiative lost during the Roosevelt years. Management presented labor representatives with a "take-it-or-leave-it," non-negotiable contract package. Managers delivered their contract offer in the form of a massive public relations campaign designed to make manufacturers appear "reasonable." Company negotiators then refused to participate in further talks with unionists. The detailed, highly specialized discussions that occurred in auto, steel, and coal negotiations—much celebrated by labor officers, academics, and liberal business leaders—were absent to a large extent in the electrical industry's industrial relations. It was a successful strategy. By the late 1950s, Boulwarism's practitioners had succeeded in separating electrical manufacturing workers from their peers laboring in those industrial sectors characterized by institutionalized and "guaranteed" collective bargaining.[73]

IUE officers fought Boulwarism, but the labor organization—itself competing with other unions for members—was not a match for increasingly powerful and savvy management teams. Union leaders ended the IUE's draining 156-day strike against Westinghouse in 1956 in victory, but GE's aggressive drive to promote back-to-work movements during a three-week strike in 1960 was successful. A. H. Raskin of the *New York Times* called it "the worst setback any union has received in a nationwide strike since the war."[74] Labor activists and the journalist Sidney Lens characterized the IUE as a "weakling" compared to employers such as GE.[75] IUE leaders, frustrated with Boulwarism, appealed to the National Labor Relations Board, which finally declared it an unfair labor practice in 1964. By then, electrical manufacturers had split the industry's wage levels from those in the high-wage, core industrial sector. IUE general counsel Irving Abramson characterized the collective bargaining agreements signed at the height of Boulwarism in the early 1960s as "utter, miserable failures" for the union.[76] In 1965, the average hourly earnings in coal mining, steel, auto, and rubber were still within pennies of each other; only in the electrical industry did workers fall "way behind," as a result of these practices.[77]

As part of their antiunion campaigns, employers resisted comparable-pay and nondiscrimination clauses in work agreements. In 1952, IUE research director David Lasser complained that GE's formal commitment to equal pay for equal work (as opposed to comparable pay) brought women little comfort. Most men and women, he pointed out, worked in separate departments and the average rate for women workers was 40 cents an hour, or 30 percent, lower than that of men. At a conference on the subject, sponsored by the U.S. Department of Labor, Lasser said that Lemuel Boulware's assurances of providing equal pay were "virtually meaningless. GE has arranged it so that very, very rarely do men and women work at the *same jobs*."[78] Even this narrower policy covered only about one-third of workers. A government report on equal pay in electrical machinery, equipment, and supplies industries revealed that, of the eighty-four contracts studied, 42 percent had equal pay clauses covering 34 percent of employees.[79]

This poor showing of equal pay guarantees had not improved by the early 1960s. At government hearings on equal pay in 1962, James Carey laid the blame at the feet of large employers, especially GE, for their non-negotiating stance. "When wage rate problems arise and when the company decides that a wage is proper there is no possibility of arbitration." Why was GE most responsible? "General Electric is twice the size of Westinghouse," Carey continued, "and they are, by far, the main factors in the determination of policy as it applies to union relations or applies to any matter in fact."[80]

The drive for the more-ambitious comparable worth met with even less success. In preparation for government hearings, David Lasser conducted a detailed study on the matter. "The results were so clear," Gloria Johnson remembered. "In most cases the highest paid women received less than the lowest paid male who happened to be a janitor. So we were arguing, based on value, [that] these women deserved better salaries." Amazingly, Lasser lost his data before he could present it publicly.[81] In place of his findings, IUE officers presented compelling anecdotal evidence of pay inequity. At the Fairmont, West Virginia, Westinghouse plant, for example, of the some 14 labor grades, women occupied labor grades 1 through 5 while men held the higher-paying grades of 6 through 14; at the Warren, Ohio, GE facilities women occupied the lowest labor grades (R-9 to R-13) and no man held a grade lower than R-12. The threat of replacing men with women continued to be an incentive to unionists as a reason to pass legislation. In 1958, for example, managers at GE's Cleveland wire plant attempted to displace men with women employees at much lower rates of pay. IUE leaders resisted the pay cut for men in this case, but GE succeeded in bringing some women in at lower rates of pay.[82]

Union leaders would go only so far in their equal pay advocacy. "Equal pay for equal work has been a demand of the IUE since the start of our union. It has been adopted at each convention and we have pressed it in all of our negotiations with the companies that we deal with," Carey assured lawmakers. Labor officers would not call a strike over the issue, however, he said: "The problem of striking over an individual wage rate is, of course, a very difficult one. Therefore, in some plants our membership has endured this discrimination for years."[83] The fact that no union ever deliberated on striking over "women's issues" indicates the limited importance of equal pay to the postwar labor movement's agenda. Carey's comment—made more as an afterthought than as a sustained consideration of the possibility of a work stoppage over the issue—neatly summarizes the peripheral nature of equality measures for women in the masculine-defined industrial world of labor relations.

As in the packinghouse industry, IUE leaders dedicated much of their effort in the period 1955–64 to countering the reorganization of production by employers. In an attempt to weaken electrical unionism's base of support, manufacturers began to disperse their operations from the East Coast and Ohio Valley region to Texas and western states. "In the fifties, the companies said they couldn't compete any longer in this Philadelphia area so they . . . decentralized," Mary Callahan recalled. "What it really was[,] was [that] they set up the different products in different areas, but all in right-to-work states, places where they wouldn't have to deal with the union." Callahan's own Local 105 went from 2,800 members during World War II to 1,800 in the 1950s, to 280 workers in 1976.[84] "We see in all our Districts," Leonard Hutson, District 9 president, observed in 1962, "shops being shut down for one reason or another and moving to another area."[85]

Employers deployed new automation as well, hoping to gain a stronger hand over their work force. Convention delegates in 1958 warned that automation was "developing into a tide that may engulf and overrun us unless provisions are made to harness and tame this new power."[86] Two years later, delegates listened to a sobering report on the matter: automation had caused significant job losses, especially in the radio and television sectors of wiring, soldering, and component assembly as well as in appliance, electronic tube, and lamp manufacturing. In addition, even in "heavy equipment" departments such as those producing generating turbines—a male-dominated work domain—automation had displaced a large number of workers. While some companies offered to pay employees trained with new skills at 95 percent of their previous pay rates, management demanded a unilateral right to assign jobs—a policy in direct violation of seniority practices. At congressional hearings on automation, James Carey reported that electrical industry employment had dropped from 925,000 in 1953 to 836,000 in February 1961. This reflected a 10 percent decline in the work force during a period when production jumped by 21 percent. Specific locals reported staggering losses. The GE Schenectady plant slashed its work force from 20,000 to 8,000 and the Westinghouse plant in East Springfield, Massachusetts, more than halved the number of workers on the payroll.[87]

Women were especially susceptible to layoffs resulting from automation and production relocation. In 1962 union head Carey noted the disproportionate burden borne by women and minority group members, ascribing this to the fact that "they haven't built up seniority. That goes for women. It goes for Negroes. It also goes even for religious minorities."[88] Participants at the 1957 IUE Women's Conference called upon union leaders to challenge the direction employers took with technological innovation. "Automation . . . is already wiping out thousands of jobs formerly held by women," they announced. "Opportunities for jobs are becoming scarce. In many of the big plants in our industries the number of women has dropped sharply and in many cases it requires 14–15 years of service for a woman to hold a job."[89] In Local 255, for example, men needed twelve years to stay on a sweeper job by the late 1950s while women needed fifteen years. Women with seniority dating back to 1941 and men with service since 1951 in Local 301 were on layoff. The UE reported similar findings: there were 3.3 percent fewer workers in the female-dominated lamp industry in 1961 than in 1956, even though production had jumped by 67 percent. "More than half of the UE locals with women workers reported problems with automation speedup and technological change," wrote the author of one UE survey. "One automatic machine displaced all 30 women in one shop; work done by women at individual work stations has been put on the assembly line with a great rate, resulting in a much greater speed of output."[90] Automation and production dispersal affected contract coverage as well. The percentage of employees working under a collective bargaining agreement decreased through the early 1960s, which resulted in a corresponding fall in the number of women covered by equal pay provisions.[91]

IUE international officers and staff attempted to ameliorate the situation, to no avail. In contract negotiations with GE in 1954, for example, union representatives asked for a cessation of building new plants that made products already being produced by the company until managers rehired laid-off employees. GE negotiators did not relent on this issue; instead, they gave workers a 2.68 percent wage increase and improved vacation and overtime benefits. As in the automobile and packinghouse workers unions, members of the IUE's International Executive Board vacillated between embracing technological innovation and fighting a rear-guard defense against its worst features. Mostly, they called for "joint committees on automation" in order to fund retraining and to slow the pace of worker displacement. While some locals such as Local 601 in Pittsburgh and Local 201 in Lynn, Massachusetts, undertook shop-floor revolts against automation, the international backed away from directly confronting management's claim to determine the means and ends of production. Only the UE—rendered a minor player by virtue of its numerical weakness—could claim to have a unionwide aggressive program to counter management's advance.[92]

As it would in other industries, automation in electrical industries provided one positive outcome for women workers: it exposed the dubious nature of job-typing by sex, thus renewing questions a few women first raised in the late 1930s and 1940s about the subjective nature of job assignments. Even more than in the packinghouse industry, as described in the next chapter, where heavier job elements and higher-skilled positions remained (although these too had been diminished), men's electrical manufacturing jobs had become considerably "lighter" and de-skilled over time. Male unionists watched this trend warily over the decades and became alarmed at its acceleration in the 1950s. Convention delegates in 1958 asked the IUE's leaders to demand from manufacturers the "abolition of area and sex wage differentials to prevent runaway operations and changing the classification of men's jobs to women's jobs in a chiseling effort to save money at the expense of employees."[93] The IUE's Carey joined the issues of comparable worth, automation, and job-typing by sex in an appeal for equal pay legislation:

> Automation is changing the character of jobs in the U.S. industry. Muscular strength is becoming secondary in many industrial operations. Women can monitor a meter needle as well as men, and can adjust dials equally well.
>
> Inevitably, many will some day be employed at tasks once limited to strong men. Unless there is equal pay legislation the age of automation could bring with it a low wage economy geared to the rising female labor supply.[94]

The "many" women to whom he referred, however, would come to have a legal claim to "men's" jobs only with the passage of the Civil Rights Act of 1964 and with it the ban on sex discrimination in employment. Until then men and women in the IUE still adhered closely to the belief in a sex-segregated workplace and the need for protective labor laws for women.

Equal Pay Legislation and Gender Inequality in the IUE, 1955–63

The IUE was in a weakened but not defeated position by the early 1960s. On the one hand, the ravages of Boulwarism, automation, and production dispersal had left the organization struggling at the bargaining table. On the other hand, the IUE remained a large union, led by a nationally known president who was committed to promoting social legislation. Unionists found that backing equal pay legislation offered them a wedge against intransigent employers. Frustrated by GE's and Westinghouse's "shocking violation of the principle of equal pay for equal work," James Carey hoped that "many employers rather than force investigations and suits flowing from equal pay legislation" would improve their contracts.[95] Advocacy for such legislation welded union leaders to the political center of national politics. It helped reinforce the belief of labor leaders and activists that the IUE was at the forefront of efforts by the U.S. Women's Bureau coalition.

IUE executive board members had supported equal pay legislation from the union's founding. What could not be accomplished at the bargaining table, they believed, must be ensured through legislation. The union's legislative office staff, convention delegates, and women activists threw their weight behind the proposal, working with the National Committee on Equal Pay (NCEP) to help pass the equal pay bill. David Lasser urged IUE locals to back the measure while James Carey joined with Walter Reuther in lobbying the newly formed AFL-CIO executive council in 1956 to support equal pay legislation, which it did.[96]

James Carey was an effective equal pay spokesperson due in large part to his ties to national and international political and labor groups. Although Carey became increasingly embroiled in internal squabbles brought on in large part by his "ungovernable temper, contentiousness, and vindictiveness," as one observer put it, his ability to draw on workplace testimonies of rank-and-file members and transnational labor issues made him an effective voice for liberal causes.[97] He chided legislators in 1962 about their claim to world leadership: "Frequently when I attend I[nternational] L[abor] O[rganization] meetings . . . I have become the target for semi-humorous needling by union leaders from other countries. . . . The question is thrown at me facetiously, 'In view of its failure to do anything about equal pay for equal work, isn't the United States more backward and underdeveloped than those countries that have signed the ILO agreement?'"[98] Carey tied the issue of sex discrimination to the more popular campaign for racial equality under the civil rights rubric. "There is . . . indisputably, a grave and continuing civil rights issue in the persistence of wage discrimination against women, even though women are no longer a minority in this country," he observed. "It is a civil rights issue that should have been resolved a long time ago, for the benefit of our national pride and prestige."[99]

IUE leaders argued through the early 1960s that equal pay for comparable work—not simply "equal work"—was necessary. "Most men and women workers are in different departments, [and] it is virtually impossible to find men and women together doing *identical work*," David Lasser noted at an equal pay conference.[100] AFL-CIO research director and NCEP chairman Anne Draper was in accord with this position, telling federation secretary-treasurer William Schnitzler:

> I would hope our position on the bill would not preclude comparisons of unlike jobs where a company has established a mechanism for making the comparisons. . . . This type of discrimination has been a major complaint of the IUE. . . . [The] IUE claims that women's jobs generally end up slotted into the lowest labor grades. Some women required to perform highly skilled tasks may nonetheless receive rates approximating the pay of male janitors. Clearly the wage determination system has scrambled the job factors to produce this result, and it would seem no great problem to rectify it on an "equal pay for equal work" principle.[101]

Draper and IUE unionists, however, rejected what she called "extreme" comparisons such as between a plant drill press operator and a business office stenographer.[102] Union head Carey believed the mechanism was already in place to deliver comparable work judgments. "Most companies have some form of job evaluation systems on which all jobs are supposed to be rated," he noted. "The use of the same standards for men and women in evaluating jobs would easily prove where unequal pay exists."[103] Comparing "men's" and "women's" jobs, in other words, would occur within specific plants and industries. In this regard, Carey and other supporters of the pending legislation differed from comparable-worth supporters in the 1980s who envisioned cross-occupational classifications.

IUE members were disappointed by the narrowing of the equal pay bill's coverage, the loss of administrative enforcement, and the substitution of "equal" for "comparable" work, but they attempted to push for the fullest enforcement possible. Carey, for one, turned his attention to promoting a loose interpretation of "equal work." "We interpret the law as meaning that it is the sum total of 'skill, effort, and responsibility' in determining equal work," he asserted soon after the law's passage. "Labor declares that the same yardstick in measuring the worth of the job should be applied to a man's job and a woman's job in the same plant. If the wage rates are not related to the value of the job, then discrimination exists."[104] Carey called on IUE Conference Board members and local unionists to assist the union's research department in furnishing the U.S. Department of Labor with examples of discriminatory practices based on sex. The lack of a comparable-worth clause and the law's allowance for unequal pay on the basis of seniority and merit and for a measuring of earnings by quality and quantity of production, however, left little room for stretching the law's limits.[105] Nevertheless, IUE activists joined other unionists in putting the best face on a modest measure. "That struggle for equal pay was a long, bitter struggle," Gloria Johnson said years later. "We did not get exactly what we wanted. . . . But it was a foot in the door, and it resulted in financial gains."[106]

In the end, the IUE leadership continued to embrace protectionism through the mid-1960s. "Women's issues" typically appeared under the heading of "family issues," as when a 1951 convention resolution called for the "safeguarding of . . . [women's] health" on the job and government tax breaks to working mothers in order to "aid them in carrying out their family responsibilities."[107] Like leaders of other unions, they opposed the Equal Rights Amendment (ERA). At the time, IUE members believed women were incapable of performing certain kinds of work or working at night for long hours. They held that the disappearance of protective measures brought by the ERA's passage would not change the social and biological conditions that made protectionism necessary; it would, however, leave women workers exposed to the demands of employers to do what they could not. Women might lose their jobs as a result. "There was such a strong fear that . . . protective labor laws . . . would be eliminated, resulting in a potential loss of women workers," Gloria Johnson explained. "If there's no law about working at night, and I can't work at night, then we [i.e., employers] don't need you. At the time these were very legitimate reasons."[108] IUE women framed their own activism, whether it be in the area of civil rights, minimum wage, or improved health and housing in relation to their responsibilities "as women." As participants to a 1957 women's conference put it: "We firmly believe that achieving [these goals] . . . is an important part of the fulfillment of our own lives and those of our families."[109]

Despite this the IUE was being carried along in the slow but discernible shift to gender equality by the early 1960s. IUE policy makers still backed protective legislation; they helped bring about the downfall of these laws, however indirectly, through service on John Kennedy's President's Commission on the Status of Women. Mary Callahan was a commission member, Gloria Johnson served as an associate to the commission's staff, and James Carey sat on the group's Committee on Civil Rights. While they did not reject protectionism, the commissioners' report and their establishing successor groups opened the way for a national debate on gender inequality.[110]

Although the IUE opposed the ban on sex discrimination in Title VII of the Civil Rights Act of 1964, James Carey at least acknowledged that the unfair treatment of women workers was implicit in early versions of the act. Carey noted the problem of gender inequality in a letter to Congressman James Roosevelt in 1962. Without endorsing a provision that included "sex" in equal employment opportunity legislation, Carey told Roosevelt that "discrimination because of sex is also common in American industry. . . . The women denied a job right because of sex are denied a key civil right."[111] Nevertheless, IUE leaders would continue their support for sex-segregated jobs, seniority lists, and wages. They would be charged with sex discrimination after 1964. They came to end these practices partly in response to the demands for change issued by their rank-and-file women. Acting on this pressure, and armed with the administrative and constitutional tools of a large organization and a commitment to equality developed in the twenty years following the end of World War II, international officers and staff members would go beyond these reforms and create an enviable Title VII compliance program in the 1970s.

5
Organized Labor, National Politics, and Gender Equality, 1964–75

Invited to testify before the Senate Subcommittee on the Equal Rights Amendment in May 1970, Olga Madar of the United Automobile Workers (UAW) described her support for gender equality. Speaking to the legislators on the eve of Mother's Day, Madar seized on the symbolism of the holiday by suggesting that its commemoration that year "may usher in a new era, for it comes at a time when a very strong tide is running in behalf of the proposition that American women, while they may like candy and roses, really need basic rights still denied them. Rights, not roses[,] is the watchword for an increasing number of American women."[1] While Madar's prediction of working-class feminism's imminent birth was, strictly speaking, premature, her overall observation on the trend toward gender equality in organized labor proved correct: the AFL-CIO endorsed the ERA for the first time in 1973 and the Coalition of Labor Union Women (CLUW) came into existence the following year.

Olga Madar's own life story told of the changes affecting working women in industrial unions in the contemporary United States. First employed in an automobile plant during World War II, she witnessed the redrawing of boundaries separating women's and men's work and the subsequent massive layoffs of women during postwar reconversion. In the supposedly unmilitant 1950s, Madar was one in a small group of women unionists who participated in the fight for what would become the Equal Pay Act of 1963 and welcomed the unexpected inclusion of a clause prohibiting sex discrimination in Title VII of the Civil Rights Act of 1964. As social and economic obstacles to equality began to erode in the late 1950s and the number of women in the paid work force jumped from 33 percent in 1960 to 38 percent in 1970, rank-and-file women challenged collective bargaining agreements that discriminated against women in areas such as hiring practices, wages, seniority, and maternity leaves.[2] Out of this discontent came a new working-class feminism. Longtime UAW officer Caroline Davis announced in the early 1970s, "Women are rebelling against discrimination. We are protesting. We are going to revolutionize society."[3] During her career, Madar rode this crest of working-class feminism. In 1966 she became the first women executive board member-at-large in the UAW; in 1974 the CLUW members elected her their first president.

The massive number of Title VII–based complaints and lawsuits brought by rank-and-file workers against their unions and employers was key to the ascendancy of support for gender equality between 1964 and 1975. Slowly, over the course of the 1950s and early 1960s, women had begun to question many of the assumptions that underlay traditional support for protective laws. The experiences of women in war plants in the 1940s had first suggested that women's secondary status in the paid labor force was a product of male prerogative and dominance rather than being self-evidently just and natural. With greater numbers of women entering the paid work force and the technological transformations of industrial jobs accelerating during the same period, the proffered reasons for such measures no longer seemed compelling. The concurrent campaign for an equal pay law underscored the growing sentiment for gender equality. The political mood of many in the nation, especially civil rights supporters, fostered this sensibility. With Title VII these individuals openly rejected job-typing by sex, unequal wage rates, and separate seniority lists; women called on their union officers to end their marginalization in the labor movement. Male unionists at the local and international union levels generally balked at such demands. They resisted revising an industrial relations system that privileged men. Out of men's opposition to change and women's resort to the courts arose a new consciousness among women unionists, one that identified the ineffectual nature of traditional union methods of addressing grievances. Solidarity, they came to realize, was hitherto masculine-defined.

The road to support for gender equality was rocky through the mid-1970s. For African-American women in unions with relatively good records of race relations, cross-racial coalitions of union feminists appeared; in unions with poor histories of race relations, minority women found few reasons or resources with which to confront sex discrimination directly and most concentrated their energies on support for the civil rights movement. Even in these situations African-American women often sought to battle gender inequality in the context of working for racial equality.

Once Title VII became law, women unionists themselves could not agree on the wisdom of completely rejecting protective labor laws. With the exception of those in the UAW, most women unionists in leadership and staff positions clung to such measures, only to see the Equal Employment Opportunity Commission

(EEOC) and courts make them invalid in response to working women's complaints and middle-class feminists' pressures for strong enforcement of Title VII. Along with male unionists, many of these women union leaders worried that new, antidiscriminatory laws might threaten the entrenched collective bargaining system they had long defended. Consequently, they viewed with alarm the EEOC's and courts' practice of ordering modifications of collective bargaining agreements without recourse to the National Labor Relations Board, the government body usually assigned to address union-management conflicts. "The once tight little ship of private adjudication," one industrial relations expert noted in 1971, "is indeed becoming a leaky vessel."[4]

With the issue of protective laws behind them in the early 1970s, working-class feminists around the country formed interunion coalitions to demand gender equality. Younger women who fought discrimination with the legal tool of Title VII joined veteran women activists and worked for the ERA's passage. They advised unions to eradicate discriminatory policies and educated women for leadership positions. These feminists remained firmly in organized labor's camp and they encouraged women to exhaust union grievance measures before resorting to the Equal Employment Opportunity Commission to resolve discrimination charges.

The Legal Battlefield for Equality: Title VII's Early Years

Title VII's prohibition of sex discrimination in employment did not receive the support of labor men and women initially. Legislators' surprising inclusion of a ban on sex discrimination in Title VII of the act called gender inequality in the workplace into significant question. Title VII sweepingly prohibited sex-segregated jobs, separate seniority lists, and dual wage scales for men and women. These cornerstones of inequality had gone unchallenged before then as liberals and unionists backed state protective laws for women that had been forged early in the century. These were necessary measures, they held, for they shielded male workers from employer-initiated competition with female workers, safeguarded working women's health, and limited women's work hours so they might attend to their domestic duties.

By the mid-1960s, however, this reasoning had lost its persuasiveness for many working women. Women questioned the unequal nature of gender relations in employment matters. Many knew of the mutability of job-typing by sex as a result of working in "men's" jobs during World War II and experiencing management's reconfiguration of work processes through automation introduced in the 1960s. They had become emboldened through their demands for equal pay. They were familiar with the story of Democratic Representative Howard W. Smith of Virginia and his successful introduction of an amendment to the pending civil rights bill that would prohibit sex discrimination. Smith's action took on added significance as older pro-ERA forces associated with the National Woman's Party (NWP) joined for the first time with prolabor congressional members such as Martha Griffiths of Michigan in the pursuit of equality. For the first time the eroding support for protectionism in the liberal camp manifested itself in clear and unambiguous backing for gender equality.[5]

The divisive issue of race—not gender—relations, however, monopolized the nation's attention in the first half of the 1960s. Many of the hallmarks of second-wave feminism such as Betty Friedan's *The Feminine Mystique* and the report of the President's Commission on the Status of Women had appeared by the time of the act's passage, but women's discontent had not yet given way to collective protest. "The tide was out in the early 1960s," one scholar notes, "for the women's movement."[6] Consideration of women's employment status held such low priority that, during extensive congressional hearings on equal employment opportunity held in mid-1963, neither legislators nor those delivering testimony mentioned sex discrimination. People at the forefront of the campaign for the Equal Pay Act of 1963 were not particularly interested in pushing further for gender equality. "I myself opposed that [i.e., incorporating a ban on sex discrimination in Title VII] at that time . . . because I was afraid it might endanger the civil rights bill," recalled labor activist and then U.S. Women's Bureau director Esther Peterson in a 1968 interview. "I just felt as an American woman I didn't want to ride the coattails of an issue that I thought was more important at that time. As it happened it didn't, and I was wrong."[7] While the passage of the Equal Pay Act of 1963 signaled a victory for activists in the National Committee on Equal Pay, that group's activities ground to a halt soon after the law went into effect.[8]

Despite their objections to the inclusion of the sex provision, federation officers strongly backed the civil rights bill, which indirectly helped further the cause of gender equality. The history of race and gender equality in the labor movement became intertwined as the history of Title VII's enforcement unfolded. Federationists did not promote gender equality at the time but they could not let that particular part of the bill derail the formidable civil rights movement or their own CIO-based members' historical commitment to racial equality. While white workers continued to practice race discrimination through the 1960s (e.g., African Americans were grossly underrepresented in the exclusionary skilled trades), union leaders such as the AFL-CIO's president George Meany threw their weight behind civil rights legislation. Meany reminded congressional members that unionists objected on moral grounds to discrimination and that it hurt union strength; he maintained that laws existed mandating that unions represent their members fairly but there was not one holding employers liable for unfair treatment of workers. The Civil Rights Act of 1964, he contended, would achieve this objective.[9]

Meany argued for the need to fight race discrimination and to protect union practices by making as few changes as possible. Labor leaders were troubled that Title VII's enforcement mechanism, the EEOC, lacked cease-and-desist powers necessary to root out race discrimination. In addition, Meany complained that the EEOC suffered from a host of problems, including a lack of adequate funding, understaffing, a high employee turnover rate, and a limited congressional mandate in which to act forcefully. Title VII's authors did not give the EEOC the power to compel employers and unions to end discriminatory practices, punish its agents, provide victims with remedies, or take violators to court. Indeed, its formal powers were woefully slim: commission members could receive written complaints (in those states with enforceable fair employment practice laws they had to defer complaints to state agencies for sixty days), investigate, issue findings of fact, and seek voluntary settlement. If they were unsuccessful in resolving the charges, EEOC representatives could either persuade the civil rights division of the Justice Department to seek court enforcement in the matter or notify individuals that they could proceed to federal court in quest of relief. Due to the sizable backlog of complaints, many charges never reached this far. Of all the complaints they tackled through 1972, equal employment agents were able to resolve charges favorably for complainants only in about 6 percent of the cases.[10]

The labor movement soon split with the civil rights movement, however, as equal employment opportunity laws went into effect. In general, labor leaders exhibited an equivocal attitude toward the equal employment policy in the commission's early years. On the one hand, they supported giving the agency cease-and-desist powers and increasing the EEOC's annual budget; on the other hand, federation leaders asked that the individual right to sue be eliminated from Title VII. Union leaders especially feared that a plaintiff's resort to judicial action would destroy the grievance procedure sanctioned by the National Labor Relations Board. Federation leaders were comfortable with their easy successes in the area of wages and benefits in the 1950s. They were wary of alienating local unions that practiced discrimination and favored conciliation and slow adjustments to labor practices, as opposed to the sudden and extensive changes lawsuits brought. In his study of equal employment opportunity, longtime NAACP legal counsel Herbert Hill contends that labor representatives pressured commission employees in 1966–67 not to force unionists to eliminate racially unequal seniority systems. Also, Hill charges that AFL-CIO staff members failed to provide the EEOC with requested equal employment information on a constituent union, the Brotherhood of Electrical Workers (IBEW); several AFL-CIO–affiliated unions, such as the Longshoremen's Union (ILWU), delayed relief to minority workers by introducing endlessly complex procedural challenges. The record varied according to union and region. There was less discrimination against women and minority men in nonreferral unions than in the traditional skilled trades running hiring halls and in the nonunion sector. Overall, labor leaders put themselves in a delicate position by attempting to balance their overall support for civil rights with a protection of the "traditional" union discriminatory practices that frequently prolonged such unfair treatment of minorities. They did not wish to upset strong, autonomous trade unions that might quit the AFL-CIO if pushed to implement sudden constitutional, contractual, or informal practices.[11]

Federationists were under little pressure to join the battle against gender discrimination, unlike race discrimination, before the mid-1960s. Consequently, they did little on its behalf. They were not alone in their belief that Title VII's ban on sex discrimination was an intrusion into the Civil Rights Act of 1964; early EEOC policy makers themselves disdained the act's sex-discrimination ban. EEOC executive director Herman Edelsberg, for example, reportedly suggested that the commission seal depict a brown rabbit above a white rabbit lying down with its head raised, with the caption "Vive la difference."[12] Franklin D. Roosevelt Jr., the commission's first—and largely absent—chairman, displayed a mocking attitude toward the sex clause. "What about sex?" a reporter grilled him at a 1965 interview. Roosevelt replied, amidst laughter: "Don't get me started. I'm all for it."[13] In an attempt to dispense with its backlog in 1966, a Budget Bureau agent recommended to the commission that "less time be devoted to sex cases since the legislative history would indicate that they deserve a lower priority than discrimination because of race and other factors."[14] Richard Berg, deputy general counsel of the EEOC in its first year, dismissed Title VII's ban on sex discrimination in 1969. He did so by counterpoising it with race discrimination, which was "by nature invidious and discriminatory while sex classification may meet the needs of the generality of both sexes." Nothing in Title VII, he claimed, "would prevent a system of classification which ignores entirely the differing capacities of the sexes."[15] This insensitivity to rooting out sex discrimination was due as much to the dearth of administrative experience in such a task as to overt hostility. Early commission staff member John Rayburn remembered that investigators "were ignorant as the devil as to sex discrimination because prior to July the 2nd [1965] it had not been illegal."[16]

Business group representatives and journalists treated the amendment with scorn as well, contributing to the government commission's poor implementation record. "I suppose we'll have to advertise for people with small, nimble fingers and hire the first male midget with unusual dexterity [who] shows up," one manager of an electronic components company told the *Wall Street Journal.*[17] The *New Republic* suggested that the sex provision be ignored; the *Wall Street Journal* echoed this view, asking its readers to imagine "a shapeless, knobby-kneed male 'bunny' serving drinks to a group of stunned businessmen in a Playboy Club" or a "matronly vice-president" chasing a male secretary around her desk.[18]

Labor officers and women union activists confined their public statements on Title VII to their unhappiness with Section 708, which asserted that state laws conflicting with the measure were invalid. For the first time ever, a congressional act threatened protectionism's existence. In 1965 some 551 such laws remained on the books.[19] Federation leaders were adamant that this provision not be enforced and they expended considerable energies to this end. "We urged you to resist any efforts to weaken or destroy protective state legislation for women workers under the guise of eliminating sex discrimination," AFL-CIO lobbyist Andrew Biemiller wrote to state federation of labor officers in March 1966.[20] Unionists in labor groups with a large female membership, such as the International Union of Electrical Workers (IUE), Amalgamated Meatcutters and Butcher Workmen, Amalgamated Clothing Workers, and the International Ladies' Garment Workers Union, took an identical position.[21] A spokesperson from the National Consumers League defended protectionism in terms understood by other organizations from the old U.S. Women's Bureau coalition. "While men may also require protection from overtime hours, as a group their need is less than that of women, who usually spend more time on family and home responsibilities," she stated.[22]

The authors of the EEOC's feeble guidelines on sex discrimination, released in November 1965, assuaged unionists' fears. In them, the commission left protective laws intact for the most part; nevertheless, women could bring their own lawsuits charging the invalidity of such measures, and commissioners encouraged state legislators to reconsider protectionism. Given the time and costly nature of private lawsuits, the former option was unlikely, as was the latter, for labor wielded considerable influence in many state legislatures. Union leaders were cheered further when, in August 1965, an EEOC-appointed committee of fourteen decided that sex-segregated want-ads, if accompanied by a disclaimer of discriminatory intent, were legal. The next year the EEOC retreated from these already-weak guidelines by eliminating the disclaimer requirement entirely. They also retreated from their policy of inviting plaintiffs to challenge protective laws on a case-by-case basis by ignoring complaints in conflict with such measures. To ease employer and union liability further, policy makers eliminated a defendant's burden to prove that separate job assignments by sex were necessary due to a "bona fide occupation qualification" (BFOQ).[23]

Union women helped change the labor movement's stance on gender equality by unloosing an avalanche of discrimination charges. Filers of sex-discrimination complaints—encouraged by EEOC employees sympathetic to aggressive Title VII enforcement—helped inspire a feminist-led drive for strong gender equality measures by demonstrating their dissatisfaction with workplace practices. Feminists in pressure groups in the late 1960s may not have been "representatives empowered by a grass-roots social movement," as the historian Hugh Davis Graham contends, but working-class women helped shape and validate the efforts of activists.[24] "Some of the early EEOC cases were filed by working-class women who were victims of discrimination and who I consider heroines," recalled the EEOC's Sonia Pressman in 1990. "They were not, by and large, founders of NOW, WEAL, and FEW, but they certainly filed some of the early leading cases."[25] The nearly 2,500 women charging sex discrimination during the EEOC's first year alone (27 percent of the total complaints) did not create a formal association; the massive protests of these "courageous union women," as the feminist Catherine East characterized them, gave those pushing the irresolute EEOC a measure of legitimacy.[26] The sex-discrimination complaints fell into several major categories, which suggested that the problem of gender inequality in employment was deep-seated: complaints on unequal employment benefits (30 percent), separate seniority lists (24 percent), unfair restrictions due to state protective laws (12 percent), and discrimination in hiring and firing (5.6 percent) appeared most frequently.[27] Even when women took these charges to court and lost, notes Karen Maschke, a political scientist, "the litigation process served as a means for mobilizing support for the legal issues at stake."[28]

Women unionists across the country rejected the inequality protective laws brought them and fought for contract changes. Sometimes rank-and-file members expressed their dissatisfaction directly to labor leaders. "As an unprotected 'man' I work a little more than women and I earn almost twice as much money," wrote one Communications Workers woman from the West Coast to George Meany following her entry into a "male" job. "'Protective laws,' sir, I do not need."[29] More important, hundreds of the complaints the EEOC received named international and local unions as defendants. Union leaders often joined women in their legal efforts when it appeared that the local might be named as a defendant party. "We filed a grievance under the normal procedure and we were laid off. The union refused to recognize it, saying that it was not a grievance procedure," the Chemical Workers' Georgianna Sellers told senators at a 1970 hearing. "The union found out that we were going to file charges with the EEOC, so they very conveniently told us that they would take us to a lawyer and file our complaint for us."[30] Looking back twenty-five years later, another woman recalled how she energized her local leadership to back her: "Another woman and myself, we got on our high horse. A lot of the girls had tried, but we had never had an equal rights law behind us before. We decided we wanted to push women's rights on the men's jobs and we just told the union, 'We're going into town to the State Equal Rights Commission and push it ourselves.' So the union decided to go with us."[31]

As the figures in table 6 indicate, no labor organization was immune to such charges. While these figures reflect an incomplete listing of complaints due to a flawed AFL-CIO-EEOC reporting system, they suggest that skilled trade groups, public-sector unions, and industrial unions priding themselves on social unionist ideals all practiced discrimination in some form.[32] Industrial union leaders with a "liberal reputation," notes Herbert Hill, "did not anticipate the extent to which labor unions would come under attack once Title VII went into effect."[33] The experiences of packinghouse and electrical unionists that are discussed in the next two chapters make clear that the character and number of complaints depended on particular unions' industrial structure, history of gender relations, and union political factionalism. Several early complaints came from Iowa packinghouse locals, for example, where women made up a smaller percentage of the membership than elsewhere in the union and where automation displaced large numbers of women disproportionately to men. The strong, militant tradition of local autonomy made it difficult for international officers and EEOC investigators to bring local leaders into compliance with the law. While electrical union locals faced charges as well, they needed to respond more sympathetically to their sizable female membership; this, and the power the international officers and staff brought to bear on guilty locals, resulted not only in fewer cases naming the union as defendant, but also in the union's working with women activists to eliminate discrimination and file suit against employers.

The split over how to enforce Title VII was not a simple example of rank-and-file women at odds with women union leaders, for public disagreements surfaced among women leaders themselves. Together they had backed protective laws, but that unity began to come undone after Title VII. At a 1966 *Los Angeles Times* forum on protectionism, for example, EEOC commissioner Aileen Hernandez, a former West Coast Garment Workers education director, spoke for the elimination of protective laws unless they could be extended to all workers. Opposing Hernandez, Ruth Miller of the Clothing Workers, chairwoman of the California Advisory Commission on the Status of Women, argued for their retention. Using the

Table 6. Sex and Sex/Race Discrimination Charges by Union (with Union Membership and Percentage of Female Membership), AFL-CIO, 1966–77

| | No. of Discrimination Charges | | | |
| | Sex | Sex and Race | Total | Percent |
Union	Sex	Race	Membership	Females
Airline Pilots	3	0	24,155	36.0
Aluminum	6	0	29,000	1.0
Asbestos	1	0	16,698	—
Bakery	5	1	149,534	22.0
Bookbinders	3	0	64,250	50.0
Brewery	1	0	50,447	10.0
Brick and Clay	1	0	18,503	1.5
Building Services	2	0	294,359[a]	28.0
Carpenters	4	0	793,000	3.0
Chemical	9	0	103,780	15.0
Telegraphers	3	0	29,732[a]	75.0
Communications	21	3	357,500	50.0
Distillery	2	0	33,656	37.5
Electrical (IBEW)	24	1	897,114	30.0
Electrical (IUE)	29	1	324,352	35.0
Elevator Construction	1	0	15,633	—
Engineers	1	0	350,000	0.05
Fire Fighters	1	0	132,634	—
Fireman and Oilers	1	0	43,000	10.0
Glass Bottle Blowers	12	0	72,000	c
Glass and Ceramic	8	1	44,824	20.0
Glassworkers, Flint	1	0	34,000	30.0
Government	4	0	60,000[a]	8.0
Hotel	3	1	459,053	32.0
Industrial	6	0	86,000	50.0
Laborers	1	0	24,000	—
Lithographers and Photoengravers	1	0	56,000	—
Machinists	22	0	903,015	c
Maritime	1	0	50,000	1.0
Meatcutters	23	0	500,000	15.0
Office and Professional	1	0	76,200	65.0
Oil, Chemical, and Atomic	12	0	173,185	4.0
Packinghouse	12	0	98,000[a]	18.0
Painters	1	0	196,487	0.20
Papermakers	19	0	144,682	8.0
Plumbing	1	0	297,023	—
Potters	1	0	16,264	18.0
Printing, Pressman	2	0	126,000	c
Pulp, Sulphite, and Paper Mill	8	0	182,795	c
Railway, Carmen	1	1	117,386	—
Railway Employees	5	1	320,000	—
Retail Clerks	10	1	552,000	c

Table 6. (cont.)

Union	Sex	Sex and Race	Total Membership	Percent Females
		No. of Discrimination Charges		
Retail, Wholesale	4	0	175,000	40.0
Rubber	16	0	203,573	c
Seafarers	3	0	85,000	1.0
Service Employees	5	1	389,000	33.0
Shoe	0	1	44,451	60.0
Stage Employees	1	0	60,000	10.0
State, County, and Municipal	4	1	364,486	c
Steel	26	1	1,120,000	c
Textile	2	0	183,000	40.0
Tobacco	5	2	32,586	55.0
Transit	2	0	134,000[a]	—
Transport	4	0	97,754	1.0
Typographical	1	0	123,310	—
Upholsterers	2	0	60,000	26.0
Woodworkers	1	0	95,596	1.0
Unknown[c]	4	0	—	—

Sources: Compliance docket summary sheets, 1967–77, Box 32, AFL-CIO Department of Civil Rights Collection, George Meany Memorial Archives, Silver Spring, Md.; U.S. Department of Labor, *Directory of National and International Labor Unions in the United States, 1969,* Bureau of Labor Statistics Bulletin 1665 (G.P.O., 1970), 18–46, 94.

Note: A dash (—) indicates that the data were not reported by the union.

a. This information is not in the 1969 report; it comes from the U.S. Department of Labor, *Directory of National and International Labor Unions in the United States, 1963,* Bureau of Labor Statistics Bulletin 1395 (Washington, D.C.: G.P.O., 1964).

b. This information was not reported by the union. The Bureau of Labor Statistics contends that these unions have at least 5 percent female membership.

c. The union name is unclear in the AFL-CIO records.

rhetoric of protectionism and difference, Miller explained her position: "One must recognize the fact that a woman's role and responsibilities are not the same as those of the male." Hernandez rejected labor's traditional position, noting that the elimination of such measures would bring women a degree of liberation: "The key to the approach of equality for women workers is not what they will be forced to do by state law, but rather what they have the freedom of choice to do." While acknowledging that this "freedom" might bring women "to accept the sometimes difficult burdens which go along with such equality," these sacrifices would be offset by the benefits that would accrue to the growing ranks of women workers because of the abolition of such laws as those limiting working hours.[34]

Labor organizations no longer concurred on the issue of protectionism either. The UAW legitimized the impressive but unorganized force of complaints filed with the EEOC and public debates on the matter by becoming the first union to oppose protectionism. In so doing it splintered decisively the solidarity of the U.S. Women's Bureau coalition. In 1965 the union's Caroline Davis asked the fledgling EEOC to develop "a policy saying that state laws affecting women cannot be used as a justification against women"; UAW representatives formalized their union's opposition to state protective laws at 1967 EEOC hearings on the matter.[35] As with IUE and UPWA women, however, unanimity of opinion on gender equality among UAW women did not exist. Emily Rosdolsky of the international staff and members of UAW Local 3 women's committee challenged their labor organization's position in support of repealing hours limitations laws by arguing that women needed protection in the area of working hours. They pressed, however, for their integration into "male" jobs closed to them.[36] There was no clear line demarcating protectionism from equality. Like many unionists, these women did not so much embrace protectionism *in toto* as occupy a middle ground between this older notion of gender relations and a newer understanding of the need for equality. Differently situated women within unions held different views on equal employment opportunity. Their age, job assignment, and family relations and responsibilities often informed their stance on gender equality.

The wider, national battle for gender equality gathered political force only with the emergence of the second-wave feminist movement in the late 1960s. Unionists played a fundamental role in defining the shape and character of this movement. UAW women, joining with upper-class women from the small, conservative National Woman's Party and younger, liberal activists, formed the National Organization for Women (NOW) in October 1966. The report of the President's Commission on the Status of Women, released in 1963, and Title VII's passage energized this new wave of feminists to protest what its members viewed as the EEOC's slowness in providing equal employment conditions for women. Unlike the radical feminists of the period, NOW members sought reform through the political system. "From the moment of its birth," writes Cynthia Harrison, "Washington politicians knew NOW was there."[37] In the organization's early years NOW members lobbied and picketed vigorously for change. "Title Seven has no teeth, EEOC has no guts," read one NOW picket sign in front of the commission's headquarters in late 1967.[38] There was cause for optimism in the heady days of the 1960s. Responding to NOW pressure, for example, President Lyndon Johnson in 1967 amended an executive order banning discrimination of the basis of race by government contractors to include a prohibition on sex discrimination.[39]

EEOC staff members sympathetic to aggressive enforcement of the prohibition on sex discrimination contributed to this "synergistic effect" on EEOC policy as well.[40] Before he left as commissioner in 1966, Richard Graham encouraged women's groups to lobby the EEOC to toughen its guidelines on sex discrimination.[41] Sonia Pressman, a Polish Jew who fled with her family from Nazi Germany, had graduated from Cornell University and the University of Miami Law School and worked at the NLRB before coming to the EEOC. At the commission she helped document disparities in employment patterns that would indicate discriminatory intent. Specifically, Pressman drafted an influential memorandum in 1966, suggesting that the commission use statistical data of an employer's work force as evidence of discrimination patterns. Building on Pressman's work and other recommendations, the EEOC legal strategy evolved into one that sought to go beyond eradicating disparate treatment in order to root out unfair labor practices that had a disparate impact on minorities and women. As staff counsel, Pressman—described later by an EEOC employee as "the champion of women at the time"—promoted the writing of forceful sex discrimination guidelines.[42] Pressman viewed weight-lifting requirements, hours limitations, and other protective measures for women workers as "ludicrous," but she felt "basically alone" at the early EEOC in her efforts to enforce the sex discrimination ban aggressively. Nevertheless, her EEOC position allowed her to fashion a critique of existing guidelines. When the commission approved a conciliation agreement at an Iowa packinghouse plant in 1966 that preserved separate jobs for men and women, she opposed the scheme as violating Title VII. For the most part her view of Title VII did not prevail at the early EEOC, but she served as a counterbalance to those who opposed strong sex discrimination enforcement.[43]

Pressman's role as a key intermediary between the commission and outside groups points to the importance individuals played in constructing the politics of gender relations. "Somehow . . . I began to be in touch with other women at other federal agencies who were like me. And we began to have a little network of sharing information [on equal employment opportunity]," she recalled in a 1993 interview.[44] Many of these women were then at the forefront of the women's movement. Pressman herself contributed to NOW's founding in an indirect, but crucial way: she advised Betty Friedan to head an effort to establish an organization for women's civil rights. NOW's founding convention occurred several months later, thanks in large part to Friedan's leadership.[45] In NOW's first few years, Pressman led what she characterized as a "double life." "I would be at the EEOC in the daytime doing my job and I would be seeing one thing after the other that the Commission didn't do for women that I thought they should." In the evening, she would gather with other NOW members at someone's house, where she would "draft a letter to the EEOC based on what I had seen that day that they didn't do. . . . I would sign it for NOW, not my name." By "sharing with these people confidential government information," Pressman helped apply pressure on intransigent commissioners to pay attention to demands for gender equality.[46]

Despite pressures on EEOC officers to reevaluate their Title VII guidelines, feminists were unable to gain direct access to commissioners. As a result, their efforts for changing commission guidelines on sex discrimination ran aground. During his tenure as chairman in 1966–67, Stephen Shulman met only with representatives from groups opposing the invalidation of protective laws, such as the National Consumers League, the American Association of University Women, and various industrial unions. To make matters worse, the two identifiably feminist commissioners at the EEOC, Aileen Hernandez and Richard Graham, left in 1966.[47]

These were temporary setbacks, however. By 1968, the cumulative effect of EEOC data pointing to the prevalence of sex discrimination and the pressure of feminists forced the recalcitrant commission to modify its policies. Commissioners returned to their original practice of determining the legality of protective laws on a case-by-case basis instead of ignoring the issue altogether; they ruled that separate retirement ages for men and women violated Title VII; and separate want-ads became unlawful. The next year, EEOC policy makers finally bowed to the varied sources of pressure for equality and released new guidelines mandating that Title VII superseded all state protective laws for women. Investigators were to interpret narrowly the act's BFOQ clause, effectively shutting off employer and union excuses for single-sex job categories.[48]

Women union activists continued to defend protectionism into the early 1970s, in part because they underestimated the new economic and social forces shaping working women's lives. Most of these activists were approaching middle age by 1969; they had been out of the work force for at least a decade. They tended to hold staff—not elected or legal—positions, which suggests that they may not have understood immediately the significance of the multitude of sex discrimination complaints filed against unions.[49] In failing to perceive the rapid political changes affecting women, women union activists suffered from a sort of "time lag." They still believed that old-line NWP members were at the forefront of efforts to invalidate protective laws. "The 'feminists,' mainly professionals," the Clothing Workers' Ruth Miller asserted in 1969, "have taken a very narrow view [of equality] and are winning because no organized effort has been made to oppose their thrust either in the courts or the community."[50] This characterization of the growing coalition for equality was sadly out of date with the new political realities of the period.

Miller's observation about the absence of organizational forums for union women, however, was accurate. Since the Equal Pay Act of 1963 there had been no national forum for labor activists. NCEP officers attempted unsuccessfully to keep their group intact to monitor equal pay and Title VII enforcement. Except for some stray efforts to assist in the passing of an equal pay measure in Maryland and in opposing a congressional act that allowed employers to have unequal wage scales based on seniority, merit, production output, or any fact other than sex (known as the Bennett amendment), the NCEP ceased its activities by the mid-1960s.[51] NCEP chairwoman and AFL-CIO staff economist Anne Draper acknowledged in a 1968 letter that "there has simply been no real continuance of the National Committee on Equal Pay, nor has a successor group been organized to co-ordinate national organizations on other problems of inequalities based on sex." Like Miller and other unionists, though, Draper failed to recognize the reordering of political affiliations; she noted, incorrectly, following the NCEP's demise, "a revival of the split along the traditional lines of groups favoring an Equal Rights Amendment . . . versus church, labor and 'liberal' organizations concerned with the maintenance of basic economic and legal benefits for women."[52]

By the decade's end, advocates of protectionism became increasingly aware of their dismal chances for reversing legal trends. Anne Draper informed male federation staff members in 1969 that, unless immediate work was undertaken to counter the "articulate and virulent" campaign of "feminist attack[s]" on protective laws, they would fail. In surveying the political landscape, Draper found that the U.S. Women's Bureau coalition had collapsed: "The traditional liberal women's organizations that have supported hours laws, etc. are pretty flabby at this point. . . . The Department of Labor is now a kind of ladies' auxiliary to the EEOC in this field. Not much support can be expected from that quarter." Neither did Draper believe that unions could contribute much to this unpromising effort: "AFL-CIO unions would probably follow 'national policy' if the national office took the lead, but with varying degrees of enthusiasm. Principal supporters of protective legislative [sic] have been the 'women's unions.' Unions with more mixed memberships might simply 'sit it out' (e.g. IAM, Steel, Transport Workers). The Auto Workers would, of course, be completely opposed."[53]

Draper's views exemplified the growing sense of futility felt by many in the liberal camp of the Democratic Party as they faced the invalidation of state protective laws for women. "Arguing against equality is enormously difficult," she wrote, "especially when an 'equality' law is already in place, vigorously promoted by its administrative agency with a stack of 'specific cases' to document its point."[54] Indeed, EEOC members had "moved faster and farther than anyone realized" toward this goal, Draper noted.[55] By December 1969, she notified the Clothing Workers' vice-president that, in the view of the federation's counsel, the trend against protectionism was "basically irretrievable"; the only hope, she wrote, lay in attempting to extend protective measures to all workers.[56]

The once-powerful bulwark in defense of protectionism collapsed in the late 1960s as key court decisions affirmed the EEOC's guidelines against sex discrimination. In *Bowe v. Colgate Palmolive Co.*, the UAW filed an *amicus curiae* brief on the plaintiff's behalf, arguing successfully that Title VII contravened state protective laws. In *Weeks v. Southern Bell*, NOW argued the first case to reach appellate court invalidating such laws. Other rulings prohibited sex-segregated union locals and job classification schemes. While not directly tied to employment issues, *Reed v. Reed* was the first case in which the Supreme Court scrutinized statutes discriminating solely on the basis of sex under the equal-protection clause.[57]

Government officers and legislators responded to the women's movement's demands for equality as well, frustrating labor officers further. The Nixon administration's secretary of labor, George Shultz, issued federal guidelines in 1971 requiring firms doing business with the government to create action plans for women's hiring and promotion; that same year Nixon issued Executive Order 11478 condemning sex discrimination in government agencies. Congressional members passed an amendment to Title VII in order to allow the EEOC to initiate suits on its own authority.[58] This last action gave the commission far-reaching power. "You had an enormous club that you could walk into federal district court with," recalled a commission administrator.[59]

In the wake of protectionism's defeat, federation leaders fought in vain to lessen union Title VII liability by weakening the EEOC. It was a rearguard defense based on the premise that undercutting federal enforcement of the law while still formally backing equal employment law would leave them in the strongest possible position with their constituent union members and the general public. Unionists continued to call for giving the EEOC cease-and-desist powers but opposed allowing the commission to institute patterns-of-practice suits without the Justice Department's approval. In addition, labor officers proposed an expansion of Title VII's coverage to include employers and unions with eight or more employees. They promoted this demand, however, only if the EEOC would be the sole enforcer of antidiscrimination. To this end, they insisted that legislators transfer the Office of Federal Contract Compliance Programs (OFCC), an enforcement agency created in 1965 to oversee the government's nondiscrimination policy of those holding federal contracts, to the EEOC. They did this, the *New York Times* said, on the "cynical belief" that the overburdened commission would be ineffective in rooting out inequality.[60] Federationists were unashamed about their attempts to dilute efforts to ensure federal equal employment opportunity, how-

ever, arguing that "unions are sometimes burdened and harassed by a multiplicity of simultaneous or successive machinery."[61] One observer described labor
leaders' response to rank-and-file demands for eradicating racial inequality as
"ambivalent." "The problem has been that after the enactment of legislation that
the AFL-CIO supported, it has not implemented the policies in a fashion that
would make possible the erosion of union discrimination in this generation."[62]

The federation's strategy may have contributed to the EEOC ineffectiveness
but it also pointed to labor's anemic condition. No longer successful at actively
promoting a program for working men and women, the AFL-CIO leadership
could only react to the changes taking place in the political and economic life of
the nation. Their power had slipped from its pinnacle in the Kennedy-Johnson
years, making them unable to resist feminists' calls for gender equality. Union
membership increases during the 1960s only kept pace with the increase in the
labor force's size; unionists failed to bring most of the burgeoning nonorganized
service sector into the fold.[63] The "inertial AFL-CIO Executive [Council]," Mike
Davis maintains, did not organize these new workers vigorously or confront the
widespread managerial speedups affecting industrial workers during this period.[64]
"The United States, it seems, is becoming less and less a labourer's country," the
political scientist Vivian Vale remarked in 1971.[65] A decrease in political power
accompanied this stagnation in membership power. The failed Johnson administration, a fractured labor vote in the 1968 presidential elections, and the
federation's subsequent failure to endorse liberal candidate George McGovern in
1972 weakened the AFL-CIO's position in the Democratic Party and sent individual unions scouting for independent electoral strategies.[66] Those struggling
for gender equality experienced a pyrrhic victory of sorts: they converted a
hobbled labor movement to their cause but in the process inherited a vehicle for
social change increasingly unable to act forcefully in the 1970s and 1980s.

The Contingencies of Class, Race, and Gender: African-American and White Women Unionists

Legal records, economic statistics, and anecdotal evidence suggest that African-
American women workers joined white women in dismantling protectionism.
In the absence of firm data on the racial identity of those filing sex discrimination charges—EEOC complaint forms did not request this—we must look to
other indices that point to the rejection by African-American women of job-typing by sex, sex-segregated workplaces, and other practices banned by Title VII.
An emerging alliance of white and black women to this end came in large measure from the success that advocates for racial equality enjoyed in bringing Afri-

can-American women into higher-paying positions in organized factories and shops in the two decades following the close of World War II. Over the course of the 1960s that trend continued, with the convergence of white and African-American women's wages: by 1970, median wages for African-American women living in the North were 95 percent of those of white women, up from 75 to 80 percent in 1960. Title VII's ban on discrimination by sex and race contributed to this progress toward parity. The closing wage gap, however, was due as much to the stagnation of white women's job status and income as to new equal employment opportunity measures. White men continued to have the highest yearly median earnings ($8,737) followed, not by white women, as in the past, but by African-American men ($5,880); white women came next ($5,078) and then African-American women ($4,009).[67]

Cross-racial efforts to battle gender inequality often proved to be the exception rather than the rule. White industrial unionists, steeped in the tradition of social unionism and civil rights support, bolstered the cause of racial and gender inequality; other labor organizations had a decidedly negative role to play in implementing Title VII. The ties between white and African-American women workers were particularly weak in unions based in the South, where black women's wages continued to lag far behind those of white women and where a high degree of racial inequality continued to exist in labor's ranks. In the North, African-American women's earnings were nearly identical to those of white women; in Virginia, North Carolina, South Carolina, and Tennessee, however, they increased only from 45 percent to a paltry 55 percent of white women's earnings. The disparity actually increased in Mississippi and Louisiana, where black women's wages dropped between 1960 and 1970 from 55 percent to around 45 to 50 percent of the earnings of white women. Other evidence points to the dismal progress of civil rights advocates in eradicating employment discrimination. In some southern plants African-American men and women were still shut out of certain employment sectors. An EEOC investigator, for example, found that one southern tobacco-processing plant had no blacks on manufacturing jobs. There were 171 craftsmen at work, none of them black; 411 white women operated machinery, but there were no black women in that job.[68]

In such circumstances, the activism and availability of legal resources offered by civil rights organizations offered an appropriate rationale to women workers in their decisions to level race-discrimination charges instead of charges of sex discrimination. When a group of African-American women employed at a Roanoke Rapids, North Carolina, textile mill filed suit in federal court in 1970, they claimed that white workers with less seniority received preferential treatment in management's rehiring scheme. Lucy Sledge, a rank-and-file leader of the women, characterized their legal action as a contribution to the civil rights movement: "it was always what was happening somewhere else—Selma, Birmingham, Montgomery—not here. So my sisters and me just wanted to do something here."[69] At the brink of reaping the benefits from long toil in the fields of civil rights, activists in the still-emerging campaign for gender equality found little fertile ground in unions where their efforts could take root.

Women like Sledge found more than just inspiration in the civil rights movement. Organizations such as the National Association for the Advancement of Colored People (NAACP) stepped in with much-needed guidance as workers sought to battle injustice. In the early 1960s the NAACP's legal department complained to the President's Committee on Equal Employment Opportunity (PCCEO) that a men's shirt manufacturing plant in South Carolina practiced race discrimination. The PCCEO, a weak precursor to the Equal Employment Opportunity Commission, enforced a federal ban on race discrimination on companies holding government contracts. On the heels of legal protests and meetings with PCCEO officials, management at this particular firm began hiring a small number of black women in seamstress jobs. The NAACP continued its role in advising African-American women after the Civil Rights Act of 1964 went into effect. A group of black women tobacco workers, for example, found NAACP staff members ready to assist them in 1965 in their complaint of unfair treatment at the hands of employers and union.[70]

The legal records of the Tobacco Workers International Union (TWIU) for the period point to the considerable barriers still dividing women workers. The TWIU's international officers' campaign for racial integration, begun in the early 1960s, had a limited effect on a union culture steeped in the tradition of local autonomy. Where African Americans in other unions used their labor organizations to battle inequality, black tobacco workers, as one labor economist put it in 1970, saw the TWIU as "antagonistic to their aspirations." Consequently, they sought redress through civil rights groups and the government; the union, "usually arguing for the status quo," faced off against its African-American members.[71]

Title VII did not mark a joining of white and black women tobacco workers to fight unfair treatment, as it did in other unions. Instead, white women defended their race-privileged place in the tobacco work force, as when a group of white women, employed by the American Tobacco Company, filed an EEOC complaint in 1967, claiming that they were "by-passed on job opportunities, by Negro employees with less departmental seniority and who were trained by us."[72] White TWIU members in general resisted the tides of change sweeping the labor movement at the time. Union convention proceedings—a useful indicator of a labor organization's positions, if not priorities, on a myriad of issues—reveal that, with one exception, the TWIU did not discuss race and sex discrimination at their meetings held in the 1960s and 1970s.[73]

Even when African-American women did not join with white women to protest gender inequality, they frequently addressed the problem of sex discrimination when they lodged race discrimination complaints. Black women charged TWIU Local 176, the international union, and the Liggett and Meyers Company with race discrimination in 1965 in the areas of seniority, wages, and apprenticeship training. The workers noted the "lack of employment of Negro women on light machine jobs" as well.[74] Five years later, and in another TWIU local, thirty-nine black women brought charges against the union and employer both for "restricting them and other Negro employees from transferring to higher paying and better jobs because of their race" and for discrimination "because of their sex."[75]

Rank-and-file workers' protests in the TWIU and other unions across the country prompted policy makers to think in new ways about equal employment opportunity enforcement. The sheer number of discrimination charges filed by white and minority women around the country awakened EEOC members to the notion that, as commissioner Richard Graham put it in 1966, "there are many [cases] where the principles are the same, where certain jobs have traditionally been for one race or the other, or one sex or the other."[76]

Beginning as early as 1967 the commission combined charges of sex discrimination and those of race discrimination in order to highlight the prevalence of these common complaints, which were pouring in from around the country. Commissioner Samuel Jackson's accusations against the TWIU and the Philip Morris Company that same year reflected this new approach to enforcing Title VII. Jackson claimed that the union and the tobacco manufacturer excluded black men from skilled and supervisory jobs; black women from office and clerical work; women in general from skilled and professional positions; and that company and union maintained separate job classification and wage scales based on sex.[77] The TWIU came under fire again from the EEOC in the 1970s when the commission expanded an existing race discrimination suit against the union and the American Tobacco Company to include all women. In his decision for the plaintiffs, the judge noted that the government had "defined the class of aggrieved women in terms similar to those used to describe the class of black employees" in job classification and wage scales based on sex.[78] The hallmark joint race and sex discrimination case came not in the tobacco industry but in communications. There, a consent decree, handed down by a U.S. district court in 1973 against American Telephone and Telegraph, forced the company to implement an affirmative action plan that eliminated unfair treatment of African-American men as well as women of both races.[79]

These workers faced similar forms of discrimination, but their situations were not identical. Unlike white women and black men, black women had the option of filing charges of either race or sex discrimination. Even with this dual recourse to justice, black women were sometimes affected by discrimination not recognized by the law. Title VII, as the legal scholar Peggie Smith notes, was a measure "developed with black men (race) and white women (sex) in mind."[80] The EEOC and courts did not always acknowledge the unique forms of discrimination African-American women encountered, which many historians have characterized as "double jeopardy."[81] A group of black women at a General Motors plant discovered this when they filed a combined race and sex discrimination lawsuit in the mid-1970s after the company's "last hired–first fired" layoff policy led to the dismissal of all black women hired after 1970 (none had been employed at the facility before the mid-1960s). The court ruled for the company. The women, it found, did not constitute a special class to be protected from employer discrimination; the plaintiffs could prevail only if they made a claim based either on racism or sexism, not a combination of both. Since GM had hired (white) female employees prior to Title VII's passage, the court recommended that the black women seek justice based on race discrimination by joining another suit underway on the matter. The implication was clear: if minority men in this particular plant had not suffered from unfair treatment—which, in fact, they had—then black women would be left without legal recourse.[82]

Embracing Equality: The Labor Movement and the ERA

"The legal status of American women," Leo Kanowitz, a law professor, wrote in 1969, "has risen to the point that it is not now far below that of American men."[83] Kanowitz's whiggish version of women's legal history was overstated, especially since the fullest expression of formal constitutional equality—the Equal Rights Amendment (ERA)—remained unenacted. The ERA had existed in one form or another since the 1920s but had failed to gather significant support when it came up for approval in Congress. When it reappeared in the late 1960s it found new life as a key component in the battle for gender equality and its chance for passage seemed promising. With the passing of the pro-ERA baton from the small, upper-class coalition of National Woman's Party supporters to a new generation of feminists, the amendment took on different meaning in the context of the second-wave feminism. These new activists were younger, and many were minority and working-class women; they pushed the boundaries of equality beyond its narrow legal confines to include a wide range of economic and social issues, including abortion rights. Nevertheless, for the vast majority of feminists committed to change through the political system and organized around groups such as NOW, the ERA remained the centerpiece of their agenda, the ultimate expression of gender equality. Renewed support for the amendment came in part as a result of political and legal changes. The EEOC and judicial decisions against protective laws, the failure to interest courts in testing the Fourteenth Amendment as a substitute for the ERA, and the Nixon administration's Women's Task Force energized receptive feminists. For the first time the ERA gained grassroots support, passed the U.S. Senate (1972), and went to states for ratification. By the time of *Roe v. Wade,* legalizing abortion in 1973, the mutual enmity between the old Women's Bureau coalition and the NWP was gone; in its place appeared a new polarization in which feminists were opposed by conservative and traditionalist women's groups.[84]

Industrial unionists, however, did not flood the pro-ERA camp during the early 1970s in a wholesale fashion. Many workers came to this political realignment reluctantly, and some, not at all. Delegates to most union conventions voted to back the amendment by 1974, but the process by which labor groups endorsed the ERA was uneven, underscoring once more that industrial structures and histories of activism on behalf of gender equality varied according to individual unions. Predictably, UAW members were the first unionists to support the proposal. The organization's Women's Bureau had long opposed protective measures for women, and its leaders were active in the founding of NOW. By the late 1960s, the union's international executive board supported strict EEOC enforcement of Title VII's ban on sex discrimination.[85] Although UAW women withdrew from NOW in 1968, "out of loyalty to the labor movement," as Nancy Gabin terms it, the automobile union's disaffiliation from the federation that same year freed the group from further obligation to oppose the ERA.[86] Members attending the UAW's 1970 convention approved proposals for the repeal of antiabortion laws, the establishment of child-care centers, and support for the ERA. Thereafter, unionists resumed their cooperative efforts with pro-ERA liberals; participants in the founding convention of the feminist-oriented National Women's Political Caucus elected the UAW's Olga Madar to its national policy council in 1971.[87]

Even though the "hoary, crippling feud over protective legislation was essentially over," as Hugh Davis Graham puts it, most unionists resisted supporting the ERA. They did so long past the point at which it had become clear that state protective laws for women were invalid.[88] Male federation leaders were especially steadfast in opposing the amendment. In his history of national civil rights policy during this period, Graham contends that, in response to a general dilution of the political power of the AFL-CIO, federation officers continued to counter the measure "in the face of snowballing sentiment in its favor." "Organized labor, having lost the great postwar campaigns to organize the South and repeal Taft-Hartley, or at least to repeal its Section 14(b) authorizing state 'right to work' laws," writes Graham, "continued to stand by its guns in defending women's protective legislation."[89] Although no direct connection can be shown between these factors, Graham's point is compelling. In rejecting the ERA in the press, at government hearings, and in union correspondence, labor leaders staked out an increasingly isolated and indefensible position. At times, they risked alienating longtime allies over the matter, as when Andrew Biemiller in 1970 reminded Bayard Rustin, head of the executive committee of the Leadership Conference on Civil Rights, that "the AFL-CIO is now and always has been on record against the Equal Rights for Women [sic] Amendment, and strenuously objects to the Leadership Conference taking a position on this question."[90] Former NOW vice-president Lucy Komisar noted in the mid-1970s that the unionists' opposition to the ERA was an "obstacle to friendship and understanding" between NOW and organized labor.[91]

Federationists assumed an almost frantic defense of protectionism in the face of abandonment by nearly every other liberal group on this issue. "It has taken the trade union movement nearly a century to build the protective laws," Biemiller wrote to one West Coast woman in 1972, "and we do not intend to see them destroyed."[92] Doris Hardesty expounded the AFL-CIO's position against the ERA in a January 1971 article in the *American Federationist.* Hardesty—a former member of the federation's Department of Civil Rights (DCR)—not only emphasized the need for continued enforcement of state protective laws but suggested that present legal measures already guaranteed gender equality to those women who sought it: "When one looks at all the things that need to be done, it seems shameful to waste so much energy over a 47-year-old proposed amendment for women's rights which most legal experts think is already covered by the 5th and 14th Amendments to the Constitution."[93] Peppering her comments with denigrating labels for ERA supporters, such as "ladies of the lib," Hardesty renewed the AFL-CIO's familiar call to legislators to pass "specific bills for specific ills."[94] Hardesty's views reflected those of the labor movement's leaders. True, the federation did not speak for unions but the federation's position on legislation generally reflected that of the labor movement. Federation leaders acknowledged that they could only require its officers and department directors—not individual unionists or constituent union heads—to abide by anti-ERA convention decisions, but they noted that several unions with a large number of union members opposed the ERA.[95]

Many women union staff members and activists, in fact, did reject the ERA in terms identical to those enunciated by their male colleagues. Most of these women came from industrial unions and had fought for equal pay legislation. They still believed, however, that justice for women workers came in the form of protective laws, not in measures demanding equal treatment with men. Despite evidence to the contrary, union activists continued to view the ERA as the work of upper-class women organized around the conservative National Woman's Party. "It is quite apparent that the leadership in support of the [equal rights] amendment is composed mainly of middle-class professional and semiprofessional women, an infinitesimal percentage of the more than 30 million in the workforce," Ruth Miller of the Clothing Workers told Congress members at a September 1970 hearing.[96] In an attempt to cast their unions' eroding position as more progressive than that of amendment backers, Miller, along with women from unions such as the Communications Workers and Garment Workers, reframed the issue for legislators. It was not an equality-inequality question but one emphasizing the labor movement's dedication to improving workers' lives as opposed to fanciful promises of equality. To this end, electrical union (IUE) officers submitted a statement to a House hearing on the ERA in 1971, decrying the amendment as "a force eliminating benefits rather than creating any."[97]

Unionists opposed to the ERA deployed some sophistication in rejecting the measure. In an appeal to common-sense reform, women union representatives agreed that many laws needed to be modified in order to reflect contemporary working women's needs. One Communications Workers representative, for example, called for a continued enforcement of state maximum hours laws but acknowledged that professional, supervisory, and executive employees should be exempted from such strictures in view of the nature of their work. Similarly, Ruth Miller recommended that job assignments by sex be eliminated. She urged her listeners to retain hours laws for women workers, however, in order to give them more time to complete their domestic tasks and other familial duties. As Miller and other unionists were fond of pointing out, the ERA did not account for the unequal sexual division at home.[98]

Those having the most to lose from the elimination of protective laws for women rejected the ERA in the fiercest manner. This was especially true for unionists in organizations with a high percentage of women members, such as the ILGWU, ACWA, and the Hotel and Restaurant Workers (HERE) union. The history of HERE women illustrates the nature of such opposition. Waitresses made up nearly 35 percent of HERE's membership, most of whom belonged to sex-segregated locals. Led by union vice-president Myra Wolfgang, HERE women practiced what Dorothy Sue Cobble calls "occupational unionism," a craft-based labor activism reminiscent not so much of the "worksite unionism" championed by CIO unionists as that of the AFL, with which they were affiliated before the

federation's merger with the CIO.[99] As their long-standing history of racial exclusivity demonstrates, waitresses were less interested than were industrial unionists in using the labor movement as a vehicle for delivering social justice. They
were, above all, practical in their demands. Hence, they supported equal pay legislation as it benefited them, but spurned the ERA for fear that it would lead to
a loss of protective measures, most noticeably in the areas of working hours.
HERE's Wolfgang characterized the amendment as a proposal promoted by
"middle class, professional woman, college girl oriented" feminists who did not
act in the best interest of working-class women.[100]

HERE unionists tested the limits of working-class feminism with their continuing support for protective laws while concurrently claiming the label of
working-class feminists. The ideal of gender equality—a main tenet of second-
wave feminism, as embodied in the ERA—never received wholehearted support
from the waitresses. "They wanted equality and special treatment and did not
see the two as incompatible," Cobble observes.[101] HERE women battled for
control over job elements with employers through contracts, hiring halls, and legal
protections predicated on the establishment of local unions with all-female memberships; a 1974 court ruling confirmed their fear that gender equality would
eliminate the practice by banning sex-segregated HERE locals, thus weakening
waitresses' decades-old practice of single-sex exclusivity.[102] For all their defense
of the seemingly antiquated protective laws for women, these unionists' astute
observations of the pitfalls of gender equality echoed the views of a small but
growing cadre of middle-class feminists who were apprehensive about pushing
for the sometimes narrow and androcentric solutions offered women at the time.
"We who want equal opportunity . . . know that frequently we obtain real equality
through a difference in treatment rather than identity in treatment [with men],"
Wolfgang observed. "We are different and remember, different does not mean
deficient."[103]

Both sides in the ERA battle traded recriminations, each charging that the other
wasted too much effort on the amendment to the detriment of other issues affecting women. "The time, energy, and money now being spent in the effort to
pass the equal rights amendment," Ruth Miller fumed, "should be channeled in
the direction of State legislatures and . . . to Federal law. There should be a coalition of all groups working for the passage and improvement of standards for
the entire work force."[104] ERA proponents countercharged that protectionists
failed to mount an adequate campaign to pass laws extending benefits such as
rest periods to male workers; also, they held that labor leaders had neglected to
help men file lawsuits under Title VII to gain labor standards equal to those of
women workers. Both sides seemed unable to find a "third way" in their search

for equality and protection. In only one instance during this period did the two coalitions join forces: NOW backed the campaign of the California-based Union WAGE (Union Women's Alliance to Gain Equality), an early working-class feminist organization, to pass a labor ERA that would extend existing protective measures to cover men.[105]

Once again, the clout of rank-and-file women unionists proved decisive in bringing their organizations to throw their weight behind equality. Leo Kanowitz noted at a government hearing that all charges brought on the subject of hours under Title VII "have been brought by women workers seeking to invalidate state hours limitation laws presently applying for women only." Given the choice, Kanowitz said, women wanted "the attractive pay."[106] At hearings in 1970, most labor leaders present testified against the ERA while women from the UAW, IUE, Amalgamated Meat Cutters, and Government Employees unions protested federation policy at a separate press conference. In Ohio, fifty women from various labor organizations attacked the AFL-CIO's stance as contrary to their interests.[107] Protectionism's remaining defenders lacked evidence with which to denounce bans on sex discrimination in employment. Asked by one congressman whether full Title VII enforcement had increased economic discrimination against women, the Clothing Workers' Ruth Miller responded that she "would not know the answer to that question."[108]

Coaxed by these new realities, longtime women activists in the labor movement came into the ERA fold. Katherine Ellickson recalled in a 1976 interview that she finally endorsed the amendment "when it became clear that state laws were going out anyhow and that the psychological effect of defeating the ERA might be bad."[109] Esther Peterson's "conversion" came only after the total eclipse of protective laws by equality legislation. As early as 1967, however, she retreated from her opposition to the ERA, arguing that it need not "be viewed as the same disruptive force we once thought it was" due to "changes that have come about and the gains women have made." Peterson, a former union staff member and then assistant secretary of labor, attributed the Equal Pay Act of 1963 and other such measures to this amelioration; however, she was still unwilling to cast aside protective laws entirely. Instead, she attempted to divert attention away from the ERA, characterizing it as superfluous: "it is foolish to spend our efforts debating the merits of the proposed Amendment at a time when we have so nearly achieved its objective [through equality legislation]."[110] Having helped engineer working-class women's battle for gender equality, she hesitated at the precipice when faced with protectionism's demise.

In 1971 Peterson reconciled herself to the need for the ERA. This came as a result of the government's nullification of protective laws and women's vast approval for the EEOC's resolve to enforce Title VII fully. She wrote to Martha Griffiths of her change of heart: "After much soul searching I have come to the conclusion that . . . the enactment of the equal rights amendment would be a constructive step. It is difficult to make this statement. I realize that it will come as a disappointment to many individuals and organizations with whom I shared the opposite view for many years. However, much has happened in the past decade to improve the prospects for women—the Equal Pay Act . . . Title 7 of the Civil Rights Act . . . and the amended Executive Order 11246." Her clarion call for equality was tempered by a suspicion that not all working women would benefit equally from such a transformation in gender relations. "History is moving in this direction [i.e., equality] and I believe women must move with it," Peterson told Griffiths. "But it entails a shared responsibility for all citizens. That is why I would urge women who have found changes in the laws to be to their advantage to make every effort to assist those who still may be exploited."[111]

In a period during which the ERA was increasingly becoming, according to one scholar, "the litmus test of whether you were for women or against them," opponents from the U.S. Women's Bureau coalition fell in line behind the amendment.[112] The Citizens' Advisory Council on the Status of Women did not back the ERA in 1967–68 despite pressure from NOW officers; they reversed their stance in 1970.[113] That year the bureau's head, Elizabeth Koontz, endorsed the amendment, justifying her move, in part, by claiming that "if protective legislation is gone or is going, then gone also is one of the major reasons why the Women's Bureau has never supported the ERA."[114] By 1972 most other coalition member organizations such as the American Association of University Women and the League of Women Voters had followed suit.[115]

Federationists and members of constituent unions endorsed the ERA in short succession in the early 1970s. The Newspaper Guild gave its approval to the amendment in 1970, the IUE and the teachers union in 1972, followed by the Garment and Clothing Workers, which backed the measure at its 1974 conventions. Perhaps in preparation for an imminent policy reversal, AFL-CIO leaders noted in their 1973 executive council report that several member unions had "disassociated themselves" from the organization's traditional anti-ERA position.[116] Later in the year, and with apparently little discord and not much discussion, federation convention delegates adopted a resolution calling the ERA "an essential step towards meeting the nation's stated goal of equality for all its citizens."[117]

By the mid-1970s, unions had become vehicles for collective action in the interest of gender equality. Some women were still against the ERA but they were in the minority. Responding to women's direct pressure on labor organizations to make gender equality the centerpiece to union policy, and to the EEOC and courts mandate in this area, unions such as the UAW, IUE, Newspaper Guild, and Woodworkers established Title VII compliance programs. These efforts, emphasizing promotion of nondiscrimination labor contracts, increased cooperation with the EEOC, and revised grievance-arbitration procedures adapted to the law's requirement, attempted to, in the words of two EEOC officers, "absorb the law of the land to the law of the shop."[118]

Support for the ERA, however, in no way ensured gender equality in unions. The Teamsters, for example—not known for their advocacy of "women's issues"— endorsed the amendment in 1970.[119] In the absence of internal pressure by union members, however, the older practice of ignoring women's demands continued to hold sway. Even in the relatively progressive UAW, argues Nancy Gabin, "the discrepancy between policy and practice remained." Union leaders cheered the EEOC's announcement that rendered state protective laws invalid but moved slowly in filing extensive charges against guilty employers.[120] When the full impact of gender equality "really starting hitting close to home," the UAW's Dorothy Haener observed, men "tended not to be all that happy with it."[121] The same reaction occurred at the federation level. On the heels of their membership's pro-ERA resolution, AFL-CIO officers did not initially provide resources to campaigns on its behalf. Mary Gereau of the ERA Ratification Council invited the federation to designate a staff member to join the group, but Andrew Biemiller declined, suggesting instead that state federation leaders might comply with her request. "Frankly we are up to our ears in work and could use two or more people to carry on here," Biemiller wrote to Gereau.[122] Only with the emergence of a national working-class feminist organization operating within the corridors of federation power would activists bring the AFL-CIO executive council to consider gender equality in an active and sympathetic light.[123]

Industrial Unions and the Emergence of Working-Class Feminism

The much-observed decline of organized labor in the 1980s began two decades earlier, hidden under the veneer of large membership rolls and healthy paychecks. As the 1960s gave way to the 1970s, labor's anemic condition became noticeable with the acceleration of deindustrialization and capital flight from high-wage regions. Women's status in unions, however, had improved; female membership increased, the AFL-CIO endorsed the ERA, and the most obvious forms of workplace discrimination had been eliminated. Women comprised an ever-growing share of both the total work force and its organized sectors, especially in the areas of educational services, medical services, and public administration. In 1956 women comprised 18.6 percent of all union members; by 1978 they claimed 24.2 percent of total membership. Title VII–inspired bans on discrimination increasingly appeared in this period. In 1965 only 28 percent of a representative sample of four hundred collective bargaining agreements contained antidiscriminatory clauses. In 1970 the figure had jumped to 46 percent; by 1975 it had risen to 74 percent.[124]

A sobering analysis of gender relations at mid-decade, however, reveals the lengths to which organized labor still needed to go to achieve workplace equality. As indicated in table 7, women may have had an increased presence on union membership rolls but their participation in leadership positions was still woefully slight. In the Amalgamated Clothing Workers in 1978, for example, women made up about 66 percent of the union's membership, but only 15 percent of the officers and board members were women. The record was usually no better in other unions. As women unionists peeled back the layers of legal inequality they found less-direct forms of discrimination, for example, in the impact of policies related to hiring, job assignment, and promotion. Even more disturbing were forms of quasi-official shop-floor inequality perpetrated by male unionists. While working-class women rejected middle-class feminist groups such as NOW on the grounds that they held highly individualistic views of women's rights—Ladies Garment Workers' staff member Evelyn Dubrow called them "elitist organizations"[125]—feminism's resurgence led working-class women, as Ruth Milkman

Table 7. Female Membership and Leadership in Labor Organizations with More Than 250,000 Members, 1978

| | Females as Percentage of | |
Organization	Total Membership	Total Officers and Board Members
National Education Association	75	55
Teamsters, International Brotherhood	25	0
Food and Commercial, United	39	3
State, County, and Municipal (AFSCME)	40	3
Clothing and Textile, Amalgamated	66	15
Service Employees	50	15
Electrical (IBEW)	30	0
Teachers (AFT)	60	25
Garment, Ladies	80	7
Communications	51	0

Sources: Coalition of Labor Union Women, Center for Education and Research, "Absent from the Agenda: A Report on the Role of Women in American Unions" (New York, mimeo, 1980); Ruth Milkman, "Women Workers, Feminism, and the Labor Movement since the 1960s," in *Women, Work, and Protest: A Century of U.S. Women's Labor History,* ed. Ruth Milkman (New York: Routledge and Kegan Paul, 1985), 306 (tables 3 and 5).

writes, "to raise their expectations" in organizing around women's issues within unions.[126]

As a result of their continuing dissatisfaction with union practices, working-class women organized into feminist groups. By the early 1970s, women were already meeting to form interunion coalitions. Workers from meatpacking, mining, and teamster locals in northern Virginia, for example, created Labor for Equal Rights Now, a group founded by Lizzie Corbin, an African-American woman. In 1970, a National Rank and File Action Conference attended by six hundred unionists drew up a "Declaration of the Rights of Women" and "Proposals for Action."[127] Having pushed their unions to support equality, rank-and-file women joined with older women activist leaders who now backed gender equality.

Cross-racial support for gender equality strengthened the emerging feminist movement. The UAW's Dorothy Haener credits Dollie Lowther Robinson, an African American, a lawyer, and a U.S. Women's Bureau member, with giving her the idea to help form the National Organization for Women. "What we need," Robinson told Haener, "[is] an NAACP for women."[128] Many African Americans active in working-class feminism, the sociologist Diane Harriford notes, brought "an impressive degree of political sophistication gained from their activity in the Civil Rights Movement, in their communities, and in their churches."[129] Veteran women industrial unionists directed the largest of these organizations, the Coalition of Labor Union Women (CLUW). Young women workers, energized by second-wave feminism, filled CLUW's ranks. *The Nation* reported that "more than half" the delegates to CLUW's founding convention in Chicago were "rank-and-filers who had never attended a union convention before."[130] While industrial unions were slowly declining in both their representation of the total work force and their political power, seasoned activists such as Gloria Johnson (IUE), Joyce Miller (ACWA), and Caroline Davis (UAW) continued to carry the social unionist banner into battle for gender equality.

These women criticized organized labor's policies but also rejected solutions that bypassed unions. "Remember, we are not each others enemies," CLUW vice-president Addie Wyatt, of the Amalgamated Meatcutters union (AMBW), told those in attendance at the Chicago meeting. "Our unions are not the enemies, because we are the unions. . . . We are telling our unions that we are ready and capable to fight."[131] CLUW members displayed admirable agility in maintaining a critical stance toward a union movement to which they were committed. While they were opposed to a "feminist union" because "we already have the structure to make change," as Gloria Johnson claimed, "if unions don't do the right thing, these women can first pursue their grievance procedure . . . then cases can be filed."[132] CLUW president Olga Madar suggested in the group's newsletter that women workers hold men "accountable through the political process" in union elections.[133]

CLUW feminists placed most of the blame for inequality with employers who, they asserted, "profit[ed] by dividing workers on sexual, racial and age lines."[134] While they educated women in general terms about Title VII, CLUW leaders did not promote the filing of charges against unions. Male union leaders had little to worry about from these activists regarding disruptive and sudden challenges to union practices. Coalition leaders decried sex discrimination in the building trades but few members belonged to such unions. They backed efforts by industrial unions such as the IUE, CWA, and UAW to institute Title VII compliance programs, endorsing the filing of supporting briefs by these labor organizations on behalf of their women members, but they did not demand the establishment of a counterpart to the federation's Department of Civil Rights in providing legal redress to women complainants.[135]

As women union activists did in the 1950s, CLUW members for the most part acted as loyal opposition within organized labor. One reporter writing on their initial convention suggested that they would "challenge" union leaders, but few men at labor's helm saw the CLUW as a "threat."[136] CLUW members supported a legislative platform that reflected a social unionist commitment to gender equality without publicly embarrassing labor leaders. Women called on Congress to back school desegregation, child-care funding, national health insurance, and the ERA. In the area of employment issues, they advocated guaranteed collective bargaining rights, improved health and safety coverage, an increased minimum wage, and extension of protective labor legislation to all workers. AFL-CIO convention participants in 1975 echoed many of these same demands. While only 2.6 percent of the convention's delegates were women (women made up around 15 percent of the federation's membership), delegates applied strong pressure for feminists issues, resulting in the adoption of a six-point program for women members that bore a striking resemblance to the coalition's demands. In addition, CLUW members were responsible for galvanizing the federation's executive board to use its clout in backing the ERA. Joyce Miller, CLUW president following Madar's retirement in the mid-1970s, for example, pressured George Meany to change the location of the AFL-CIO's convention from Florida, where legislators had not ratified the amendment, to Washington, D.C., in 1977.[137]

Gender inequality continued in unions across the United States, most noticeably in the marginalization of women from leadership ranks. Moreover, while organized workers played an important part in contributing to the campaign for gender equality, feminism had not blanketed the working class in the United States in the same way, across all regions and industrial sectors. Activism at the national level to a large extent masked the uneven progress and varied experiences of unionists struggling over gender issues at the union and local level. The support black women workers gave to feminists workers is a case in point. No single factor points to the likelihood that strong, cross-racial feminism would take root. An analysis focused solely on region, for example, falters in the light of considerable evidence of white and black women workers joining together in the South. One example is the textile industry: as white men left that particular work force in the late 1960s, African-American women moved into their jobs; these women not only supported unionization but often convinced younger, more hesitant white women to join them.[138] Southern textile workers were not alone. The Amalgamated Clothing Workers, regarded as among the "most progressive unions with respect to civil rights," had a strong presence in the South and in the CLUW.[139] Interestingly, while race relations in southern-based ACWA locals lacked the animosity found in the TWIU, Puerto Rican and other Latina ACWA members in New York, New Jersey, and Philadelphia went to court over alleged union and employer discrimination.[140]

Myra Wolfgang warned male federationists at the CLUW's founding convention that the figurative "foot" that women had in the door of labor leadership "is not a ballet slipper hiding twinkle-toes . . . [but] a marching shoe, and it intends to march jointly with the men of the labor movement." This marked a new understanding in labor's ranks about the importance of gender equality and the means by which it would be achieved.[141] Such clarion calls for activism, however, belied the uneven progress toward equality. Women in hundreds of locals across the country came to demand equality in the period 1965–75. Their decision and ability to do so, however, was a result of many factors, including their age and employment status. Just as in the years preceding Title VII's passage, the membership composition and institutional history of their unions, as well as the regions and industrial structures in which they worked, shaped the parameters of each labor organization's history of gender equality.

6

Rank-and-File Militancy in the Service of Anti-Equality: Title VII and the United Packinghouse Workers, 1964–75

Writing about the status of women workers in the *Annals of the American Academy of Political and Social Science* in 1968, Alice Cook reported that, "since the last summary of this subject was assembled for the *Annals* [1947], only numbers and a few events have changed, not trends."[1] Cook's dismal report failed to mention specifically two key events affecting women workers: the passage of Title VII of the Civil Rights Act of 1964, forbidding, among other things, sex discrimination, and the establishment of the National Organization for Women (NOW). Their histories are interconnected: when Dorothy Haener of the United Automobile Workers (UAW) and other, mostly middle-class activists formed NOW in 1966, they lobbied the Equal Employment Opportunity Commission (EEOC) to invalidate state protective laws for women when they violated Title VII. This the EEOC did in 1969.

Much of the credit for the change in EEOC policy must go to rank-and-file women unionists. By charging their labor organizations and employers with discrimination, they helped to shape working-class feminism and gave credence to NOW's efforts. While all unions were affected by Title VII, its impact varied widely from union to union. Some industrial unions, among them the United Rubber Workers and International Chemical Workers, became embroiled in lawsuits; others, such as the UAW and the International Electrical Workers, not only faced fewer charges but actually joined with women unionists to fight for vigorous enforcement.[2]

The history of the United Packinghouse Workers of America (UPWA) from the time of Title VII's passage through the mid-1970s, when the most obvious forms of sex discrimination had been eliminated, illustrates the "confrontationalist" nature of gender relations in unions. The UPWA's history and organizational structure stretching back to its early days explain in large part the construction of gender ideology within its ranks. Strong, militant local unionists experienced divisiveness as rank-and-file men and women opposed the enactment of Title VII. This contrasted sharply, for example, with the UAW, where the Women's Bureau joined forces with a powerful international office against discrimination. In addition to the legacy of local autonomy in the UPWA, job losses in the meatpacking industry beginning in the mid-1950s led to a confrontation between men and laid-off women. Many of these UPWA women with decades of seniority were thrown out of jobs while younger men retained their positions in sex-segregated workplaces. These factors, and the continued belief by the UPWA's international leadership in the necessity of protective labor laws for women, helped create a high level of hostility among men toward the full implementation of Title VII.

Women persisted in spite of obstacles to equality. Even in the midst of active federal government pressure on unions to end discrimination, sex-segregated packinghouses remained. Employers and unions renegotiated labor agreements, ridding contracts of blatantly discriminatory measures. They replaced them with a job classification scheme that retained sex-segregated workplaces. The history of Title VII in the UPWA provides a window through which to examine the complicated and changing relationships of women to their unions. Their bitter and prolonged battles in the courts, union halls, and on the shop floor also help explain the emergence of working-class feminism in the 1970s, as unionists began promoting gender equality as a result of their experiences with equal employment opportunity law.[3]

Legal Challenges to Gender Inequality in the UPWA

UPWA women were not at the center of the feminist resurgence sweeping the country. They welcomed Title VII, however, as a solution to their increasingly precarious position in the packinghouse work force. By filing complaints against their union, women forced the equality issue to the surface at the local level, helping to usher in a reconceptualization of social unionism's agenda. Most sex discrimination charges came from the large Iowa locals that made up much of District 3 (see table 8). There, women constituted only 13 percent of the rank and file, while they made up 20 percent of the union's total membership. The massive mechanization and reorganization schemes that management had begun to institute a decade before affected meatpacking employees in District 3 especially, displacing women workers at almost twice the rate of men. Male union leaders had failed to prevent further job losses or to address "women's concerns," for the most part. Women unionists' proposals to the international for support were

Table 8. Sex Discrimination Charges Filed against the UPWA, 1964–75

	EEOC Case Number	Date	Resulting Court Case (if any)
District 2			
Local 167 (St. Paul, Minn.)	6-4-2606, et al.	10/11/67	Sokolowski v. Swift & Co., 1 FEP Cases 611
	7-3-133, et al.	06/30/69	—
District 3			
Local 1 (Ottumwa, Iowa)	5-7-212, et al.	03/28/66	Freese v. John Morrell, 1 FEP Cases 662
	7-2-117, et al.	08/05/68	—
Local 8 (Omaha)	YKC9–112	01/13/72	Borovac v. AMBW Local 8 and Armour, 13 FEP Cases 296
Local 46 (Waterloo, Iowa)	5-8-411, et al.	12/21/65	—
	—	—	Peterson v. Rath FEP Cases 1054
Local 89 (Des Moines)	7-5-225	05/25/68 (no cause ruling)	—
Local 679 (Webster City, Iowa)	5-12-2855, et al.	11/21/68	
District 5			
Local 324 (Ft. Worth, Tex.)	6-11-8981	10/18/67	—

Sources: Discrimination Case Files, AFL-CIO Department of Civil Rights Collection, George Meany Memorial Archives, Silver Spring, Md.; Lexus/Nexus Computer Search.

Notes: The data include old UPWA locals after their merger with the Amalgamated Meatcutters and Butcher Workmen's union in 1968. The date given is the date of the EEOC decision; the first numeral in the case number is the year the complaint was filed (e.g., 5-8-411: filed in 1965).

"pretty much the same as have been approved many times at conventions," admitted the UPWA's *Staff Letter* editor in 1965. "The ladies' beef is that we seem to do so little about it."[4]

Ironically, the UPWA's championing of the Civil Rights Act of 1964—deemed by unionists as key legislation in battling racism—helped bring Title VII to the attention of women members fighting sex discrimination. The packinghouse union continued to oppose unequal pay rates and worksite discrimination on the basis of race and national origin by filing EEOC complaints on behalf of minority workers.[5] Union men, however, were unprepared for the challenge brought by women workers against practices of wage inequality, separate seniority lists, and male-controlled job recruitment practices. This opened up in the UPWA "a new problem in a rather unexpected vein," as the author of the 1966 officers' report admitted.[6] At first, the international office seemingly took no action to implement Title VII's ban on sex discrimination. "WE SUGGEST THAT ALL LOCALS MOVE

VERY CAUTIOUSLY," read a July 1965 memorandum from union president Ralph Helstein to UPWA officers. "There is absolutely no reason for wild haste. The law has no criminal provision."[7]

A few months later, however, recently unemployed UPWA women in District 3 packing locals in Ottumwa and Waterloo pooled their money, sought legal counsel, and contacted the EEOC to complain of employer and union discrimination.[8] "We had an awful time with our women, because they were fighting for survival," recalled a longtime union member.[9] The women hired Dave Dutton, a Waterloo lawyer and local civil rights activist, who believed he came to the attention of the workers by way of his father's ministry in a local church. A recent graduate of the University of Iowa Law School, Dutton admired the women for being among the first in the country to demand their rights on the basis of Title VII. "They were not neophytes," he said. "They were tough minded and tough physically in every respect. They were certainly outspoken."[10]

As shown by the experiences of UPWA Iowa women in Ottumwa and Waterloo described here, those attempting to assert their rights under Title VII faced recalcitrant unionists who offered long-term and creative opposition to equal employment opportunity demands. When eight laid-off Local 1 women at the 2,273-employee Morrell plant in Ottumwa filed charges with the EEOC in late 1965, alleging sex discrimination, for example, their employer and union officers were in the process of amending a labor contract with an agreement that they believed put them in compliance with Title VII requirements.[11] General Agreement 16, as it was known, was in fact a creative evasion of the law's requirement to consider employees "on the basis of individual capacities and not on the basis of any characteristics generally attributed to any group."[12] The contract revision instituted a single seniority list for the plant and individual lists for departments but did not eradicate separation of jobs according to sex. Instead, union leaders and management reformulated previous "male" and "female" categories into three "bona fide occupation groups" called the "ABC system," which effectively preserved Morrell's sex-segregated workplace. The ABC system—found in other large packing firms as well—was cloaked in the aura of scientific objectivity. It was reminiscent of an earlier classification scheme employed by the electrical industry whereby men and women were placed in "heavy" and "light" jobs, respectively.[13] The architects of the new system defined group "A" jobs, intended for men, as "primarily of interest to males because on the basis of job content they consist of physical and/or environmental demands such that the normal male would be and the normal female would not be qualified to perform the jobs or learn them within a reasonable time."[14] The agreement placed women in "B" jobs for similar reasons; both men and women could apply for "C" positions because "the normal male and normal female" were deemed suitable for them.[15] Union officers and Morrell management hoped that the new jobs opened to women in the "C" category, as well as the agreement's disclaimer that "no job shall be listed in any category because of an intention to discriminate against an employee on account of sex," would absolve them of discrimination charges.[16]

The ABC system's framers created an elaborate scheme that perpetuated sex-segregated packinghouses. Workers could "cross groups" (i.e., women into "A" jobs, men into "B" jobs) only in unusual circumstances. The authors of the agreement noted that "the company will consider the special aptitudes of the claimants and make such assignments unless the ability to perform the job or learn it within a reasonable time is found not to exist."[17] In the case of layoffs, employees with plant seniority (which took longer to attain than departmental seniority) could "bid" or displace workers with less seniority in jobs considered "available" to them. By limiting women to "B" and "C" jobs, workers would, for the most part, remain segregated by sex. Men would be employed at jobs paying higher wages and women would be grouped in lower-wage jobs.

Negotiations over the plan's approval were difficult. Records of those negotiations reveal the varied obstacles employers and union leaders constructed to deflect challenges to inequality. While both company and union leaders were publicly committed to eliminating discriminatory practices, both parties did as little as possible to change the status quo. Employers were as obstinate as male workers in opening up even a small number of positions to women. Morrell officials initially claimed that increased numbers of women on the payroll would entail exorbitant maternity payments, a weak argument as most of the women affected by General Agreement 16 were past childbearing age. Implementation of Title VII, Morrell management then suggested, could affect the company's solvency. The proliferation of smaller, independent packers employing nonunion workers already caused major packing companies such as Morrell and Rath to fear for their economic survival. Retraining workers under the ABC system would raise labor costs, they argued, already a sizable chunk of operating expenses in the industry's organized sector. And, although a company would continue to hear union grievances over production issues, management refused to bargain over its perceived right to restructure the workplace (including introducing automation and combining jobs). The maintenance of industrial peace, characterized by long-term contracts and cooperative relations with the UPWA, had arrived in the packinghouse industry only in the mid-1960s. Morrell and Company was intent on preserving such quiescence.[18]

Perhaps the most telling feature of the new plan was the entirely subjective manner in which the ABC framers classified packinghouse jobs. Morrell, UPWA leaders, and an EEOC "referee" met to discuss job assignments. Ethel Jerred, a participant in some of the meetings, recalled that "we went over department by department, job by job, and job descriptions to see whether that [particular job] would fit into A category, B category, or C category."[19] What criteria they used is uncertain; many of the designations were arbitrary and depended on local labor tradition. "This is a problem that can keep you awake at night," reported Ottumwa's *Local One Bulletin* in the midst of efforts to amend the union's contract with Morrell.[20] An EEOC ruling in 1968 found that while women had participated in initial attempts to classify ABC jobs, local officers subsequently reclassified some positions without the women's input.[21] Waterloo's Local 46 leadership publicly recruited members' opinions on the matter: "If you know of jobs in your department that are within the capabilities of performance of either the average male or female employee, please let the Committee, your department steward, the union office, Labor relations office, or your department foreman know about it."[22] "In our plant," a chief steward in Waterloo later noted, "we have some jobs classified A that in other plants are classified C or are normally available to women."[23] One worker from Cedar Rapids who had assisted in the reclassification effort said that "if I thought my wife couldn't do the job" then he would place it in the "A" category.[24] Women delegates from the Morrell plant discovered industry-wide variation in classification while touring a Sioux Falls, South Dakota, packinghouse in 1969: "They have two other classifications . . . [and] they are: C.F. for women before [the] law, C.M. for men before [the] law."[25]

Local union officers responded to Title VII's prohibition on sex discrimination with acrimony from the outset. Their hostility stemmed from a rejection of the very idea of sex equality in employment: "I've always been a believer that if the man's the head of the house he should have the job," Local 1 president Jesse Merrill maintained years after.[26] Virgil Bankson, chief steward and the local leadership's strongest opponent of the plan, claimed in the late 1970s that "there's more divorces over women taking men's jobs than anything else."[27] At the international level, union officers in Chicago continued their decades-old practice of not forcing locals to honor union resolutions and principles of equality on "women's issues." The UPWA's Chicago office formally supported the ban on sex discrimination, sending Edward Filliman—originally from Local 1—as the Chicago headquarters representative to assist in negotiations over the ABC system. According to Dave Dutton, however, the international leadership, fearful of alienating the militant and independent-minded District 3 locals, attempted to "put on two faces" in handling the situation.[28] International leaders reassured their women members that the union would not condone sex discrimination; the international then helped craft an agreement that did just that. UPWA president

Helstein soothed the fears of hostile Waterloo workers in April 1966 by reminding them of the plan's limited scope. "We would like to make as few changes as
is possible in order to find ourselves in full compliance, so that the practices which
you have been able to pursue in the past will be continued with a minimum
amount of disruption," he told them.[29] Overall, union officers viewed the appearance of Title VII and women's rights as unfortunate. They looked forward
to ending, as they put it in their 1966 convention report, the "harassment of
complaints, lawsuits, and mass meetings on the issue."[30]

Helstein, in fact, continued to embrace the notion that protective measures
for women were necessary. When questioned at the Waterloo meeting on how
the ABC system could deliver equal rights while still distinguishing jobs by a
worker's sex, he responded, "There are jobs they [i.e., women] can't do. Single
job lists are not equal. . . . The tradition of the trade union movement has always been . . . to say that equality has to have something to it. It's got to mean
equality in terms of what a person can do."[31] EEOC commissioners—unsympathetic to full enforcement of the proscription on sex discrimination during the
agency's first three years in existence—sanctioned the new plan for similar reasons. "This provision has the dual effect of insuring all employees their rights
under Title VII," claimed the EEOC's *Second Annual Report,* "while at the same
time, protecting the employer and employees from unwanted and unnecessary
adjustments in plant organization."[32]

The UPWA's Helstein attempted to heal the division within the labor organization by appealing to union solidarity. This was no easy task: the employer-initiated changes in the workplace had devastated the union's ranks. Helstein, nevertheless, asked the divided membership to have patience with the ABC system.
"There are going to be a lot of headaches with it yet, but we have had these before and we will sweat them through. . . . What is required is that this be given
time to work."[33] District 3 men and women, however, became dispirited with the
meatpacking union's declining fortunes, even blaming the usually popular Helstein for the slide in rank-and-file morale. Reporting to the union president on
the district's 1966 convention, UPWA publications director Les Orear noted that
the president's failure to visit the embattled locals on a regular basis had contributed to growing factionalism. "Shake hands and chat with people early in the
game, rather than making a college try to save the situation at the last minute,"
Orear counseled.[34] Notwithstanding the charisma Helstein could bring to bear
in his speeches to UPWA members, the local officers kept international representatives at arm's length; packinghouse leaders in Chicago in turn refrained from
forcing solutions or policing agreements once in place unless made to do so by
the EEOC.[35]

In their campaign to secure equality, women did not seek to destroy the principle of seniority, a key tenet of industrial unionism. Rather, they called for plantwide seniority to replace the prevailing sex-segregated and unequal department seniority systems that determined the order of layoffs. There is no evidence to indicate that unionists at the time believed that this was a clash between the union's commitment to equality and its defense of seniority. Those in opposition to Title VII–related changes countered the plaintiffs on the traditional grounds that women were unsuited to some industrial work. Their immediate concerns for their own jobs aroused much of this sentiment. Younger men with little seniority, in fact, were the most hostile to the ABC system, as it threatened to displace them with older women who had accumulated significant seniority. When Ottumwa unionists approved General Agreement 16 in late March 1966, men attempted to obstruct the women's return to the packinghouse by engaging in "bidding" schemes for available jobs. Bankson remembered how the ABC system operated in the plant the day following its implementation: "Very next day she blowed, right on the hog kill. The men bid all the C jobs, and there wasn't no B jobs. There wasn't anything left but A jobs, and every time a woman would try to take a job some bunch of guys would talk an older guy into bumping her out, and first thing you know they're all out on the street again."[36] The returning women met with a barrage of hostile acts designed to frustrate their reincorporation into the work force. In addition to being "outbid" by several men, the women found that they were required to choose jobs that had been identified with numbers but with no description of the requirements of the positions. As a result, they often took jobs only to discover they either could not perform the tasks or did not want the particular job. Also, the women found that "C" jobs had been "manipulated." "Heavy elements" had been added through an arrangement worked out between Local 1 officers and Morrell's management in hopes of discouraging the women from returning to the packinghouse. Union officers and company personnel managers denied women access to department seniority lists—necessary documents for workers to consult in attempting to determine their potential bidding positions.[37] Male workers, Ethel Jerred said, "would not do anything to help them at all. Written grievances were thrown in the wastebasket."[38]

By April 1966, Ottumwa women had become disillusioned with the possibility of a traditional union-based solution to their complaints. Joined by an additional twelve women bumped out of jobs by the ABC system, they brought suit in federal district court in Des Moines after the EEOC reported its unsuccessful attempt at conciliation. Beyond the loss of jobs, these women had few commonalities that marked them off from other female employees at Morrell. As indicated in table 9, the employment pattern of the plaintiffs and their spouses fol-

Table 9. Occupational Status of Local 1 UPWA Women's Spouses

	All Women		Plaintiffs	
	No.	%	No.	%
Not at Morrell	52	43	9	45
Morrell employee	33	27	5	25
Female head of household	14	12	1	5
Unknown[a]	22	18	5	25
Totals	121	100	20	100

Sources: Ottumwa City Directory (1966), State Historical Society of Iowa, Iowa City, Iowa; Female Employee Roster, Trimble Notebook, Box 1, Amalgamated Meatcutters and Butcher Workmen Collection, State Historical Society of Iowa, Iowa City, Iowa.
Note: Data include only women with plant seniority.
a. No listing; may have lived outside directory area.

lowed closely that of the plant as a whole. Two of the plaintiffs were African American; the ethnicity of the others is unknown. All had worked at Morrell at least six years and some as many as fifteen years or more. There were equal numbers of women in the sausage and bacon departments.[39]

The plaintiffs' complaint charged the company and union with persistent sex discrimination: "the defendants over the past years have established a general practice of arbitrarily classifying jobs according to sex, of combining jobs for the sole purpose of excluding women from said jobs, of refusing to recognize plant seniority of women, of placing women on layoff and refusing to recall women while men with less seniority than said women were working regularly and of hiring new male employees while women remained on layoff, which practices continue to the date of this petition."[40] In addition, the women charged the UPWA with unfair representation of its women members by conspiring with Morrell to deny the plaintiffs their rights. Dutton included the international union in the suit, claiming it wasn't "acting with enough power or authority." He hoped to push the international into taking a stronger stand for women workers' rights.[41] The plaintiffs asked for back pay and benefits accrued since July 2, 1965 (Title VII's effective date), attorney's fees, and an injunction preventing company and union from future discrimination on the basis of sex.[42]

As the swirl of legal activities initiated by the plaintiffs threatened to deplete the coffers of employer and union, both defendant parties requested a dismissal of the charges. Morrell's motion for dropping the suit centered on the fact that only seven of the twenty-one women filing against their employer in federal court had participated in bringing charges against the defendant with the EEOC—a procedural prerequisite, the company insisted. In addition, Morrell's legal counsel claimed that an EEOC letter reporting the agency's inability to eradicate discriminatory practices, dated March 28, 1966, did not appear to take into account General Agreement 16's provisions of March 23, 1966.[43] A flurry of memoranda from the UPWA to the court argued for dismissal for three reasons. The union contended that none of the plaintiffs had filed initial charges against the UPWA; allegations of unfair representation were supposed to be handled by the National Labor Relations Board (NLRB)—not the EEOC; and the charges against the union were "so vague and ambiguous that defendants cannot reasonably be required to frame a response."[44] Next, UPWA lawyers suggested that a person's sex was a bona fide occupation qualification (the aforementioned BFOQ) in job assignments. Here, union lawyers referred to the exception noted in Title VII that excused certain forms of discrimination. It was to be used only in rare cases when necessary to assert "authenticity of genuineness," such as roles for actors or actresses, but UPWA officers claimed that the very nature of packinghouse work allowed for job-typing by sex. While an individual woman might have cause for filing a sex discrimination grievance, the union lawyers argued that group determinations of discrimination in this case were "virtually meaningless."[45] The industrial relations situation at the Morrell plant was characterized by "the kind of complexity which requires administrative investigation, analysis and determination" of each specific charge.[46] Of the three reasons given for dismissal, this last one was perhaps the weakest. Title VII's BFOQ provision was carefully and strictly limited by the EEOC. In the early years of Title VII's existence, however, few court decisions existed, leaving the union with an opportunity to test the legal waters on the matter.[47]

As they did in hundreds of cases, officials in the AFL-CIO Department of Civil Rights became involved in the sex discrimination charge against the Ottumwa local. The AFL-CIO nearly always proved helpful to its constituent unions in this regard for many reasons, chief among them to defend union treasuries from defense awards. As defenders of protective labor laws, enemies of the Equal Rights Amendment, and, at best, lukewarm supporters of Title VII's ban on sex discrimination, representatives of the Department of Civil Rights, under the directorship of William Pollard, worked assiduously to prevent women's cases from reaching the courtroom by urging informal conciliation. To this end, the AFL-CIO's familiarity with the political and bureaucratic labyrinth of federal government operations served them well in their support for unions whenever possible. The UPWA Local 1 case was no exception. Acting on its agreement with the EEOC that all complaints affecting constituent unions be forwarded to Pollard's office, the AFL-CIO opened its own file on the Ottumwa charge when it was registered in April 1966. While the AFL-CIO's Department of Civil Rights did not intervene as extensively as in other cases, on at least two occasions UPWA attorney

Eugene Cotton accompanied Pollard on a visit to the EEOC to discuss the Ottumwa matter. Unfortunately, no proceedings of their meetings exist. In addition to these interventions, Cotton felt comfortable enough about Pollard's "insider" status to write requesting that he locate EEOC general counsel opinion letters he thought relevant to his defense of the meatpacking union.[48]

The courtroom drama of the women's legal battle was short lived. The women had failed to include the union in their charges with the EEOC; a hearing on November 16, 1966, forced them to drop all charges against the UPWA. Moreover, the judge determined that a union's failure to represent the women fairly was in fact within the NLRB's jurisdiction, not the EEOC's. The court did not address the union's dubious "BFOQ" argument. Judge Roy Stephenson denied Morrell's motion, ruling that the packinghouse company knew of the charges for over ten months and had been granted a sixty-day stay order after all twenty plaintiffs had filed suit.[49] Company lawyers received a time extension from Stephenson, allowing them to negotiate and arbitrate further with the plaintiffs. On July 12, 1968, the case formally closed when the court found Morrell to be in compliance with Title VII. The company paid each plaintiff $450 as full settlement of claims and reimbursed Dave Dutton with "reasonable fees for services rendered . . . to plaintiffs."[50]

Evading Equality: The UPWA, EEOC, and the Shop Floor, 1968–73

Women workers persisted in their fight for bidding rights on available jobs through continued legal action and by developing informal support networks. "I think it is the woman's place to decide when she can qualify for a job and not qualify for a job," one woman told delegates at the UPWA's 1966 convention. "Let's band together at this convention and go back home and stick up for our rights."[51] Despite harassment from men in the local, including an occasion when her house was broken into and red paint splattered about, Ethel Jerred said, "I made up my mind that we'd paid our dues all those years, we were entitled to just as much as any male that walked through that door . . . because that's what the union stands for."[52] Jerred was not a plaintiff, but she supported the women. Fourteen of the original complainants, joined by two additional women, renewed charges of sex discrimination along lines of the 1966 case. The EEOC contended in August 1968 that Local 1 "did not provide for a systematic, equitable, and expeditious procedure for resolving disputes concerning job classifications."[53] The agency's new indictment against the meatpacking local came less than a month after the first case closed, sending the union's leadership back into conciliation meetings with its women members. Frequent conferences with Filliman, the EEOC, and the complainants resulted in a partial opening of jobs for women throughout the plant. In this regard, the EEOC's strengthened guidelines and judicial rulings against sex discrimination after 1968 put the UPWA on legally shaky ground. In the first Ottumwa case, the union argued its innocence on the basis of a "BFOQ" exemption and held that aggrieved parties could pursue claims of union breaches of fair representation only through NLRB procedures. Now, however, this position was no longer valid.[54] The force of federal intervention along with the feminist movement's condemnation of sexism by the late 1960s invigorated Iowa women unionists in their battle for equality.

As indicated in table 8, Ottumwa women were not the only UPWA members to file sex discrimination charges, although most complaints came from within District 3. The complaints substantively echoed those of the Local 1 women but Title VII had been enacted differently at each industrial site. In fact, crucial factors such as the timing of complaints in relation to legal changes in EEOC policy and the character of local union politics produced distinctive Title VII experiences in UPWA locals elsewhere in Iowa and across the country. At Waterloo Local 46, for example, approval of the ABC plan was especially difficult due to the small percentage of women within the total membership and the relatively open and free deliberations that accompanied the new system's approval proceedings. The union represented over three thousand workers at the Rath plant, but only 14 percent were women. Unlike Local 1, where the union executive board pushed through the ABC plan, only to sabotage its implementation on the shop floor, the Waterloo leadership held several general membership meetings to discuss the employment changes soon after the first thirty-six of what would be fifty-nine women filed complaints with the EEOC in 1965. In January 1966 the local's membership rejected the conciliation agreement due to men's fears that a single seniority list would cause them to lose their jobs. "It's beginning to seem that irregardless [sic] of what we do, we are not making anyone happy," the editor of the union's newsletter grumbled.[55] Only after intensive efforts by labor representatives from Washington and the international, and with a lawsuit hanging over the local, did the membership approve the women's return to work.[56]

The intervention of the international office and the AFL-CIO's Department of Civil Rights in Waterloo throughout the period underscores the important role played by high-ranking labor officers who became active in UPWA sex discrimination cases. William Pollard of the AFL-CIO engineered several meetings between UPWA attorney Eugene Cotton, Ralph Helstein, and the EEOC's Kenneth Holbert during the first six months of 1966 in order to help avoid a courtroom struggle between the union and the plaintiffs. During this time, Helstein attempted to stave off final approval by the EEOC's conciliator for litigation by the women. In early March 1966 he suggested to Pollard that he would place the local union under trusteeship and force the ABC plan on the unwilling rank and file in Waterloo. The UPWA's president hoped to delay court action with this promise of vigorous intervention. Local 46 records do not mention Helstein's threat. Whether Helstein ever intended to achieve such a coup—or whether he could have—is unclear; it certainly would have been a stunning reversal of international union policy of noninterference with its locals regarding most matters. By March 18, 1966, union counsel Eugene Cotton had convinced the EEOC not to send the plaintiffs letters advising them to file suit; he promised to intensify efforts to arrive at a resolution.[57]

When the women finally went to federal district court, Judge Edward J. McManus approved the UPWA's plea for additional time to persuade those who were unconvinced of the worth of the ABC plan, granting a trial delay until June 7, 1966. Meetings organized by Pollard with the women's attorney, Dave Dutton, and personal appearances by Helstein in the Waterloo local in April 1966 resulted in the plan's approval. Evaluating his efforts in 1972, Pollard highlighted the significance of his Waterloo agreement by noting that "we assisted in [the] first conciliation agreement in the meat packing industry involving sex."[58] Disagreements over the system's application, however, did not end. As late as 1970, union officials in the AFL-CIO's Washington office were still acting as intermediaries in Local 46 disputes between men and women over enforcement of the ABC plan.[59]

Women in plants that were similar to District 3 locals in industrial structure and work-force composition filed discrimination charges. Eighteen laid-off women in the South St. Paul Local 167 in District 2 appealed to the EEOC in 1966, using language similar to that used by Iowa women. "This is a grave situation for all of us!!" they wrote to the EEOC's Franklin D. Roosevelt Jr. concerning the union and company employment policy that put them out of work. "Our protection for our jobs and equal rights lies in your hands. We beg for your assistance. . . . Since Union [sic] tells us that their efforts with Swift & Company have proven futile, we must turn the matter over to you."[60] Commissioners found that management and leaders of the 2,600-member local (of which 11 percent were women) were guilty of having created an ABC system that did not provide such essential features as the right to "cross over" to jobs in their categories.[61]

There were few EEOC complaints filed in locals outside of District 3. The reasons for this vary. In some locals, such as those with members engaged in canning, women made up the majority of the work force and thus there was little immediate sexual division of labor to challenge. For other locals, massive layoffs and even entire plant closings did not allow for prolonged struggles over job-typing by sex and unequal seniority. In 1955 Wilson closed its Chicago plants, putting three thousand workers on the street; between 1956 and 1963, employers closed sixteen plants in Chicago, Fort Worth, and Sioux City. In Chicago alone, five thousand workers lost their jobs in the early 1960s when Armour shut its flagship plant.[62]

Women's experiences with filing sex discrimination complaints and court cases led many to begin pushing for permanent changes in union policies and practices. District 3 conventions were important sites of contention over Title VII enactment. The "Women's Activities Committee Report" presented at the district's 1968 meeting, for example, renewed discussions among workers of what the union's upper-echelon leadership ought to do to ensure equality. The committee made several recommendations. These included calls for the international to establish a pattern for Title VII guidelines that would "apply to all locals and [be] enforced if necessary by international union action" and for the district to develop job classification guidelines "where minor heavy elements would be removed from jobs thereby making them more available to all union members." The discussion that followed indicated that, dating back to the union's early years, men—and some women—had been resistant to "interference" by district and international officers in local affairs.[63]

Debate also pointed to divisions among the men over how to ensure fairness to all in reclassifying jobs. Many men supported the women because they were their spouses (see table 10), and the loss of a partner's relatively high-paying job would severely reduce a man's standard of living. A significant minority of delegates stubbornly held that the ABC system was fair and had been arrived at objectively. Fred Nolting, president of Local 46, for example, rose to object to removing heavy elements from jobs in order to make them available to women. Other men contended that job reclassification by employers and the union to discourage women

Table 10. Occupational Status of Local 46 UPWA Women's Spouses

	Number	Percent
Not at Rath	15	25.4
Rath employee	22	37.3
Female head of household	9	15.3
Unknown[a]	13	22.0
Totals	59	100.0

Source: Waterloo City Directory (1966) State Historical Society of Iowa, Iowa City, Iowa. No roster of all women workers at Waterloo's Rath plant is available.

a. No listing; may have lived outside directory area.

from "A" jobs gave management further ground in the labor organization's losing battle to control shop-floor conditions. A St. Joseph, Missouri, male delegate noted the burden companies placed on men by loading up certain jobs. "When the jobs were combined the companies put [in] from five to ten percent of the job elements they knew from a physical standpoint the women could not perform," he said. "In many instances we have older employees among the men who would not be able to perform some of these operations."[64] Notwithstanding objections by Nolting and others, convention delegates adopted the committee's report that would have made gender equality more obtainable. The UPWA's merger with the Amalgamated Meatcutters and Butcher Workmen's union (AMBW) two months later and the reorganization of the district system under AMBW control, however, short-circuited the enactment of the report's recommendations.

The turbulence of this period cannot be characterized as a simple struggle of men versus women, for not all packinghouse women supported gender equality. Employment status was clearly an overriding factor in determining a woman's decision to support those bringing lawsuits; by the mid-1960s most packinghouse women employees in large plants had at least ten years' seniority, but not all were immediately threatened by displacement. Violet Bohaty, a Morrell employee, believed that the women bringing the suit were "troublemakers."[65] The sole woman department steward in the plant, Sue Smith, didn't approve of their action either, "but I never did mistreat the girls over it."[66] Many older women workers in Iowa meatpacking plants were "satisfied with the jobs they had."[67] In one case, a group of women Rath workers in Waterloo's UPWA Local 46, angry at being forced to "float around the plant on different C jobs," protested job changes to the NLRB.[68] Dutton claimed they were not only fearful of being "thrown into new jobs, but also afraid of losing departmental seniority when being moved around."[69] In several instances resentment ran high. "I know a couple of women who were best friends all of their lives and really became bitter enemies over that," recalled a Waterloo woman.[70]

For those women who joined with local leaders and men in resisting the drive for equality, gender still shaped their experiences and work relations. As Patricia Cooper argues in her study of electrical workers in the 1930s who were divided over job-typing by sex, women who accepted the sexual division of labor did so within the context of a gender ideology that shaped their identities. "The faces of gender were many," Cooper writes. "They were sculpted by the system of occupational segregation and workers' varied experiences at the plant and elsewhere."[71] Boundaries between men's and women's jobs remained arbitrary, inviting contestation over job reclassification. Many women formally supported equality as embodied in Title VII but still looked to older, sex-segregated job lists as a way of defending their positions in the shrinking manufacturing employment market. Here, packinghouse workers shared with Cooper's women electrical workers—and many women in general—the same overlapping and contradictory attitudes regarding the shift from protectionism to equality in the workplace.[72]

The hostilities experienced by women moving into new meatpacking jobs continued outside the EEOC's purview. "When one of the [returning] girls would walk into the lunchroom, everybody else would get up and walk out," a Morrell official related to a *Wall Street Journal* reporter in 1966.[73] As a sign of protest, men often refused to extend assistance to women in need of help on the shop floor, as Ethel Jerred discovered while splitting hog backs at the Morrell plant in the early 1970s. It was a "knife job," requiring knowledge of how to sharpen large butcher knives. "No, the men wouldn't sharpen my knife," said Jerred, who first came to work at Morrell in 1943, "but I didn't care because I had a husband who was a trimmer, and he taught me how to keep my knife sharp."[74] Ruth Morrow moved to the "pork cut" department and encountered harassment there as well. She recalled, "Sometimes someone who didn't particularly think you should be doing that job would stand out there and throw those great big hogs all at once. There was no way you could keep them from falling off the table on the floor. . . . It just so happened that one time a meat inspector was standing there, and he went and got the foreman, and he said, 'now, you find out who's doing that and we'll not have any more of that.'"[75] Women coming into these jobs for the first time "had to walk in together. . . . Try to find a friend so that if you had problems you had somebody to go get help."[76] As laid-off women were brought back into the Morrell plant, many of the younger men supporting Bankson's intransigence lost their jobs, thus easing tension between workers.[77]

Male workers unable to complete work assignments often received understanding from their coworkers; women in similar situations were told that job equality entailed no relief from individual tasks due to difficult circumstances. "A male alcoholic who complained of 'sick feelings' was allowed to transfer to a new department and a new job with union and management approval," reported two scholars writing about discrimination in the packinghouse industry. "A woman who was faced with the choice between risk of severe physical injury or layoff was told that the seniority system could not permit her to take a less demanding job."[78] Title VII could do little to ease this type of treatment, which occurred daily on the packinghouse floor.

Fighting for gender equality was arduous and long-term work. Recourse to federal antidiscrimination plans did not always deliver sought-after justice. A second case involving Waterloo UPWA women, *Petersen v. Rath,* begun in 1969, points to the inability of the ABC system to eradicate sex discrimination. Two

Rath women workers claimed that both company and union prevented them from applying for "A" jobs in the plant's cafeteria by refusing them information and aid on job availability. The plaintiffs, Dorothy Petersen and Patricia Youngblut, with attorney Dave Dutton, exposed the inequality of the tripartite job classification system by calling Dr. Leon Smith from the University of Iowa's Motor Performance Research Laboratory to present his findings on the women's physical capabilities. Smith concluded, among other things, that Petersen and Youngblut were "well above average for woman [sic]" and "compared well with a large group of men."[79] Smith also noted that the plaintiffs "were extremely strong and had no problem with endurance" as they possessed "mesomorphic" or low center of gravity in their bodies, which was ideal for lifting. The men who received the women's cafeteria jobs, on the other hand, were described by Dutton as "neither average nor above average physical specimens."[80] One of the men the attorney described as "diabetic and on appearance, a slender and even frail looking individual."[81] The U.S. Court of Appeals decided in favor of the women in 1972, maintaining that the UPWA was guilty of "adher[ing] to a policy of never transferring a woman to an 'A' job regardless of her individual capabilities."[82]

Dutton explained to the court what many women packinghouse workers already well understood: "The situation created is even more insidious than the one it replaced, for when an employee now complains of discrimination the Company and Union both point to the 'ABC' Agreement as approved by the Equal Employment Opportunity Commission and claim that the anti-discrimination arm of the federal government has approved their seniority system. In fact, the female employees at the Rath Packing Company are just as restricted in their work opportunities and have even more difficulty gaining relief than before."[83] In January 1972, in a decision regarding a small Armour packing local in Omaha, the EEOC declared the ABC system to be "inconsistent with the requirements of Title VII."[84] EEOC chairman William H. Brown explained to the union's attorney that, while the agency once approved of the scheme, recent judicial decisions required employers and unions to "prove that he/she has factually-determined reasonable cause to believe that all or substantially all persons of the other sex would be unable to perform the job involved safely and efficiently, or that the job requires specific physical characteristics necessarily possessed only by one sex." The ABC job system, Brown wrote, did not meet these requirements.[85]

Despite its illegality, the system remained part of the employment structure in Iowa's packinghouses at least until the mid-1970s. "If someone told us to go to hell, there was nothing we could do about it," Ralph Helstein admitted, "but we would try to get people to bid according to their sex on the two jobs that were attuned to them."[86] Few cases went to trial due to the willingness of companies, union, and women workers to accept arbitration settlements. The EEOC's back-log of cases, which ran into the thousands by the early 1970s, may have helped encourage women complainants to participate in nonlitigative conciliation efforts, especially when organized labor and employers could delay relief to workers for extensive periods by introducing complex challenges of a procedural nature.[87] Whether in or out of the courtroom, however, the uneven effectiveness of Title VII–inspired labor policies perpetuated sex discrimination in the workplace.

Waterloo Local 46 president Lyle Taylor's meeting with women workers in February 1973 demonstrates the continuing nature of packinghouse sex discrimi-nation. Called in the midst of employment cutbacks and on the heels of the *Petersen v. Rath* case, the stormy meeting followed weeks of male workers' "crossing over" to "B" jobs for the first time. Taylor claimed that the local leadership "red-circled the 'B's' and we tried and hold the men off and kick their head in every time they looked at them, figuring we'll keep those jobs for the women a lot longer."[88] Taylor also claimed that the women's lawsuit changed this arrangement. "The men started waking up and saying, 'Hey, if they can sue us to get an A job, what the heck are we staying away from the B jobs for?' . . . . [It's] going to open wide now, because you opened a kettle of worms in front of all these men."[89]

Women in attendance presented Taylor with a different picture of the situa-tion at Rath. Heavy elements had been added to "A" jobs, they charged, and, as "B" jobs were being eliminated at a faster rate than other positions, women were pushed into "A" jobs. Furthermore, the company allowed men replaced by other workers with higher seniority rights to stay in their departments, when possible, in order to retain what management viewed as valuable skills. Women were shipped out of the diminishing "B" departments when men outbid them or the company scaled down its operations. Consequently, they lost department seniority while men retained their seniority.

The ABC system's maddening design, laden with special exceptions and local addenda, could work for women in some cases. Taylor promised, for example, to enforce a little-known part of their labor contract that made men with low seniority who were on "C" jobs switch positions with women on undesirable "A" jobs. This, and his vow to persuade the local's bargaining committee to revert to a pre-1972 system whereby certain "C" jobs were "frozen" or reserved for women, points to the local—and often confusing—variations of the ABC system. It also demon-strates that women were often caught between demanding a job classification sys-tem that reserved certain positions for them (i.e., freezing "C" jobs) and a desire for full formal equality. Both men and women struggled to maintain employment in a period of economic sluggishness, but a gendered contract and legal system resulted in significantly different experiences for them as workers.

Working-Class Feminism in a Decaying Union

The historical significance of these working women's experiences lies not so much in the specific legal battles they initiated as in the process by which they accepted and attempted to bring about gender equality. Instead of abandoning the cause of unionism, women embraced it in new ways. Unfortunately, an accompanying drop in the total percentage of unionized employees in the work force and lackluster organizing efforts in female-dominated industries undercut improvements in women's status within the labor movement. Victory for UPWA women, whether it be against employers or union discrimination, was often slow in arriving and incomplete when it came. In the Cedar Rapids local, for example, men and women workers found progressively fewer employment opportunities in the Wilson plant as the company continued its outsourcing of jobs to smaller operations and combined remaining positions.[90] The situation was even bleaker in Local 1. Morrell's management initiated an offensive that left UPWA members reeling. "They are still combining and eliminating jobs at a rapid and programmed pace," a Sioux Falls, South Dakota, union officer reported to Bankson in 1971. "It appears that the new breed now calling the shots for Morrell expect more for less. They have no scruples or decency about their methods. A person can be working well beyond his limitations and still they expect more."[91] The company had threatened to close the Ottumwa plant since the mid-1960s, citing inefficiency as its reason. Despite an employee wage freeze and job-combining, the plant closed in 1973. At the time it ceased operations only one woman held union office.[92]

Packinghouse leaders continued their impassive advocacy for gender equality into the 1970s. Following the UPWA's merger with the AMBW in 1968, convention resolutions continued to condemn sex discrimination and encourage women's rights committees, all with minimal results. At the 1970 annual meeting of District 11 (formally, District 3), only 7 of the 128 delegates (5 percent) were women. District convention delegates did not approve the formation of a separate "women's" committee until 1976. As the next chapter will illustrate, this contrasted sharply with the actions of unions such as the UAW and the IUE, which boasted of having a successful Title VII compliance program in addition to a sizable number of women activists in local and international office. The international established a women's affairs department in 1973 but moved slowly to embrace gender equality. Two years after the department's establishment, staff members finally were in contact with the IUE to inquire how to develop an effective program for women members. However, this did little to bring the union to the forefront of the battle for women's rights. UPWA women found little support when looking to the larger labor movement, as the Iowa Federation of Labor was slow to address packinghouse women's concerns. The state federation's conventions—important annual forums for discussion of labor issues—did not openly deliberate the ABC system's unfairness until 1974 when the newly established Committee of Women Trade Unionists condemned it.[93]

If UPWA locals lagged behind other unions in rooting out the most obvious forms of sex discrimination, women made noticeable advances in dismantling inequality during Title VII's first decade. "In the long run," Ethel Jerred said, "I think the women had proven to the men that we came up there as ladies. . . . There were more women on the cut and the kill and down through there, and they were holding their own."[94] Local 1 president Jesse Merrill admitted that "most women in there was no different than us. They was down there to make a living, you know."[95] The lesson of Title VII was not lost on Ottumwa women after the plant's closing, when many workers found themselves unemployed. Frances Calhoun, a steward of the local's clerical workers, became interested in welding in the early 1970s after "doing some reading in the library." She discovered that "a lot of women had done welding in shipyards during World War II. I convinced myself that . . . a woman can do this if she's hungry enough and I was beginning to get pretty hungry by then."[96] For a woman to become a welder a decade earlier would have been nearly unthinkable.

By the mid-1970s, working-class feminists around the country had formed interunion coalitions in which packinghouse women participated. The most notable of these was the Coalition of Labor Union Women (CLUW). Addie Wyatt, a longtime UPWA Chicago activist, played a prominent role in CLUW's formation and sat on the group's executive board. At least one Iowa packinghouse local sent women delegates to the organization's first convention.[97] As the present UPWA case study exemplifies, campaigns to promote women's issues to unionists were mostly initiated by women themselves. "You started thinking for yourself," Julia Naylor remembered about women's participation in union politics after Title VII's early years.[98] Fort Dodge UPWA Local 31 members elected Jane Burleson, an African-American woman, as recording secretary and steward, and she served throughout the 1970s. She also sat on the State Federation of Labor's Human Relations Committee in 1973. Burleson ran for office, she said, "just to give them some opposition, because we still got chauvinist men! Even though we're supposed to be union brothers and sisters, we still have that."[99] The events of the critical period 1964–80 demonstrate how the force of government legislation, economic crises, and budding working-class feminism created change; they also indicate the tenacious nature of gender inequality in the face of such challenges.

7

"A Genuine Good Faith Effort": Women and Equal Employment Opportunity in the International Union of Electrical Workers, 1964–80

When asked in a 1976 interview which labor organizations had made the most progress in the area of women's equality, Katherine Ellickson, a longtime activist, AFL-CIO staff member, and government officer, singled out the International Union of Electrical Workers (IUE), a 300,000-member AFL-CIO union, for commendation. The IUE, she said, "played a notable part in advancing the cause of women in avoiding cases before the courts when necessary."[1] Ellickson was undoubtedly referring to the union's Title VII compliance program—a comprehensive and vigorous antidiscrimination plan. Unlike other unions that focused on racial inequality, the IUE's membership included only 3.7 percent African-American men; minority and white women made up approximately 35 percent of the membership. Most of the IUE's efforts flowed in the direction of supporting gender equality. At the time of Ellickson's observation, in fact, the union was a plaintiff in several high-profile cases over sex discrimination in job assignment, wages, and benefits. In particular, the Supreme Court heard a case in 1976 filed by the IUE charging that employer insurance plans constituted sex discrimination under Title VII of the Civil Rights Act of 1964.[2]

While the electrical workers union had given considerable attention to "women's" issues since its inception in 1949, its move to the forefront of the fight for gender equality came in the decade following Title VII's passage. How did this union—which, until the early 1970s, supported protective labor laws for women, opposed the Equal Rights Amendment (ERA), and was found liable in several sex discrimination cases—come to create a model Title VII compliance program? The answer lies, in part, in the IUE's history of gender relations in the 1950s. Women electrical workers wielded significant power by their sheer numbers. Male unionists feared that, in an industry threatened by female substitution in "male" jobs, women's low wages would damage their positions. Therefore, they promoted equal pay campaigns and played a major role in the passage of the Equal Pay Act of 1963. In addition, the union leadership sponsored conferences for women workers, hired women staff members at the international level, and sent women organizers into IUE locals during this period. The cumulative effect of this activity by the 1960s could be found in the union's growing commitment to the ideal of gender equality.

This predisposition to equality, however, did not result instantly in a vigorous practice of equality in the IUE. Union executive board and staff members, joined by male leaders at the local level who were sympathetic to their objectives, faced a series of discrimination charges filed by rank-and-file women workers and came to embrace the antidiscrimination policies of the Equal Employment Opportunity Commission (EEOC) as their own. They were able to do so because the IUE's centralized structure gave them substantial authority. The advocacy of equality and the defense of class interests, they maintained, were not mutually exclusive goals. "We have saved this IUE money which has saved this IUE being charged with failure to meet the EEOC standard," International Executive Board (IEB) member Mary Callahan reminded convention delegates in 1972.[3] By instituting a compliance program within the realm of collective bargaining practices, unionists hoped to defend the traditional arbitration system, dissuade members from filing costly charges against the organization, and deliver justice to all workers. As Callahan noted, "If we don't do it ourselves somebody else is going to do it for us."[4]

The key to the IUE leadership's success in promoting gender equality lay in the ability of international staff members, especially those in the legal department and the social action department, to enforce equal employment mandates. To do this, union leaders used their constitutional power over local unions to institute the IUE's compliance program at the district and local levels. IUE activists in turn brought their feminist ideals and the electrical workers' compliance strategy to other women unionists. They helped form the Coalition of Labor Union Women in 1974, the national organization of labor women demanding gender equality.

Dissatisfaction with Difference: The Challenge to Gender Inequality in the IUE, 1964–73

"History has proven that it [Title VII] was probably the best thing that ever happened to the Civil Rights Act," IUE officer and activist Gloria Johnson acknowledged in a 1993 interview.[5] In the 1960s, however, the union's leaders balked at the attempts of government officers to enforce Title VII fully by overriding state protective measures for women. IUE representatives publicized their position on the matter at government hearings and in correspondence to public officials. Joined by other members of the U.S. Women's Bureau coalition, they asked EEOC chairman Franklin D. Roosevelt Jr. in 1965 to preserve protective laws "because . . . [they have] greatly improved [women's] . . . economic position, provided essential protection from exploitation, and promoted their health, safety and well-being. There are still many differences between men and women which amply justify existing differential legislation."[6] Electrical workers argued that, where these laws were found to be "outmoded, ineffective, and discriminating," they should be repealed;[7] they asked that laws be retained where they "do not discriminate against women or prevent their job opportunities."[8] IUE leaders rejected the ERA firmly, characterizing it as "a force eliminating benefits rather than creating any."[9]

Many rank-and-file women were not in accord with the IUE leadership's position on these matters. Their dissatisfaction with the union's defense of protectionism came at a time when job security was increasingly elusive in the electrical industry. The problems faced by IUE members in the 1950s, such as management's refusal to negotiate contracts (Boulwarism), the introduction of automation, and the decentralization of electrical manufacturing, had not lessened over the next decade. Although the National Labor Relations Board (NLRB) had declared Boulwarism illegal in 1964, union negotiators continued to face obstinate employers at the bargaining table until 1969, when the union finally joined forces with its parent organization and rival, the United Electrical Workers, and other labor organizations to roll back General Electric's (GE) proposition to dismantle national contracts.[10] Employers were by no means defeated, however; they intensified their dispersal of production to nonunion regions and firms. Even when electrical manufacturing plants with an IUE presence remained open, management "subcontracted" work out to small firms with nonunion work forces. Subcontracting, IUE general counsel Irving Abramson noted in 1966, had become a "creeping paralysis" to the union's strength.[11] This union's membership had not been decimated as in the packinghouse industry, but its growth, one industrial relations expert observed in the mid-1960s, was "substantially below the potential in the dynamically growing industries comprising the IUE jurisdiction."[12]

Internal factionalism plagued the IUE as well, weakening the union even further. At the center of controversy, IUE president James Carey faced off with secretary-treasurer Al Hartnett and then battled District 3 head Paul Jennings. Jennings went on to become president in 1965 following a recount of the previous year's ballots by the U.S. Department of Labor. Carey's differences with his opponents were essentially personality feuds that centered on minor squabbles over dues increases. One journalist noted that, following a strike defeat in the early 1960s, Carey had become "more tense, sometimes short-tempered. He had a fist fight with the union secretary [Hartnett] in his office. It was said that he brought on a strike which could have been avoided and in which the union was at a disadvantage."[13] Even with Carey's departure the union was still plagued by a leadership crisis during Jennings's early years at the helm as he oversaw the ouster of District 3 officers in 1967. These union leaders, in charge of eighty-one thousand members in New York, New Jersey, Baltimore, and Philadelphia, misused thousands of dollars of union funds.[14]

As with working women employed in other industrial sectors, IUE women came to reject protectionism as detrimental to their interests. Angry over the practice of segregating jobs by sex, unequal pay, denial of overtime, and separate seniority lists, women in several locals filed sex discrimination charges against employers and the IUE (see table 11). Women fashioned Title VII into an effective tool for securing gender equality. "What has happened to Paragraph 7 of the Civil Rights Bill?" three Dayton, Ohio, women members asked president Jennings in a letter in August 1965. "They keep telling us this would help us solve the problem and since going into effect in July we have heard nothing about it."[15] These women and others filed sex discrimination charges with the EEOC.

While the IUE's history of Title VII enforcement lacked the animosity found in the record of the packinghouse experience, women faced ample hostility from local male unionists who resisted modifying their work practices. "The labor movement is a real cross-section of America, and so you're going to find some biases and resistance to change and we certainly did see it during that time," Gloria Johnson admitted years later.[16] After filing charges with the EEOC in 1967, for example, a woman from Local 717 in Youngstown, Ohio, told the government official investigating her complaint that union officers "continually harassed" her; the woman told how a shop steward threatened her, telling her that "men were waiting for her," and "would take care of me."[17] When Local 707 women in Cleveland went to the EEOC the next year, they noted that "complaints to our union officers have been met with sneers, statements we are 'nothing but trouble' and refusals to take any action to protect our job rights."[18] In the mid-1970s, union counsel Winn Newman reviewed for Paul Jennings the "substantial harassment" IUE women had faced in filing discrimination charges. "You know about the suit by women alleging that Union officers called them lesbians," Newman wrote. "There were also incidents involving women who tried to get men's jobs—slashing of tires of women, gun shots in their homes, placement of rats on machines, a strike when women went on jobs for the first time. I've never attempted to collect all of these items but there may be more."[19]

As indicated in table 11, there are no readily discernible geographical, mem-

Table 11. Sex Discrimination Charges Filed against the IUE, 1964–75

Local	EEOC Case Number	Date	Local Membership	Women as Percentage of Total
103 (Camden, N.J.)	YNYO-166	04/19/71	n.a.	
	YNYO-058	07/27/71	n.a.	
260 (Bristol, Conn.)	5-10-2423	conciliated	764	68.7
272 (Cambridge, Mass.)	NY68-12-568, et al.	03/28/69	260	55.0
438 (Newark, N.J.)	6-1-539	05/16/66	1,500	50.0
601 (East Pittsburgh, Pa.)	5-10-2103	05/25/66	n.a.	
	034-61076-2[a]	03/05/76[b]	n.a.	
	034-61074-6[a]	03/05/76	n.a.	
707 (Cleveland, Ohio)	YCL9-085	12/23/70	n.a.	
717 (Warren, Ohio)	CL7-2-261U, et al.	07/10/68 (no cause ruling)	7,927	61.8
	YCL1-311	06/14/72		
787 (Richardson, Tex.)	TAU9-0600, et al.	05/02/70	2,500	60.0
801 (Dayton, Ohio)	5-11-2563	03/10/66	12,000	8.3
	CL7-2-226, et al.	06/16/69		
	YCLO-091	05/12/71 (no cause ruling)		
804 (Vandalia, Ohio)	YCL9-090	06/18/71	550	45.4
810 (Dayton, Ohio)	6-3-1500	03/04/68 (no cause ruling)	215	5.1
1022 (Zion, Ill.)	CH7-3-183, et al.	04/17/68	n.a.	
1581 (Buffalo, N.Y.)	YNY9-148	11/16/71	4,500	24.8

Sources: Discrimination Case Files, AFL-CIO Department of Civil Rights Collection, George Meany Memorial Archives, Silver Spring, Md.; Lexus/Nexus Computer Search; "Breakdown of IUE Female Membership by District and Local," Jennings Binder, August 18, 1967, group 2, International Union of Electrical Workers Collection, Rutgers University Libraries, New Brunswick, N.J.
a. A charge number is given since the EEOC case number is not available.
b. Charge date; decision date not available.

bership, or employer patterns related to the filing of charges. Many of the complaints, however, centered on the denial of overtime work to women. At first glance, it appears that union leaders accused of discriminatory treatment were merely following state hours limitations for women. In 1965–66 several women complained to the EEOC that they were denied high-paying extra work on Sunday at the General Motors Frigidaire plant in Dayton, Ohio. The complainants, who were some of the approximately 11 percent of women in the 13,200-person work force, went first to Local 801 president Joe Shump with their grievance. Shump, who later claimed he "bent over backwards to resolve these matters," protested that he could not violate Ohio statutes on women's working hours. "It is beyond me what can be done unless the state laws are changed," Shump explained to the IUE's General Motors Conference Board chairman, David Fitzmaurice. "Let me hasten to add," Shump continued, "the laws were enacted in the 30s and supported by the Ohio AFL-CIO, as they are protection for the females."[20]

Shump's point about state protective laws was technically correct, but the local leader neglected to address the women's charge that union leaders, in collusion with plant managers, reconstructed the work week to end on Sunday, thus circumventing their opportunity to work on that day, since they would have already reached the maximum hours permitted by law. In December 1965, Delores Fickert, joined by twenty-nine other women, charged that employer and union "had established work shifts and overtime schedules and procedures which discriminate against female employees and limit their promotional opportunities."[21] Beyond being denied extra shifts, the Dayton women were frustrated with their treatment by union officers in general. "It seems as though whenever a female calls for representation, it is never processed to the full extent," Fickert wrote to Paul Jennings at the time.[22] The EEOC found cause on the women's behalf on the question of overtime. While commission guidelines on applying Title VII to sex discrimination during this period left protective measures intact unless challenged in court, the EEOC's Aileen C. Hernandez found that the company and union had "not fully explored the possibilities within Title VII and the Ohio state laws for providing equal opportunity to male and female employees."[23]

Evidently union officers and company managers did not consider negative findings incentive enough to change their employment practices. Two years later, fourteen more women from the local filed charges on the same grounds. Overtime conditions did not improve until new EEOC guidelines invalidating protective laws appeared in 1969.[24] Women in Local 801 were still trying to collect back pay in the early 1970s as a result of the discrimination, to no avail; district and appellate courts ordered that payment of attorney's fees was appropriate but not a monetary payment for the women themselves, "in view of the uncertainty as to whether the Ohio statutes were invalidated and the lack of any final court decisions in validating these statutes."[25]

Union leaders also violated Title VII by maintaining sex-segregated job classifications and denying women positions in line with plantwide seniority. Julia Kuc of East Pittsburgh Local 601 bid on an available job but her employer, with the union's approval, gave the position to a man with three years' less seniority. A similar situation existed at the electrical workers' local in Cleveland where three women fought against discrimination in the areas of pay, promotion, and access to jobs.[26] An EEOC investigator in 1968 found that the Vandalia, Ohio, IUE unit representing American Machine and Foundry Company workers "acquiesced" to a woman's layoff despite the fact that she was eligible to "bump" a man with less seniority for an inspector position. At this worksite, managers—with the local's sanction—required women, but not men, to take mechanical aptitude tests for certain jobs. While men were given thirty days to learn a higher-skilled job, the plant's industrial relations manager bragged that "he can usually tell in a day if a woman would perform the job." He claimed, further, that "women are not qualified for inspection work" and that he "sees no sense in trying to train them when . . . a man can do the job with just a little training."[27]

In at least two cases IUE officers agreed to end separate job and seniority lists, only to replace them with a classification scheme designed to discourage women workers from applying for former "male" jobs. At a Bristol, Connecticut, electrical manufacturing plant in 1967, Derek C. Bok, then a Harvard law professor and EEOC-appointed conciliator, hammered out an agreement that eliminated "men's" and "women's" jobs. Bok instead placed positions in either a "Class I" or "Class II" category. Requirements for the first group of jobs—"relatively light *Effort,* seldom necessitating lifting or otherwise exerting forces over twenty-five pounds . . . . [working] where *Responsibility* of operator for either product or process is held to a minimum"—were remarkably similar to those of traditional "women's" jobs. Likewise, Class II job descriptions served the same euphemistic purposes for former "men's" jobs. Those jobs involved "considerable physical ability" and "substantial *Responsibility*"; workers should expect to find conditions involving "temperature, cleanliness, relative humidity, odors, noise, flavors, light and others that depart from the optimum or desirable ones." Bok's scheme effectively left the sex-segregation job system in Bristol intact, while guaranteeing that women and men would have equal opportunity to bid for jobs based on seniority and competence. His agreement gave bidding preference to those workers applying to jobs within their "class."[28]

The EEOC conciliation agreement in 1968 between Local 1022 in Zion, Illinois, Warwick Electronics, and women complainants was considerably more blatant in relegating men and women to specific jobs. Workers in Zion toiled under an "HML" classification plan, which was similar to the packinghouse industry's ABC system. The text of the conciliation agreement was not subtle in its message: while employer and local union officers promised that "jobs or job training . . . shall be made on an individual basis without regard to . . . sex," they exempted specific jobs (i.e., matron, janitor, general maintenance, operator/set-up and repair) from this pledge on the grounds that these positions required either men or women only and thus fell under Title VII "bona fide occupational qualification" (BFOQ) provision. The remaining positions were designated as

"Heavy," "Medium," or "Light"; essentially, the first and last categories were updated "men's" and "women's" job lists, while "medium" positions came from both classifications. Employees could bid "down" on jobs (i.e., move from an "M" to an "L" job) with relative ease, but upgrading was more difficult. Besides facing a thicket of paper work, workers with such ambitions confronted the potentially insurmountable challenge of being responsible for all jobs within that classification: "It is understood . . . that once an employee is placed and qualifies on any job classification, the employee is required to be able to perform, and if required by the Company, he shall perform all functions of that classification [on] any job within that classification consistent with the terms of the collective bargaining agreement in effect between the Company and the Union."[29]

In addition to these requirements, the "HML" plan's authors placed further restrictions on employment mobility. Citing Illinois hours laws and the company's need to maintain acceptable profit margins, they insisted that many jobs have a minimum percentage (and some times a maximum percentage) of male workers. At least 50 percent and no more than 75 percent of the "operator, shipping, truck" positions, for example, were to be filled by men; 70 percent but no more than 90 percent of the "machine operator, heavy" positions ,were to be filled by men, while the "solderer" job need not be held by any men.[30]

Because union and EEOC records are incomplete, it is difficult to know how women fared under these transparent attempts to maintain sex-segregated worksites. In at least one case, a Local 1022 woman complained of seniority violations and the chief steward's unwillingness to advocate on her behalf two years after the conciliation agreement was implemented.[31] Some IUE women did not support gender equality measures because they threatened their job security, however limited it might be. Local 1081 women in DeKalb, Illinois, protested to union leaders that women were assigned jobs "normally [considered] men's work, and is to [sic] heavy for them to perform," only to have GE management respond that Title VII required no distinctions between men and women in job assignments.[32] One Dayton woman with twenty-one years' seniority in the plant was distraught to discover that she had been put on the assembly line, "which I think is a job for the male employees," while younger women did "bench work." "I have filed grievances on this, but it seems that our local officers are not interested in older employees," she wrote to IUE leader Mary Callahan in 1966.[33] Few IUE women appear to have defended the older sex-segregated industrial relations system outright. It is not surprising that many IUE women opposed equal employment opportunity policy, however, given the "lighter," more-automated nature of their work and their overriding need to maintain a relatively high-paying union job as the American labor movement began to decline.

The international leadership's handling of sex discrimination complaints in the period between Title VII's passage and the establishment of the union's compliance program in 1973 could be characterized as uncertain and lacking focus rather than as overtly hostile to complainants' charges. Official union policy held that protective laws for women workers might need to be reformed but generally served a good purpose. To this end, union head Paul Jennings could hardly side with those filing charges, especially when their complaints disrupted the usual practice of conducting private grievance procedures. Jennings underestimated the damage that union liability in these cases could have on the financial health and morale of the IUE. When Delores Fickert wrote the union head in late 1965, angrily telling him that if he supported the local in its treatment of women workers requesting overtime, "then I don't know what our union stands for anymore," Jennings responded with near indifference, telling her the matter was best handled at the district and local levels.[34] When another woman contacted Jennings with a similar complaint, he refused to meet with her, suggesting that she "make full use of the formal Grievance Procedure incorporated in your collective bargaining agreement."[35] Such responses indicate that IUE officers were not energized in the mid-1960s to do battle on behalf of gender equality.

Nevertheless, union leaders had to address women's concerns if for no other reason than that women made up 35 percent of the IUE's total membership.[36] "Our industry employs a large percentage of women workers," James Carey noted in 1964. "When their standards are improved, those for the entire industry are improved—so everyone benefits. . . . Their gains are beneficial to all."[37] The author of the union's 1972 *Officers' Report* put it in even more forthright terms: "Even if the IUE were not moved by injustice to the victims of race and sex discrimination, a rational attempt to protect the wage standards of our male members would require that IUE mount an attack on race and sex discrimination."[38]

As they pondered the conundrum of protectionism or equality, IEB members and negotiators pursued their longtime goal of pay equity. Since the 1930s, male electrical workers had worried that they would be replaced by women who worked in lower-paying and similar if not identical jobs. The United Electrical Workers filed the first pay equity case with the War Labor Board near the end of World War II.[39] Thereafter, the IUE campaigned vigorously for passage of what became the Equal Pay Act of 1963. Although disappointed with its narrow coverage of "equal work," IUE members bargaining with employers continued to propose methods for "upgrading" women's rates. "The problem is when you have a washroom attendant paid the same as common labor and then you put a woman on the job and call it a matron job and pay a lower rate," Local 301 president and union negotiator Leo Jandreau lectured GE representatives in 1969. "You can't justify this and it shows your bankrupt attitude on this."[40] Unionists' proposals for a national wage structure, full automatic progression of women's rates, and a firm practice whereby no job rate would be less than the rate paid to a common laborer were rejected by employers through the early 1970s.[41]

Union demands in other areas of specific interest to women met with disappointing results, as well. IUE negotiators had their most success in securing disability benefits arising from pregnancy. In 1960 they persuaded GE to raise the coverage amounts for pregnant workers, and management agreed to treat pregnancy as a disability. IUE representatives, however, were unsuccessful in obtaining sickness and accident benefits for members disabled by complications of pregnancy or childbirth.[42] In the more costly and far-reaching areas of equality, unionists made few advances. During both 1966 and 1969 negotiations, GE refused to discuss placing guarantees for equal employment in all labor agreements. "Reference to Title VII doesn't belong in the contract any more than referring to the constitution belongs in the contract," the company spokesperson informed the IUE team in 1969.[43] Trying to increase their strength in relation to that of electrical manufacturers, union leaders spent considerable time attempting to win plantwide seniority, job bidding, and procedures for posting available positions in national contracts. While auto, steel, rubber, and coal international unionists enjoyed national contracts, the IUE leadership obtained labor agreements that left key issues such as wage rates and seniority levels to local supplemental agreements. By eliminating discrimination, unionists hoped to enhance the power of the IEB: "The thrusts of the IUE's proposals," counsel Winn Newman explained, "was to put into the National Agreement minimum protections based on plantwide seniority which would be implemented at the local level, rather than leave this important aspect of job security exclusively to local negotiations." Here, too, the union was only partially successful: GE agreed finally in 1973 that, while posting procedures would still be decided by union and employer representatives, both the international union office and top company officials would have veto power over these supplemental agreements.[44] As the union limped through the early 1970s it increasingly turned away from the negotiating table and toward the EEOC and courts in order to gain members' demands.

Through their legal actions at the local level and their growing organizational strength at the international level, IUE women played a significant part in bringing the union to endorse the principle of gender equality. As they had for the United Automobile Workers (UAW), the international's women's conferences served as a platform for expressing growing discontent over gender inequality and for discussions of Title VII–related issues affecting the whole labor movement. In the mid-1960s, union leaders renamed the Department of Civil Rights the

Social Action Department (SAD). They enlarged its responsibilities to reflect the wide range of social programs of concern to the union besides those of support for racial equality (African Americans made up no more than 5 percent of their membership). The new department's jurisdiction included "women's" issues, so SAD directors William Gary and Gloria Johnson sponsored regular sessions for women workers at their annual meetings. At their 1966 Conference on Civil Rights for All People through Community Action, for example, conveners held a workshop on women in industry that included presentations on women's rights under the Equal Pay Act of 1963 and Title VII. Following an IEB proposal that a National Women's Conference be held every second year, SAD members gathered to consider "The Status of the IUE Woman, Her Responsibilities, Contributions, and Goals." Over two hundred women attended the meeting; they heard speakers representing the IUE, other unions, the EEOC, and the U.S. Department of Labor. In this same period, Districts 1 and 3, representing workers from the southeastern and Middle Atlantic states, as well as the IUE's Canadian district held their own women's conferences. With the formal establishment of a women's department in the SAD in 1972, representatives from districts, industry conference boards, and the head of women's activities, Gloria Johnson, intensified their efforts to create women's councils in every district and local.[45]

The resolutions coming out of these meetings in the period 1965–72 reflect increasing support for gender equality. Women participating in the 1967 meeting echoed convention delegates' resolution calling on the IUE's IEB to "examine state protective laws in an effort to determine whether or not such laws are protective or discriminate." Moreover, they went even further than the general body and all but rejected protectionism by demanding that "job discrimination based on the sex or race of the worker should be completely abolished, and . . . women should have access to all jobs and be given that [sic] same promotional opportunities as men, providing they are capable of doing the job." Although they stopped short of calling for an end to protective laws, the women asked that the union's legal department study the meaning of a recent decision in which the courts for the first time ruled that Title VII contravened state protective laws.[46]

Rank-and-file women in some IUE locals enjoyed a friendly and supportive environment in which to formulate their demands for gender equality. In many locals women held union office. In 1966, 562 women held office, 18 of them serving as local presidents; the next year the number of office holders jumped to 840 and by the decade's end it rose again to 1,467. In the absence of complete data on the union (e.g., the total number of offices available), these numbers are little more than impressionistic, but they do indicate women's overall presence and growing influence in the electrical union.[47] Women workers expressed their demands in other ways as well. When management at the Bacharach Instrument Company in Pittsburgh refused to improve the wage levels of those working in traditional "women's" jobs, for example, women "put on a strong battle" at a Local 630 meeting and defeated the company's proposed labor agreement. Subsequently, the women got the union to file charges with the EEOC and a lawsuit based on the Equal Pay Act of 1963 in order to protest this unfair treatment.[48]

Even before the international instituted its compliance program in 1973, local union leaders across the country filed sex discrimination charges on behalf of women members. In 1967 the IUE local in Louisville, Kentucky, successfully demonstrated to the EEOC that the NOPCO Chemical Company discriminated against women by never having more than three women on its payroll of forty workers at any one time. Local 782 officers in Tyler, Texas, prevailed in a challenge to GE's practice of refusing to hire anyone less than 5' 7" tall, a policy that unfairly and unnecessarily eliminated the majority of women and Mexican-American applicants. Local 509 officers were plaintiffs in a case argued before the New York Human Rights Division in the early 1970s that resulted in a ruling directing General Motors to pay disability and accident benefits for all periods of a woman's absence due to pregnancy. Sometimes unionists went to court to defend men's rights, as in 1969 when IUE Local 425 filed EEOC charges and a class action suit against Sperry Rand, asking that the company cease its discriminatory practice against male employees by setting their retirement age higher than that of women. Unlike the United Packinghouse Workers, IUE locals did not fare better on "women's issues" in one specific geographical region or industrial sector. Just as in cases where the IUE local faced women's complaints of unequal treatment, there is no discernible pattern to the aggressive actions of electrical workers' locals to battle sex discrimination.[49]

Union leaders began to file sex-based wage discrimination complaints during this period. This was a litigation field that would increasingly occupy members of the legal department in the 1970s. Mansfield, Ohio, unionists charged Westinghouse with paying women twelve cents an hour less than men working on substantially the same assembly jobs. When the case closed in 1977, the court ordered the employer to increase the pay scale for nine jobs held mostly by women and to pay workers $166,000 in back wages. A similar ruling came from the GE Fort Wayne, Indiana, plant where the union obtained $350,000 in back pay and $1 million annually in future "upgrading" of pay for some two thousand employees at the plant working in "women's" jobs.[50]

There continued to be conflict between men and women, however, as IUE leaders moved toward endorsing gender equality over protective laws. While IUE representatives spoke against the ERA during 1970 congressional hearings, for example, several women electrical unionists appeared with workers from the UAW, Meatcutters, and Government Employees unions at a protest press conference reported in the *New York Times*.[51] The change in official policy on the ERA came in June 1972 when a convention resolutions committee observed that the influx of large numbers of women into low-paying jobs continued "by custom and by the law where hoary legal precedents and outdated statutes place women at an economic disadvantage." Taking notice of the EEOC's and courts' negative rulings on protective laws, they observed that "the basis upon which many labor unions relied, in formerly opposing the Equal Rights Amendment, no longer exists." Delegates asked the IEB to "re-examine" its historical opposition to the ERA,[52] which it did in December 1972 by backing the ERA for the first time.[53]

The IUE'S Model Title VII Compliance Program

The prospects for achieving gender equality improved in the IUE in 1972 with the arrival of general counsel Winn Newman, who brought with him a new approach to dealing with Title VII. Instead of reacting in a piecemeal fashion to government mandates, the union would, in the words of Newman, "pursue . . . a militant program of ferreting out all discrimination and utilizing all available orderly legal procedures to correct the discrimination found." By embracing the requirements of federal law, making a "genuine good faith effort" to fight unfair treatment, and eliminating union liability, international leaders intended to fuse EEOC guidelines with traditional grievance practices.[54] Their plan, the IUE's "Title VII Compliance Program," required union locals to eliminate discrimination in contracts. Just as important, it asked rank-and-file members to work with the union in processing complaints and to go through established arbitration procedures before seeking government relief from discrimination. "We were saying that going outside the IUE is not the first step, it's the last step," Gloria Johnson remarked years later.[55] By all accounts the scheme was successful: as mentioned in chapter 4, IUE leaders had filed more than five hundred charges of sex and race discrimination with the EEOC and over fifty lawsuits that named the union or its locals as plaintiffs against employers by 1981. Equally impressive was the near disappearance of cases with the IUE as defendant. After 1973 the IUE paid out practically no money in damages for discrimination.[56]

The two key figures in the implementation of the electrical union's program were its general counsel, Winn Newman, and an associate counsel, Ruth Weyand. Newman, a University of Wisconsin law school graduate, worked at the IUE briefly in the early 1960s and returned to head the legal department in 1972 when general counsel Irving Abramson retired.[57] Newman was responsible for the over-all development of the IUE's antidiscrimination policy. "Every program or policy has to have a very strong advocate," Gloria Johnson observed, "and Winn Newman 'birthed' this program. . . . He was very close to it. He played a strong role in the filing of charges and going to court and winning big bucks for our people."[58] Unlike the cautious heads of union legal departments during the period, who were often hostile to rank-and-file members using equal employment opportunity laws, Newman embraced such measures and moved to bring the IUE into alignment with the new mandates for equality.

Drawing from his work on the EEOC staff in the mid-1960s, Newman brought a valuable awareness of federal equal employment opportunity policy to his job at the IUE. As the commission struggled to decrease its sizable complaint back-log and develop effective guidelines, Newman pushed the EEOC to process complaints more quickly by providing defendant unions and employers with copies of charges immediately after they arrived at the agency. This would give respondents an opportunity to answer to investigators in writing on the complaints' merits. Thereafter, EEOC representatives, he suggested, should be able to seek withdrawal of unmerited charges and settle cases in the field without having to render formal decisions. Commission officials less sympathetic to the labor movement rejected Newman's recommendation on the grounds that releasing a complainant's name before a formal investigation might result in harassment of workers.[59]

The IUE counsel understood the potential liability that unions faced from the tougher EEOC guidelines and judicial rulings that appeared by the early 1970s. Such measures left labor organizations, with employers, responsible not only for obvious and direct discriminatory practices, but also for being a party to contracts and behavior that had an unequal, "disparate impact" on workers. In *Griggs v. Duke Power* (1971), for example, the Supreme Court found that supposedly neutral employment policies and practices (in this case, requiring a high school diploma and job testing) could be in violation of Title VII on the grounds of its disparate impact on women and minorities.[60] Newman followed these court decisions closely. Accordingly, he told delegates at the union's 1972 convention that "we are running into court decisions . . . which make it clear that we need to do a couple of things that we may not now be doing."[61]

The following year Newman introduced his sweeping compliance program. In designing it he considered Title VII as "general[ly] consistent with trade union principles" because it provided labor groups with a "valuable tool . . . to obtain what they were not able to get at the bargaining table through traditional means."[62] His plan was thorough and systematic; it called for local unions, assisted by field staff and district officers, to conduct midcontract reviews of labor agreements and work practices. The legal department helped in this endeavor by providing locals with a checklist of the most obvious forms of discrimination. The international would request concurrently from employers data on the sex, race, and national origin of new employees and workers applying for jobs within plants. If local officers detected a violation of equal employment law, they then were to request a meeting with management to bargain for its elimination using the international office's suggested model contract language; employers not providing requested data, or those not meeting demands to make necessary changes to work agreements, faced EEOC charges or vigorous prosecution of lawsuits under Title VII and the Equal Pay Act of 1963.[63]

Newman's efforts lent IUE negotiators an extra measure of legitimacy as they continued their efforts at the bargaining table to gain equality guarantees. Beginning with national contract negotiations in 1973, the union used employment data to push for better treatment of pregnant workers, plantwide seniority, and job posting for all available jobs. In their discussions with GE that year, union negotiators presented overwhelming evidence that entry-level pay rates for women were approximately 75 cents an hour less than those for men; men held most upper-level jobs, as well. Union leaders were able to gain increased pay for those working in traditionally "women's" positions, but GE balked at mandatory job-posting procedures for plants. Instead, the company agreed to meet with IUE representatives on a plant-by-plant basis to negotiate local settlements on the issue. Unionists accepted this compromise under protest but made clear their intention to pursue the matter through the EEOC or courts. By 1976 they had secured some job-posting agreements with GE, covering 92 percent of their members working in GE facilities.[64]

The success of this top-down program lay in getting locals to follow international directives. In this regard, the union leadership did well. Unlike the packinghouse workers union, the IUE international had considerable control over local unions. Local leaders collected dues and signed supplemental work agreements, but the union's constitution had become progressively more restrictive in the area of local autonomy since the 1950s. In the late 1950s, members gave the international new powers to place an administrator in charge of a local when it was "involved in a controversy which adversely affects the welfare of its membership, in a manner which threatens the local's existence."[65] International officers made use of this clause. They placed Local 1022 in Zion, Illinois, in trusteeship in 1972, for example, for refusing to forward the international's share of dues and for its local leaders' financial mismanagement of funds. When Local 717 went on strike in 1972 without first giving notice to the IUE president, as the constitution required, the international's secretary-treasurer threatened to withhold strike benefit payments.[66]

Union officers usually had only to bring informal pressure to bear on locals that were recalcitrant about implementing the compliance scheme. Most times, the threat of financial liability proved effective. "As you know, we have many situations in which local unions resist our recommendations—we hear that the membership won't stand for it, will strike, disaffiliate, revolt, etc.," Newman reported to Jennings in 1975. "It continues to amaze me how pliant the local leadership and membership become after they are sued and are really made to understand that the International policy is in their best interests."[67] Newman's influence over local employment practices was strengthened considerably in the late 1970s when the National Labor Relations Board ruled that electrical manufacturers must provide requested data on the race and sex of job applicants as well as on hiring, promotion, and wage rates to the Washington office directly, since, as Newman put it, the requests "related in no small measure to matters of national bargaining, the IUE Conference Board, as distinguished from the local union."[68]

Despite this increased flow of power to the international office, IUE staff members in the legal and social action departments faced immediate internal and external obstacles to eradicating gender inequality. During the compliance program's early years, local and district leaders were delinquent in forwarding employment information to union headquarters, even in the face of a series of reminders sent to them from the Washington office. Shortly after the call went out for local-by-local progress reports on antidiscrimination measures, Paul Jennings complained to district leaders that the responses were "slow" in arriving and were "insufficiently detailed."[69] Following a 1974 directive to district presidents to assign a staff member to the compliance program, Winn Newman grumbled that many reports were still overdue. "IUE is operating under a serious threat of heavy liability," he warned Jennings and secretary-treasurer Dave Fitzmaurice.[70] Six months later Newman noted that 109 locals had not yet submitted reports, and that in one case, a union representative erroneously advised the international that an employer had refused to supply information on employment matters when, in fact, it had. The union filed a charge against the company, which, Newman pointed out, "caused a waste of the Board's time as well as ours, embarrassment and damage to the Union."[71]

The reporting problem seemed to be bureaucratic in nature, revealing indirect resistance to fighting discrimination rather than an overt widespread hostility to the Title VII compliance scheme. By delaying the filing of requested information or engaging in sloppy reporting, local and district union leaders placed a low priority on implementing the plan in its early years. Such lackluster commitment to the scheme was damaging to the union's financial health, not to mention women's economic status. When a woman worker from Local 826 at Otis Elevator wrote to the union to tell of discriminatory conditions and received a form letter response advising her to pursue the grievance through normal local union procedures, Newman fretted that "members who receive such stock response to their complaints may determine that their best recourse is to file complaints with the EEOC against both the company and the union rather than to seek aid from the union. . . . It is important that we resolve the sex discrimination issue as soon as possible so that it will not be joined in the suit." Newman recommended to international officers that Title VII–based complaints be referred automatically to the legal or social action department.[72]

In addition to these concerns, Newman had to contend with IUE president Paul Jennings's attempt to cut the legal department's budget, thus threatening the effectiveness of the compliance program. When Jennings discussed reducing the organization's in-house legal staff in 1975, Newman bristled, warning Jennings that this would lead to "considerable delay" in processing Title VII–related correspondence.[73] He told the union head that such a reduction would lessen the time the department had to study contracts to find discriminatory clauses, thus undercutting the whole program. Newman hinted that Jennings was acting unconstitutionally; Newman did not believe, he wrote the president, that "local constitution review can be discontinued without convention action." Newman urged Jennings to consider the compliance program as a wise investment:

> In addition to the fact that it continues to provide the least costly method of providing the greatest benefits to ⅓ of our members [i.e., women] . . . our survey of other unions' Title VII expenditures for legal services and back pay shows that the program has saved IUE money far exceeding its pxpenditures [sic]. Although the extent of discrimination is as great or greater in the electrical industry than in any other industry, IUE has no money for settlements, thus indicating that we have been on the right track. UAW has recently joined the growing number of unions who have adopted the IUE program.[74]

The choice, Newman said in a report to the IEB, was not "whether we wish to do the right thing, but rather, whether we prefer to engage in a preventive action or far more costly defensive action."[75] While Jennings did not relent on his order to lay off one department lawyer, he did allow for the transfer of some of the compliance program's workload to the social action department as well as for the retention of outside counsel to handle more cases. His solution did not please Newman, but neither did it gut the compliance program.[76]

Newman's complaints about the poor record of district and local reporting tapered off after 1975 due to the international's success in cajoling union officers to comply with policy. The general counsel commended IEB members in August 1975 for deciding to "bring about compliance . . . once and for all and to do it on an immediate crash basis program."[77] While it is unclear to what specific "crash" program Newman was referring, top IUE officers moved decisively that year to settle cases against the union. Finding that Local 502 in St. Mary's, Pennsylvania—characterized as "perhaps one of the worst in our Union"—was liable for allowing unequal pay, separate seniority, and department seniority to exist, Newman suggested that Jennings and Fitzmaurice take strong action, "with an eye towards scheduling a high level meeting at the earliest possible date . . . [aimed at] *directing* that the Local comply with IUE policy." He proposed that the union agree to have an approved arbitrator rewrite the local's work agreement so that it meet Title VII requirements.[78]

In most of the cases in which plaintiffs named the IUE as a party to practicing discrimination, union representatives were able to convince the women, EEOC, and courts to allow the labor organization to realign its position from that of defendant to plaintiff.[79] In the first three years of the IUE's compliance program, however, EEOC members frequently attempted to group the union with employers as a matter of course when they assisted individuals or when they leveled their own charges. Unlike the complaints filed in the 1960s and the smaller number in the 1970s where investigators uncovered IUE locals' guilt in practicing discrimination, commissioners in these cases named the union as liable without examining closely the multiple ways their compliance scheme functioned to fight inequality.

IUE leaders were genuinely surprised when the EEOC, in launching a major discrimination case against four large electrical manufacturers in 1973, held the IUE and other labor organizations responsible as well. They did this, Newman pointed out to the EEOC's general counsel, Abner Sibal, in 1976, "without making any attempt to determine the role of the IUE or any of the other large labor organizations named as respondents." Instead, he fumed, "all were lumped together and charged." Newman acknowledged that IUE negotiators had signed discriminatory work agreements with employers but held that they did so under protest and subsequently pursued legal action to protest the unfair contract. He argued to Sibal that, "except for calling a strike when the IUE's most strenuous bargaining efforts were unsuccessful," the leadership has acted with maximum effort to end discrimination. A work stoppage over discrimination, he suggested to Sibal, was not required nor was there any reason to believe it would be successful.[80] This last issue points to the possibilities and limitations inherent in contemporary industrial relations in the United States. Why didn't the IUE—

or any other union—consider calling a strike in opposition to sex discrimination? In the masculine-defined world of management-union conflict, "women's issues" remained at the margins, something to be discussed, introduced into collective bargaining talks, and even brought to the courtroom, but never worthy of a work stoppage.

The government filed charges against the electrical union not because it believed that the IUE was specifically guilty of discrimination but rather because it suspected that organized labor contributed to workplace inequality. This perception stemmed largely from the generally poor relations between the EEOC commissioners and organized labor in the first half of the 1970s. Many government officers did not believe that labor unions acted in their membership's best interest or that established collective bargaining practices helped erase discrimination in a fundamental way. Unlike the NLRB, whose members were generally sympathetic to labor, EEOC members tended to be younger and had less of a connection to unions. They were not predisposed to see things in the same manner as union leaders. Some EEOC members' own experiences led them to this general outlook. Seeking to investigate discrimination charges filed against the International Brotherhood of Electrical Workers in August 1973, for example, the EEOC's deputy chief of national programs, David Copus, sought assistance repeatedly from union officers and the AFL-CIO's Department of Civil Rights representatives. Federationists were "of absolutely no help," recalled Copus. "They did not even acknowledge receipt of the Commission's letter."[81] For their part, labor leaders became frustrated with the commission's immense backlog of complaints, EEOC members' inability (and refusal at times) to forward copies of charges to the federation and international union offices so they could attempt conciliation, and its outright hostility to unions, based on political and class differences. "Why does the EEOC bypass the civil rights machinery . . . unions have created to make sure unions do all they can to ensure justice in the workplace?" the AFL-CIO's William Pollard grumbled publicly in 1972. "Is it any wonder that we suspect union-busting is involved?"[82]

Newman held that the IUE's Title VII program assisted in the enforcement of equal employment laws. He explained continuing inequality as a result of initial hiring and job assignment, over which the union had no ultimate control or legal responsibility. Calling it the "linchpin of intraplant wage inequalities," Newman told EEOC commissioners in 1980 that "what happens to the newly hired employee is our concern from the minute that they report for work in the job to which they are assigned." Nevertheless, the IUE pressed for hiring and job assignment data from employers for the "very therapeutic" effect it had on pressuring employers to improve their employment record.[83] To continue to charge the union with discrimination, Newman said, would injure women workers by draining union treasuries. "The imposition of monetary liability on IUE would require that its female and minority members either pay increased union dues to meet that liability or suffer a reduction in the services available to them from the union."[84] In short, Newman argued that the interests of union officers and women members were the same.

Newman succeeded in persuading the commission that equal employment opportunity law and union practices could be inextricably linked to satisfy both the unionists' demands for collective bargaining and the federal government's requirement that Title VII be enforced. With the IUE's proven litigation efforts, the arrival of the more labor-sympathetic Eleanor Holmes Norton as chair of the EEOC in 1977, and commissioners' subsequent adoption of its "Resolution on Title VII and Collective Bargaining," the union no longer worried that they would be named automatically as defendants in equal employment opportunity cases.[85]

The filing of charges and lawsuits—not contract negotiations and grievance bearings—was the most effective tool in the electrical union's antidiscriminatory arsenal. Newman told those gathered at an EEOC hearing in 1980 of his success: "I think the relief we have gotten has come about virtually entirely as a result of either the filing of charges, litigation or the threat of litigation. This is not to say that we have not settled a great many things as a result of filing grievances, but it is always with the idea that if we don't settle, there will be a charge or a lawsuit that follows."[86] When they went to court, union leaders had a coordinated strategy to maximize the scope of the ruling and increase the judgment amount. In order to accomplish this, Newman asked local officers to forward all discrimination information to the international's legal department; they were not to settle charges for small monetary amounts or to drop charges.[87] Newman, in turn, gave "substantial publicity" to pay equity suits, as a way of "stimulat[ing] additional complaints of discrimination."[88]

Legal department members were most successful in fighting pregnancy discrimination. After years of extracting only partial gains at the bargaining table for pregnant workers, unionists filed suits against GE, Westinghouse, and General Motors. They did so even before the EEOC mandated in 1972 that pregnancy disabilities were to be treated by employers as standard disabilities.[89] In their most widely publicized case, *Gilbert v. General Electric,* union leaders won district court and court of appeals judgments before the U.S. Supreme Court reversed its decision in 1976. The justices maintained that "an exclusion of pregnancy from a disability-benefits plan providing general coverage is not a gender-based discrimination."[90] IUE members were livid. Upon the urging of labor, feminist, and civil rights groups, congressional members decried the *Gilbert* decision as well and began crafting legislation to modify Title VII in addressing this area of employment discrimination. In 1978, Congress passed the Pregnancy Discrimination Act, which stated that employers cannot treat pregnancy more or less favorably than other worker disabilities.[91]

Pay equity remained a key concern to IUE members through the 1970s. Wage data indicated that startling inequity still remained between men and women. Statistics revealed, for example, that 90.2 percent of women electrical workers' pay was below the common rate of pay in Newark, Ohio, but only 4.4 percent of men's pay had this same low rate; in Syracuse, New York, 75.4 percent of women fell into the same category while only 4.4 percent of men shared this fate.[92] "We . . . have still existing serious problems around rate discrimination," Winn Newman revealed to convention delegates in 1972. "I mean here, where women not only do the same jobs as men, but where women do jobs that are substantially equivalent to that of the men's jobs, or where women are deprived of the job."[93]

As their predecessors had done thirty years earlier with the War Labor Board, IUE members resorted to judicial and administrative bodies to seek relief from pay inequity. In the 1970s their protest against such treatment in their own industry struck a responsive chord with women in other employment sectors, giving rise to the comparable-worth pay movement. "The roots of the contemporary movement for pay equity can be found in the IUE's efforts since 1969 to litigate structural wage inequities," it was observed in a study from the mid-1980s.[94] Workers in industrial, service, and clerical unions as well as middle-class professional women embraced comparable worth as a response to the deep, structural inequality in workplace practices and the increasing feminization of poverty despite the appearance of federal guarantees of equal employment opportunity.

Newman and Ruth Weyand initiated a number of pay equity cases over the course of the decade, with promising results. In 1973 they filed an EEOC charge alleging wage structure bias and discrimination against women and minorities at over thirty Westinghouse locations. Two years later they began four lawsuits challenging the wages paid to woman workers at factories in Fairmont, West Virginia; Buffalo, New York; Bloomfield, New Jersey; and Trenton, New Jersey. Under the threat of similar action GE managers at their Youngstown, Ohio, facility agreed to increase the rates of pay for twenty-one jobs in a total of twenty-five labor grades.[95]

Working-Class Feminism in the IUE, 1975–80

The union's Title VII compliance program—created in response to women workers' demands for equality—further legitimized the commitment of activists within the union to working-class feminism. By publicizing discrimination and taking aggressive action against unfair treatment of unionists on the bases of sex and race, international leaders sent a clear message to local members that the IUE would use union resources to back campaigns for equality. "The support of union officers, the executive board, and legal staff in countering sex and race discrimination made a big difference in the IUE," Gloria Johnson commented two decades after the implementation of the Title VII compliance program. "It meant financial support, it meant strong resolutions, strong affirmative action programs, it meant implementation of strong anti-discrimination policy."[96] The willingness of women to seek legal redress was clearly a decisive factor in the matter. One scholar writing in the 1970s from a decidedly critical stance grudgingly noted that the IUE international's role was "on balance" a "positive one" in pursuing equality, but credited this in large measure to "threatened litigation by EEOC as well as to a substantial female constituency in its ranks."[97] At the time of the program's establishment in the early 1970s, electrical unionists established a women's department within the SAD. Its functions included developing educational materials, holding training sessions and conferences, representing the IUE at non-IUE events, and working with the legal department in carrying out the organization's affirmative action program. By the middle of the decade most districts and some regional bodies had held SAD conferences and local unions were appointing their own representatives to the women's department.[98]

Developing and sustaining a viable program to promote gender equality was challenging work even within the relatively progressive IUE. It was easiest at the international level where leaders backed such efforts with money and newspaper coverage. The IEB, for example, signed the union as a supporter of the ERA Ratification Council, a loosely based coalition of women activists from professional, religious, educational, and labor groups, and contributed money to ERAmerica, an organization constituted along similar lines. Gloria Johnson was the IUE's representative on the Labor Committee for ERA. In addition, the IUE leadership supported the designation of an International Women's Year in 1976; the social action department's William Gary recommended to president Jennings that the union publish a special pamphlet to commemorate the event.[99] "Not only would such a publication be fitting and proper for the women in the IUE, but I feel that it could also be used as an effective organizing tool what with the emphasis being placed on the hiring of women and minorities," Gary told Jennings.[100] By the mid-1970s few unions could match the IUE's commitment to gender equality.

As is clear from the uneven record of local union compliance with Title VII, the cause of gender equality fared less well across IUE locals. In 1974, for example, one Local 717 woman in Warren, Ohio, asked Paul Jennings to add an assembly of local women representatives to meet at international and district social action department gatherings. This would, she wrote, "help to increase the number of IUE women in active union roles, something the IUE and local unions have not as yet attained."[101] Women in this Ohio local joined with men sympathetic to their underrepresentation in leadership and organized a "Female Study Group" to examine labor contracts, industrial relations, and the union's history in general. Despite such promising signs, much work still needed to be done. They reported to Jennings that, although women made up 60 percent of the 14,000-member local, only 6 percent of the 129 elected officers were women. "There seems in our elected officials a great deal of the men holding office [that] are not interested in a balance of power between the sexes," rank-and-file member Charlotte Ingalls informed Jennings. She continued: "You may feel that my attitudes are naive but I feel there is a great need for a new pure idealism and a need for new blood to be infused into the union structure. . . . I will continue with the moral support of my sisters to further the cause of good unionism at all cost[,] personal or otherwise."[102] Such pressure for locals to embrace equality on a scale commensurate with that of the international resulted in 1977 in a constitutional amendment requiring all locals to have social action chairpersons.[103]

Incongruencies between union policy and implementation were not unique to the IUE. The equally progressive United Electrical Workers' "militant rhetoric [was] rarely matched by its concrete practice," as one former UE member in the Westinghouse local in Hamilton, Ontario, put it. He reported that, when women transferred to "men's" jobs in the mid-1970s, men "refused to show them the jobs or hassled them in other ways." The passing of the Ontario Human Rights Code in 1970—the province's counterpart to Title VII—and the UE's progressive record "mask[ed]" a male resistance within the unions and on the shop floor that . . . [didn't] surface publicly."[104]

Like most working-class feminists of the period, IUE activists rejected middle-class women's approach to feminism as much as they decried intransigent male unionists. "There was agreement that women's organizations for the most part were not addressing issues of concern to working women," Gloria Johnson recalled in a 1993 interview.[105] Unionists charged that groups such as the National Organization for Women (NOW) did not expend much energy on economic issues that concerned lower-paid working women; when they did—for example, advocating strong EEOC enforcement—they ignored the valuable role labor played by educating its members on equality and by offering the grievance as a tool to fighting discrimination. Johnson spoke in 1974 of the need to avoid forming a "feminist union" along NOW lines: "We already have the structure to make change. . . . If there are women who feel unions are not doing enough then it points up the need for them to become more involved and initiate change. . . . If unions don't do the right thing, these women can first pursue their grievance procedure and if there is some problem there, then cases can be filed."[106] Labor unions, Johnson and her peers believed, were part of the solution to inequality, not its cause.

Electrical worker unionists were early and influential supporters of the Coalition of Labor Union Women (CLUW). Gloria Johnson was on the agenda committee for CLUW's founding convention held in 1974 and sat on its executive board with Mary Callahan. At the state level, IUE women served as CLUW conveners in New York, New Jersey, West Virginia, Kentucky, and Minnesota. Representatives from the international office participated in the feminist group's activities, as well. In 1975, for example, assistant general counsel Carol Jeffries spoke at a CLUW-sponsored sex discrimination workshop. The union's Winn Newman advised CLUW on legal matters. CLUW members adopted for use a "Program to Implement the CLUW Resolution on Discrimination in Employment," modeled after the IUE's compliance program. As a sign of how careful they were not to interfere with internal union policy and practices, CLUW officers recommended their compliance plan to international unions but did not set up their own separate program that would involve CLUW chapters in implementing the plan at the local level.[107]

By 1980 IUE activists could look with pride to their efforts for gender equality. "Winn [Newman] has done landmark work through your Union on equal pay for comparable worth, on pregnancy disability, and so many other things that benefit working women," CLUW president Joyce Miller told IUE convention delegates that year. "I think that your Union . . . has done landmark work on legislation and stands second to no other union in the AFL-CIO."[108] Ruth Weyand became the EEOC's Equal Pay Act counsel in the late 1970s, supervising pay equity litigation by the twenty-three agency district offices across the country. She died in 1986.[109] Newman left the IUE in the early 1980s but continued to advocate on behalf of comparable worth as counsel for the American Federation of State, County, and Municipal Employees and other organizations until his death in 1994. "He really was a revolutionary," said Judith Lichtman, head of the Women's Legal Defense Fund, shortly after he died. "He was willing to use creatively the resources of the trade union movement on behalf of its women members and to provide the leadership, as well as his organizing skills and his legal ability. He was a master at using litigation for social change."[110]

Feminists were still divided throughout the 1970s, however, on how best to achieve equality. NOW activists angered CLUW women with their proposal that union seniority be bypassed during layoffs in order to increase the numbers of underrepresented workers. Mary Callahan spoke for many women unionists who viewed such efforts with unease: "I think those [middle-class] women can't understand that a contract is a benefit to a woman as well as a man. They are of the opinion that you go in and pick certain things that are just for us and you set up a dual [seniority] line . . . just for women and men. . . . Union women don't see it that way. They see it that a union is a union, that's what it is, unity of sexes, of the races, what have you."[111] While this divisive issue threatened to undo the fragile coalition between working-class and middle-class feminists, the battle for pay equity, the ERA, and reproductive rights became a joint project that helped tie activists from both camps to the cause of equality.

Conclusion:
From Equality to Equity

The 1970s were a time of a guarded optimism for women unionists. Long accustomed to being marginalized in the labor movement, women saw their concerns gain prominence as they moved into leadership positions. This transformation came about after three decades of economic, social, and legal changes that gave rise by the early 1970s to support for gender equality. Women's proportion of total union membership climbed to 37 percent in the early 1990s from 17 percent in 1950. As this study has shown, women themselves (assisted by well-placed men) ushered in these changes by challenging labor market segregation and inequality. They worked for the passage of the Equal Pay Act of 1963, filed Title VII–based sex discrimination charges, and lobbied their union officers to endorse the Equal Rights Amendment (ERA). The Coalition of Labor Union Women's (CLUW) membership continued to increase steadily, from around six thousand members in the late 1970s to eighteen thousand members in the mid-1980s. CLUW members tended to be activists, staff members, and office holders within their own international and local unions.[1]

Even while their own unions declined in strength over the decade, industrial union activists, in particular, observed with satisfaction labor leaders taking up the cudgels of working-class feminism. Armed with the social unionist ideal upon which their labor organizations were founded in the 1930s, many of these women worked for political and legal changes to improve working women's status. Their efforts had begun to pay off by the 1970s. "We make gains slowly, but surely," the CLUW's Olga Madar noted confidently in 1975.[2] Significantly, these industrial unionists mobilized on behalf of equality from within the labor movement, embracing the notion that, as Nancy Gabin puts it, unions were "arenas for collective action in the interest of gender equality."[3] Women unionists believed their cause was inextricably linked with that of labor and they were more likely to vote for unionization than were men.[4] "We realized really what the union was doing and how much it means to us," one rank-and-file packinghouse woman said of the period. "We learned by it too . . . we became educated. Before, we took it for granted."[5]

Yet not all was uniform in this progression to equality. In unions such as the United Packinghouse Workers (UPWA), where fierce competition for jobs combined with a male-dominated union resistant to government and international leadership dictates, men threw up procedural and shop-floor barriers to full implementation of Title VII. While women in the International Electrical Workers (IUE) union encountered similar resistance from rank-and-file men, they were able to use their sizable share of the IUE's membership, as well as the top leadership's commitment to gender equality, in order to create an impressive record of support for pay equity, pregnancy benefits, and unified job lists and wage scales for women workers. Women fared the worst in the skilled trades, such as welding and carpentry, where their percentage as a total of these occupations increased not at all between the 1970s and 1990s.[6]

With the massive layoffs during the economic recession in the mid-1970s, the uneasy coalition of working-class feminists and activists in groups dominated by the middle class, such as the National Organization for Women (NOW), threatened to come undone. During the economic downturn, NOW, the Equal Employment Opportunity Commission (EEOC), and other organizations proposed that the traditional collective bargaining guarantee of "last-hired, first-fired" be suspended in order to preserve the recent hiring gains of women and minorities. This plan met with scorn from male union leaders and CLUW members alike. "The problem caused by the recession has kept our department working on the double. The attack on Seniority has been endless," William Pollard of the AFL-CIO Department of Civil Rights reported to his colleagues in December 1975.[7] Rejecting a proposal by EEOC commissioners to use worksharing, reduction of hours, voluntary early retirement, and rotating layoffs instead of the usual seniority principles in determining job retention, the IUE's Winn Newman declared that such a plan would "penalize workers for the discriminatory acts of the employer."[8] Assistant counsel Robert Friedman was more blunt in attacking the plan's proponents: "The eradication of illegal discrimination has to be accomplished within the context of the collective bargaining agreement. . . . EEOC could not care less about the collective bargaining agreement."[9]

CLUW members echoed these sentiments, decrying the commission's scheme as, in Olga Madar's words, "supportive of management's long opposition to seniority systems and a return to the law of the jungle at the workplace."[10] Working-class feminists such as Madar attempted to negotiate between feminism and the gender-neutral goals of social unionism by emphasizing equal treatment of all workers: "I am not about to let the leftists, the corporate managements [*sic*] and the women's organizations destroy the seniority systems. I am for affirmative action and yes, quotas, if necessary; but I think that can be done without injury to a current workforce. . . . The only official CLUW position is a statement saying that 'Brother and Sister workers should not be penalized for the past discrimination of management.'"[11] In a letter to NOW's president, Karen DeCrow, Madar defended her position by drawing on her work experience in the 1940s, when women strove to gain their place in the seniority system. "You may be too young to recall what happened to working women after World War II," she lectured DeCrow. "The seniority systems were violated in both organized and unorganized workplaces and affected both women and older men."[12] Catherine Conroy of the Communications Workers of America spoke for many union women in asserting that "you cannot just stomp on seniority."[13]

The debate over seniority and affirmative action points to the fault lines among union women and between liberal groups in general. At the 1975 CLUW convention, for example, union leaders faced vigorous, but ultimately unsuccessful, opposition from some of their own members who thought Olga Madar "too timid" in challenging male union leaders over women's demands; these dissidents argued for a modification of established seniority practices in order to stave off the firing of recently hired minority men and women and white women workers.[14] If some union women sided with the EEOC position on layoff policy, there were cases in which union women backed organized labor's position against other groups. For example, one African-American woman who belonged to the Amalgamated Clothing Workers in the South said in a 1977 interview: "It was just getting to the place where black people within the unions were getting seniority because those who were white were retiring and we're building up seniority and now we have it over some of the younger whites." She singled out the NAACP in particular for its support of preferential layoffs, reminding her listeners that "seniority is one of the most sacred things we have in our contract."[15]

The various liberal camps averted a damaging break over the issue with the Supreme Court's *Franks v. Bowman Transportation* ruling in 1976. In their decision the justices left intact the traditional seniority system but ordered that measures be taken to provide a "rightful-place" remedy (i.e., retroactive seniority to the date of discrimination) for victims of unequal treatment.[16] A few months after the decision, William Pollard reported to the AFL-CIO's civil rights committee that "our non-discrimination seniority systems are not under the heavy attack we previously experienced." Pollard attributed this cessation of hostilities to the strengthened dialogue with civil rights leaders concerning the labor movement's support for affirmative action, its backing of the Humphrey-Hawkins Full Employment Bill as a way of directing attention to worker security, and the *Franks* decision. Before it was watered down, the Humphrey-Hawkins Bill of 1978 gave a legal guarantee of a job.[17] If any question remained about the seniority system's legal viability, the *Teamsters v. U.S.* decision in 1977 eased unionists' concerns further when the Court ruled that "an otherwise neutral, legitimate seniority system does not become unlawful under Title VII simply because it may perpetuate pre–[Civil Rights] Act discrimination."[18]

Supporters of gender equality bridged many of their other differences as well. The arrival of Eleanor Holmes Norton as chair of the EEOC in 1977 ended the poor relationship unionists had had with the commission since its inception. Labor leaders had been angry with EEOC members for a number of reasons, chief among them the government's formidable backlog of cases, chronic inability and unwillingness to send copies of discrimination charges to union headquarters, and the practice of naming unions along with employers in charges and lawsuits. By the late 1970s they believed this had ended finally. Unionists praised Norton's attempt to process complaints more quickly. In addition, she shared workers' charges with union officers so that they might solve the issue through conciliation, and she ended the policy of routinely naming unions in all charges.[19] "The Commission has gone through 15 years of tremendous internal turmoil," Winn Newman told U.S. senators at a 1981 hearing. "We are at a point now in the Commission where guidelines have been established in most every area, where the basic pattern for enforcing the law is in reasonably good shape. Systems have been established for taking care of the backlog that was so horrible 4 years ago."[20]

CLUW and NOW activists moved closer together in the 1970s on issues previously of concern to only one or the other organization. Their united effort to pass the ERA and to win recognition for comparable worth undoubtedly helped them firm up their ties in other areas. NOW members, for example, came to endorse minimum-wage legislation and National Labor Relations Act reform, two items of key importance to organized labor. For their part, CLUW delegates supported abortion rights at their 1977 convention, a position the AFL-CIO was not willing to take, much to NOW members' chagrin.[21] With women constituting an ever-growing share of the work force, "the labor movement's commitment to women increasingly will be one that redounds to its own benefit," one NOW leader observed during the period. Professional and middle-class women would gain from blue-collar women's battle against inequality for, "as their consciousness and feeling of solidarity is raised, feminist women will be more ready to organize into unions to fight for their rights than other white-collar workers who reject such organizations for ideological reasons."[22] By the decade's end, one scholar noted, "the growing identity of CLUW as part of the women's movement was . . . evident in its alliance with women's organizations on a range of social, political and economic issues."[23]

Even though they overcame these obstacles, feminists faced even greater difficulty in having to respond to continuing inequality. While the most obvious forms of sex discrimination, such as job assignment by sex and separate seniority lists, had been eradicated, the ratio of female-to-male earnings did not rise from the 1950s to the early 1980s.[24] The inability of the law of equality to provide relief was most discouraging to those who had struggled in the first decade of the legal existence of equal employment opportunity. Sonia Pressman, an EEOC counsel and early NOW member, noted: "There were some studies done which were depressing because they showed that where a company had charges filed against it . . . and they conciliated them, that they did business very much the same after that. . . . [Employers] would settle this particular question or case and go on like they had before."[25] The reasons for this failure were many: the inability of the EEOC to issue cease-and-desist orders, the commission's institutional instability, economic recession, an ever-expanding unorganized sector of women workers, the ERA failure to gain approval, and the onset of the conservative Reagan years.[26]

Women unionists responded to these setbacks by developing new strategies to attack the deep structural causes of inequality. The campaign for comparable worth—a plan for redressing the persistent disparity between men's and women's wages—emerged in the late 1970s. Backed by the EEOC, NOW, CLUW, and several politicians, comparable-worth supporters proposed to undercut the value of male wages by making it expensive to maintain unofficial sex-segregated jobs. Although initial support came from the IUE's drive for pay equity, comparable-worth advocates represented workers in the growing service sector of the economy, especially in occupational groups with large female memberships such as nursing, clerical work, and teaching. The moment of industrial unionism's dominance in the labor movement passed as industrial jobs dried up. Between 1958 and 1968 there were four million new manufacturing jobs; in the period 1978–83 the manufacturing sector of the economy lost three million jobs. This changing of the guard was evident in the CLUW's composition, where older industrial unionists held the top positions while the bulk of the membership and new leadership came from service unions.[27]

Despite the unfulfilled promise of equality, industrial unionists could claim a significant influence on gender relations in the United States. Even as service and public sector unionists gained more authority, and as many feminists turned their attention to improving women workers' lot in female-dominated jobs instead of confronting directly sex-segregated employment and job hierarchies, industrial activists left a significant imprint on contemporary work relations. In a few short years they had overseen the transformation of the union's support for protective laws for women to one of gender equality. Likewise, unionists brought the women's movement to recognize the centrality of workplace concerns in the wider struggle for equality.

The process of change was incomplete and uneven, marked by varying records of confrontation and accommodation to equality demands within specific unions. This variation stemmed from members' daily encounters with the organization, labor politics, and the composition of their union's work force. If the changes affecting union policy at the national level were not entirely of the labor activists' own making, unionists contributed in meaningful ways to shaping the character of that change. Women confronted the inequality embedded in the wage structure and occupational segregation and, in the process, transformed the labor movement. With the arrival of Ronald Reagan as U.S. president in 1981, they would face a new set of challenges brought on by conservative politicians and policy makers hostile to many of the core precepts of equal employment opportunity. The renewed instability of the EEOC, open attacks on affirmative action, and a general backlash against feminism threatened the gains made in the previous two decades. The labor movement entered a new, more defensive phase in the 1980s from which it has yet to emerge.

Rank-and-file women were central to the story of the emergence of gender equality in the 1960s and 1970s. They used the imperfect legal tools at their disposal to influence their job security, wages, and work environment, and they forced women activists and union staff members to reevaluate their defense of protectionism. They continued to be a vital force for improving women's rights in the 1980s and 1990s. "We do not want separate little unequal, unfair laws and separate little unequal, low-paid jobs," Georgianna Sellers of the Chemical Workers told congressional committee members in 1970. "We want full equality." That this equality had not yet arrived did not seem to trouble Sellers, for women had a new sense of their power and there was "no one more aware of the power of women than women—especially working women."[28]

Notes

Introduction

1. Alice Kessler-Harris, *Out to Work: A History of Wage-Earning Women in the United States* (New York: Oxford University Press, 1982); Nancy F. Gabin, *Feminism in the Labor Movement: Women and the United Auto Workers, 1935–1975* (Ithaca, N.Y.: Cornell University Press, 1990); Dorothy Sue Cobble, *Dishing It Out: Waitresses and Their Unions in the Twentieth Century* (Urbana: University of Illinois Press, 1991), and "Recapturing Working-Class Feminism: Union Women in the Postwar Era," in *Not June Cleaver: Women and Gender in Postwar America, 1945–1960,* ed. Joanne Meyerowitz (Philadelphia: Temple University Press, 1994), pp. 57–83; Ruth Milkman, "Women Workers, Feminism, and the Labor Movement since the 1960s," in *Women, Work, and Protest: A Century of U.S. Women's Labor History,* ed. Milkman (New York: Routledge, 1985), pp. 300–322; Lisa A. Kannenberg, "From World War to Cold War: Women Electrical Workers and Their Union, 1940–1955" (M.A. thesis, University of North Carolina at Charlotte, 1990); Bruce R. Fehn, "Striking Women: Gender, Race and Class in the United Packinghouse Workers of America (UPWA), 1938–1968" (Ph.D. diss., University of Wisconsin–Madison, 1991).

2. Betty Talkington, interview by Merle Davis, Des Moines, May 5, 1983, Iowa Labor History Oral Project, State Historical Society of Iowa, Iowa City, Iowa. Unless otherwise noted, all interviews consulted were in transcript form.

3. Various labor law scholars have written on the late nineteenth century. See, for example, William E. Forbath, *Law and the Shaping of the American Labor Movement* (Cambridge, Mass.: Harvard University Press, 1991), and Daniel R. Ernst, *Lawyers against Labor: From Individual Rights to Corporate Liberalism* (Urbana: University of Illinois Press, 1995).

4. A general discussion of protective laws is found in Kessler-Harris, *Out to Work,* pp. 180–214; Susan Lehrer, *Origins of Protective Labor Legislation for Women, 1905–1925* (Albany: State University of New York Press, 1987); Joan Hoff, *Law, Gender, and Injustice: A Legal History of U.S. Women* (New York: New York University Press, 1991); and Lise Vogel, *Mothers on the Job: Maternity Policy in the U.S. Workplace* (New Brunswick, N.J.: Rutgers University Press, 1993).

5. Margaret Drier Robins, "Newspaper Woman Protests against 'Maternal Legislation,'" *Life and Labor* 10, no. 30 (March 1920): 86. My thanks to Eric Karolak for providing this article.

6. Marjorie B. Turner, *Women and Work* (Los Angeles: University of California, Los Angeles, Institute of Industrial Relations, 1964), p. 21.

7. National Women's Trade Union League pamphlet, quoted in Kessler-Harris, *Out to Work*, p. 209.

8. Quoted in Kessler-Harris, *Out to Work*, p. 202.

9. Kessler-Harris, *Out to Work*, p. 202.

10. Ibid., p. 189.

11. Alice Kessler-Harris, "The Paradoxes of Motherhood: Night Work Restrictions in the United States," in *Protecting Women: Labor Legislation in Europe, the United States, and Australia, 1880–1920,* ed. Ulla Wikander, Alice Kessler-Harris, and Jane Lewis (Urbana: University of Illinois Press, 1995), p. 341; Vogel, p. 29; Sara M. Evans, *Born for Liberty: A History of Women in America* (New York: Free Press, 1989), p. 192.

12. Evans, p. 192.

13. Quoted in William Chafe, *Women and Equality* (New York: Oxford University Press, 1977), p. 56.

14. A discussion of the shifting meaning of the "wage" and the "provider" is found in Alice Kessler-Harris, *A Woman's Wage: Historical Meanings and Social Consequences* (Lexington: University Press of Kentucky, 1990).

15. Quoted in Chafe, p. 53.

16. Quoted in Vivien Hart, *Bound by Our Constitution: Women, Workers, and the Minimum Wage* (Princeton: Princeton University Press, 1994), p. 114.

17. Quoted in Chafe, p. 56.

18. Quoted in Kessler-Harris, *Out to Work*, p. 212.

19. Nancy Cott, "Historical Perspectives: The Equal Rights Amendment in the 1920s," in *Conflicts in Feminism,* ed. Marianne Hirsch and Evelyn Fox Keller (New York: Routledge, 1991), p. 54.

20. Sidney Lens, *The Crisis of American Labor* (New York: Sagamore Press, 1959), p. 55.

21. The figures for union membership and wages come from Foster Rhea Dulles and Melvyn Dubofsky, *Labor in America: A History,* 4th ed. (Arlington Heights, Ill.: Harlan Davidson, 1984), pp. 365, 381.

22. Elizabeth Faue, "'Anti-Heroes of the Working-Class': A Response to Bruce Nelson," *International Review of Social History* 41 (1996): 383.

23. Paula Giddings, *Where and When I Enter: The Impact of Black Women on Race and Sex in America* (New York: William Morrow, 1984), p. 307. Giddings's view is typical of that of scholars who consider black women and feminism. See Jacqueline Jones, *Labor of Love, Labor of Sorrow: Black Women, Work, and Family, From Slavery to the Present* (New York: Vintage, 1986), pp. 232, 315; Bonnie Thornton Dill, "Race, Class and Gender: Prospects for an All-Inclusive Sisterhood," *Feminist Studies* 9, no. 1 (Spring 1983): 134; Chafe, p. 54.

24. Clipping, *Wall Street Journal,* January 5, 1974, box 9, folder 13, Coalition of Labor Union Women Collection, Walter Reuther Archives of Labor History and Urban Affairs, Wayne State University, Detroit, Mich.

Chapter 1: Beyond the Doldrums

1. Pauline Newman, interview by Barbara Wertheimer, New York City, November 1976, box 1, folder 6, Pauline Newman Collection, Schlesinger Library, Radcliffe College, Cambridge, Mass. (hereafter, Newman Collection).

2. This quotation is the title of chapter 11 in Alice Kessler-Harris's *Out to Work: A History of Wage-Earning Women in the United States* (New York: Oxford University Press, 1982).

3. William Chafe, *Women and Equality* (New York: Oxford University Press, 1977), p. 172.

4. Gladys Dickason, "Women in Labor Unions," *Annals of the American Academy of Political and Social Science* 251 (May 1947): 77.

5. Ibid., pp. 70–71.

6. Stella Nowicki [Vicki Starr], quoted in *Rank and File: Personal Histories by Working Class Organizers,* ed. Alice and Staughton Lynd (Boston: Beacon Press, 1973), pp. 67, 90.

7. Nancy F. Gabin, *Feminism in the Labor Movement: Women and the United Auto Workers, 1935–1975* (Ithaca, N.Y.: Cornell University Press, 1990), p. 5.

8. Gladys Poese Ehlmann, quoted in Nancy Baker Wise and Christy Wise, *A Mouthful of Rivets: Women at Work in World War II* (San Francisco: Jossey-Bass, 1994), p. 182.

9. Susan Hartmann, *The Home Front and Beyond: American Women in the 1940s* (Boston: Twayne, 1982), p. 92; Sherna Berger Gluck, *Rosie the Riveter Revisited: Women, the War, and Social Change* (Boston: Twayne, 1987), p. 261.

10. A. G. Mezerik, "Getting Rid of the Women," *Atlantic Monthly,* June 1945, p. 84; Marye Stumph, quoted in Gluck, p. 65.

11. Philip S. Foner, *Women and the American Labor Movement: From the First Trade Unions to the Present* (New York: Free Press, 1982), p. 391.

12. Mezerik, p. 81.

13. Jacqueline Jones, *Labor of Love, Labor of Sorrows: Black Women, Work and the Family from Slavery to the Present* (New York: Vintage, 1986), pp. 235, 264–66; Karen Tucker Anderson, "'Last Hired, First Fired': Black Women Workers during World War II," *Journal of American History* 69 (June 1982): 82–97; Barbara S. Griffith, *The Crisis of American Labor: Operation Dixie and the Defeat of the CIO* (Philadelphia: Temple University Press, 1988); M. Melinda Chateauvert, "Marching Together: Women of the Brotherhood of Sleeping Car Porters, 1925–1957" (Ph.D. diss., University of Pennsylvania, 1992), pp. 5, 205, 214.

14. Jones, p. 257.

15. Sara M. Evans, *Born for Liberty: A History of Women in America* (New York: Free Press, 1989), p. 229

16. Helen Studer, quoted in Gluck, p. 192.

17. Evans, pp. 230–31.

18. Gabin, p. 126.

19. Quoted in William H. Chafe, *The Paradox of Change: American Women in the Twentieth Century* (New York: Oxford University Press, 1991), pp. 179–80.

20. Ferdinand Lundberg and Marynia F. Farnham, M.D., *Modern Woman: The Lost Sex* (New York: Harper, 1947), p. 370.

21. Jennifer Colton, "Why I Quit Working," *Good Housekeeping*, September 1951, quoted in *America's Working Women: A Documentary History—1600 to the Present*, ed. Rosalyn Baxandall, Linda Gordon, and Susan Reverby (New York: Vintage, 1976), p. 300.

22. Kessler-Harris, *Out to Work*, pp. 498–99.

23. Annie Stein, "Postwar Jobs for Women: Two New Studies," *Life and Labor Bulletin* 60 (March 1945): 3.

24. Mezerik, pp. 81, 83.

25. Vera-Mae Widmer Fredrickson, quoted in Wise and Wise, p. 169.

26. Testimony of Joseph A. Beirne, U.S. Congress, House, Committee on Education and Labor, *Equal Pay for Equal Work: Hearings before Subcommittee No. 4 of the Committee on Education and Labor, House of Representatives, on H.R. 4273 and H.R. 4408*, 80th Cong., 2d sess., 1948, p. 225. See also Testimony of Frieda S. Miller, ibid., p. 154. In the period 1945–75 women did not hold any major offices in the Communications Workers of America and never held more than one of the union's seven to nine directorships. See Stephen Norwood, *Labor's Flaming Youth: Telephone Operators and Worker Militancy, 1878–1923* (Urbana: University of Illinois Press, 1990), p. 209.

27. Evans, p. 240.

28. Margaret A. Hickey, "The Rights of Women Workers Must Be Protected in Peace as in War," *Life and Labor Bulletin* 57 (December 1944): 1.

29. "Women Losing Better Paid War Industry Jobs," *Life and Labor Bulletin* 66 (November 1945): 4.

30. Kessler-Harris, *Out to Work*, p. 297.

31. Ibid., p. 286.

32. Ibid., p. 276.

33. Mezerik, p. 80.

34. Alice Peurala, interview by Elizabeth Balanoff, Chicago, September 30, 1977, Twentieth Century Trade Union Women: Vehicle for Social Change, Oral History Project, Institute of Labor and Industrial Relations, University of Michigan/Wayne State University, Detroit, Mich. (hereafter, Twentieth Century Trade Union Women Project).

35. Interview with Lillian Hatcher, Twentieth Century Trade Union Women Project, quoted in Gabin, p. 140.

36. Mary Callahan, interview by Alice M. Hoffman and Karen Budd, Philadelphia, Pa., May 7, 1976, Twentieth Century Trade Union Women Project.

37. Dellie Hahne, quoted in Studs Terkel, *The Good War: An Oral History of World War Two* (New York: Pantheon, 1984), p. 41.

38. Lola Weixel, quoted in Ruth Milkman, *Gender at Work: The Dynamics of Job Segregation by Sex during World War II* (Urbana: University of Illinois Press, 1987), p. 103.

39. Mezerik, p. 80.

40. Testimony of Joseph A. Beirne, *House Hearings,* 1950, p. 17.

41. Testimony of Lewis B. Schwellenbach, U.S. Congress, House, Committee on Education and Labor, *Equal Pay for Equal Work: Hearings before Subcommittee No. 4 of the Committee on Education and Labor, House of Representatives, on H.R. 4273 and H.R. 4408,* 80th Cong., 2d sess., 1948, p. 106.

42. Milkman, *Gender at Work,* p. 147.

43. Joanne Meyerowitz, "Introduction: Women and Gender in Postwar America, 1945–1960," in *Not June Cleaver: Women and Gender in Postwar America, 1945–1960,* ed. Meyerowitz (Philadelphia: Temple University Press, 1994), p. 4.

44. Cynthia Harrison, *On Account of Sex: The Politics of Women's Issues, 1945–1968* (Berkeley: University of California Press, 1988), pp. 89–91; Leila Rupp and Verta Taylor, *Survival in the Doldrums: The American Women's Rights Movement, 1945 to the 1960s* (New York: Oxford University Press, 1987; reprint, Columbus: Ohio State University Press, 1990), pp. 12–18; Claudia Goldin, *Understanding the Gender Gap: An Economic History of American Women* (New York: Oxford University Press, 1990), pp. 174–84; Baxandall, Gordon, and Reverby, p. 405.

45. Mary Baker and Margarita Salazar McSweyn, quoted in Gluck, pp. 234, 94; James B. Carey to Alvine King, April 9, 1964, box 8, group 2, International Union of Electrical Workers (IUE) Archives, Special Collections and University Archives, Rutgers University Libraries, New Brunswick, N.J. (hereafter, IUE Archives).

46. Richard C. Wilcox, "Women in the American Labor Force: Employment and Unemployment," in U.S. Congress, Senate, *Studies in Unemployment: Prepared for the Special Committee on Unemployment Problems, Pursuant to S. Res. 196,* 86th Cong., 2d sess., 1960, pp. 169–76.

47. Ibid.

48. William H. Chafe, *The American Woman: Her Changing Social, Economic, and Political Roles, 1920–1970* (New York: Oxford University Press, 1972), pp. 219–20.

49. Jones, p. 234.

50. Wilcox, p. 124.

51. U.S. Department of Labor, *Directory of Labor Unions in the United States, 1953,* Bureau of Labor Statistics Bulletin 1127 (G.P.O., 1953), p. 46; Katherine P. Ellickson, interview by Philip Mason, Washington, D.C., December 15, 1974, Walter Reuther Archives of Labor and Urban Affairs, Wayne State University, Detroit, Mich. (hereafter, Reuther Archives); Gabin, pp. 87, 143; Kim Moody, *An Injury to All: The Decline of American Unionism* (New York: Verso, 1988), p. 23.

52. Leonard R. Sayles and George Strauss, *The Local Union: Its Place in the Industrial Plant* (New York: Harper, 1953), pp. 213–14.

53. Catherine Conroy, interview by Elizabeth Balanoff, Milwaukee, Wis., August/December 1976, Twentieth Century Trade Union Women Project.

54. Gabin, p. 180.

55. Katherine P. Ellickson to Victor Reuther, September 28, 1954, box 58, folder 9, CIO Washington Office Collection, 1950–56, Reuther Archives.

56. Dorothy Haener, interview by Lyn Goldfarb, Lydia Kleiner, and Christine Miller, Detroit, Mich., 1978, Twentieth Century Trade Union Women Project.

57. Florence Peterson interview, Twentieth Century Trade Union Women Project, quoted in Gabin, p. 165.

58. Katherine P. Ellickson, interview by Dennis East, Detroit, Mich., January 10, 1976, Reuther Archives.

59. A good summary of the CIO's and AFL's competing visions of labor's role in society can be found in Moody, pp. 58–59. For a history of corporativism in the CIO see Nelson Lichtenstein, "From Corporativism to Collective Bargaining: Organized Labor and the Eclipse of Social Democracy in the Postwar Era," in *The Rise and Fall of the New Deal Order, 1930–1980*, ed. Steve Fraser and Gary Gerstle (Princeton: Princeton University Press, 1989), pp. 122–52, and Dennis A. Deslippe, "'A Revolution of Its Own': The Social Doctrine of the Association of Catholic Trade Unionists in Detroit, 1939–1950," *Records of the American Catholic Historical Society of Philadelphia* 102, no. 4 (Winter 1991): 19–36.

60. Harrison, pp. xiii, 7–9. Dorothy Sue Cobble points to this mistaken belief in Harrison's otherwise excellent treatment of the period. See Cobble's "Recapturing Working-Class Feminism: Union Women in the Postwar Era," in *Not June Cleaver: Women and Gender in Postwar America, 1945–1960,* ed. Joanne Meyerowitz (Philadelphia: Temple University Press, 1994), p. 83 n. 80.

61. Many of these women are mentioned in a U.S. Women's Bureau report in 1953. See U.S. Department of Labor, *The Status of Women in the United States, 1953,* Women's Bureau Bulletin 249 (G.P.O., 1953), pp. 23–24.

62. Typescript, "War and Postwar Problems of Women Workers from the Women's Bureau Union Study," n.d. [1946], box 6, folder 131, Frieda Miller Collection, 1909–73, Schlesinger Library, Radcliffe College, Cambridge, Mass. (hereafter, Miller Collection); Amy Kesselman, *Fleeting Opportunities: Women Shipyard Workers in Portland and Vancouver during World War II and Reconversion* (Albany: State University of New York Press, 1990), pp. 17–18, 20, 110–11.

63. Women made up 75 percent of the ILGWU's ranks and 40 percent of the HERE. Figures are for 1958 as Lucretia Dewey reports in "Women in Labor Unions," *Monthly Labor Review* 94, no. 2 (February 1971): 43.

64. Nancy Pratt Vanderbeek, interview by Dennis Deslippe, Detroit, Mich., May 7, 1992, Oral Labor History Collection, State Historical Society of Iowa, Iowa City, Iowa.

65. Frieda Miller to William Green, February 10, 1950, box 7, folder 142, Miller Collection.

66. Charles S. Johnson and Preston Valien, "The Status of Negro Labor," in *Labor in Postwar America,* ed. Colston E. Warne et al. (New York: Remsen Press, 1949), p. 560.

67. Philip S. Foner, *Women and the American Labor Movement: From World War I to the Present* (New York: Free Press, 1980), pp. 346–47.

68. Jones, pp. 266–67.

69. Dorothy Sue Cobble, *Dishing It Out: Waitresses and Their Unions in the Twentieth*

Century (Urbana: University of Illinois Press, 1991), pp. 80, 158; Gary M. Fink, ed., *Labor Unions* (Westport, Conn.: Greenwood, 1977), pp. 392–93.

70. Quoted in Dolores Janiewski, "Seeking 'a New Day and a New Way': Black Women and Unions in the Southern Tobacco Industry," in *"To Toil the Livelong Day": America's Women at Work, 1780–1980,* ed. Carol Groneman and Mary Beth Norton (Ithaca, N.Y.: Cornell University Press, 1987), p. 171.

71. Richard Love, "In Defiance of Custom and Tradition: Black Tobacco Workers and Labor Unions in Richmond, Virginia, 1937–1941," *Labor History* 35 (Winter 1994): 31. For the TWIU's race relations history see also Ray Marshall, *The Negro and Organized Labor* (New York: Wiley, 1965), p. 189, Janiewski, pp. 161–78, and Foner, p. 322.

72. Philip R. Shays to R. J. Petree, February 23, 1961, series 1, box 42, Tobacco Workers Union Collection, Special Collections University of Maryland Library, College Park, Md.

73. Typescript, "Contract Employment Cases: Examples of Corrective Actions," n.d. [1962], box 5, White House Central Files: George Reedy, Lyndon B. Johnson Presidential Papers, 1963–69, Lyndon Baines Johnson Library, Austin, Tex.

74. Quoted in Kathleen Anne Laughlin, "Backstage Activism: The Policy Initiatives of the Women's Bureau of the U.S. Department of Labor in the Postwar Era, 1945–70" (Ph.D. diss., Ohio State University, 1993), pp. 184–85.

75. Nancy F. Cott, *The Grounding of Modern Feminism* (New Haven: Yale University Press, 1987), p. 125.

76. "Why Take Off Your Head to Cure a Headache!" *Life and Labor Bulletin* 55 (October 1944): 1.

77. Quoted in Harrison, p. 44. Barney was Elizabeth Cady Stanton's granddaughter and Harriot Stanton Blatch's daughter.

78. Quoted in Rupp and Taylor, p. 144.

79. Ibid.

80. Clipping, New York Trade Union League *Bulletin,* March 1938, box 55, folder 19, American Federation of Labor–Congress of Industrial Organizations Department of Legislation Collection, George Meany Collection, George Meany Memorial Archives, Silver Spring, Md.

81. Esther Peterson, interview by Paige Mulhollan, Washington, D.C., November 25, 1968, Lyndon Baines Johnson Library, Austin, Tex., transcript in carton 2, Esther Peterson Collection, 1940, 1952–86 (unprocessed), Schlesinger Library, Radcliffe College, Cambridge, Mass. By the early 1960s, NWP representatives told Congress that they supported equal pay legislation but they spent most of their testimony speaking on behalf of the ERA. See Testimony of Anita Pollitzer, U.S. Congress, House, Committee on Education and Labor, *Equal Pay for Equal Work: Hearings before the Select Subcommittee on Labor of the Committee on Education and Labor, House of Representatives, on H.R. 8898; H.R. 10226, Part 2,* 87th Cong., 2d sess., 1962, p. 327, and Testimony of Leila M. Holt, U.S. Congress, House, Committee on Education and Labor, *Equal Pay for Equal Work: Hearings before the Select Subcommittee on Labor of the Committee on Education and Labor, House of Representatives, on H.R. 8898; H.R. 10226, Part 2,* 87th Cong., 2d sess., 1962, p. 143.

82. Quoted in Harrison, p. 27.

83. Ibid., p. 31.

84. Ibid., p. 32. See also Rupp and Taylor, pp. 63, 74.

85. Katherine P. Ellickson to Nancy Jewell Cross, November 23, 1955, box 92, folder 7, Katherine P. Ellickson, 1929–68 Collection, Reuther Archives. The lowering of the age was a long-standing goal. See "Social Security Amendments," *Life and Labor Bulletin* 64 (July 1945): 2–3.

86. U.S. Department of Labor, *Maternity Protection of Employed Women,* Women's Bureau Bulletin No. 240, Washington, D.C., 1952; Wilcox, p. 167; Lise Vogel, *Mothers on the Job: Maternity Policy in the U.S. Workplace* (New Brunswick, N.J.: Rutgers University Press, 1993); Minutes, U.S. Women's Bureau Labor Advisory Committee Meeting, May 15, 1953, box 8, folder 120, Newman Collection.

87. Laughlin, pp. 60–61; Susan M. Hartmann, "Women's Employment and the Domestic Ideal in the Early Cold War Years," in *Not June Cleaver: Women and Gender in Postwar America, 1945–1960,* ed. Joanne Meyerowitz (Philadelphia: Temple University Press, 1994), p. 95; Esther Peterson, "Widening Range of Women's Work in the United States," *Free Labor World* 75 (September 1956): 20–23, 48.

88. Minutes, U.S. Women's Bureau Labor Advisory Committee Meeting, December 8, 1950, box 8, folder 120, Newman Collection. Their efforts proved fruitless; the Eisenhower administration eliminated the Wage Stabilization Board that considered their request.

89. Quoted in U.S. Congress, House, Committee on Education and Labor, *Legislative History of the Equal Pay Act of 1963 (Amending Section 6 of the Fair Labor Standards Act of 1938, as amended),* 88th Cong., 1st sess., 1963, p. 63.

90. Carol Riegleman Lubin and Ann Winslow, *Social Justice for Women: The International Labor Organization and Women* (Durham, N.C.: Duke University Press, 1990), pp. 93–97; Shirley Tillotson, "Human Rights Law as Prism: Women's Organizations, Unions, and Ontario's Female Employees Fair Remuneration Act, 1951," *Canadian Historical Review* 72 (December 1991): 532–57; typescript, "Highlights of the Conference of British Trade Union Women," n.s. [Frieda Miller], May 28, 1946, box 6, folder 140, Miller Collection; Testimony of James B. Carey, U.S. Congress, House, Committee on Education and Labor, *Equal Pay for Equal Work: Hearings before the Select Subcommittee on Labor of the Committee on Education and Labor, House of Representatives, on H.R. 8898; H.R. 10226, Part 1,* 87th Cong., 2d sess., 1962, p. 175.

91. William Schnitzler, "Why Less Pay for Women Workers?" *Bakers and Confectioners Journal* 65 (March 1950): 12, quoted in Alice Kessler-Harris, *A Woman's Wage: Historical Meanings and Social Consequences* (Lexington: University Press of Kentucky, 1990), p. 109.

92. James C. Nix, "Equal Pay for Equal Work," *Monthly Labor Review* 74, no. 1 (January 1952): 43.

93. Figures cited in David F. Noble, *Forces of Production: A Social History of Industrial Automation* (New York: Oxford University Press, 1984), pp. 249–50. For a general dis-

cussion of automation, see James R. Bright, *Automation and Management* (Cambridge, Mass.: Harvard University Press, 1958); Michael Harrington, "The Advance of Automation," *Commonweal* 62 (May 20, 1955): 175–78; and Bernard Karsh, "Automation's Brave New World . . . ," *Nation,* October 5, 1957, pp. 212–13.

94. Quoted in Noble, p. 250.

95. U.S. Congress, Senate, *Report of the Special Committee on Unemployed Problems, Pursuant to S. Res. 196,* 86th Cong., 2d sess., 1960, p. 46.

96. Harold L. Sheppard and James L. Stern, "Impact of Automation and Workers in Supplier Plants," *Labor Law Journal* 8 (October 1957): 717.

97. U.S. Department of Labor, *Case Studies of Displaced Workers: Experiences of Workers after Layoff,* Bureau of Labor Statistics Bulletin No. 1408 (G.P.O., 1964), p. 7.

98. Richard A. Beaumont and Roy B. Helfgott, *Management, Automation, and People* (New York: Industrial Relations Counselors, 1964), pp. 49–50.

99. Jones, p. 211; clipping, *New York Times,* "Negro Seniority Raises Broad Rights Issues," December 13, 1964, box 25, folder 102, AFL-CIO Department of Civil Rights, Discrimination Case Files Collection, George Meany Memorial Archives, Silver Spring, Md.; Bruce R. Fehn, "Striking Women: Gender, Race and Class in the United Packinghouse Workers of America (UPWA), 1938–1968" (Ph.D. diss., University of Wisconsin–Madison, 1991), pp. 160, 256, 290; Janiewski, p. 177.

100. See James B. Atleson, *Values and Assumptions in American Labor Law* (Amherst: University of Massachusetts Press, 1983), especially, pp. 2, 7, 47, 95, 101, 114, 160–70.

101. Howell John Harris, *The Right to Manage: Industrial Relations Policies of American Business in the 1940s* (Madison: University of Wisconsin Press, 1982), p. 203. For an example of union-employer contracts' giving unions considerable control over production decisions in the early 1940s, see Steve Jeffreys, "'Matters of Mutual Interest': The Unionization Process at Dodge Main, 1933–1939," in *On the Line: Essays in the History of Auto Work,* ed. Nelson Lichtenstein and Stephen Meyer (Urbana: University of Illinois Press, 1989), pp. 121–22. John Zerzan argues that union leaders always embraced technology and centralization to the detriment of Luddism, antiwork, and anti-authoritarianism among rank-and-file workers. See his "Organized Labor versus 'The Revolt against Work': The Critical Contest," *Telos* 21 (Fall 1974): 194–206; "Unionization in America," *Telos* 27 (Spring 1976): 147–56; and "Taylorism and Unionism," *Fifth Estate,* November 1976.

102. Charles D. Stewart, "Social Implications of Technological Progress," *Monthly Labor Review* 79, no. 12 (December 1956): 1417.

103. Marjorie B. Turner, *Women and Work* (Los Angeles: UCLA, Institute of Industrial Relations, 1964), p. 21.

104. Ibid., pp. 19–20.

105. Mrs. W. B. McPherson to the NLRB, January 7, 1954, special file, box 1052. The letter was forwarded to the Women's Bureau [files]; quoted in Kessler-Harris, *Out to Work,* p. 308.

106. Testimony of Esther Peterson, *House Equal Pay Hearings,* 1962, part 1, p. 27.

107. Testimony of Jacob Clayman, U.S. Congress, Senate, Committee on Labor and

Public Welfare, *Equal Pay Act of 1963: Hearings before the Subcommittee on Labor of the Committee on Labor and Public Welfare, United States Senate, on S. 882 and S. 910,* 88th Cong., 1st sess., 1963, p. 88.

108. Kessler-Harris, *A Woman's Wage,* p. 112.

109. U.S. Department of Labor, *Handbook of Women Workers, 1975,* Women's Bureau Bulletin No. 297 (G.P.O., 1975), pp. 9, 11, 17, 18; Elizabeth Faulkner Baker, *Technology and Women's Work* (New York: Columbia University Press, 1964), p. 205

110. Nancy Pratt, "When Women Work," *American Federationist,* August 1957, p. 9.

111. Gabin, pp. 158–60, 180–87. The UAW leadership in 1944 even called for the retention of unified seniority lists in such plants where lists were already in effect.

112. Boris Shishkin to George Meany, May 27, 1957, box 26, folder 1, AFL, AFL-CIO Office of the President, George Meany (1952–1960), George Meany Memorial Archives, Silver Spring, Md. Shiskin raised this issue at the insistence of Matthew Woll, leader of the photoengravers union. In 1956 Woll also asked the members of the AFL-CIO Civil Rights Committee that they give the ERA a "serious policy review." Nothing came of this either; Woll died shortly thereafter. See Minutes, AFL-CIO Civil Rights Committee Meeting, March 1, 1957, box 58, group 2, IUE Archives.

113. William F. Schnitzler, "A New World for Working Women," *American Federationist,* August 1963, p. 19.

114. Ruth Moore to "Dear Ike," quoted in Kessler-Harris, *Out to Work,* p. 310.

115. Gabin, p. 184.

116. Ibid.

117. Baker, p. 440.

118. Katherine P. Ellickson, interview by Joan Walsh Goldman, La Jolla, Calif., May 4, 1979, AFL-CIO Merger Oral History Collection, George Meany Memorial Archives, Silver Spring, Md.

119. Katherine P. Ellickson, interview by Dennis East, Detroit, Mich., January 10, 1976, Reuther Archives.

120. *Problems of Working Women: Summary Report of a Conference Sponsored by Industrial Union Department, AFL-CIO,* June 12–14, 1961, p. 3, box 95, folder 34, Ellickson 1929–68 Collection, Reuther Archives.

121. Ibid., p. 56.

122. Ibid., p. 60.

123. Ibid., p. 49.

124. Chafe, *Women and Equality,* p. 95.

Chapter 2: Prospects for Equality

1. George Meany, "What Labor Means by 'More,'" *Fortune,* March 1955, p. 92.

2. Ibid., pp. 92–93, 172, 174, 176.

3. Ibid., p. 92.

4. Kathleen Anne Laughlin, "Backstage Activism: The Policy Initiatives of the Women's

Bureau of the U.S. Department of Labor in the Postwar Era, 1945–1970" (Ph.D. diss., Ohio State University, 1993), pp. 9, 110–11.

5. Cynthia Harrison, *On Account of Sex: The Politics of Women's Issues, 1945–1968* (Berkeley: University of California Press, 1988), pp. 40–47; Alice Kessler-Harris, *Out to Work: A History of Wage-Earning Women in the United States* (New York: Oxford University Press, 1982), pp. 304–5; James C. Nix, "Equal Pay for Equal Work," *Monthly Labor Review* 74, no. 1 (January 1952): 41–45.

6. Alice Kessler-Harris, *A Woman's Wage: Historical Meanings and Social Consequences* (Lexington: University Press of Kentucky, 1990), p. 100. See also, ibid., pp. 92–101, and Harrison, p. 96, for a general description of the early comparable worth campaign.

7. Testimony of Leo Teplow, U.S. Congress, House, Committee on Education and Labor, *Equal Pay for Equal Work for Women: Hearings before a Special Subcommittee of the Committee on Education and Labor, House of Representatives, on H.R. 1584 and H.R. 2438,* 81st Cong., 2d sess., 1950, p. 55.

8. Harrison, p. 45; see also pp. 47–50.

9. Testimony of T. R. Owens, U.S. Congress, Senate, Committee on Education and Labor, *Equal Pay for Equal Work: Hearings before a Subcommittee of the Committee on Education and Labor, United States Senate, on S. 1178,* 79 Cong., 1st sess., 1945, p. 172.

10. Testimony of Clifford McAvoy, *Senate Hearings, 1945,* p. 161.

11. Testimony of Joseph A. Beirne, *House Hearings, 1950,* p. 11.

12. Testimony of Helen Blanchard, *House Hearings, 1950,* pp. 30–31.

13. For a statement of the CIO's opposition to the FLSA coverage mandated by Bolton's bill and its support of the Murray-Morse Bill, see Thomas Burke to Frances P. Bolton, August 11, 1953, box 78, folder 14, and Anthony W. Smith to Robert Oliver, April 6, 1954, box 78, folder 14, both in CIO Washington Office Collection, 1950–56, Walter Reuther Archives of Labor and Urban Affairs, Wayne State University, Detroit, Mich. (hereafter, CIO Collection); Minutes, NCEP meetings, April 16, 1954, National Committee on Equal Pay Collection (unprocessed), George Meany Memorial Archives, Silver Spring, Md. (hereafter, NCEP Collection [unprocessed]).

14. [Thomas Burke and Robert Oliver (by Anthony W. Smith)] to James P. Mitchell, January 18, 1954, box 78, folder 14, CIO Collection.

15. Harrison, p. 49; Ronald W. Schatz, *The Electrical Workers: A History of Labor at General Electric and Westinghouse, 1923–60* (Urbana: University of Illinois Press, 1983), p. 126.

16. Harrison, pp. 47, 83; Winifred G. Helmes to Helen Loy, October 15, 1954, box 1, folder 8, Alice K. Leopold Collection, Schlesinger Library, Radcliffe College, Cambridge, Mass. (hereafter, Leopold Collection). Helmes wrote: "You may know that in some cases labor people are critical of Alice."

17. Nancy Pratt Vanderbeek, interview by Dennis Deslippe, Detroit, Mich., May 7, 1992, Oral Labor History Collection, State Historical Society of Iowa, Iowa City, Iowa (hereafter, OLHC).

18. Quoted in Julia Greene, "The Strike at the Ballot Box: Politics and Partisanship in the American Federation of Labor, 1881–1916" (Ph.D. diss., Yale University, 1989), p. 105.

19. Greene, 100–174; William Forbath, *Law and the Shaping of the American Labor Movement* (Cambridge, Mass.: Harvard University Press, 1991), pp. 128–58; Christopher L. Tomlins, *The State and the Unions: Labor Relations, Law, and the Organized Labor Movement in America, 1880–1960* (New York: Cambridge University Press, 1985), pp. 74–95.

20. Quoted in Tomlins, p. 76.

21. Tomlins, pp. 138–47; Kenneth Casebeer, "The Workers' Unemployment Insurance Bill: American Social Wage, Labor Organization, and Legal Ideology," in *Labor Law in America: Historical and Critical Essays,* ed. Christopher L. Tomlins and Andrew J. King (Baltimore: Johns Hopkins University Press, 1992), pp. 234–36. See, generally, James A. Gross, *The Making of the National Labor Relations Board: A Study in Economics, Politics, and the Law* (Albany: State University of New York Press, 1974), and Irving Bernstein, *The New Deal Collective Bargaining Policy* (Berkeley: University of California Press, 1950).

22. Testimony of Joseph A. Padway, *Hearings before the Committee on Education and Labor, U.S. Senate, National Labor Relations Act and Proposed Amendments,* 76th Cong., 1st Sess. (Washington, D.C., 1939), p. 713, quoted in Tomlins, p. 188.

23. Mike Davis, *Prisoners of the American Dream: Politics and Economy in the History of the US Working Class* (London: Verso, 1986), p. 71.

24. Walter J. Mason to Tony Sender, May 7, 1948, box 16, folder 54, American Federation of Labor–Congress of Industrial Organizations Department of Legislation Collection, George Meany Collection, George Meany Memorial Archives, Silver Spring, Md. (hereafter, AFL-CIO Legislation Collection).

25. Forbath, p. 55. See also, Susan Lehrer, *Origins of Protective Labor Legislation for Women, 1905–1925* (Albany: State University of New York Press, 1987), pp. 141–83.

26. Testimony of Lewis G. Hines, U.S. Senate, *Equal Pay Hearings, 1945,* pp. 126, 123.

27. George Meany to Frances Bolton, June 11, 1953, box 55, folder 20, AFL-CIO Legislation Collection.

28. Adelia B. Kloak to Miss Ambursen et al., December 10, 1951, box 6, folder 138, Miller Collection; U.S. Department of Labor, *Report of the National Conference on Equal Pay,* Women's Bureau Bulletin 242 (G.P.O., 1952), pp. 4–5.

29. [Katherine Ellickson and Nancy Pratt], "Comments on Federal Equal Pay Legislation—Chronology of AFL Convention Action on Equal Pay for Equal Work Legislation," May 25, 1956, box 17, folder 1, AFL-CIO Legislation Collection.

30. [William C. Hushing] to George Riley, April 24, 1951, box 16, folder 54, AFL-CIO Legislation Collection.

31. George Meany to Frances Bolton, June 6, 1953, box 55, folder 20, AFL-CIO Legislation Collection.

32. The AFL leadership supported the Full Employment Bill in 1945 as well. See Margaret Weir, *Politics and Jobs: The Boundaries of Employment Policy in the United States* (Princeton: Princeton University Press, 1992), pp. 46, 194 n. 64.

33. Minutes, NCEP, May 12, 1955, NCEP Collection (unprocessed); Dorothy Sue Cobble, *Dishing It Out: Waitresses and Their Unions in the Twentieth Century* (Urbana: University of Illinois Press, 1991), pp. 154–55.

34. Andrew J. Biemiller to George Meany, April 16, 1954, box 15, folder 2, AFL-CIO Office of the President, George Meany Collection, George Meany Memorial Archives, Silver Spring, Md. (hereafter, Meany Collection). Appointing people who fit this category may not have always been possible. On at least one occasion AFL officers in Washington, D.C., sent an ILGWU representative to a Women's Bureau meeting. See George Meany to James P. Mitchell, May 4, 1954, box 15, folder 2, Meany Collection.

35. U.S. Department of Labor, *Equal Pay Conference, 1952*, p. 7.

36. Kessler-Harris, *A Woman's Wage*, p. 155 n. 52; Harrison, p. 91. While much of the explanation for the passage of legislation lay in the political dominance of the Republican Party in these years, a general lessening of public support for equal treatment for men and women undoubtedly contributed to the lethargic legislative record of the period. Public support for women's participation in the labor force increased at 2.2 percent per year between 1938 and 1946; it slowed to 0.7 percent between 1946 and 1969. A similar pattern existed for support for a woman as president: it grew 3.8 percent a year between 1945 and 1949 but slowed to 0.3 percent between 1949 and 1969. See Paul Burnstein, *Discrimination, Jobs, and Politics: The Struggle for Equal Employment Opportunity in the United States since the New Deal* (Chicago: University of Chicago Press, 1985), p. 50.

37. Kessler-Harris, *A Woman's Wage*, p. 111.

38. Harrison, p. 51.

39. Kim Moody, *An Injury to All: The Decline of American Unionism* (New York: Verso, 1988), p. 61. Figures are from Davis, p. 95 n. 73.

40. Quoted in Sidney Lens, "George Meany's Troubled Legacy," *The Progressive*, December 1979, p. 26.

41. Katherine P. Ellickson, interview by Joan Walsh Goldman, La Jolla, Calif., May 4, 1979, AFL-CIO Merger Oral History Collection, George Meany Memorial Archives, Silver Spring, Md.

42. Alan Draper, *A Rope of Sand: The AFL-CIO Committee on Political Education, 1955–1967* (New York: Praeger, 1989), pp. 24–39; Moody, pp. 59–61.

43. Davis, p. 64.

44. Nancy Pratt's recollection of this policy is vague but she claims that the International Ladies Garment Workers Union support for equal pay laws was the most crucial factor in changing Meany's mind on the subject. See Vanderbeek, interview, OLHC.

45. Katherine P. Ellickson, interview by Philip Mason, Washington, D.C., December 15, 1974, Walter Reuther Archives of Labor and Urban Affairs, Wayne State University, Detroit, Mich. (hereafter, Reuther Archives). Ellickson worked in the AFL-CIO Social Security department after the 1955 merger. Boris Shishkin (AFL) was to run the Research Department but became ill; he later headed the Civil Rights Department. See Vanderbeek, interview, OLHC.

46. [Katherine Ellickson and Nancy Pratt], memorandum, "Federal Legislation to Provide Equal Pay for Equal Work," February 1956, box 17, folder 1, AFL-CIO Legislation Collection.

47. Ellickson, interview, December 15, 1974, Reuther Archives. For Pratt and Ellickson's report, see [Katherine Ellickson and Nancy Pratt], "Memorandum on Responses from State Bodies on Equal Pay Legislation," May 24, 1956, box 17, folder 1, AFL-CIO Legislation Collection.

48. American Federation of Labor–Congress of Industrial Organizations, *The AFL-CIO Position in Support of Equal Pay,* Publication No. 44 (Washington, D.C.: AFL-CIO, 1956), pp. 3–4.

49. Memorandum, "Comments on Federal Equal Pay Legislation," n.a., May 25, 1956, box 17, folder 1, AFL-CIO Legislation Collection.

50. *Stollar et al. v. Continental Can Company, Inc.,* Pennsylvania Court of Common Pleas, Washington County, No. 185, February term, 1960, October 7, 1960, 41 LC 50,081. The Glass Bottle Blowers Association announced its support for equal pay legislation at U.S. Congress, Senate, Committee on Education and Labor, *Equal Pay for Equal Work: Hearings before a Subcommittee of the Committee on Education and Labor, United States Senate, on S. 1178,* 79 Cong., 1st sess., 1945, pp. 181–82.

51. *Thelma Stollar et al. v. Continental Can Company, Inc.; Shirley Mae Blouir et al. Appellants, v. Same,* Pennsylvania Superior Court, Nos. 57 and 58, December 14, 1961, 43 LC 50,415. See also *Thelma Stollar et al. v. Continental Can Company, Inc., Shirley Mae Blouir et al. Plaintiffs v. Same,* Nos. 157, Pennsylvania Supreme Court, Western District, April 17, 1962, 44 LC 50,507.

52. Alan Draper, "Do the Right Thing: The Desegregation of Union Conventions in the South," *Labor History* 33 (Summer 1992): 343–56; Hugh Davis Graham, *The Civil Rights Era: Origins and Development of National Policy, 1960–1972* (New York: Oxford University Press, 1990), pp. 82–83; Herbert Hill, "The Equal Employment Opportunity Acts of 1964 and 1972: A Critical Analysis of the Legislative History and Administration of the Law," *Industrial Relations Law Journal* 2 (1977): 34–35; Tomlins, pp. 317–26.

53. Vanderbeek, interview, OLHC.

54. George Riley to Lorraine Hedberg, June 30, 1960, box 17, folder 7, AFL-CIO Legislation Collection; Minutes, NCEP meeting, February 28, 1957; Nancy Pratt to Stanley Ruttenberg, January 2, 1957; and Anne Draper to Peter Henle and George Riley, May 19, 1959, all in NCEP Collection (unprocessed). See also, George Riley to Gloria Johnson, February 16, 1960, box 17, folder 7, AFL-CIO Legislation Collection.

55. George Riley to Andrew Biemiller, February 27, 1959, box 17, folder 6, AFL-CIO Legislation Collection.

56. George Riley to Barbara Hornum, November 20, 1959, box 17, folder 6, AFL-CIO Legislation Collection.

57. George Riley to Lorraine Torres, May 31, 1962, NCEP Collection (unprocessed).

58. George Riley to Edith Rogers, February 1, 1957; George Riley to Edith Green, February 1, 1957; and George Riley to James Roosevelt, February 1, 1957, all in box 17, folder

7, AFL-CIO Legislation Collection; Nancy Pratt, "When Women Work," *American Federationist,* August 1957, p. 9.

59. Minutes, NCEP meeting, February 28, 1957, NCEP Collection (unprocessed).

60. Harrison, p. 51.

61. American Federation of Labor–Congress of Industrial Organizations, *Report of the Executive Council, Second Convention* (Atlantic City, N.J., 1957), p. 269.

62. Harrison, pp. 33–38, 47, 50, 83; Robert Oliver et al. to James P. Mitchell, February 11, 1955, box 92, folder 7, Katherine P. Ellickson, 1929–68 Collection, Walter Reuther Archives of Labor and Urban Affairs, Wayne State University, Detroit, Mich. (hereafter, Ellickson, 1929–68 Collection); Alice K. Leopold to Frances Tuckerman Freeman, June 10, 1957, NCEP Collection (unprocessed); Andrew Biemiller to George Meany, April 16, 1954, box 15, folder 2, AFL-CIO Office of the President, Meany Collection; George Riley to Katherine Ellickson, July 9, 1957, and Alice Leopold to William Schnitzler, January 23, 1957, both in box 17, folder 1, AFL-CIO Legislation Collection; Alice K. Leopold, "Federal Equal Pay Legislation," *Labor Law Journal* 6 (January 1955): 9.

63. Testimony of Esther Peterson, U.S. Congress, House, Committee on Education and Labor, *Equal Pay for Equal Work: Hearings before the Select Subcommittee on Labor of the Committee on Education and Labor, House of Representatives, on H.R. 8898; H.R. 10226, Part 1,* 87th Cong., 2d sess., 1962, p. 81.

64. Gloria Johnson, interview by Dennis Deslippe, Washington, D.C., June 8, 1993, Reuther Archives.

65. Press release, U.S. Department of Labor, March 12, 1956, box 1, folder 4, Leopold Collection.

66. Minutes, NCEP meetings for January 13, 1955, July 11, 1955, and May 19, 1959, all in NCEP Collection (unprocessed).

67. Hyman H. Bookbinder to Pauline Eisinger, February 19, 1957, box 17, folder 2, AFL-CIO Legislation Collection. See also, Harrison, pp. 37–38, and Leila J. Rupp and Verta Taylor, *Survival in the Doldrums: The American Women's Rights Movement, 1945 to the 1960s* (New York: Oxford University Press, 1987; reprint, Columbus: Ohio State University Press, 1990), pp. 144–53.

68. Hyman Bookbinder to Boris Shishkin, November 6, 1957, box 17, folder 3, AFL-CIO Legislation Collection.

69. Nancy Pratt to Stanley Ruttenberg, January 2, 1957, NCEP Collection (unprocessed).

70. There is no record that Meany responded. See Nina B. Price to George Meany, n.d. [November 1957], box 17, folder 3, AFL-CIO Legislation Collection. The NWP leadership tried this tactic with other opposition groups. See Rupp and Taylor, p. 142.

71. Tom Harris to Andrew Biemiller, January 19, 1960, box 17, folder 7, AFL-CIO Legislation Collection.

72. Vanderbeek, interview, OLHC.

73. Harrison, pp. 91, 123; Irwin N. Gertzog, *Congressional Women: Their Recruitment, Treatment, and Behavior* (New York: Praegers, 1984), p. 149.

74. Gertzog, p. 117.

75. Quoted in U.S. Congress, House, Committee on Education and Labor, *Legislative History of the Equal Pay Act of 1963 (Amending Section 6 of the Fair Labor Standards Act of 1938, as amended)*, 88th Cong., 1st sess., 1963, p. 67. See also Claudia Dreifus, "Women in Politics: An Interview with Edith Green," *Social Policy* 2, no. 5 (January/February 1972): 19–20.

76. Quoted in Robert Zieger, "George Meany: Labor's Organization Man," in *Labor Leaders in America*, ed. Melvyn Dubofsky and Warren Van Tine (Urbana: University of Illinois Press, 1987), p. 339.

77. Zieger, pp. 338–39, and idem, *American Workers, American Unions, 1920–1985* (Baltimore: Johns Hopkins University Press, 1986), pp. 166, 184–86; Harrison, pp. 70–72; Moody, p. 83.

78. Minutes, NCEP meeting, April 6, 1961, NCEP Collection (unprocessed); Minutes, "Meeting in Esther Peterson's Office on Equal Pay Bill," March 2, 1961, box 92, folder 11, Katherine P. Ellickson, 1929–68 Collection, Reuther Archives.

79. Esther Peterson to W. Willard Wirtz, February 13, 1963, carton 8, folder 215, Esther Peterson Collection, 1910–84, Schlesinger Library, Radcliffe College, Cambridge, Mass. (hereafter, Peterson, 1910–84 Collection).

80. George Riley to Arthur Goldberg, July 18, 1961, box 17, folder 8, AFL-CIO Legislation Collection.

81. George Riley to Esther Peterson, July 18, 1961, box 17, folder 8, AFL-CIO Legislation Collection.

82. George Riley to Lorraine Torres, July 18, 1961, NCEP Collection (unprocessed).

83. Harrison, pp. 91–105; Testimony of William F. Schnitzler, U.S. Congress, Senate, Committee on Labor and Public Welfare, *Equal Pay Act of 1963: Hearings before the Subcommittee on Labor of the Committee on Labor and Public Welfare, United States Senate, on S. 882 and S. 910*, 88th Cong., 1st sess., 1963, pp. 121–22.

84. Testimony of William F. Schnitzler, *Senate Equal Pay Hearings*, 1963, p. 124.

85. Anne Draper to William Schnitzler, April 11, 1963, box 17, folder 9, AFL-CIO Legislation Collection. See also, Nancy F. Gabin, *Feminism in the Labor Movement: Women and the United Auto Workers, 1935–1975* (Ithaca, N.Y.: Cornell University Press, 1990), pp. 32, 63–64, 190–92.

86. Minutes, NCEP meeting, August 6, 1962, NCEP Collection (unprocessed).

87. Andrew Biemiller to Dear Congressman, May 22, 1963, box 17, folder 9, AFL-CIO Legislation Collection; Harrison, p. 103.

88. Kenneth Meiklejohn to Andrew Biemiller, May 28, 1963, box 17, folder 9, AFL-CIO Legislation Collection.

89. Quoted in U.S. Congress, House, Committee on Education and Labor, *Equal Pay for Equal Work: Hearings before the Select Subcommittee on Labor of the Committee on Education and Labor, House of Representatives, on H.R. 8898; H.R. 10226, Part 1*, 87th Cong., 2d sess., 1962, p. 223.

90. Mr. Randolph, quoted in *House Equal Pay Act of 1963 Legislative History*, 1963, p. 53.

91. Caroline Davis to Esther Peterson, n.d., reel 59, Department of Labor Papers, John F. Kennedy Library, quoted in Harrison, p. 104.

92. Dorothy Haener, pp. 59–62, Twentieth Century Trade Union Women Oral History Project: Vehicle for Social Change, Oral History Project, Institute of Labor and Industrial Relations, University of Michigan/Wayne State University, Detroit, Mich., quoted in Gabin, p. 188.

93. Ad Hoc Committee to NCEP members, April 6, 1964, NCEP Collection (unprocessed).

94. Esther Peterson to W. Willard Wirtz, February 13, 1963, carton 8, folder 215, Peterson, 1910–84 Collection.

95. Quoted in *Legislative History of the Equal Pay Act of 1963 (Amending Section 6 of the Fair Labor Standards Act of 1938, as Amended),* 88th Cong., 1st sess., 1963, pp. 76–77.

96. Harrison, pp. 104–5. See also, Morag MacLeod Simchak, "Equal Pay in the United States," *International Labour Review* 103 (June 1971): 553.

97. Claudia Goldin, *Understanding the Gender Gap: An Economic History of American Women* (New York: Oxford University Press, 1990), p. 201.

98. Harrison, pp. 104–5.

99. George Meany to James Roosevelt, January 29, 1962, box 55, folder 21, AFL-CIO Legislation Collection.

100. U.S. Congress, Senate, *Report of the Special Committee on Unemployment Problems, Pursuant to S. Res. 196,* 86th Cong., 2d sess., 1960.

101. Jo Freeman, "How 'Sex' Got into Title VII: Persistent Opportunism as a Maker of Public Policy," *Law and Inequality: A Journal of Theory and Practice* 9, no. 2 (March 1991): 163–84.

102. Harrison, pp. 109–37; Kessler-Harris, *Out to Work,* p. 313; Rupp and Taylor, pp. 166–74; Graham, pp. 313, 206–7; and Jane Sherron DeHart, "The New Feminism and the Dynamics of Social Change," in *Women's America: Refocusing the Past,* 4th ed., ed. Linda K. Kerber and Jane Sherron DeHart (New York: Oxford University Press, 1995), pp. 545–46.

103. Ellickson, "The PCSW," unpublished manuscript, cited in Rupp and Taylor, p. 172.

Chapter 3: The Roots of Discontent

1. Virgil Bankson, interview by Paul Kelso, Ottumwa, October 18, 1978, Iowa Labor History Oral Project, State Historical Society of Iowa, Iowa City, Iowa (hereafter, ILHOP).

2. "Sex and Equal Employment Rights," *Monthly Labor Review* 90 (August 1967): iii. A concise history of Title VII is included in Ralph J. Lindgren and Nadine Taub, *The Law of Discrimination* (St. Paul, Minn.: West Publishing, 1988), pp. 109–29. Karen J. Maschke's *Litigation and Women Workers* (New York: Praeger, 1989) also offers an overview of the law and women in the twentieth century.

3. Upton Sinclair, *The Jungle: The Lost First Edition,* edited with an introduction by Gene DeGruson (Memphis: St. Luke's Press, 1988), pp. 119–20.

4. U.S. Department of Labor, *Progress toward Equal Pay in the Meat-Packing Industry,* Women's Bureau Bulletin 251 (1953), p. 3; Research Department notes, "Statistics on

Women in Food Industry," n.d. [1959], box 512, folder 10, United Packinghouse Workers of America Collection, State Historical Society of Wisconsin, Madison, Wis. (hereafter, UPWA-SHSW Collection). A disproportionate presence of women in the lowest three wage brackets existed at Armour (74.3 percent women to 35.7 percent men) and Swift (68.6 percent women to 22.7 percent men). No figures exist for the other large packing companies but anecdotal evidence suggests a similar pattern.

5. Quoted in *America's Working Women: A Documentary History—1600 to the Present,* ed. Rosalyn Baxandall, Linda Gordon, and Susan Reverby (New York: Vintage, 1976), p. 271. For general histories of the UPWA, see Gary M. Fink, ed., *Labor Unions* (Westport, Conn.: Greenwood, 1977), pp. 269–72; David Brody, *The Butcher Workmen: A Study of Unionization* (Cambridge, Mass.: Harvard University Press, 1964), pp. 38, 161, 233; and Roger Horowitz's, "The Path Not Taken: A Social History of Industrial Unionism in Meatpacking, 1930–1960" (Ph.D. diss., University of Wisconsin–Madison, 1990). Horowitz discusses the UPWA in Iowa in "'It Wasn't a Time to Compromise': The Unionization of Sioux City Packinghouses, 1937–1942," *Annals of Iowa* 50 (Fall 1989/Winter 1990): 241–68. The UPWA and race are examined in Eric Brian Halpern, "'Black and White, Unite and Fight': Race and Labor in Meatpacking, 1904–1948" (Ph.D. diss., University of Pennsylvania, 1989), and Bruce R. Fehn, "Striking Women: Gender, Race and Class in the United Packinghouse Workers of America (UPWA), 1938–1968" (Ph.D. diss., University of Wisconsin–Madison, 1991). Alice Kessler-Harris discusses the family-wage ideal in the 1930s and working-class women's demand for "necessity" wages for family stability in *A Women's Wage: Historical Meanings and Social Consequences* (Lexington: University Press of Kentucky, 1990), pp. 78–79.

6. Typescript, "Early History of Local No. 3," February 11, 1957, United Food and Commercial Workers, box 43, Local P-3 Collection (unprocessed), State Historical Society of Iowa, Iowa City, Iowa (hereafter, Local P-3 Collection [unprocessed]).

7. Horowitz, "'It Wasn't a Time to Compromise,'" p. 242.

8. Kerry Napuk to All officers and district directors, "Analysis of U.S. Membership, March 1966," October 3, 1966, box 471, folder 3, UPWA-SHSW Collection; District Council No. 3, United Packinghouse Workers of America, CIO, *Minutes, Seventh Annual Constitutional Convention* (Des Moines, Iowa, 1953), p. 36 (all District 3 convention and international convention proceedings in Local P-3 Collection [unprocessed]); clipping, "Women's Activities," District 3 *Blade,* March 1965, Amalgamated Meatcutters and Butcher Workmen, Local P-1, box 1, Jerred Collection, State Historical Society of Iowa, Iowa City, Iowa (hereafter, P-1 Jerred Collection). District 1 was made up of locals in Michigan, Indiana, Kentucky, Ohio, and Illinois; District 2 represented workers in North Dakota, South Dakota, Wisconsin, and Minnesota; District 3 included packing locals found in Iowa, Nebraska, Missouri, Kansas, and Colorado.

9. Kerry Napuk to all officers and district directors, "Analysis of U.S. Membership, March 1966," October 3, 1966, box 471, folder 3, UPWA-SHSW Collection.

10. William B. Gould, *Black Workers in White Unions: Job Discrimination in the United States* (Ithaca, N.Y.: Cornell University Press, 1977), p. 402; David J. Garrow, *Bearing the*

Cross: Martin Luther King, Jr., and the Southern Christian Leadership Conference (New York: Vintage, 1988), pp. 63, 90, 97, 465, 511; Roger Horowitz, *"Negro and White, Unite and Fight!": A Social History of Industrial Unionism in Meatpacking, 1930–90* (Urbana: University of Illinois Press, 1997), esp. chapters 6–8; F. Ray Marshall, *The Negro and Organized Labor* (New York: Wiley, 1965), pp. 179–83.

11. Addie Wyatt, United Packinghouse Workers of America Oral History Project, 1985–1986 interview, State Historical Society of Wisconsin, Madison, Wis. (hereafter, UPWAOHP), quoted in Fehn, p. 178.

12. Fehn, p. 221.

13. Mary Ashlock, interview by Merle Davis, Mason City, November 17, 1981, Iowa Labor History Oral Project, State Historical Society of Iowa, Iowa City, Iowa (hereafter, ILHOP).

14. Ibid.; Elizabeth "Sue" Smith, interview by Merle Davis, Ottumwa, September 15, 1981, ILHOP. Smith noted that "knife jobs" were both "heavy" and involved "dexterity"; as such, they were considered highly skilled and reserved for men.

15. Quoted in Fehn, p. 149. Nowicki also went by the name "Vicki Starr." See Fehn, pp. 129–34, for a discussion of UPWA wartime history.

16. "Swift PWOC News," n.d. [December 1942], quoted in Fehn, p. 127.

17. The UPWA offered the NWLB an additional reason for eliminating pay differentials: "Surely women cannot be attracted to the industry during this period of crisis by perpetuating the injustice of unequal pay for similar work." See Brief, submitted by UPWA, CIO to NWLB, in the matter of UPWA and Swift and Company (111-5544-D), Armour and Co. (111-5760-D), Wilson and Co. (111-6000-D), Cudahy Packing Co. (111-5763-D), and John Morrell and Co. (111-5914-D), 1943, box 35, Local P-3 Collection (unprocessed). See Fehn, p. 147, for a partial list of UPWA equal pay wartime grievances.

18. See Ruth Milkman, *Gender at Work: The Dynamics of Job Segregation by Sex during World War II* (Urbana: University of Illinois Press, 1987), pp. 99–127.

19. United Packinghouse Workers of America, CIO, *Proceedings, Eighth Constitutional Convention* (Denver, Colo., 1952), pp. 118.

20. United Packinghouse Workers of America, AFL-CIO, *Proceedings, Thirteenth Constitutional Convention* (Minneapolis, Minn., 1962), p. 88.

21. United Packinghouse Workers of America, AFL-CIO, *Proceedings, Fifteenth Constitutional Convention* (Los Angeles, Calif., 1966), p. 77.

22. Ralph Helstein, interview by Merle Davis, Chicago, May 5, 1983, ILHOP.

23. Ethel Jerred, interview by Merle Davis, Ottumwa, October 5, 1981, ILHOP.

24. William E. Forbath discusses such notions in *Law and the Shaping of the American Labor Movement* (Cambridge, Mass.: Harvard University Press, 1991), pp. 53, 55, as does Alice Kessler-Harris in *Out to Work: A History of Wage-Earning Women in the United States* (New York: Oxford University Press, 1982), pp. 180–205.

25. Sylvester Ames, interview by Paul Kelso, Waterloo, March 10, 1978, ILHOP; Helstein, interview, ILHOP.

26. Milkman, p. 19.

27. David Brody, "The Uses of Power, I: Industrial Battleground," in his *Workers in Industrial America: Essays on the Twentieth Century Struggle* (New York: Oxford University Press, 1980), p. 197. The literature on labor's failure to establish a more radical agenda for postwar industrial relations is large. For a helpful overview see Nelson Lichtenstein, "From Corporatism to Collective Bargaining: Organized Labor and the Eclipse of Social Democracy in the Postwar Era," in *The Rise and Fall of the New Deal Order, 1930–1980,* ed. Steve Fraser and Gary Gerstle (Princeton: Princeton University Press, 1989), pp. 122–52.

28. Richard Price, interview by Merle Davis, Waterloo, July 9, 1981, ILHOP.

29. Harold W. Davey, "Present and Future Labor Relations Problems in the Meat Packing Industry," *Labor Law Journal* 18 (December 1967): 750.

30. District Council No. 3, *Minutes* (1953), p. 4.

31. Wilson J. Warren, "The Heyday of the CIO in Iowa: Ottumwa's Meatpacking Workers, 1937–1954," *Annals of Iowa* 51 (Spring 1992): 363–89. Before 1950, Warren says, 60 percent of Local 1 members lived in the neighborhood immediately surrounding the Morrell plant.

32. United Packinghouse Workers of America, CIO, *Proceedings, Sixth Constitutional Convention* (Estes Park, Colo., 1949), pp. 157.

33. UPWA, *Proceedings* (1952), p. 117. For an example of pre-UPWA activism by women in the packinghouses see James R. Barrett, *Work and Community in the Jungle: Chicago's Packinghouse Workers, 1894–1922* (Urbana: University of Illinois Press, 1987), pp. 260–61.

34. Ercell Allen, interview, UPWAOHP, quoted in Fehn, p. 135.

35. Local 46 *Newsletter,* July 7, 1950, box 1, folder 1, Local 46 Collection, State Historical Society of Iowa, Iowa City, Iowa (hereafter, UPWA Local 46 Collection).

36. United Packinghouse Workers of America, AFL-CIO, *Proceedings, Thirteenth Constitutional Convention* (Minneapolis, Minn., 1962), p. 94.

37. UPWA, *Proceedings* (1949), p. 158.

38. District Council No. 3, United Packinghouse Workers of America, AFL-CIO *Minutes, Eleventh Annual Constitutional Convention* (Cedar Rapids, Iowa, 1957), p. 15.

39. Elizabeth Faue, "Paths of Unionization: Community, Bureaucracy, and Gender in the Minneapolis Labor Movement of the 1930s," in *Work Engendered: Toward a New History of American Labor,* ed. Ava Baron (Ithaca, N.Y.: Cornell University Press, 1991), p. 299. See Faue's *Community of Suffering and Struggling: Women, Men, and the Labor Movement in Minneapolis, 1915–1945* (Chapel Hill: University of North Carolina Press, 1991), pp. 4–15, for a discussion of the gendered community and workplace in labor history.

40. District Council No. 3, UPWA, CIO, *Minutes, Fifth Annual Constitutional Convention* (Sioux City, Iowa, 1951), p. 1. See Warren, p. 282, for a discussion of the "wide circles of social affiliations" manifested in packinghouse men's domination of fraternal groups such as the Eagles, Moose, American Legion, and Veterans of Foreign Wars.

41. U.S. Congress, Senate, Committee on Education and Labor, *Equal Pay for Equal Work: Hearings before a Subcommittee on Education and Labor, United States Senate, on S. 1178,* 79th Cong., 1st sess., 1945, pp. 181–82; U.S. Congress, House, Committee on Edu-

cation and Labor, *Equal Pay for Equal Work for Women: Hearings before a Special Subcommittee of the Committee on Education and Labor, House of Representatives, on H.R. 1584 and H.R. 2438*, 81st Cong., 2d sess., 1950, pp. 46–49. See Fehn, pp. 204–38, for a history of equal pay in the UPWA. Cynthia Harrison summarizes the significance of the Equal Pay Act of 1963 in *On Account of Sex: The Politics of Women's Issues, 1945–1968* (Berkeley: University of California Press, 1988), pp. 89–105.

42. U.S. Department of Labor, *Progress Toward Equal Pay*, p. 16.

43. Ibid., p. 16.

44. Fehn, p. 223.

45. Ibid., pp. 204–38.

46. United Packinghouse Workers of America, AFL-CIO, *Proceedings, Twelfth Constitutional Convention* (Chicago, Ill., 1960), p. 104.

47. Robert Schutt to Addie Wyatt, May 15, 1959, box 512, folder 10, UPWA-SHSW Collection. The international office found in 1960 that Chicago women meatpacking workers earned an average per week gross salary of $87.93 as compared to $117.24 for men, a difference of $29.31. See Fehn, p. 299 n. 55.

48. UPWA, *Proceedings* (1962), p. 79. The UPWA also supported state and federal Fair Employment Practices legislation campaigns being carried out by local unions to ensure jobs rights for women workers. See United Packinghouse Workers of America, AFL-CIO, *Proceedings, Tenth Constitutional Convention* (Cincinnati, Ohio, 1956), p. 131.

49. UPWA, *Proceedings* (1956), p. 125.

50. District Council No. 3, *Minutes* (1953), p. 26.

51. Ibid., p. 30. Minority women's rights continued to be a focus of the UPWA. See UPWA, *Proceedings: Officers' Report* (1956), p. 53.

52. Fehn, p. 237.

53. UPWA, *Proceedings* (1956), p. 135.

54. Ibid., pp. 114–15.

55. UPWA, *Proceedings* (1952), p. 120.

56. UPWA, *Proceedings* (1960), p. 122. The demand for the international to take control of women's programs is on page 105.

57. United Packinghouse Workers of America, CIO, *Proceedings, Ninth Constitutional Convention* (Sioux City, Iowa, 1954), p. 68.

58. Ibid., pp. 70, 71.

59. Ibid., p. 76. See also UPWA, *Proceedings* (1956), p. 139, for Lasley's exact restatement of this position.

60. Ibid., p. 79. Helstein maintained in 1958 that he would treat the women's activities committee resolutions as mere recommendations and warned that the international's implementation of them would depend on available funds and feasibility. See United Packinghouse Workers of America, AFL-CIO, *Proceedings, Eleventh Constitutional Convention* (New York, 1958), p. 23. The international did develop meetings for women. Beginning in 1953 it held national women's conferences at the same time as its biennial contract meetings. See Fehn, p. 220.

61. Warren (p. 24) suggests UPWA could equivocate on this issue as well.

62. United Packinghouse Workers of America, AFL-CIO, *Proceedings, Fourteenth Constitutional Convention: Officers' Report* (Kansas City, Kans., 1964), p. xxxix. See Fehn, p. 246, for information on UPWA women's networking with each other. Wyatt sat on the PCSW's "Committee on Protective Labor Legislation." Of the group's thirteen members, one other woman came from the AFL-CIO: Bessie Hillman, vice-president of the Amalgamated Clothing Workers of America. See Harrison, p. 235. Statistics on women officers in District 3 are found in District Council No. 3, United Packinghouse Workers of America, *Minutes, Nineteenth Annual Constitutional Convention* (Ottumwa, Iowa, 1965), p. 25. The report regarding the district's first women's conference is noted in District Council No. 3, United Packinghouse Workers of America, *Minutes, Thirteenth Annual Constitutional Convention: Officers' Report* (Denver, Colo., 1959), p. 5.

63. Pamphlet, "Women in the UPWA: An Analysis by the Projects Committee," February 10, 1965, box 188, folder 7, UPWA-SHSW Collection; typescript, "Report of Panel on Union Participation and Representation of Women Workers, 1955," n.s. [prepared for Joint Wage and Contract, Anti-Discrimination and Women's Activities Conference, Chicago, Ill.], box 454, folder 8, UPWA-SHSW Collection.

64. District Council No. 3, United Packinghouse Workers of America, *Minutes, Ninth Annual Constitutional Convention* (Waterloo, Iowa, 1955), p. 43.

65. District Council No. 3, *Minutes* (1957), p. 15.

66. District Council No. 3, United Packinghouse Workers of America, *Minutes, Seventeenth Annual Constitutional Convention* (Omaha, Nebr., 1963), p. 16.

67. Untitled folder, "Special Report," December 17, 1951, United Packinghouse Workers of America, box 1, Local 1 Collection, State Historical Society of Iowa, Iowa City, Iowa.

68. Ibid.

69. Report, "UPWA Local 46 Women's Conference," April 21, 1953, United Packinghouse Workers of America, box 1, folder 1, Local 46 Collection; see District Council No. 3, *Minutes* (1957), p. 16, for mention of the inactivity of the women's committee of Local 46. For a general overview of the UPWA's efforts on behalf of minority women, see Fehn, pp. 152–203. For local activity of this type in District 3 consult Minutes, Membership committee meeting, September 20, 1955, box 1, Local P-3 Collection (unprocessed); clipping, "Newsnotes," District 3 *Blade,* January 1954, box 1, P-1 Jerred Collection; District Council No. 3, *Minutes, Sixth Annual Constitutional Convention* (Denver, Colo., 1952), p. 4; District Council No. 3, *Minutes* (1953), p. 32; District Council No. 3, *Minutes* (1957), pp. 25–27.

70. See UPWA, *Proceedings* (1958), p. 231, for an example of women's acknowledging male support in women's programs in District 1; "I can say, truthfully, the men have stood behind us one hundred per cent in District 1. We are proud of our men. We have no complaints to make" (UPWA, *Proceedings* [1962], p. 81).

71. UPWA, *Proceedings* (1958), p. 228.

72. Ibid.

73. District Council No. 3, *Minutes* (1963), p. 17.

74. Ibid., p. 19.

75. Ibid.

76. Jerred, interview, ILHOP.

77. Rachel Maerschalk, interview by Gregory Zieran, Dubuque, September 3, 1981, ILHOP.

78. Julia Naylor, interview by Merle Davis, Fort Dodge, August 7, 1981, ILHOP.

79. Jane Burleson, interview by Merle Davis, Fort Dodge, August 5, 1981, ILHOP; Fink, p. 271; Davey, p. 774; Warren, pp. 385–89. District Council No. 3, *Minutes* (1959), p. 35; see also UPWA, *Proceedings* (1966), p. 81 (District 3 director Hart): "in my particular district we have more bigger [*sic*] plants and that is where we have had a problem . . . over this issue [i.e., technological displacement of women]."

80. Rachel Maerschalk, interview by Gregory Zieran, Dubuque, September 3, 1980, ILHOP.

81. Lucille Bremer, interview by Merle Davis, Waterloo, June 2, 1982, ILHOP.

82. Jerred, interview, ILHOP.

83. District Council No. 3 *Minutes* (1959), p. 35; Fink, p. 271.

84. Stephen Meyer, "Technology and the Workplace: Skilled and Production Workers at Allis-Chalmers, 1900–1941," *Technology and Culture* 29 (October 1988): 840.

85. Ed Nixon, interview by Gregory Zieran, Des Moines, March 4, 1981, ILHOP. The origins of the Bedaux system are discussed in David Montgomery, *The Fall of the House of Labor: The Workplace, the State, and American Labor Activism, 1865–1925* (New York: Cambridge University Press, 1987), pp. 440–41.

86. Maerschalk, interview, September 3, 1980, ILHOP; Bremer, interview, ILHOP; Jerred, interview, ILHOP; UPWA, *Proceedings* (1958), p. 224. According to Bruce Fehn (p. 257), the proportion of women employed in packinghouses dropped from 23 percent in the early 1950s to 14 percent in 1955, but this seems unusually low. The UPWA reported in 1965 that 15,557 of its 73,957 members were women (21 percent). See District Council No. 3, *Minutes* (1965), p. 25. U.S. Women's Bureau head Esther Peterson cites the packinghouse industry as one of several industries where the level of displacement on account of automation was high. See International Union of Electrical Workers, AFL-CIO, *Proceedings, Tenth Constitutional Convention* (Cleveland, Ohio, 1962), p. 40.

87. Letter, Ralph Helstein to All Affiliates, September 3, 1963, box 1, folder 5, UPWA Local 46 Collection. For the UPWA's plan to counter automation, see vertical file: Automation, pamphlet, "Progress Report, Automation Committee (1961)," Walter Reuther Archives of Labor History and Urban Affairs, Wayne State University, Detroit, Michigan.

88. Quoted in Fehn, p. 260.

89. Ibid.

90. UPWA, *Proceedings* (1958), p. 227.

91. See UPWA, *Proceedings* (1956), pp. 68–85, for debates on the issue. See also UPWA, *Proceedings* (1960), p. 111, for a restatement of the policy.

92. Fehn, p. 270; clipping, "Women Lay Plans to Combat Automation," District 3 *Blade,* February 1959, box 1, P-1 Jerred Collection; typescript, NLRB charge against em-

ployer, July 17, 1962, box 2, folder 16, UPWA Local 46 Collection [Note: the NLRB's decision in this matter is unknown]; Grievance #207, August 10, 1964, Grievance #223, September 4, 1964, Grievance #248, November 6, 1965, box 1, folder 39, UPWA Local 46 Collection.

93. District Council No. 3, *Minutes* (1959), p. 32.

94. District Council No. 3, *Minutes* (1963), p. 17.

95. UPWA, *Proceedings* (1954), p. 69.

96. UPWA, *Proceedings* (1960), p. 104. As early as 1954 convention delegates had begun calling for laws to be passed "to insure equal job rights for women workers" and for "full and effective enforcement of the protective laws" for women. See UPWA, *Proceedings* (1954), pp. 83–84.

97. UPWA, *Proceedings* (1966), p. 78.

98. UPWA, *Proceedings* (1964), p. 46.

99. Ibid.

100. UPWA, *Proceedings* (1956), p. 127.

Chapter 4: Accounting for Equality

1. Herbert Hammerman and Marvin Rogoff, "The Union Role in Title VII Enforcement: Liability and Opportunity," *Civil Rights Digest* 7 (Spring 1975): 22, 30.

2. Winn Newman and Carole W. Wilson, "The Union Role in Affirmative Action," *Labor Law Journal* 32 (June 1981): 328.

3. Kim Moody, *An Injury to All: The Decline of American Unionism* (New York: Verso, 1988), pp. xv, 58.

4. James J. Matles and James Higgins, *Them and Us: Struggles of a Rank-and-File Union* (Englewood Cliffs, N.J.: Prentice-Hall, 1974), p. 37. For accounts of the UE's origins, see Matles and Higgins, pp. 32–53; Ronald W. Schatz, *The Electrical Workers: A History of Labor at General Electrical and Westinghouse, 1923–60* (Urbana: University of Illinois Press, 1983), pp. 63–64; John Bennett Sears, "Labor Opposition to the Cold War: The Electrical Unions and the Cold War Consensus" (Ph.D. diss., Temple University, 1988), pp. 37–46; Gary M. Fink, ed. *Labor Unions* (Westport, Conn.: Greenwood, 1977), pp. 80–83.

5. Schatz, pp. 63–64, 92–99.

6. Patricia Cooper, "The Faces of Gender: Sex Segregation and Work Relations at Philco, 1928–1938," in *Work Engendered: Toward a New History of American Labor,* ed. Ava Baron (Ithaca, N.Y.: Cornell University Press, 1991), p. 330. On job-typing by sex in the electrical industry, also see Schatz, pp. 30–32. Schatz reports (p. 29) that African-American men and women and other minorities made up less than 1 percent of the industry's work force in 1930; as late as 1960 that figure had climbed only to 3 percent.

7. Cooper, pp. 334–35; Alice Kessler-Harris, *A Woman's Wage: Historical Meanings and Social Consequences* (Lexington: University Press of Kentucky, 1990), pp. 57–80. Like all industrial unions, the UE opposed the Equal Rights Amendment. See pamphlet, "The Road to Equality," n.d. [1948], National Commission on the Status of Women, box 55, folder 9, American Federation of Labor–Congress of Industrial Organizations Depart-

ment of Legislation Collection, George Meany Memorial Archives, Silver Spring, Md. (hereafter, AFL-CIO Legislation Collection).

8. Cooper, p. 349. See Ruth Milkman, *Gender at Work: The Dynamics of Job Segregation by Sex during World War II* (Urbana: University of Illinois Press, 1987), pp. 3, 8, 51, 112, 116–17, 151, for a comparison of automobile and electrical manufacturing and different rates of hiring women.

9. Schatz, p. 33.

10. Mary Callahan, interview by Alice M. Hoffman and Karen Budd, Philadelphia, Pa., May 7, 1976, Twentieth Century Trade Union Women: Vehicle for Social Change, Oral History Project, Institute of Labor and Industrial Relations, University of Michigan/Wayne State University, Detroit, Mich. (hereafter, Twentieth Century Trade Union Women Project).

11. Quoted in Barbara M. Wertheimer and Anne H. Nelson, *Trade Union Women: A Study of Their Participation in New York City Locals* (New York: Praeger, 1975), p. 48.

12. Lisa Kannenberg, "The Impact of the Cold War on Women's Trade Union Activism: The UE Experience," *Labor History* 34 (Spring–Summer 1993), p. 310.

13. Linda Nyden, "Women Electrical Workers at Westinghouse Electric Corporation's East Pittsburgh Plant, 1907–1954" (M.A. thesis, University of Pittsburgh, 1975), p. 58, quoted in Philip S. Foner, *Women and the American Labor Movement: From World War I to the Present* (New York: Free Press, 1980), p. 318.

14. Quoted in Milkman, p. 35.

15. Lisa A. Kannenberg, "From World War to Cold War: Women Electrical Workers and Their Union, 1940–1955" (M.A. thesis, University of North Carolina at Charlotte, 1990), pp. 16–20. It is difficult to gauge how the Communist Party's promotion of women's rights influenced UE policy. Kannenberg suggests it was significant in that the UAW and UE were the most attentive of unions to women's concerns and were labor organizations with a strong left-wing influence. This does not explain, however, the unremarkable record of other CP union strongholds, such as the International Fur and Leather Workers, or the IUE's good record. Nancy F. Gabin notes that neither the left or right wing of the UAW advocated for women's rights very seriously in the 1940s. See her *Feminism in the Labor Movement: Women and the United Auto Workers, 1935–1975* (Ithaca, N.Y.: Cornell University Press, 1990), p. 146.

16. *New York Times,* September 30, 1943, quoted in Foner, p. 376.

17. Gladys Dickason, "Women in Labor Unions," *Annals of the American Academy of Political and Social Science* 251 (May 1947): 72; Kannenberg, "From World War to Cold War," pp. 22–44.

18. Kannenberg, "From World War to Cold War," p. 33.

19. Ibid., pp. 22–24. Kannenberg asserts that the UE leadership displayed "an intent to eliminate the whole category of separate 'female jobs'" (p. 24), but her evidence does not demonstrate this.

20. Dickason, p. 73; Milkman, pp. 42–48, 77–83; Kannenberg, "From World War to Cold War," pp. 31–36.

21. Testimony of Ruth Roemer, U.S. Congress, House, Committee on Education and Labor, *Equal Pay for Equal Work for Women: Hearings before Subcommittee No. 4 of the Committee on Education and Labor, House of Representatives, on H.R. 4273 and H.R. 4408,* 80th Cong., 2d sess., 1948, p. 201.

22. Ibid., pp. 198–205.

23. Ruth Young, "Women in the UE," *Life and Labor Bulletin* 52 (May 1944): 1.

24. Milkman, p. 113; Kannenberg, "From World War to Cold War," pp. 36–37; Schatz, p. 121.

25. Callahan interview, Twentieth Century Trade Union Women Project.

26. Milkman, pp. 144–48; Schatz, pp. 125–27; Kannenberg, "From World War to Cold War," p. 46.

27. Quoted in Fink, p. 79.

28. On the IUE-UE split, see Schatz, pp. 76, 225; Sears, pp. 85–91; Robert H. Zieger, *American Workers, American Unions, 1920–1985* (Baltimore: Johns Hopkins University Press, 1986), p. 112; Mark McColloch, "The Shop-Floor Dimension of Union Rivalry: The Case of Westinghouse in the 1950s," in *The CIO's Left-Led Unions,* ed. Steve Rosswurm (New Brunswick, N.J.: Rutgers University Press, 1992), pp. 184–85. On the Association of Catholic Trade Unionists rivalry with the UE's right wing, see Matles and Higgins, pp. 200–202; Schatz, pp. 181–83; Patrick J. McGeerer, *Rev. Charles Owen Rice: Apostle of Contradiction* (Pittsburgh: Duquesne University Press, 1989), pp. 92–135; Steve Rosswurm, "The Catholic Church and the Left-Led Unions: Labor Priests, Labor Schools, and the ACTU," in *The CIO's Left-Led Unions,* ed. Rosswurm (New Brunswick, N.J.: Rutgers University Press, 1992), pp. 132–33; Mike Davis, *Prisoners of the American Dream: Politics and Economy in the History of the US Working Class* (London: Verso, 1986), p. 80; and Douglas P. Seaton, *Catholics and Radicals: The Association of Catholic Trade Unionists and the American Labor Movement from Depression to Cold War* (Lewisburg, Pa.: Bucknell University Press, 1981).

29. Kannenberg, "From World War to Cold War," p. 46.

30. Ibid., pp. 50–63; Schatz, pp. 126–27. Not so for Local 617 (Sharon, Pa.). There, single women led the effort to ban married women from the work force; pressure from Local 617 married women, District 6 leaders, and UE GEB members turned this policy around.

31. Quoted in Milkman, p. 149.

32. International Union of Electrical Workers-CIO, *Proceedings, Fourth Annual Convention* (Pittsburgh, Pa., 1952), p. 363. Sears provides the two unions' memberships (pp. 81, 233; in thousands). IUE: 1949 = 0; 1950 = 71; 1951 = 203; 1952 = 231; 1953 = 266; 1954 = 282; 1955 = 284; 1960 = 271; 1962 = 270. UE: 1949 = 428; 1950 = 233; 1951 = 222; 1952 = 215; 1953 = 203; 1954 = 182; 1955 = 133; 1960 = 59; 1962 = 55.

33. Gloria Johnson, interview by Dennis Deslippe, Washington, D.C., June 8, 1993, Walter Reuther Archives of Labor and Urban Affairs, Wayne State University, Detroit, Mich. (hereafter, Reuther Archives).

34. *Who's Who in America,* vol. 2, 1978–79 (Chicago: Marquis Publishing, 1978), p. 1,894. As an activist in Americans for Democratic Action (an anticommunist liberal group), Lasser marshaled his abilities on behalf of the newly created IUE. Specifically, Lasser

nurtured IUE contacts with public officials in order to publicize the potential loss of government contracts at UE worksites. See Sears, p. 107.

35. Gloria Johnson, interview, Reuther Archives.

36. Minutes, NCEP meetings: January 9, 1953, April 6, 1954, May 19, 1954, January 3, 1955, April 12, 1955, July 11, 1955, all in National Committee on Equal Pay Collection (unprocessed), George Meany Memorial Archives, Silver Spring, Md. (hereafter, NCEP Collection [unprocessed]). Ben Sigal (IUE legal counsel) participated in discussions with CIO legislative representatives on the need for an equal pay law. See, for example, Anthony W. Smith to Robert Oliver, April 8, 1954, box 78, folder 14, CIO Washington Office Collection, 1950–56, Reuther Archives.

37. U.S. Department of Labor, *The Status of Women in the United States, 1953,* Women's Bureau Bulletin No. 249 (G.P.O., 1953); Gloria Johnson, interview, Reuther Archives; Callahan interview, Twentieth Century Trade Union Women Project. Another rank-and-file member, Evelyn McGarr (described by Johnson as a "very powerful woman"), from Montreal, held the position of secretary-treasurer of Canada's District 5; in 1960 McGarr began to serve on the IEB.

38. Katherine P. Ellickson, interview by Dennis East, Detroit, Mich., January 10, 1976, Reuther Archives.

39. James B. Carey and Al Hartnett to IUE Executive Board Members, May 3, 1957, box 2186, group 1, International Union of Electrical Workers (IUE) Archives, Special Collections and University Archives, Rutgers University Libraries, New Brunswick, N.J. (hereafter, IUE Archives).

40. Typescript, "Program of National IUE-AFL-CIO Women's Conference," June 1957, box 2186, group 1, IUE Archives.

41. International Union of Electrical Workers, AFL-CIO, *Proceedings, Tenth Constitutional Convention* (Cleveland, Ohio, 1962), pp. 22–24.

42. Callahan interview, Twentieth Century Trade Union Women Project.

43. Kathleen McNee to Al Hartnett, March 27, 1956, box 2075, group 1, IUE Archives.

44. Marjorie McKeown to Milton Weihrauch, April 7, 1954, box 275, group 1, IUE Archives.

45. Kathleen McNee discusses her bowling and birthday party activities in letters to Al Hartnett, April 28, 1956 and May 6, 1956, both in box 2075, group 1, IUE Archives.

46. Ruth Frank to Al Hartnett, May 22, 1951, box 2072, group 1, IUE Archives. Carey fired Frank soon after for chronic overcharging of her expense vouchers. See James Carey to Ruth Frank, June 18, 1951, box 2072, group 1, IUE Archives.

47. Rosemary Mannie, Organizers Report, District 10, IUE-CIO, November 24, 1953, box 2075, group 1, IUE Archives.

48. Rosemary Mannie to Al Hartnett, March 23, 1954, box 2075, group 1, IUE Archives.

49. Mary Lou Sauer to Al Hartnett, April 24, 1950, box 2077, group 1, IUE Archives.

50. Typescript, [David Lasser], "Summary of Collective Bargaining Negotiations between IUE-CIO and GE, 1949–54," n.d., box 2006, group 1, IUE Archives; International Union of Electrical Workers, AFL-CIO, *Proceedings, Ninth Constitutional Convention*

(Miami Beach, Fla., 1960), pp. 280–84, and *Proceedings, Eighth Constitutional Convention* (Philadelphia, Pa., 1958), p. 349.

51. Agreement, Between Philco Corp., Sandusky, Ohio, and International Union of Electrical, Radio and Machine Workers, AFL-CIO, Local 701, 1960, box 175, group 1, IUE Archives.

52. McColloch, pp. 195–96.

53. Foner, p. 413.

54. Kannenberg, "From World War to Cold War," p. 74.

55. Ibid., pp. 85–89; McColloch, pp. 194–99.

56. United Electrical Radio and Machine Workers of America, *Report of the General Officer, 1950*, p. 50.

57. Schatz, pp. 126–27; Kannenberg, "From World War to Cold War," pp. 50–63.

58. Mary Lou Sauer to Al Hartnett, April 23, 1950, box 2077, group 1, IUE Archives. According to Mark McColloch, when the IUE won the Sharon election, discrimination against married women resumed (see McColloch, p. 239 n. 93).

59. Robert Alfred Lorentz discusses IUE local autonomy in his "Electrical Insurgency in an International Union: The Influence of Local Union Size and Dispersion in the IUE" (Ph.D. diss., Syracuse University, 1986), p. iv.

60. International Union of Electrical Worker's *Constitutions*, 1950–51, 1959, 1977, all in box 220, group 2, IUE Archives. Before 1959 this revocation involved a complex process; thereafter, Carey could act with three IEB members to suspend locals prior to a hearing. This action would stay in effect until the next regular board meeting.

61. Benjamin C. Sigal to James Carey, August 13, 1959, box 2016, group 1, IUE Archives.

62. Schatz, pp. 195, 216–17; Seaton, pp. 60–61; Fink, p. 79; David Lasser to James Carey and Al Hartnett, July 9, 1959, box 2015, group 1, IUE Archives; Sears, pp. 11, 27, 200–201, 235; McColloch, pp. 188–93.

63. Schatz, pp. 185, 225–26.

64. Mary Lou Sauer to Al Hartnett, April 23, 1950, box 2077, group 1, IUE Archives.

65. Rosemary Mannie to Al Hartnett, March 23, 1954, box 2075, group 1, IUE Archives.

66. Terry Copp, *The IUE in Canada: A History* (Elora, Ont.: Cumnock Press, 1980), p. 46.

67. Sears, pp. 47, 80–81, 150, 213–16, 233; Zieger, pp. 133–34; Schatz, pp. 229–30.

68. Kannenberg, "From World War to Cold War," p. 95.

69. United Electrical, Radio and Machine Workers of America, *24th Convention Proceedings* (Chicago, Ill., 1959), p. 242.

70. United Electrical, Radio and Machine Workers of America, *25th Convention Proceedings* (Atlantic City, N.J., 1960), p. 323.

71. Kannenberg, "The Impact of the Cold War," p. 323.

72. IUE, *Proceedings* (1960), p. 281. The 35 percent female membership figure is constant throughout 1945–80. See, for example, International Union of Electrical Workers, AFL-CIO, *Proceedings, Fifteenth Constitutional Convention: Officers' Report* (Washington, D.C., 1972), p. 454.

73. Schatz, pp. 169–74; Matles and Higgins, p. 250; Davis, pp. 119–24. For a pro-management perspective of Boulwarism, see Peter Brimlow, "A Look Back at Boulwarism," *Forbes,* May 5, 1989, pp. 239–48.

74. *New York Times,* October 25, 1960, quoted in Davis, p. 124. See also Sears, pp. 241–43, on IUE strikes during this period.

75. Sidney Lens, *The Crisis of American Labor* (New York: Sagamore Press, 1959), p. 254.

76. International Union of Electrical Workers, AFL-CIO, *Proceedings, Twelfth Constitutional Convention* (Bal Harbour, Fla., 1966), p. 57.

77. Moody, p. 68.

78. Typescript, Statement of David Lasser, Research Director, IUE-CIO, Representing the CIO at Equal Pay for Equal Work Conference, U.S. Department of Labor, March 31–April 1, 1952, box 2087, group 1, IUE Archives.

79. This compared to 17 percent of agreements in all industry groups, covering 26 percent of all workers. See James C. Nix, "Equal Pay for Equal Work," *Monthly Labor Review* 74, no. 1 (January 1952): 43.

80. Testimony of James B. Carey, U.S. Congress, House, Committee on Education and Labor, *Equal Pay for Equal Work: Hearings before the Select Subcommittee on Labor of the Committee on Education and Labor, House of Representatives, on H.R. 8898; H.R. 10226, Part 1,* 87th Cong., 2d sess., 1962, pp. 175, 181.

81. Gloria Johnson, interview, Reuther Archives.

82. Testimony of James B. Carey, *House Equal Pay Hearings,* 1962, p. 175; Ruth Weyand to Jane M. Picker, December 10, 1993, box 239, group 2, IUE Archives.

83. Carey, 1962 testimony, pp. 174–75.

84. Callahan interview, Twentieth Century Trade Union Women Project.

85. IUE, *Proceedings* (1962), p. 350.

86. IUE, *Proceedings* (1958), p. 344.

87. IUE, *Proceedings* (1960), p. 306; David F. Noble, *Forces of Production: A Social History of Industrial Automation* (New York: Oxford University Press, 1984), pp. 249–50; Testimony of James B. Carey, U.S. Congress, House, *Impact of Automation on Employment: Hearings before the Subcommittee on Unemployment and the Impact of Automation of the Committee on Education and Labor, House of Representatives,* 87th Cong., 1st sess., March/April 1961, p. 259. Carey noted other job losses at the hearing. For GE plants: Lynn, Mass., went from 16,000 to 8,000 workers; the GE Bloomfield, N.J., plant closed; Bridgeport, Conn., dropped by nearly 50 percent; and Pittsfield, Mass., and Fort Wayne, Ind., plants cut one-third of their work forces. At Westinghouse, the East Pittsburgh plant cut 32.1 percent while the Lima, Ohio, facility slashed its employee roster by 55.6 percent and Mansfield, Ohio, by 60.7 percent, and the Sharon, Pa., plant dropped 25.4 percent.

88. Testimony of James B. Carey, *House Automation Hearings,* 1962, p. 270.

89. Typescript, "Program of National IUE-AFL-CIO Women's Conference," June 1957, box 2186, group 1, IUE Archives.

90. *Labor Fact Book 16: A People's Almanac* (New York: Labor Research Association/International Publishers, 1963), p. 42.

91. Memorandum, [David Lasser], "Facts on Day Letter of February 4," n.d. [1958], box 2015, group 1, IUE Archives; Testimony of James B. Carey, *House Equal Pay Hearings, Part 1,* 1962, p. 182.

92. Memorandum, "Summary of Collective Bargaining Negotiations between IUE-CIO and GE, 1949–54," n.a., n.d., box 2006, group 1, IUE Archives; "The First 'Automation' Strike," *Fortune,* December 1955, pp. 57–58; IUE, *Proceedings* (1958), pp. 132–33; IUE, *Proceedings* (1962), pp. 364–65; Noble, pp. 249–52.

93. IUE, *Proceedings* (1958), pp. 132–33.

94. Testimony of James B. Carey, U.S. Congress, House, *Equal Pay Act: Hearings before the Special Subcommittee on Labor of the Committee on Education and Labor, House of Representatives, on H.R. 3861, 4269, and Related Bills,* 88th Cong., 1st sess., March 1963, p. 110.

95. Typescript, James B. Carey, "Statement on Equal Pay Legislation," n.d. [1956], box 46, group 2, IUE Archives.

96. International Union of Electrical Workers, AFL-CIO, *Legislative Handbook,* 1958–59, box 2077, group 1, IUE Archives; typescript, "Program of national IUE-AFL-CIO Women's Conference," June 1957, box 2186, group 1, IUE Archives; David Lasser to IUE, IEB, and GE/Westinghouse Locals, April 5, 1962, box 218, group 2, IUE Archives; IUE *Proceedings:* 1958, 1960, and 1962, pp. 349, 316, and 373, respectively; David Lasser to Paul Sifton, February 2, 1956, box 46, group 2, IUE Archives.

97. Jack Barbash, *American Unions: Structure, Government and Politics* (New York: Random House, 1967), p. 97.

98. Testimony of James B. Carey, *House Equal Pay Hearings, Part 1,* 1962, p. 177.

99. Ibid., p. 178. Carey chaired the federation's Civil Rights Committee; he quit in 1957, charging that AFL-CIO president George Meany did not provide enough staff support and that Meany developed civil rights policy without his group's input. See Memorandum, James B. Carey, Report on AFL-CIO Civil Rights Committee, March 1, 1957, box 58, group 2, IUE Archives.

100. Typescript, Statement of David Lasser, Research Director, IUE-CIO, Representing the CIO at Equal Pay for Equal Work Conference, U.S. Department of Labor, March 31–April 1, 1952, box 2087, group 1, IUE Archives.

101. Anne Draper to William F. Schnitzler, April 11, 1963, box 17, folder 9, AFL-CIO Collection.

102. Ibid.

103. Typescript, Statement of James B. Carey to AFL-CIO Executive Council Meeting on Equal Pay Legislation, n.d. [1956], box 46, group 2, IUE Archives.

104. Memorandum, Report of President to IUE International Executive Board Meeting Participants, December 18–19, 1963, box 36, group 2, IUE Archives. For the IUE's negative reaction to a weakening of the legislation in Congress in 1962, see IUE, *Proceedings: Officers' Report* (1962), p. 572.

105. Memorandum, Report of President to IUE International Executive Board Meeting Participants, December 18–19, 1963, box 36, group 2, IUE Archives.

106. Gloria Johnson, interview, Reuther Archives.

107. International Union of Electrical Workers, AFL-CIO, *Proceedings, Third Annual Convention* (Buffalo, N.Y., 1951), pp. 157–58.

108. Gloria Johnson, interview, Reuther Archives.

109. Program, National IUE-AFL-CIO Women's Conference, Washington, D.C., June 17–18, 1957, box 2186, group 1, IUE Archives.

110. Cynthia Harrison, *On Account of Sex: The Politics of Women's Issues, 1945–1968* (Berkeley: University of California Press, 1988), pp. 138–65, 229–36.

111. James B. Carey to James Roosevelt, January 17, 1962, box 145, group 2, IUE Archives. For background on proto–Title VII legislation see Hugh Davis Graham, *The Civil Rights Era: Origins and Development of National Policy, 1960–1972* (New York: Oxford University Press, 1990), p. 98.

Chapter 5: Organized Labor, National Politics, and Gender Equality

1. U.S. Congress, Senate, Committee on the Judiciary, *The "Equal Rights" Amendment, Hearings before the Subcommittee on Constitutional Amendments of the Committee on the Judiciary on S.J. Res. 61,* 91st Cong., 2d sess., 1970, p. 593.

2. Figures are from U.S. Department of Labor, *Handbook of Women Workers, 1975,* Women's Bureau (Washington, D.C., 1975), pp. 9, 11, 17, 18. There was a corresponding increase in women's union membership. In 1956 women comprised 18.6 percent of total union membership; by 1978 they claimed 24.2 percent of the total. See Ruth Milkman, "Women Workers, Feminism, and the Labor Movement since the 1960s," in *Women, Work, and Protest: A Century of Women's Labor History,* ed. Milkman (New York: Routledge and Kegan Paul, 1985), p. 304.

3. *Detroit Free Press,* June 26, 1972, quoted in Nancy F. Gabin, *Feminism in the Labor Movement: Women and the United Auto Workers, 1935–1975* (Ithaca, N.Y.: Cornell University Press, 1990), p. 223.

4. Jean T. McKelvey, "Sex and the Single Arbitrator," *Industrial and Labor Relations Review* 24 (April 1971): 353.

5. For a general discussion on the passage of the sex discrimination ban in Title VII, see Charles and Barbara Whalen, *The Longest Debate: A Legislative History of the 1964 Civil Rights Act* (Cabin John, Md.: Seven Locks Press, 1985), pp. 15–17; Jo Freeman, "How 'Sex' Got into Title VII: Persistent Opportunism as a Maker of Public Policy," *Law and Inequality: A Journal of Theory and Practice* 9, no. 2 (March 1991): 163–84; Susan M. Hartmann, *From Margin to Mainstream: American Women and Politics since 1960* (Philadelphia: Temple University Press, 1989), pp. 63–71; Philip S. Foner, *Women and the American Labor Movement: From World War I to the Present* (New York: Free Press, 1980), pp. 481–82; Donald Allen Robinson, "Two Movements in Pursuit of Equal Employment Opportunity," *Signs* 4 (Spring 1979): 416–17; Carl M. Brauer, "Women Activists, Southern Conservatives, and the Prohibition of Sex Discrimination in Title VII of the 1964 Civil Rights Act," *Journal of Southern History* 49 (1983): 37–57; Leila Rupp and Verta Taylor, *Survival in the Doldrums: The American Women's Rights Movement, 1945 to the 1960s* (New

York: Oxford University Press, 1987; reprint, Columbus: Ohio State University Press, 1990), pp. 177; Cynthia Harrison, *On Account of Sex: The Politics of Women's Issues, 1945–1968* (Berkeley: University of California Press, 1988), pp. 179–80; Patricia G. Zelman, *Women, Work, and National Policy: The Kennedy-Johnson Years* (Ann Arbor, Mich.: UMI Research Press, 1980), pp. 63–71; Sally J. Kenney, *For Whose Protection? Reproductive Hazards and Exclusionary Policies in the United States and Britain* (Ann Arbor: University of Michigan, 1992), pp. 139–84: Kathleen Esther Nuccio, "The Equal Employment Opportunity Commission, 1964–1984: A Life Cycle Model" (Ph.D. diss., Bryn Mawr Graduate School of Social Work and Social Research, 1987), pp. 77–87, 110–15.

6. Robinson, p. 414.

7. Esther Peterson, interview by Paige Mulhollan, Washington, D.C., November 25, 1968, Lyndon Baines Johnson Library, Austin, Tex., transcript in carton 2 of the Esther Peterson Collection, 1940, 1952–86 (unprocessed), Schlesinger Library, Radcliffe College, Cambridge, Mass. Organizations in the U.S. Women's Bureau Coalition generally rejected the inclusion of "sex" as well. See, for example, American Association of University Women to Carl Albert, February 9, 1964, box 69, folder 21, Legislative Series, Carl Albert Collection, Carl Albert Center, University of Oklahoma, Norman, Okla.

8. Peterson interview by Mulhollan, Schlesinger Library; Minutes, NCEP meeting, June 14, 1965, National Committee on Equal Pay Collection (unprocessed), George Meany Memorial Archives, Silver Spring, Md. (hereafter, NCEP Collection [unprocessed]).

9. On race discrimination and civil rights activism in the labor movement, see Robert H. Zieger, *American Workers, American Unions, 1920–1985* (Baltimore: Johns Hopkins University Press, 1986), pp. 51–53, 82, 174–82; Kim Moody, *An Injury to All: The Decline of American Unionism* (New York: Verso, 1988), pp. 59, 75; Hugh Davis Graham, *The Civil Rights Era: Origins and Development of National Policy, 1960–1972* (New York: Oxford University Press, 1990), p. 103; Herbert Hill, "The Equal Employment Opportunity Acts of 1964 and 1972: A Critical Analysis of the Legislative History and Administration of the Law," *Industrial Relations Law Journal* 2 (Spring 1977): 34–35, 35 n. 147, 63–64; Robert Korstad and Nelson Lichtenstein, "Opportunities Found and Lost: Labor, Radicals, and the Early Civil Rights Movement," *Journal of American History* 75 (December 1988): 786–811; Alan Draper, "Do the Right Thing: The Desegregation of Union Conventions in the South," *Labor History* 33 (Summer 1992): 343–56. For the federation's backing of the Civil Rights Act of 1964, see Graham, p. 139; Zieger, p. 176; Moody, p. 75; Andrew Biemiller to Adam Clayton Powell, July 8, 1963, and George Meany to All Members of House Judiciary Committee, August 20, 1963, both in box 17, folder 9, Andrew Biemiller to Officers of State and Local Central Bodies, January 26, 1964, box 10, folder 17, all in the American Federation of Labor–Congress of Industrial Organizations Department of Legislation Collection, George Meany Memorial Archives, Silver Spring, Md. (hereafter, AFL-CIO Legislation Collection); pamphlet, "Labor Looks at Congress, 1963" (AFL-CIO Publication 77E, 1964), George Meany Memorial Archives, Silver Spring, Md.

10. Robinson, p. 421; Graham, pp. 177, 203; Nuccio, pp. 130–43; B. Dan Wood, "Does

Politics Make a Difference at the EEOC?" *American Journal of Political Science* 34 (May 1990): 507.

11. Pamphlet, *Labor Looks at Congress, 1965* (AFL-CIO Publication 77G, 1965), George Meany Memorial Archives, Silver Spring, Md.; Hill, pp. 34–35, 35 n. 147, 63–64; Farrell E. Bloch, "Discrimination in Nonrefferal Unions," in *Equal Rights and Industrial Relations,* ed. Leonard J. Hawsman et al. (Madison, Wis.: Industrial Relations Research Association, 1979), p. 118.

12. Harrison, p. 189.

13. Quoted in Graham, p. 211.

14. Ibid., p. 204.

15. Richard K. Berg, "Title VII: A Three Years' View," *Notre Dame Lawyer* 44 (February 1969): 330 n. 110, 331.

16. Quoted in Equal Employment Opportunity Commission, *Making a Right a Reality: An Oral History of the Early Years of the EEOC, 1965–1972* (Washington, D.C.: EEOC, 1990), p. 7.

17. Quoted in Harrison, p. 189.

18. Ibid., pp. 188–89.

19. Irvin D. Solomon, *Feminism and Black Activism in Contemporary America: An Ideological Assessment* (New York: Greenwood, 1989), p. 48.

20. Andrew J. Biemiller to State Central Body Officers, March 31, 1966, box 44, folder 24, AFL-CIO Legislation Collection.

21. Barbara Allen Babcock et al., *Sex Discrimination and the Law: Causes and Remedies* (Boston: Little, Brown, 1975), pp. 263–68; Dorothy I. Height to Luther Holcomb, July 28, 1966, box 55, folder 22, AFL-CIO Legislation Collection.

22. Quoted in Babcock et al., p. 266.

23. Harrison, pp. 187–91; Graham, pp. 213–18; Nuccio, pp. 143–67.

24. Graham, p. 225.

25. Sonia Pressman Fuentes, interview by Sylvia Danovitch, Potomac, Md., December 27, 1990, Equal Employment Opportunity Commission, transcript in author's possession. Pressman was referring to the National Organization for Women (NOW), the Women's Equity Action League (WEAL), and Federally Employed Women (FEW).

26. Catherine East, "The Current Status of the Employment of Women," in *Women in the Workforce: Proceedings of a Conference Sponsored by the Division of Personnel Psychology of the New York State Psychological Association, November 1970,* ed. Mildred E. Katzell and William C. Byham (New York: Behavioral Publications, 1972), p. 11.

27. Summary memorandum, "8,854 Job Discrimination Complaints Filed with EEOC in First Year," n.d., box 7, folder 8, Katherine Ellickson Collection, 1921–78, Walter Reuther Archives of Labor and Urban Affairs, Wayne State University, Detroit, Mich. (hereafter, Reuther Archives); Graham, pp. 228–29.

28. Karen J. Maschke, *Litigation, Courts, and Women Workers* (New York: Praeger, 1989), p. 103. See also, Ann Corinne Hill, "Protection of Women Workers and the Courts: A

Legal Case History," *Feminist Studies* 5 (Summer 1979): 261, and Jo Freeman, *The Politics of Women's Liberation: A Case Study of an Emerging Social Movement and Its Relation to the Policy Process* (New York: David McKay, 1975), pp. 164–66.

29. Ginger Timberlake to George Meany, August 26, 1972, box 55, folder 22, AFL-CIO Legislation Collection.

30. Testimony of Georgianna Sellers (for the League for American Working Women), U.S. Congress, Senate, Committee on the Judiciary, *The "Equal Rights" Amendment: Hearings, before the Committee on the Judiciary,* 91st Cong., 2d sess., May 1970, p. 590.

31. Interview with anonymous woman, quoted in Brigid O'Farrell and Suzanne Moore, "Unions, Hard Hats, and Woman Workers," in *Women and Unions: Forging a Partnership,* ed. Dorothy Sue Cobble (Ithaca, N.Y.: ILR Press, 1993), p. 75.

32. The UAW left the AFL-CIO in 1968 and is not listed in Appendix 4. Nevertheless, even this progressive union practiced sex discrimination. See Gabin, pp. 196–97.

33. Herbert Hill, "Black Workers, Organized Labor, and Title VII of the 1964 Civil Rights Act: Legislative History and Litigation Record," in *Race in America: The Struggle for Equality,* ed. Herbert Hill and James E. Jones Jr. (Madison: University of Wisconsin Press, 1993), p. 313.

34. Clipping, *Los Angeles Times,* March 7, 1966, box 44, folder 22, AFL-CIO Legislation Collection.

35. Quoted in Gabin, p. 191. The International Chemical Workers testified against protective laws at the hearings as well. See Babcock et al., p. 263.

36. Gabin, pp. 202–5.

37. Harrison, p. 201.

38. *New York Times,* December 14, 1967.

39. On NOW's early years, see Hartmann, pp. 56–60; Rupp and Taylor, pp. 166, 179–80; Harrison, p. 192, 194–97; Jane Sherron DeHart, "The New Feminism and the Dynamics of Social Change," in *Women's America: Refocusing the Past,* 4th ed., ed. Linda K. Kerber and Jane Sherron DeHart (New York: Oxford University Press, 1995), pp. 548–54.

40. Harrison, p. 208.

41. Graham, p. 225.

42. Dorothy Howze, quoted in Equal Employment Opportunity Commission, *Making a Right,* p. 17. See Graham, pp. 244–45, for background on Pressman.

43. Sonia Pressman Fuentes, interview by Dennis Deslippe, Potomac, Md., November 23, 1993, Reuther Archives.

44. Ibid.

45. Harrison, p. 193; Robinson, pp. 423 n. 30, 428–31.

46. Fuentes, interview, Reuther Archives. For a discussion of female government employees' connection with NOW, see also Michele Ingrassia, "NOW and Then," *Newsday,* October 29, 1991, p. 61.

47. Graham, pp. 228–32; Robinson, pp. 413–33; Harrison, pp. 193–95. Subsequent to leaving the EEOC, both Graham and Hernandez were elected to the NOW leadership.

48. Graham, pp. 228–32.

49. On the small number of women in elected union office and the larger number in appointed positions, see Lucretia M. Dewey, "Women in Labor Unions," *Monthly Labor Review* 94 (February 1971): 44–47.

50. Ruth Miller to Howard Samuel, November 21, 1969, carton 9, folder 294, Esther Peterson Collection, 1910–84, Schlesinger Library, Radcliffe College, Cambridge, Mass. (hereafter, Peterson Collection, 1910–84).

51. Minutes, NCEP meetings: December 16, 1964, December 28, 1964, June 14, 1965; Clarence Lundquist to Anne Draper, April 9, 1965; Anne Draper to Franklin D. Roosevelt Jr., June 30, 1965; Anne Draper to NCEP members, September 15, 1965; Gloria Johnson and Mary C. Baily to All interested organizations, January 24, 1966, all in NCEP Collection (unprocessed).

52. Anne Draper to Sara Feder, February 14, 1968, NCEP Collection (unprocessed). The NCEP did not disband formally until 1974.

53. Anne Draper to Andrew Biemiller, Don Slaiman, and Tom Harris, carton 9, folder 294, Peterson Collection, 1910–84.

54. Ibid.

55. Anne Draper to Howard D. Samuel, December 22, 1969, carton 9, folder 294, Peterson Collection, 1910–84.

56. Ibid. Federation lobbyist Andrew Biemiller was still trying to save women's protective laws in 1970 but Draper thought it futile. See Anne Draper to Andrew Biemiller, January 16, 1970, carton 9, folder 294, Peterson Collection, 1910–84.

57. *Bowe v. Colgate Palmolive Co.*, 416 F. 2d 711, 718 (1969); *Weeks v. Southern Bell*, 408 F. 2d 228 (1969); *Rosenfeld v. Southern Pacific Co.*, 293 F. Supp. 1219 (1968); *Evans v. Sheraton Park Hotel*, 5 FEP Cases 393 (1972); *Reed v. Reed*, 404 U.S. 71 (1971).

58. Joan Hoff, *Law, Gender, and Injustice: A Legal History of U.S. Women* (New York: New York University Press, 1991), pp. 234–35, 245–48.

59. Ronnie Blumenthal, quoted in Equal Employment Opportunity Commission, *Making a Right*, p. 20.

60. *New York Times*, May 9, 1971.

61. Memorandum, n.a., September 29, 1970, box 34, AFL-CIO Department of Civil Rights, Discrimination Case Files Collection, George Meany Memorial Archives, Silver Spring, Md. See also, Andrew J. Biemiller to Dear Senator, January 18, 1972, box 17, folder 10, AFL-CIO Legislation Collection.

62. William B. Gould, *Black Workers in White Unions: Job Discrimination in the United States* (Ithaca, N.Y.: Cornell University Press, 1977), p. 17.

63. Graham K. Wilson, *Unions in American National Politics* (New York: St. Martin's, 1979), p. 2. In the nonagricultural work force, unions represented 29.8 percent of the workers in 1962; that percentage decreased to 26.7 percent in 1972.

64. Mike Davis, *Prisoners of the American Dream: Politics and Economy in the History of the US Working Class* (London: Verso, 1986), p. 129.

65. Vivian Vale, *Labour in American Politics* (New York: Barnes and Noble, 1971), p. 125.

66. Davis, pp. 100–101, 132–36.

67. Jacqueline Jones, *Labor of Love, Labor of Sorrow: Black Women, Work, and Family, From Slavery to the Present* (New York: Vintage, 1986), p. 302; Paul Burnstein, *Discrimination, Jobs, and Politics: The Struggle for Equal Employment Opportunity in the United States since the New Deal* (Chicago: University of Chicago Press, 1985), p. 149; Patricia Gurin, "The Role of Worker Expectancies in the Study of Employment Discrimination," in *Women, Minorities, and Employment Discrimination,* ed. Phyllis A. Wallace and Annette M. Lamond (Lexington, Mass.: Lexington Books, 1973), p. 15; Catherine East, "The Current Status of the Employment of Women," in *Women in the Workforce: Proceedings of a Conference Sponsored by the Division of Personnel Psychology of the New York State Psychological Association, November 1970, New York,* ed. Mildred E. Katzell and William C. Byham (New York: Behavioral Publications, 1972), p. 9 n. 26; Jane Riblett Wilke, "The Decline of Occupational Segregation between Black and White Women," *Research in Race and Ethnic Relations: A Research Annual, 4,* ed. Cora Bagley Marrett and Cheryl Leggon (Greenwich, Conn.: JAI Press, 1982), pp. 67–89.

68. Jones, p. 302; Gurin, p. 15; EEOC Decs., Case No. 6-4-4066, *Josephine D. Wells v. Liggett and Meyers Tobacco Co.,* May 29, 1967, series 1, box 42, Tobacco Workers International Union Collection, University of Maryland Library, Special Collections, College Park, Md. (hereafter, TWIU Collection).

69. Quoted in Jones, p. 303.

70. Typescript, "Contract Employment Cases: Examples of Corrective Actions," n.d. [1962], box 5, White House Central Files, Aides Files: George Reedy, Lyndon B. Johnson Presidential Papers, 1963–69, Lyndon B. Johnson Presidential Library, Austin, Tex.; EEOC Complaint, *Dorothy P. Robinson et al. v. Lorillard and Co. and TWIU Local 317,* December 2, 1965, series 1, box 42, TWIU Collection.

71. Herbert R. Northrup, "The Negro in the Tobacco Industry," in *Negro Employment in Southern Industry: A Study of Racial Policies in Five Industries,* ed. Herbert R. Northrup and Richard L. Rowan (Philadelphia: University of Pennsylvania Press, 1970), part 3, pp. 85, 91. For a general note about black workers using using civil rights organizations for support in court cases, see Bruce Nelson, "Class, Race and Democracy in the CIO: The 'New' Labor History Meets the 'Wages of Whiteness,'" *International Review of Social History* 41 (1996): 374.

72. The EEOC did not find for the white complainants. See EEOC Discr. Charge, #AT7-1-26-30, *Geraldine H. Quick et al. v. TWIU Local 182 and American Tobacco Co.,* January 11, 1967; EEOC Decs., Case No. #6-1-68, *Blair Hallet et al. v. American Tobacco Co., and TWIU Local 182,* September 27, 1967, both in series 1, box 42, TWIU Collection. For another example of white workers' claiming unfair hiring of African-American workers in the TWIU, see EEOC Decs., Case #YATO-192, *Roy S. Yeatts, William B. Ware, Ben T. Allen v. American Tobacco Co. and TWIU Local 192* (Reidsville, N.C.), May 14, 1970, series 1, box 1, TWIU Collection.

73. The one exception came at the TWIU's 1968 convention when a group of Local 317 delegates, led by Dorothy Robinson, a plaintiff in a discrimination lawsuit brought

against employer and union, attempted to introduce a proposal that would bring union leaders to support equal employment opportunity laws, especially at the local level. The group was unsuccessful, however. With no debate on the proposal, delegates rejected the measure. See Tobacco Workers International Union, AFL-CIO, CLC, *Proceedings: Fourteenth Regular Convention* (Chicago, Ill., 1968), p. 106.

74. EEOC Discr. Charge, *TWIU Local 208 v. Liggett and Meyers Co.*, Durham, N.C., TWIU Local 176, and TWIU International, July 20, 1965.

75. EEOC Determination, Case No. YDC2-194, *Louise Lewis et al. v. Philip Morris, Inc. and TWIU Local 203*, Richmond, Va., August 23, 1973, series 1, box 43, TWIU Collection.

76. Clipping, *Daily Labor Report*, "Remarks of Richard A. Graham, Equal Employment Opportunity Commission, Speech to Annual Conference of American Management Association, Chicago, Ill.," n.d. [1966], box 44, folder 24, AFL-CIO Legislation Collection. The EEOC was not the only interested organization noting the similarity between race discrimination and sex discrimination; according to the IUE's Officer's Report for 1974, "the roadblocks are virtually the same for race and sex discrimination and . . . a unified effort must be made to remove them." International Union of Electrical Workers, AFL-CIO, *Proceedings, Sixteenth Constitutional Convention: Officers' Report* (Chicago, Ill., 1974), p. 411.

77. EEOC Commission's Charges, *Samuel Jackson v. Philip Morris Co. and TWIU Local 16*, October 26, 1967, series 1, box 42, TWIU Collection.

78. *Patterson v. American Tobacco Co.*, 535 F. 2d 262 (1976).

79. Charles L. Betsey, "Litigation of Employment Discrimination under Title VII: The Case of African American Women," *American Economic Review* 84, no. 2 (May 1994): 99. On the AT&T case also see the essays in *Equal Employment Opportunity and the AT&T Case*, ed. Phyllis A. Wallace (Cambridge, Mass.: MIT Press, 1976).

80. Peggie R. Smith, "Separate Identities: Black Women, Work, and Title VII," *Harvard Women's Law Journal* 14 (Spring 1991): 22.

81. See, for example, William H. Chafe, *Women and Equality: Changing Patterns in American Culture* (New York: Oxford University Press, 1977), p. 52.

82. *Emma Degraffenreid v. General Motors*, 413 F. Supp. 142 (E.D. Mo. 1976).

83. Leo Kanowitz, *Women and the Law: The Unfinished Revolution* (Albuquerque: University of New Mexico Press, 1969), p. 197.

84. Harrison, pp. 204–9; Graham, pp. 393–94, 418–19; Freeman, pp. 209–11; DeHart, p. 457; Hartmann, pp. 66–70; Rupp and Taylor, pp. 182–84; Irwin N. Gertzog, *Congressional Women: Their Recruitment, Treatment, and Behavior* (New York: Praeger, 1984), pp. 150–51.

85. Foner, p. 482; Gabin, pp. 198–200; Harrison, p. 203; Carol Kates, "Working Class Feminism and Feminist Unions: Title VII, the UAW and NOW," *Labor Studies Journal* 14 (Summer 1989): 41–43.

86. Gabin, p. 201. Gabin asserts that the UAW's break with the AFL-CIO allowed them to endorse the ERA. See Gabin, p. 201 n. 16.

87. Ibid., pp. 208–9; Hartmann, pp. 75–76; Kates, p. 42.

88. Graham, p. 410.

89. Ibid., p. 208; Andrew Battista, "Political Divisions in Organized Labor, 1968–1988," *Polity* 24 (Winter 1991): 173–97.

90. Quoted in Graham, p. 208. See also Zieger, pp. 187–92, and Moody, pp. 79–94, for background information on the federation's weak political and industrial relations positions after 1966.

91. Lucy Komisar, "Where Feminism Will Lead: An Impetus for Social Change," *Civil Rights Digest* 6, no. 3 (Spring 1974): 9.

92. Andrew J. Biemiller to Dolores Doninger, May 15, 1972, box 55, folder 22, AFL-CIO Legislation Collection.

93. Doris Gibson Hardesty, "The Continuing Fight for Women's Rights," *American Federationist*, January 1971, p. 15.

94. Ibid., p. 13.

95. Ibid., p. 15; Andrew J. Biemiller to Emily Stoper, March 24, 1972, box 17, folder 10, AFL-CIO Legislation Collection.

96. Testimony of Ruth Miller, U.S. Congress, Senate, Committee of the Judiciary, *Equal Rights 1970: Hearings before the Committee on the Judiciary, United States Senate, on S.J. Res. 61 and 231*, 91st Cong., 2d sess., September 1970, p. 230.

97. Submitted Statement of the International Union of Electrical Workers, U.S. Congress, House, Committee on the Judiciary, *Equal Rights for Men and Women, 1971: Hearings before Subcommittee No. 4 of the Committee on the Judiciary, House of Representatives, on H.J. Res. 35, 208, 916, and Related Bills*, 92d Cong., 1st sess., 1971, pp. 331–43.

98. Testimony of Mrs. Eloise M. Basto [Special Representative, Communications Workers of America], U.S. Congress, Senate, Committee on the Judiciary, *The "Equal Rights" Amendment: Hearings before the Subcommittee on Constitutional Amendments of the Committee on the Judiciary, United States Senate, on S.J. Res. 61*, 91st Cong., 2d sess., May 1970, p. 355; Testimony of Ruth Miller, *Senate Equal Rights Hearings*, September 1970, pp. 230–32. See also, Submitted Statement of Evelyn Dubrow [Legislative Representative, International Ladies Garment Workers Union], *Senate Equal Rights Hearings*, May 1970, pp. 642–43.

99. Cobble, pp. 4–10.

100. Testimony of Myra K. Wolfgang, *Senate Equal Rights Hearings*, May 1970, p. 317.

101. Cobble, p. 10.

102. Ibid., pp. 80, 158; *Evans v. Sheraton Park Hotel*, 5 FEP Cases, 503 F. 2d 177 (1974).

103. Quoted in Cobble, p. 151. For a discussion of radical feminists' misgivings about the ERA along similar lines, see Alice Echols, *Daring to Be Bad: Radical Feminism in America, 1967–75* (Minneapolis: University of Minnesota Press, 1989), pp. 200, 366 n. 36.

104. Testimony of Ruth Miller, *House Equal Rights Hearings*, 1971, p. 257.

105. Babcock et al., pp. 277–78, 281; Moody, p. 275; Foner, p. 501.

106. Quoted in *New York Times*, September 12, 1970.

107. *New York Times*, September 15, 1970; Foner, pp. 482–84.

108. Testimony of Ruth Miller, *House Equal Rights Hearings,* 1971, p. 263.

109. Katherine P. Ellickson, interview by Dennis East, Detroit, Mich., January 10, 1976, Reuther Archives. Ellickson claimed in this 1976 interview that she supported the ERA "not long after" 1967; in 1970, however, she called the ERA "a vague[,] high sounding but ineffectual addition to our Constitution." See typescript, Katherine P. Ellickson, Statement of the National Consumers League before the Senate Judiciary Committee on the Equal Rights Amendment, September 10, 1970, box 7, folder 15, Ellickson Collection, 1921–78.

110. Typescript, Esther Peterson, Address to the AFL-CIO National Auxiliaries Convention, December 11, 1967, box 1, folder 2, Peterson Collection, 1910–84.

111. Esther Peterson to Martha Griffiths, October 12, 1971, box 2, Esther Peterson Collection, 1960–88, Schlesinger Library, Radcliffe College, Cambridge, Mass.

112. Gertzog, p. 204.

113. Harrison, pp. 206, 305 n. 43.

114. Typescript, Elizabeth Duncan Koontz at Women's Organizations Consultation Meeting on the 50th Anniversary of the Women's Bureau, February 26, 1970, box 55, folder 22, AFL-CIO Legislation Collection. See also Graham, p. 409, and Hartmann, p. 103, on background to the Department of Labor's position on the ERA in the late 1960s and early 1970s.

115. Hartmann, p. 103; Diane Balser, *Sisterhood and Solidarity: Feminism and Labor in Modern Times* (Boston: South End Press, 1987), p. 103; Hoff, p. 235; Kessler-Harris, *Out to Work,* p. 315.

116. American Federation of Labor–Congress of Industrial Organizations, *Proceedings, Tenth Constitutional Convention: Volume II: Report of the Executive Council* (Bal Harbour, Fla., 1973), pp. 109–11.

117. American Federation of Labor–Congress of Industrial Organizations, *Proceedings: Tenth Constitutional Convention,* [vol. 1] (Bal Harbour, Fla., 1973), pp. 388–89.

118. Herbert Hammerman and Marvin Rogoff, "The Union Role in Title VII Enforcement: Liability and Opportunity," *Civil Rights Digest* 7, no. 3 (Spring 1975): 27.

119. Submitted Statement of James R. Hoffa, *Senate Equal Rights Hearings,* September 1970, p. 402. For examples of sex discrimination court cases involving the Teamsters, see *Holiday v. Red Ball Motor Freight,* 11 FEP Cases 567 (1974); *International Brotherhood of Teamsters v. U.S.,* 431 U.S. 324 (1977); and *Macklin v. Spector Freight Systems, Inc.,* 478 F. 2d 979 (DC. Cir. 1973). For an account of the Teamsters' poor civil rights record, see Gould, pp. 365–71.

120. Gabin, p. 208.

121. Dorothy Haener, interview by Lyn Goldfarb, Lydia Kleiner, and Christine Miller, Detroit, Mich., 1978, Twentieth Century Trade Union Women: Vehicle for Social Change, Oral History Project, Institute of Labor and Industrial Relations, University of Michigan, Ann Arbor, Mich./Walter Reuther Archives of Labor History and Urban Affairs, Wayne State University, Detroit, Mich. (hereafter, Twentieth Century Trade Union Women Project).

122. Andrew J. Biemiller to Mary Condon Gereau, December 6, 1973, box 17, folder 10, AFL-CIO Legislation Collection.

123. Phyllis S. Glick, "Bridging Feminism and Trade Unionism: A Study of Working Women's Organizing in the United States" (Ph.D. diss., Brandeis University, 1983), p. 349.

124. Milkman, pp. 304–7; "Note: Union Liability for Employer Discrimination," *Harvard Law Review* 93 (February 1980): 712 n. 60.

125. Evelyn Dubrow, interview by Lydia Kleiner, Washington, D.C., August 21, 1976, Twentieth Century Trade Union Women Project.

126. Milkman, p. 309.

127. Foner, pp. 486, 498–500.

128. Haener interview, Twentieth Century Trade Union Women Project.

129. Diane Harriford, "Comment," in *Women and Unions: Forging a Partnership*, ed. Dorothy Sue Cobble (Ithaca, N.Y.: ILR Press, 1993), p. 404.

130. Judy Baston, "The Voice of Women," *Nation*, April 13, 1974, p. 451.

131. CLUW *News*, Winter 1975, box 13, folder 1, Coalition of Labor Union Women Collection, Walter Reuther Archives of Labor History and Urban Affairs, Wayne State University, Detroit, Mich. (hereafter, CLUW Collection).

132. Clipping, Philadelphia *Inquirer*, January 29, 1974, box 1, folder 5, CLUW Collection.

133. CLUW *News*, Summer 1975, box 13, folder 1, CLUW Collection.

134. Pamphlet, "Statement of Purpose, Structure and Guidelines, adopted by Coalition of Labor Union Women Founding Conference, March 23–24, 1974, Chicago, Illinois," box 1, folder 17, CLUW Collection.

135. See, for example, the charges that "union contracts don't begin to protect women from discriminatory practices" (Memo, n.a., n.d. [1973–74], box 1, folder 16, CLUW Collection). CLUW dropped its official naming of unions as suspect parties in discrimination complaints with employers in 1977 (see typescript, Resolutions Passed, 1977 convention, box 11, folder 10, CLUW Collection).

136. Baston, p. 452.

137. CLUW *News*, Winter 1975, box 13, folder 1; Press Release, "Founding Convention—CLUW, Pick-Congress Hotel, Chicago, Ill., March 23–24, 1974, 1974," box 1, folder 1; clipping, AFL-CIO *News*, October 11, 1975, box 8, folder 6, all in CLUW Collection; Glick, p. 366.

138. Mary Frederickson, "Heroines and Girl Strikes: Gender Issues and Organized Labor in Twentieth-Century American South," in *Organized Labor in Twentieth-Century South*, ed. Robert Zieger (Knoxville: University of Tennessee Press, 1991), p. 98.

139. F. Ray Marshall, *Labor in the South* (Cambridge, Mass.: Harvard University Press, 1967), p. 73.

140. *Miranda v. Clothing Workers Local 208*, 10 FEP 557 (1974); *Cubas v. Rapid American Corp.*, 13 FEP Cases 794 (1976).

141. American Federation of Labor–Congress of Industrial Organizations, *Proceedings, Eleventh Constitutional Convention* (San Francisco, Calif., 1975), p. 442.

Chapter 6: Rank-and-File Militancy in the Service of Anti-Equality

1. Alice Cook, "Women and American Trade Unions," *Annals of the American Academy of Political and Social Science* 375 (January 1968): 125.

2. For examples of Title VII–inspired cases where the United Rubber Workers and the International Chemical Workers were defendants, see *Bowe v. Colgate-Palmolive Co.,* 1 FEP Cases 210, and *Taylor v. Goodyear Tire and Rubber Co.,* 6 FEP Cases 50.

3. The history of the UAW's Women's Bureau is found in Nancy F. Gabin, *Feminism in the Labor Movement: Women and the United Auto Workers, 1935–1975* (Ithaca, N.Y.: Cornell University Press, 1990), pp. 144–54, and Carol Kates, "Working Class Feminism and Feminist Unions: Title VII, the UAW and NOW," *Labor Studies Journal* 10 (Winter 1986): 28–45. There is a growing literature on women and unions after 1945, although few authors deal specifically with Title VII and women at the union local level. See, for example, Cynthia Harrison, *On Account of Sex: The Politics of Women's Issues, 1945–1968* (Berkeley: University of California Press, 1988); Alice Kessler-Harris, *A Women's Wage: Historical Meanings and Social Consequences* (Lexington: University Press of Kentucky, 1990); Diane Balser, *Sisterhood and Solidarity: Feminism and Labor in Modern Times* (Boston: South End Press, 1987); and Ruth Milkman, "Women Workers, Feminism, and the Labor Movement since the 1960s," in *Women, Work, and Protest: A Century of U.S. Women's Labor History,* ed. Milkman (New York: Routledge and Kegan Paul, 1985), pp. 300–322.

4. UPWA, *Staff Letter* no. 7, February 19, 1965, box 188, folder 3, United Packinghouse Workers of America Collection, State Historical Society of Wisconsin, Madison, Wis. (hereafter, UPWA-SHSW Collection).

5. See, for example, EEOC Decs., Case No. 7-2-901, Rafael Flores et al., *UPWA Local 1206 and Flores v. Farmers' Cooperative Compress,* Lubbock, Tex., March 17, 1967, box 15, folder 102, AFL-CIO Department of Civil Rights Collection, George Meany Memorial Archives, Silver Spring, Md. (hereafter, DCR Collection).

6. United Packinghouse Workers of America, AFL-CIO, *Proceedings: Fifteenth Constitutional Convention, Officers' Report* (Los Angeles, Calif., 1966), p. xxiii.

7. Ralph Helstein to Local unions, field representatives, international representatives, district director, July 1, 1965, box 468, folder 3, UPWA-SHSW Collection.

8. The charges were announced in the local press: Waterloo *Daily Courier,* February 24, 1966; Ottumwa *Courier* n.d. [April 1966]; Dubuque *Telegraph Herald,* September 11, 1966, all clippings in Elizabeth "Sue" Smith Scrapbook, Amalgamated Meatcutters and Butcher Workman P-1 Collection, State Historical Society of Iowa, Iowa City, Iowa (hereafter, AMBW P-1 Collection). In Dubuque, women cited only the employer for discriminatory practices.

9. Richard Price, interview by Merle Davis, Waterloo, July 9, 1981, Iowa Labor Oral History Project, State Historical Society of Iowa, Iowa City, Iowa (hereafter, ILHOP).

10. Dave Dutton, interview by Dennis Deslippe, Waterloo, August 8, 1989, Oral Labor History Collection, State Historical Society of Iowa, Iowa City, Iowa (hereafter, OLHC).

11. Labor Agreement, John Morrell and Company and Local 1 UPWA (1967–70), Labor Collection, State Historical Society of Iowa, Iowa City, Iowa (hereafter, SHSI Labor Collection). UPWA membership figures are from Kerry Napuk to All officers and district directors, October 3, 1966, box 471, folder 3, UPWA-SHSW Collection.

12. 42 U.S.C. 2000e et seq.

13. See, for example, Ruth Milkman, *Gender at Work: The Dynamics of Job Segregation by Sex during World War II* (Urbana: University of Illinois Press, 1987), pp. 15–20; Ronald W. Schatz, *The Electrical Workers: A History of Labor at General Electric and Westinghouse, 1923–60* (Urbana: University of Illinois Press, 1983): pp. 30–33; and Patricia Cooper, "The Faces of Gender: Sex Segregation and Work Relations at Philco, 1928–1938," in *Work Engendered: Toward a New History of American Labor*, ed. Ava Baron (Ithaca, N.Y.: Cornell University Press, 1991), pp. 336–44. Swift and Co. first proposed the ABC system to Helstein. See Minutes (by Edward Filliman), Meeting with Morrell and Local 1, December 28, 1965, box 1, folder 1, AMBW P-1 Collection.

14. Labor Agreement, John Morrell and Company and Local 1 UPWA (1967–70), SHSI Labor Collection.

15. Ibid.

16. Ibid.

17. Ibid.

18. Ethel Jerred, interview by Merle Davis, Ottumwa, October 5, 1981, ILHOP; Harold Davey, "Present and Future Labor Relations Problems in the Meat Packing Industry," *Labor Law Journal* 18 (December 1967), p. 748. The argument concerning retraining costs was used widely by companies. See *New York Times,* May 27, 1967. Production control is discussed in M. V. Link to Dave Hart, July 5, 1965, Trimble Notebook, box 1, AMBW P-1 Collection; Harry Hansel to Dave Hart, August 4, 1965, box 25, folder 8, AMBW P-1 Collection.

19. Jerred, interview, ILHOP.

20. *Local One Bulletin,* February 21, 1966, box 23, AMBW P-1 Collection.

21. EEOC decision, Case No. KC 7-2-117, *Puffinharger et al. v. Morrell and Local 1 UPWA,* August 14, 1968, box 25, folder 9, AMBW P-1 Collection.

22. Local 46, *UPWA Bulletin,* April 27, 1966, box 468, folder 3, UPWA-SHSW Collection.

23. Charles Mueller, interview by Merle Davis, Waterloo, July 3, 1981, ILHOP.

24. Robert Heaverlo, interview by Paul Kelso, Cedar Rapids, March 1, 1979, ILHOP.

25. Miscellaneous notes, August 1969, Elizabeth "Sue" Smith Scrapbook, AMBW P-1 Collection.

26. Jesse Merrill, interview by Merle Davis, Ottumwa, September 16, 1981, ILHOP.

27. Virgil Bankson, interview by Paul Kelso, Ottumwa, October 18, 1978, ILHOP.

28. Dutton, interview, OLHC.

29. Audio tape, meeting with Ralph Helstein and Local 46 members, April 18, 1966, box 7, Local 46 Collection, State Historical Society of Iowa, Iowa City, Iowa (hereafter, UPWA Local 46 Collection).

30. UPWA, *Officers' Report* (1966), p. 55.

31. Ibid. Helstein made this argument on more than one occasion. See UPWA, *Proceedings* (1966), p. 85.

32. U.S. Equal Employment Opportunity Commission, *Second Annual Report of the Equal Employment Opportunity Commission* (Washington, D.C.: G.P.O., 1968), p. 12.

33. UPWA, *Proceedings* (1966), p. 86. Helstein also urged patience in his talk to Waterloo workers. See audio tape, Helstein and Local 46 members, UPWA Local 46 Collection.

34. Les Orear to Ralph Helstein, July 11, 1966, box 472, folder 3, UPWA-SHSW Collection.

35. Each local had to approve the ABC plan individually. See Jesse Prosten to all Swift locals, November 29, 1965, box 15, folder 23, DCR Collection.

36. Virgil Bankson, Ottumwa, October 18, 1978, ILHOP.

37. Dave Dutton to Local 1 officers, April 18, 1966, box 25, folder 8, AMBW P-1 Collection.

38. Ethel Jerred, Ottumwa, October 5, 1981, ILHOP.

39. Clipping, Ottumwa *Courier*, n.d. [April 1966], Elizabeth "Sue" Smith Scrapbook, AMBW P-1 Collection; Female Employee Roster, Trimble Notebook, box 1, AMBW P-1 Collection; Dutton, interview, OLHC.

40. Complaint, April 8, 1966, *Freese v. John Morrell* Case File 7-1823-C-1, U.S. Court of Appeals, Eighth Circuit Records, St. Louis, Mo. (hereafter *Freese v. Morrell* Case File).

41. Dutton, interview, OLHC.

42. Complaint, April 8, 1966, *Freese v. Morrell* Case File.

43. Motion for Stay of Defendant Morrell, April 29, 1966; Affidavit in Support of Stay, April 29, 1966; Defendant Motion to Dismiss, August 19, 1966; Morrell Memo to Dismiss, October 5, 1966; Supplemental Motion to Dismiss, October 24, 1966, all in *Freese v. Morrell* Case File.

44. UPWA Motion to Dismiss Count 1, August 22, 1966, *Freese v. Morrell* Case File.

45. UPWA Supplemental Motions to Dismiss, October 24, 1966, *Freese v. Morrell* Case File.

46. Ibid.

47. Ralph J. Lindgren and Nadine Taub, *The Law of Discrimination* (St. Paul, Minn.: West Publishing, 1988), pp. 126–49 passim.

48. The meeting dates were April 20, 1966, and March 17, 1967. See present status form, registered April 5, 1966; Eugene Cotton to William Pollard, October 5, 1966, both in UPWA folders, box 22, DCR Collection.

49. *Freese v. John Morrell and Company,* 1 FEP Cases 665. For a case initiated by Minnesota women for similar reasons see *Sokolowski v. Swift and Company,* 286 F. Supp. 775 (1968).

50. Order of Dismissal, July 12, 1968, *Freese v. Morrell* Case File.

51. UPWA, *Proceedings* (1966), p. 77.

52. Ethel Jerred, Ottumwa, October 5, 1981, ILHOP.

53. EEOC complaint, Case No. KC 7-2-117, *Morrell and Local 1, UPWA v. Puffinharger,* August 5, 1968, box 25, folder 9, AMBW P-1 Collection.

54. Babcock et al., pp. 366–67; Hugh Davis Graham, *The Civil Rights Era: Origins and Development of National Policy, 1960–1972* (New York: Oxford University Press, 1990), p. 232; Karen J. Maschke, *Litigation and Women Workers* (New York: Praeger, 1989), pp. 40–51; Joan Hoff, *Law, Gender, and Injustice: A Legal History of U.S. Women* (New York: New York University Press, 1991), p. 235; Lindgren and Taub, pp. 126–49; Harrison, pp. 201–8. In 1969, the EEOC declared state protective laws for women invalid in most cases, especially where they clashed with Title VII mandates. Iowa did not have any such laws at the time.

55. Clipping, "What Hath Rath Wrought? A Waterloo," *Chicago Daily News,* May 10, 1966, box 468, folder 3, UPWA-SHSW Collection; Morris Y. Kinne to Kenneth Holbert, January 17, 1966, box 15, folder 23, DCR Collection; Local 46 *Newsletter,* May 18, 1966, box 1, folder 1, UPWA Local 46 Collection.

56. Waterloo *Daily Courier,* June 16, 1966.

57. See present status form, registered December 16, 1965, William Pollard to Don Slaiman, January 26, 1966, both in box 15, folder 23, DCR Collection.

58. William Pollard to Don Slaiman, January 19, 1972, box 33, DCR Collection.

59. Discrimination case files, Local 46 notes, box 15, folder 23, DCR Collection; Waterloo *Daily Courier,* February 24, 1966, April 7, 1966, May 4, 1966, June 13, 1966, June 16, 1966. The women's case (*L. Ackerman et al. v. Rath Packing Co.,* 66-C-504-EC) did not come to trial. The disposition of their demands for back pay is not known.

60. Rosemary Sokolowski et al. to Franklin D. Roosevelt Jr., March 29, 1966, box 22, DCR Collection.

61. EEOC Decs., Case No. 6-4-2606-2625, *Sokolowski et al. v. Swift and Co. and UPWA Local 167,* South St. Paul, Minn., October 11, 1967, box 22, DCR Collection.

62. Research Department Report, August 1956, "Economic Case for 1956 Contract Demands," box 1, folder 6, UPWA Local 46 Collection; Bruce R. Fehn, "Striking Women: Gender, Race and Class in the United Packinghouse Workers of America (UPWA), 1938–1968" (Ph.D. diss., University of Wisconsin–Madison, 1991), p. 290.

63. District Council No. 3, UPWA, *Minutes, Twenty-Second Annual Constitutional Convention* (Omaha, Nebr., 1968), pp. 14–16.

64. Ibid., pp. 15–16. See also Dutton, interview, OLHC, and audio tape, Helstein and Local 46, UPWA Local 46 Collection, for similar observations of how ABC reclassification burdened male workers.

65. Violet Bohaty, interview by Merle Davis, Ottumwa, September 15, 1981, ILHOP.

66. Elizabeth "Sue" Smith, interview by Merle Davis, Ottumwa, September 15, 1981, ILHOP.

67. Ibid.

68. Mary Ashlock, interview by Merle Davis, Mason City, November 17, 1981, ILHOP.

69. Dutton, interview, OLHC.

70. Lucille Bremer, interview by Merle Davis, Waterloo, June 2, 1982, ILHOP.

71. Cooper, p. 350.

72. Ibid., pp. 336–50.

73. Clipping, *Wall Street Journal,* September 22, 1966, box 468, folder 3, UPWA-SHSW Collection.

74. Jerred, interview, ILHOP. For examples of harassment against women at the Omaha Swift local, see Fehn, p. 300 n. 64.

75. Ruth Morrow, interview by Merle Davis, Ottumwa, September 8, 1981, ILHOP.

76. Ibid.

77. Dutton, interview, OLHC.

78. Dorothy Remy and Larry Sawers, "Economic Stagnation and Discrimination," in *My Troubles Are Going to Have Trouble with Me,* ed. Karen Brodkin Sacks and Dorothy Remy (New Brunswick, N.J.: Rutgers University Press, 1984), p. 109.

79. Court notes, n.d. [April 1971], *Petersen v. Rath* Case File 69-C-512-EC, U.S. Court of Appeals, Eighth Circuit Records, St. Louis, Mo. (hereafter, *Petersen v. Rath* Case File). Dr. Leon Smith's findings were also noted in Plaintiff's Brief and Argument, March 12, 1971, *Petersen v. Rath* Case File.

80. Ibid.

81. Ibid.

82. See *Petersen v. Rath Packing Company* 9 FEP Cases 1057.

83. Plaintiff's Reply Brief, April 5, 1971, *Petersen v. Rath* Case File.

84. William H. Brown to Irving M. King, March 30, 1972, box 15, folder 103, DCR Collection.

85. Ibid. The cases Brown referred to, including *Rosenfeld v. Southern Pacific Co.,* 444 F. 2d 1219 (1971), rejected defense pleas that jobs with long hours and weight-lifting classifications were unsuitable for women on the basis of a "BFOQ" exemption from Title VII.

86. Ralph Helstein, interview by Merle Davis, Chicago, May 5, 1983, ILHOP. The ABC system was in place in 1974. Labor contracts after that date do not specifically mention it, but oral history interviews suggest that it remained in place, at least on an informal basis, until the late 1970s. See Labor Agreement, Rath Packing Company and Amalgamated Meat Cutters and Butcher Workmen of North America, September 22, 1973, SHSI Labor Collection, and Iowa Federation of Labor, AFL-CIO, *Proceedings of Nineteenth Convention* (Sioux City, Iowa, 1973), p. 24.

87. Herbert Hill, "The Equal Employment Opportunity Acts of 1964 and 1972: A Critical Analysis of the Legislative History and Administration of the Law," *Industrial Relations Law Journal* 2 (Spring 1977): 34–35, 42, and "The Equal Opportunities Commission: Twenty Years Later," *Journal of Intergroup Relations* 11 (Winter 1983): 57–58.

88. Audio tape, February 1973 ABC Meeting, box 7, UPWA Local 46 Collection.

89. Ibid.

90. See grievance #60, April 30, 1973, grievance #163, October 31, 1973, grievance #52, April 5, 1975, Third Step Grievance Binder, 1973–74, grievance #112, August 21, 1972,

Second Step Grievance Binder, 1972 (no box number), both in Local P-3 Collection (unprocessed), State Historical Society of Iowa, Iowa City, Iowa (hereafter, Local P-3 Collection [unprocessed]).

91. Francis Krier to Virgil Bankson, July 7, 1971, box 2, AMBW P-1 Collection.

92. Bankson journal entries: January 21, 1969, January 30, 1969, February 3, 1969, March 4, 1969, April 18, 1969, box 2A, AMBW P-1 Collection, Bankson Journals Collection; grievance #979, May 2, 1971, grievance #285, September 28, 1971, grievance #288, September 28, 1971, grievance #971, February 9, 1972, grievance #975, February 9, 1972, grievance #297, February 28, 1972, grievance #996, October 26, 1972, grievance #1004, January 18, 1973, Grievance Binder, 1971–73, box 9, AMBW P-1 Collection.

93. Russell Lasley to William Pollard, January 23, 1969, UPWA folders, box 22, DCR Collection; Patrick E. Gorman, to Paul Jennings, February 18, 1975, box 156, group 2, International Union of Electrical Workers (IUE) Archives, Special Collections and University Archives, Rutgers University Libraries, New Brunswick, N.J.; District No. 11, Amalgamated Meatcutters and Butcher Workmen of America, Minutes, *Second Annual Constitutional Convention* (Sioux City, Iowa, 1970), p. 2; District No. 11, Amalgamated Meatcutters and Butcher Workmen of America, *Minutes, Seventh Annual Constitutional Convention* (Des Moines, Iowa, 1976), p. 26; Herbert Hammerman and Marvin Rogoff, "The Union Role in Title VII Enforcement: Liability and Opportunity," *Civil Rights Digest* 7 (Spring 1975): 22–33; Iowa Federation of Labor, *Proceedings* (1974), pp. 24–25.

94. Ethel Jerred, Ottumwa, October 5, 1981, ILHOP.

95. Jesse Merrill, Ottumwa, September 15, 1981, ILHOP.

96. Conversations with former employees of John Morrell and Company, January 14, 1974, box 24, AMBW P-1 Collection.

97. Minutes, regular unit meetings, March 5–6, 1974 (no box number), Local P-3 Collection (unprocessed).

98. Julia Naylor, interview by Merle Davis, Fort Dodge, August 7, 1981, ILHOP.

99. Jane Burleson, interview by Merle Davis, Fort Dodge, August 5, 1981, ILHOP. See also, Iowa Federation of Labor, AFL-CIO, *Proceedings of Eighteenth Convention* (Waterloo, Iowa, 1973), pp. 24.

Chapter 7: "A Genuine Good Faith Effort"

1. Katherine P. Ellickson, interview by Dennis East, Detroit, Mich., January 10, 1976, Walter Reuther Archives of Labor and Urban Affairs, Wayne State University, Detroit, Mich. (hereafter, Reuther Archives).

2. *General Electric Co. v. Gilbert*, 429 U.S. 125 (1976). Of the union's total membership, African-American women made up 10.2 percent. See William B. Gould, *Black Workers in White Unions: Job Discrimination in the United States* (Ithaca, N.Y.: Cornell University Press, 1975), p. 405.

3. International Union of Electrical Workers, AFL-CIO, *Proceedings, Fifteenth Constitutional Convention* (Washington, D.C., 1972), p. 191.

4. Ibid. Sympathetic EEOC members also noted this strategy with approval. See

Herbert Hammerman and Marvin Rogoff, "The Union Role in Title VII Enforcement: Liability and Opportunity," *Civil Rights Digest* 7 (Spring 1975): 33.

5. Gloria Johnson, interview by Dennis Deslippe, Washington, D.C., June 8, 1993, Reuther Archives.

6. Olga Margolin to Franklin D. Roosevelt Jr., July 30, 1965, quoted in Barbara Allen Babcock et al., *Sex Discrimination and the Law: Causes and Remedies* (Boston: Little, Brown, 1975), p. 262.

7. Statement of International Union of Electrical Workers, U.S. Congress, House, Committee on the Judiciary, *Equal Rights for Men and Women, 1971, Hearings before Subcommittee No. 4 of the Committee on the Judiciary, House of Representatives, on H. J. Res. 35, 208, 916, and Related Bills,* 92d Cong., 1st Sess., 1971, p. 597.

8. IUE, AFL-CIO, *Proceedings, Twelfth Constitutional Convention* (Bal Harbour, Fla., 1966), p. 235. For other examples of IUE support for protective laws, see IUE, AFL-CIO, *Proceedings, Thirteenth Constitutional Convention* (New York, N.Y., 1968), pp. 283, 287, and *Proceedings, Fourteenth Constitutional Convention* (Houston, Tex., 1970), p. 191; Dorothy I. Height to Luther Holcomb, July 28, 1966, box 55, folder 22, American Federation of Labor–Congress of Industrial Organizations Department of Legislation Collection, George Meany Memorial Archives, Silver Spring, Md.; Report, Social Action Department to International Executive Board, May 27 and 28, 1967, box 5, group 2, International Union of Electrical Workers (IUE) Archives, Special Collections and University Archives, Rutgers University Libraries, New Brunswick, N.J. (hereafter, IUE Archives).

9. Statement of IUE, *House Equal Rights Hearings,* 1971, p. 597.

10. Gary M. Fink, ed., *Labor Unions* (Westport, Conn.: Greenwood, 1977), p. 80; James J. Matles and James Higgins, *Them and Us: Struggles of a Rank-and-File Union* (Englewood Cliffs, N.J.: Prentice-Hall, 1974), pp. 257, 263, 281; John Bennett Sears, "Labor Opposition to the Cold War: The Electrical Unions and the Cold War Consensus" (Ph.D. diss., Temple University, 1988), pp. 261–80.

11. IUE, *Proceedings* (1966), p. 64. Abramson noted that "GE applied Boulwarism with more vigor and in a more egregious fashion during the 1969 negotiations than it did in 1960." See his "The Anatomy of Boulwarism with a Discussion of Forkosch," *Catholic University of America Law Review* 19, no. 4 (Summer 1970): 461–62.

12. Jack Barbash, *American Unions: Structure, Government and Politics* (New York: Random House, 1967), p. 98. The IUE and UE's membership (in thousands): IUE = 270 (1962), 291 (1965), 309 (1970), 296 (1973), 224 (1980), 172 (1983); UE = 55 (1962), NA (1965, 1970), 90 (estimate-1973), 89 (1980), 54 (1983). See Sears, p. 233.

13. Patrick Flynn, "The Winner, Paul Jennings," *The Sign* (October 1965): 24. Also on Carey's fall from power see "Leadership Feud Rocks IUE," *Business Week,* August 18, 1962; Robert Alfred Lorentz, "Electrical Insurgency in an International Union: The Influence of Local Union Size and Dispersion in the IUE" (Ph.D. diss., Syracuse University, 1986), pp. 36–38; Sears, pp. 38–45; Matles and Higgins, p. 253; Barbash, p. 98.

14. Typescript, *Star-Ledger* (Newark, N.J.), September 26, 1967, box 5, group 2, IUE Archives.

15. Margaret Craig, Mary Ehren, and Alma Dickensheets to Paul Jennings, August 2, 1965, box 8, group 2, IUE Archives. On IUE's support for the Civil Rights Act of 1964, see IUE, *Proceedings, Tenth Constitutional Convention* (Cleveland, Ohio, 1962), pp. 317–18, and Memorandum, Report of President [Carey] to IUE, IEB Meeting, December, 18–19, 1963, box 36, group 2, IUE Archives.

16. Gloria Johnson, interview, Reuther Archives.

17. EEOC Decs. Case No. CL 7-2-261U and 6-2-946U, *Katherine K. Raschak v. IUE Local 7171,* Youngstown, Ohio, June 2, 1967, box 42, group 2, IUE Archives.

18. EEOC Complaint, Case No. YCL9-0011, July 8, 1968, box 5, folder 58, AFL-CIO Department of Civil Rights, Case Files Collection, George Meany Memorial Archives, Silver Spring, Md. (hereafter, DCR Collection).

19. Winn Newman to Paul Jennings, February, 7, 1975, box 156, group 2, IUE Archives.

20. Joe Shump to David J. Fitzmaurice, December 6, 1965, box 8, group 2, IUE Archives.

21. EEOC Decs., Case No. 5-11-2563, *Fickert et al. v. GM, Frigidaire Division and IUE Local 801,* Dayton, Ohio, March 10, 1966, box 5, folder 77, DCR Collection.

22. Delores E. Fickert to Paul Jennings, December 6, 1965, box 8, group 2, IUE Archives. See also Margaret W. Call to Your Honor [Paul Jennings], September 20, 1965, box 8, group 2, IUE Archives, for a similar complaint from another Local 801 woman.

23. EEOC Decs., Case No. 5-11-2563, *Fickert et al. v. GM, Frigidaire Division and IUE Local 801,* Dayton, Ohio, March 10, 1966, box 5, folder 77, DCR Collection.

24. EEOC Decs. Case No. CL7-2-226, *McKinney et al. v. General Motors, Frigidaire Division and IUE Local 801,* Dayton, Ohio, June 16, 1969, box 5, folder 78, DCR Collection.

25. *Ridinger v. GE and IUE Local 801,* 3 FEP Cases 280, 7 FEP Cases 566, 569. For examples of other decisions where the EEOC found the IUE guilty of denying women overtime, see EEOC Decs., Case No. YNYO-058, *Harris et al. v. RCA and IUE Local 103,* Camden, N.J., July 27, 1971, box 5, folder 15, and EEOC Conciliation Agreement, Case No. NY 68-12-568-U, *EEOC and Sawtell et al. v. IUE Local 272,* Cambridge, Mass., March 3, 1971, box 5, folder 36, both in DCR Collection.

26. EEOC Decs., Case No. 5-10-2103, *Kuc v. Westinghouse and IUE Local 601,* East Pittsburgh, Pa., May 25, 1966, box 5, folder 46, and EEOC Decs., Case No. YCL9-085, *Bethel et al. v. GE and IUE Local 707,* Cleveland, Ohio, December 23, 1970, box 5, folder 58, both in DCR Collection.

27. EEOC Decs., Case No. YCL9-090, *Ramsey v. American Machine and Foundry Co. and IUE Local 804,* Vandalia, Ohio, June 18, 1971, box 5, folder 83, DCR Collection.

28. Typescript, Stipulation 67-1, Between Ingraham Co. and IUE Local 260, Bristol, Conn., February 26, 1967, box 85, group 2, IUE Archives.

29. EEOC Conciliation, Case No. CH7-3-183 et al., Between Mollie Wierzbicki et al. and Warwick Electronics/IUE Local 1002, Zion, Ill., April 17, 1968, box 5, folder 101, DCR Collection.

30. Ibid.

31. Rosalie Swadish to Mr. [Paul] Jennings, January 5, 1970, box 178, group 2, IUE Archives.

32. Grievance summary sheet, Report on Local 1081, IUE (DeKalb GE), Grievance #100, n.d. [1967], box 5, group 2, IUE Archives.

33. Maurine W. Keys to Mrs. Callahan, November 3, 1966, box 8, group 2, IUE Archives.

34. Delores E. Fickert to Paul Jennings, December 28, 1965, box 8, group 2, IUE Archives.

35. Paul Jennings to Louise W. Fryman, April 26, 1966, box 8, group 2, IUE Archives.

36. This statistic is for 1968. In 1958 women made up 40 percent and in 1981 36–38 percent of the total membership. See Lucretia M. Dewey, "Women in Labor Unions," *Monthly Labor Review* 94, no. 2 (February 1971): 43; Gloria Johnson and Odessa Komer, "Education for Affirmative Action: Two Union Approaches," in *Labor Education for Women Workers,* ed. Barbara Mayer Wertheimer (Philadelphia: Temple University Press, 1981), p. 205.

37. James B. Carey to Alvine Krug, April 9, 1964, box 8, group 2, IUE Archives.

38. IUE, *Proceedings* (1972), p. 457.

39. Ruth Milkman, *Gender at Work: The Dynamics of Job Segregation by Sex during World War II* (Urbana: University of Illinois Press, 1987), pp. 42–48, 77–83; Lisa A. Kannenberg, "From World War to Cold War: Women Electrical Workers and Their Union, 1940–1955" (M.A. thesis, University of North Carolina at Charlotte, 1990), pp. 31–36; Gladys Dickason, "Women in Labor Unions," *Annals of the American Academy of Political and Social Science* 251 (May 1947): 73.

40. Transcript, IUE-GE Negotiations, October 10, 1966, box 218, group 2, IUE Archives.

41. Memorandum, Winn Newman to EEOC, n.d. [1974], box 218, group 2, IUE Archives.

42. Ibid.

43. Transcript, IUE-GE Negotiations, 1969, box 218, group 2, IUE Archives. Only in 1976 did GE relent and agree to include an antidiscrimination clause in its contracts.

44. Memorandum, Winn Newman to EEOC, n.d. [1974], box 218, group 2, IUE Archives.

45. Nancy F. Gabin, *Feminism in the Labor Movement: Women in the United Auto Workers, 1935–1975* (Ithaca, N.Y.: Cornell University Press, 1990), pp. 198–99; IUE, *Proceedings: President's Report* (1966), p. 305, and *Proceedings: President's Report* (1970), p. 376; typescript, Program, IUE Women's Conference, October 9–10, 1967, box 6, group 2, IUE Archives; Johnson and Komer, p. 208.

46. Typescript, n.a. [Gloria Johnson], Report of Social Action Department to IEB, December 4–6, 1967, box 35, group 2, IUE Archives. The case was *Bowe v. Colgate-Palmolive Co.,* 1 FEP Cases 201, 416 F. 2d 711, 718 (1969).

47. Alice H. Cook, "Women and American Trade Unions," *Annals of the American Academy of Political and Social Science* 375 (January 1968): 130; Johnson and Komer, p.

207. The available data breaks down this way: in 1966, 18 women were IUE local presidents; 108, secretaries; 272, executive board members; and 108, trustees (also, 43 were chief stewards and 595 were shop stewards). There is no specific information on 1967 offices but in 1969 (with 40 percent of the locals responding) 17 were presidents; 76, secretaries; 130, trustees; and 391, executive board members.

48. Ruth Weyand to Paul Jennings, January 31, 1975, box 156, group 2, IUE Archives.

49. IUE, *Proceedings: Officers' Report* (1972), pp. 463–64; EEOC Decs., Case No. 6-7-6426, *Local 741 IUE v. NOPCO Chemical Co.,* Louisville, Ky., August 1, 1967, box 5, folder 66, DCR Collection; U.S. District Court, Eastern District, Texas, Complaint No. 5452, *Allen v. GE,* Tyler, Tex., February 18, 1972, box 218, group 2, IUE Archives; Winn Newman to Abner Sibal, June 30, 1976, box 33, DCR Collection; *Lynch v. Sperry Rand,* 6 FEP Cases 1306. On pre-1973 IUE litigation, see EEOC Decs., Case No. YCL-2-228, Local 704, *IUE v. GE,* Bucuyrus, Ohio, box 218, group 2, IUE Archives.

50. *Rinehart v. Westinghouse,* 4 EPD Par 7520 (1971); Winn Newman and Carole W. Wilson, "The Union Role in Affirmative Action," *Labor Law Journal* 32 (June 1981): 331–32.

51. Philip S. Foner, *Women and the American Labor Movement: From World War I to the Present* (New York: Free Press, 1980), p. 483.

52. IUE, *Proceedings* (1972), pp. 188–89.

53. International Union of Electrical Workers, AFL-CIO, *Proceedings, Sixteenth Constitutional Convention* (Chicago, Ill., 1974), pp. 180–81.

54. Winn Newman to Abner Sibal, June 6, 1976, box 33, DCR Collection.

55. Gloria Johnson, interview, Reuther Archives.

56. Newman and Wilson, p. 238.

57. *Martindale-Hubbell Law Dictionary,* vol. 4, DC150P.

58. Gloria Johnson, interview, Reuther Archives.

59. Draft, Winn Newman, "Temporary Experimental Procedural Changes," July 27, 1966, Winn Newman to Herman Edelsberg, August, 2, 1966; Winn Newman to Commissioners Hernandez and Jackson, August 4, 1966; Winn Newman to Commissioner Hernandez, August 12, 1966; Winn Newman to Commissioner Jackson, October 3, 1966, all in box 33, DCR. The commission claimed to have cause to fear harassment of workers. Reacting to a decades-old pattern of such behavior in Philadelphia, for example, EEOC district director Thomas Hadfield wrote to the AFL-CIO: "The danger of retaliations to charging parties is so great that in good conscience, I cannot unilaterally order copies of various charges automatically mailed to [the federation in] Washington." See Thomas P. Hadfield to William E. Pollard, November 18, 1974, box 32, DCR Collection.

60. *Griggs v. Duke Power Co.,* 401 U.S. 424 (1971).

61. IUE *Proceedings* (1972), p. 87.

62. Typescript, Winn Newman, "Comments on Westinghouse Electric Corporation, 239, NLRB No. 19; East Dayton Tool and Die Corporation, 239 NLRB, No. 20, October 31, 1978," December 27, 1978, box 9, folder 1, Coalition of Labor Union Women

Collection, Walter Reuther Archives of Labor History and Urban Affairs, Wayne State University, Detroit, Mich. (hereafter, CLUW Collection).

63. Hammerman and Rogoff, pp. 27–28, 30–31; Winn Newman to Abner Sibal, June 30, 1976, box 33, DCR Collection.

64. Ibid. See also, IUE, *Proceedings, Seventeenth Constitutional Convention: Officers' Report* (Miami Beach, Fla., 1976), p. 564.

65. International Union of Electrical Workers, AFL-CIO, *Constitution* (1959), box 220, group 2, IUE Archives.

66. David J. Fitzmaurice to Edward Harrison, June 13, 1972, box 175, and David Fitzmaurice to Joseph Eibl, January 30, 1972, box 178, both in group 2, IUE Archives. The Zion plant closed in 1974.

67. Winn Newman to Paul Jennings, August 26, 1975, box 156, group 2, IUE Archives.

68. Typescript, Winn Newman, "Comments on Westinghouse Electric Corporation, 239, NLRB No. 19; East Dayton Tool and Die Corporation, 239 NLRB, No. 20, October 31, 1978," December 27, 1978, box 9, folder 1, CLUW Collection.

69. Paul Jennings to IUE District Presidents, May 25, 1973, box 218, group 2, IUE Archives.

70. Winn Newman to Paul Jennings and Dave Fitzmaurice, January 23, 1975, box 156, group 2, IUE Archives.

71. Typescript, Winn Newman, Report to IUE IEB, July 27, 1975, box 156, group 2, IUE Archives.

72. Winn Newman to Paul Jennings, Dave Fitzmaurice, and William Brady, January 14, 1975, box 156, group 2, IUE Archives.

73. Winn Newman to Paul Jennings, November 21, 1975, box 156, group 2, IUE Archives.

74. Winn Newman to Paul Jennings, November 10, 1975, box 156, group 2, IUE Archives.

75. Typescript, Winn Newman, Report to IUE IEB, July 27, 1975, box 156, group 2. Newman reported that the 36,000-member Tobacco Workers' union shelled out $300,000 in back pay and $225,691 in outside counsel fees; the Steelworkers were ordered to pay $4 million plus a share of the $30.9 million to be paid by the steel industry as a result of guilty verdicts in discrimination cases.

76. For an example of the legal department's farming-out of cases, see Ruth Weyand to Jane M. Picker, box 239, group 2, IUE Archives. Newman worried that social action department members would not be able to handle compliance work "since so much of the work has moved from program and policy to the legal phase"; he was concerned that a "certain amount of duplication" would occur as well. See Winn Newman to Paul Jennings, December 9, 1975, box 156, group 2, IUE Archives.

77. Winn Newman to Peter S. diCicco, August 4, 1975, box 156, group 2, IUE Archives.

78. Winn Newman and Boren Chertkov to Paul Jennings and David Fitzmaurice, March 6, 1975, box 156, group 2, IUE Archives. The IUE local in Bristol, Connecticut—

found to be in violation of Title VII for maintaining separate seniority lists for men and women (see EEOC Decision, Case No. 5-10-2423, *Owns v. Ingraham*, January 20, 1966 [conciliated], box 5, folder 36, DCR Collection)—was again charged with the same discrimination in the 1970s. See Winn Newman to Paul Jennings, February 18, 1975, box 170, group 2, IUE Archives.

79. See, for example, *IUE v. Westinghouse*, 14 FEP Cases 950 and *Crawford v. GE* (Local 731, Memphis, Tenn.). Employers tried to convince the EEOC that the union should be named as defendant in several cases (e.g., Winn Newman and Ruth Weyand to Paul Jennings et al., September 9, 1975, box 156, group 2, IUE Archives); they even attempted to get IUE leaders to accept and defend discriminatory contracts, a recommendation rejected firmly by the union. "GE was caught with its pants down and now you are worried," assistant IUE counsel Robert Friedman lectured GE negotiators in 1973. See Transcript, IUE-GE Negotiations, April 12, 1973, box 218, group 2, IUE Archives.

80. Winn Newman to Abner Sibal, June 30, 1976, box 33, DCR Collection. See William A. Carey to Winn Newman, December 28, 1973, box 5, folder 42, DCR Collection for the EEOC's opinion that calling a strike over discrimination in contracts was not required. The announcement of the EEOC filing this case is found in Philip Shabecoff, "Job Bias Charged to 4 Companies and Major Unions," *New York Times*, September 18, 1973.

81. Quoted in Herbert Hill, "The Equal Employment Opportunity Acts of 1964 and 1972: A Critical Analysis of the Legislative History and Administration of the Law," *Industrial Relations Law Journal* 2 (September 1977): 63–64. See also, Benjamin W. Wolkinson, *Blacks, Unions, and the EEOC: A Study of Administrative Futility* (Lexington, Mass.: Lexington Books, 1973), especially pp. 18–20.

82. Industrial Relations Research Association, *Proceedings, Twenty-Fifth Anniversary Meeting* (Toronto, 1972), p. 376.

83. EEOC, *Hearings* (1980), pp. 48–49. Newman could exaggerate on occasion. He told the EEOC in 1976, for example, that when the union formed in 1949, "terms and conditions of employment for employees . . . had already been set." Winn Newman to Abner Sibal, June 30, 1976, box 33, DCR Collection. This, however, does not account for the varied and changing seniority practices at the local level where married women in some plants faced discriminatory layoff. See Agreement, Between Philco Corp., Sandusky, Ohio, and International Union of Electrical, Radio and Machine Workers, AFL-CIO, Local 701, box 175, group 1, IUE Archives, and Mark McColloch, "The Shop-Floor Dimension of Union Rivalry: The Case of Westinghouse in the 1950s," *The CIO's Left-Led Unions*, ed. Steve Rosswurm (New Brunswick, N.J.: Rutgers University Press, 1992), pp. 195–96.

84. Winn Newman to Abner Sibal, June 30, 1976, box 33, DCR Collection.

85. Newman and Wilson, pp. 338–39.

86. U.S. Equal Employment Opportunity Commission, *Hearings on Job Segregation and Wage Discrimination, Hearings before the Equal Employment Opportunity Commission*, 1980, p. 52. On the union's Title VII related court activity, in general, see Karen O'Connor, *Women's Organizations' Use of the Courts* (Lexington, Mass.: Lexington Books, 1980), pp.

114–15; Susan M. Hartmann, *From Margin to Mainstream: American Women and Politics since 1960* (Philadelphia: Temple University Press, 1989), pp. 100, 115; Karen J. Maschke, *Litigation, Courts, and Women Workers* (New York: Praeger, 1989), p. 87; Newman and Wilson, pp. 323–31.

87. Winn Newman to All IUE Local Union Presidents, October 15, 1975, box 156, group 2, IUE Archives. On at least one occasion, Newman wanted the IUE to join another union's suit that promised better back pay than the IUE's pending case. In 1975 he suggested to Jennings that the union give "serious consideration" to joining a UE suit against GE for pay equity; the UE's action—filed four years before the IUE's charge—would bring substantially greater compensation to the plaintiffs. See Winn Newman to Paul Jennings, June 16, 1975, box 156, group 2, IUE Archives.

88. Winn Newman to Abner Sibal, June 30, 1976, box 33, DCR Collection.

89. Even before the initiation of their compliance program, IUE leaders had filed pregnancy discrimination cases in the late 1960s and early 1970s. See, for example, *Kupczyk v. Westinghouse,* New York SDHR Case No. CSF 15206-67, March 3, 1969; Winn Newman to Abner Sibal, June 30, 1976, box 33, DCR Collection. The IUE also filed *amicus curiae* briefs on the matter. See *Cleveland Board of Education v. LaFleur,* 414 U.S. 631 (1974); *Aiello v. Geduldig,* 94 S. Ct. 2485 (1974); IUE, *Proceedings: Officers' Report* (1976), p. 578; Newman and Wilson, p. 328; Joan Hoff, *Law, Gender, and Injustice: A Legal History of U.S. Women* (New York: New York University Press, 1991), p. 294.

90. *GE v. Gilbert,* 429 U.S. 125 (1976).

91. Newman and Wilson, p. 329; Hoff, p. 297.

92. Newman and Wilson, pp. 334–35.

93. IUE, *Proceedings* (1972), p. 87.

94. Lisa Portman, Joy Ann Grunne, and Eve Johnson, "The Role of Labor," in *Comparable Worth and Wage Discrimination: Technical Possibilities and Political Realities,* ed. Helen Remick (Philadelphia: Temple University Press, 1984), p. 223. For background discussion, see Alice Kessler-Harris, *A Woman's Wage: Historical Meanings and Social Consequences* (Lexington: University Press of Kentucky, 1990), pp. 113–29.

95. Newman and Wilson, pp. 331–33. See also, Richard B. Freeman and Jonathan S. Leonard, "Union Maids: Unions and the Female Labor Force," in *Gender in the Workplace,* ed. Clair Brown and Joseph A. Pechman (Washington, D.C.: Brookings Institution, 1987), p. 205, and Norma M. Riccucci, *Women, Minorities, and Unions in the Public Sector* (Westport, Conn.: Greenwood, 1990), pp. 144, 148.

96. Gloria Johnson, "Comments," in *Women and Unions: Forging a Partnership,* ed. Dorothy Sue Cobble (Ithaca, N.Y.: ILR Press, 1993), p. 97.

97. Gould, p. 405.

98. IUE Social Action Department, *Newsletter* 5, no. 3, July–August 1975, box 156, group 2, IUE Archives; IUE, *Proceedings* (1974), pp. 180–81, 411.

99. IUE, *Proceedings* (1974), pp. 180–81; Gloria Johnson to Paul Jennings, January 8, 1976, and Bill Gary to Paul Jennings, May 14, 1975, both in box 156, group 2, IUE Archives.

100. Bill Gary to Paul Jennings, May 14, 1975, box 156, group 2, IUE Archives.

101. Marion M. Cook to Paul Jennings, December 10, 1974, box 175, group 2, IUE Archives.

102. Charlotte H. Ingalls to President Jennings, April 7, 1975, box 175, group 2, IUE Archives.

103. Johnson and Komer, p. 208.

104. Stan Gray, "Sharing the Shop Floor: Women and Men on the Assembly Line," *Radical America* 18, no. 5 (September/October 1984): 70–71.

105. Gloria Johnson, interview, Reuther Archives.

106. Clipping, *Philadelphia Inquirer,* January 29, 1974, box 1, folder 5, CLUW Collection.

107. Agenda Committee to National Conference Planning Committee, January 18, 1974, box 1, folder 1, CLUW Collection; Mary Callahan, interview by Alice M. Hoffman and Karen Budd, Philadelphia, Pa., May 7, 1976, Twentieth Century Trade Union Women: Vehicle for Social Change, Oral History Project, Institute of Labor and Industrial Relations, University of Michigan/Wayne State University, Detroit, Mich. (hereafter, Twentieth Century Trade Union Women Project); Joyce Miller to CLUW officers, August 7, 1974, box 1, folder 4 and CLUW *News* 1, no. 1 (Winter 1975), box 13, folder 1, both in CLUW Collection; Glick, pp. 354–57. Johnson became CLUW president in 1993. The union backed the CLUW, officially. See IUE, *Proceedings* (1974), p. 183, and *Proceedings* (1976), p. 64.

108. International Union of Electrical Workers, AFL-CIO, *Proceedings, Nineteenth Constitutional Convention* (Detroit, Mich., 1980), pp. 179–80.

109. Clipping, EEOC News, "EEOC Posthumously Honors Civil Rights Advocate Ruth Weyand," November 25, 1986, clipping files, Schlesinger Library, Radcliffe College, Cambridge, Mass.

110. Judy Mann, "A Gentleman and a Lawyer," *Washington Post,* July 8, 1994, p. E-3.

111. Callahan interview, Twentieth Century Trade Union Women Project.

Conclusion

1. Ruth Milkman, "Women Workers, Feminism, and the Labor Movement," in *Women, Work, and Protest: A Century of U.S. Women's Labor History,* ed. Milkman (New York: Routledge and Kegan Paul, 1985), p. 304; Ruth Needleman, "Raising Visibility, Reducing Marginality: A Labor Law Reform Agenda for Working Women of Color," paper presented for the U.S. Department of Labor, Women's Bureau, October 1993, p. 17 (ms in author's possession); Linda M. Blum, *Between Feminism and Labor: The Significance of the Comparable Worth Movement* (Berkeley: University of California Press, 1991), p. 43 n. 23.

2. Clipping, unidentified newswpaper, n.s., n.d. [1975], Olga Madar note, box 7, folder 9, Coalition of Labor Union Women Collection, Walter Reuther Archives of Labor History and Urban Affairs, Wayne State University, Detroit, Mich. (hereafter, CLUW Collection).

3. Nancy F. Gabin, *Feminism in the Labor Movement: Women and the United Auto Workers, 1935–1975* (Ithaca, N.Y.: Cornell University Press, 1990), p. 231.

4. Dorothy Sue Cobble, "Introduction: Remaking Unions for the New Majority," in *Women and Unions: Forging a Partnership,* ed. Cobble (Ithaca, N.Y.: ILR Press, 1993), pp. 9–10. On the significant wage differentials by race and sex between the union and non-union work force, see Farrell E. Bloch, "Discrimination in Nonreferral Unions," in *Equal Rights and Industrial Relations,* ed. Leonard Hausman et al. (Madison, Wis.: Industrial Relations Research Association, 1977), p. 116.

5. Lucille Bremer, interview by Merle Davis, Waterloo, June 2, 1982, Iowa Labor History Oral Project, State Historical Society of Iowa, Iowa City, Iowa.

6. See Paula Ries and Anne J. Stone, eds., *The American Woman, 1992–93: A Status Report* (New York: Norton, 1992).

7. William Pollard to Civil Rights Committee, December 8, 1975, box 32, AFL-CIO Department of Civil Rights Collection, George Meany Memorial Archives, Silver Spring, Md. (hereafter, DCR Collection). See also, Alfred W. Blumrosen and Ruth G. Blumrosen, "Layoff or Work Sharing: The Civil Rights Act of 1964 in the Recession of 1975," *Civil Rights Digest* 7, no. 3 (Spring 1975): 35–40.

8. Typescript, [Winn Newman], March 27, 1975, box 156, group 2, International Union of Electrical Workers Collection, Rutgers University Library, New Brunswick, N.J. (hereafter, IUE Archives). On the EEOC's plan, see U.S. Department of Labor, *Daily Labor Reports,* no. 58, March 25, 1975, box 156, group 2, IUE Archives.

9. Robert Friedman to Winn Newman, July 23, 1975, box 156, group 2, IUE Archives.

10. Quoted in an unidentified press clipping, n.d. [1975], box 14, folder 11, CLUW Collection. For the CLUW's official statement against violating seniority in layoff, see CLUW *News* 1, no. 2 (Summer 1975), box 13, folder 1, CLUW Collection.

11. Olga Madar to Jerry Parsh, March 17, 1975, box 14, folder 11, CLUW Collection.

12. Olga Madar to Karen DeCrow, May 5, 1975, box 14, folder 12, CLUW Collection. Not all CLUW women opposed preferential layoff. See Philip S. Foner, *Women and the American Labor Movement: From World War I to the Present* (New York: Free Press, 1980), p. 526.

13. Catherine Conroy, interview by Elizabeth Balanoff, August/December 1976, Milwaukee, Wis., Twentieth Century Trade Union Women: Vehicle for Social Change, Oral History project, Institute of Labor and Industrial Relations, University of Michigan/Wayne State University, Detroit, Mich. (hereafter, Twentieth Century Trade Union Women Project).

14. Eileen Shanahan, "Union Women Hold Mainstream Course," *New York Times,* December 8, 1975, p. 39.

15. Fannie Neal, interview by Marlene Hunt Rikard, unknown location, May 27, 1977, Twentieth Century Trade Union Women Project.

16. *Franks v. Bowman Transportation Co.,* 96 S. Ct. 1251 (1976).

17. William E. Pollard to Civil Rights Committee, September 21, 1976, box 32, DCR Collection.

18. *IBT v. U.S.,* 431 S. Ct. 353-54 (1977).

19. For union records on the dismal AFL-CIO–EEOC relationship, see for example,

William E. Pollard to Don Slaiman, September 9, 1971, and January 25, 1971, both in box 32, DCR Collection; Gloria Johnson, interview by Dennis Deslippe, Washington, D.C., June 8, 1993, Walter Reuther Archives of Labor History and Urban Affairs, Wayne State University, Detroit, Mich. (hereafter, Reuther Archives). On Eleanor Holmes Norton's changes affecting labor unions, see Eleanor Holmes Norton to William Pollard, February 2, 1978, box 33; Eleanor Holmes Norton to Thomas Donahue, April 15, 1980, box 33; and William E. Pollard to Civil Rights Committee, January 22, 1981, box 32, all in DCR Collection.

20. Testimony of Winn Newman, U.S. Congress, Senate, Committee on Labor and Human Resources, *Sex Discrimination in the Workplace, 1981: Hearings: Before the Committee on Labor and Human Resources, U.S. Senate*, 97th Cong., 1st sess., 1981, p. 213. See also, Peggy Lamson, "Eleanor Holmes Norton Reforms the Equal Employment Opportunity Commission," in *Women Leaders in American Politics*, ed. James David Barber and Barbara Kellerman (Englewood Cliffs, N.J.: Prentice-Hall, 1986), pp. 340–44.

21. Phyllis S. Glick, "Bridging Feminism and Trade Unionism: A Study of Working Women's Organizing in the United States" (Ph.D. diss., Brandeis University, 1983), pp. 347, 351–52; Minutes, CLUW National Officers Council Meeting, August 28, 1979, box 14, folder 6, and typescript, Resolutions Passed, 1977 Convention, box 11, folder 10, both in CLUW Collection.

22. Lucy Komisar, "Where Feminism Will Lead: An Impetus for Social Change," *Civil Rights Digest* 6, no. 3 (Spring 1974): 9.

23. Glick, p. 385. See also, Cobble, "Introduction," p. 4.

24. Claudia Goldin, *Understanding the Gender Gap: An Economic History of American Women* (New York: Oxford University Press, 1990), pp. 58, 212–17; Brigid O'Farrell and Suzanne Moore, "Unions, Hard Hats, and Women Workers," in *Women and Unions: Forging a Partnership*, ed. Dorothy Sue Cobble (Ithaca, N.Y.: ILR Press, 1993), p. 70; Andrea H. Beller, "The Effects on Women's Earnings of Enforcement in Title VII Cases," *Monthly Labor Review* 100, no. 3 (March 1977): 56–57. Bellar reports that enforcement of sex discrimination bans during 1967–74 caused women's earnings in 1974 to be 4.7 percent higher than they otherwise would have been; she characterized Title VII as having a "significant impact" on women's earnings but her study considers only a short time period.

25. Sonia Pressman Fuentes, interview by Dennis Deslippe, Potomac, Md., November 23, 1993, Reuther Archives.

26. See Susan H. Hartmann, *From Margin to Mainstream: American Women and Politics since 1960* (Philadelphia: Temple University Press, 1989), especially chapters 5–7.

27. Sara M. Evans and Barbara J. Nelson, *Wage Justice: Comparable Worth and the Paradox of Technocratic Reform* (Chicago: University of Chicago Press, 1989), pp. 29–37; Ann Snitow, "Pages from a Gender Diary: Basic Divisions in Feminism," *Dissent* (Spring 1989): 213–15, 223–24 n. 20; Glick, pp. 313–14.

28. Testimony of Georgianna Sellers (for the League for American Working Women), U.S. Congress, Senate, Committee on the Judiciary, *The "Equal Rights" Amendment: Hearings, before the Committee on the Judiciary*, 91st Cong., 2d sess., May 1970, p. 577.

Index

DENNIS A. DESLIPPE is a lecturer in the Department of History of
the Australian National University, Canberra.

Worker City, Company Town: Iron and Cotton-Worker Protest in Troy
and Cohoes, New York, 1855–84   *Daniel J. Walkowitz*
Life, Work, and Rebellion in the Coal Fields: The Southern West
Virginia Miners, 1880–1922   *David Alan Corbin*
Women and American Socialism, 1870–1920   *Mari Jo Buhle*
Lives of Their Own: Blacks, Italians, and Poles in Pittsburgh,
1900–1960   *John Bodnar, Roger Simon, and Michael P. Weber*
Working-Class America: Essays on Labor, Community, and American
Society   *Edited by Michael H. Frisch and Daniel J. Walkowitz*
Eugene V. Debs: Citizen and Socialist   *Nick Salvatore*
American Labor and Immigration History, 1877–1920s: Recent European
Research   *Edited by Dirk Hoerder*
Workingmen's Democracy: The Knights of Labor and American
Politics   *Leon Fink*
The Electrical Workers: A History of Labor at General Electric and
Westinghouse, 1923–60   *Ronald W. Schatz*
The Mechanics of Baltimore: Workers and Politics in the Age of Revolu-
tion, 1763–1812   *Charles G. Steffen*
The Practice of Solidarity: American Hat Finishers in the Nineteenth
Century   *David Bensman*
The Labor History Reader   *Edited by Daniel J. Leab*
Solidarity and Fragmentation: Working People and Class Consciousness
in Detroit, 1875–1900   *Richard Oestreicher*
Counter Cultures: Saleswomen, Managers, and Customers in American
Department Stores, 1890–1940   *Susan Porter Benson*
The New England Working Class and the New Labor History   *Edited
by Herbert G. Gutman and Donald H. Bell*
Labor Leaders in America   *Edited by Melvyn Dubofsky and
Warren Van Tine*
Barons of Labor: The San Francisco Building Trades and Union Power in
the Progressive Era   *Michael Kazin*
Gender at Work: The Dynamics of Job Segregation by Sex during World
War II   *Ruth Milkman*
Once a Cigar Maker: Men, Women, and Work Culture in American
Cigar Factories, 1900–1919   *Patricia A. Cooper*
A Generation of Boomers: The Pattern of Railroad Labor Conflict in
Nineteenth-Century America   *Shelton Stromquist*
Work and Community in the Jungle: Chicago's Packinghouse Workers,
1894–1922   *James R. Barrett*

The Female Economy: The Millinery and Dressmaking Trades, 1860–
1930   *Wendy Gamber*
"Negro and White, Unite and Fight!": A Social History of Industrial
Unionism in Meatpacking, 1930–90   *Roger Horowitz*
Power at Odds: The 1922 National Railroad Shopmen's Strike
Colin J. Davis
The Common Ground of Womanhood: Class, Gender, and Working
Girls' Clubs, 1884–1928   *Priscilla Murolo*
Marching Together: Women of the Brotherhood of Sleeping Car
Porters   *Melinda Chateauvert*
Down on the Killing Floor: Black and White Workers in Chicago's
Packinghouses, 1904–54   *Rick Halpern*
Labor and Urban Politics: Class Conflict and the Origins of Modern
Liberalism in Chicago, 1864–97   *Richard Schneirov*
All That Glitters: Class, Conflict, and Community in Cripple
Creek   *Elizabeth Jameson*
Waterfront Workers: New Perspectives on Race and Class   *Edited by*
Calvin Winslow
Labor Histories: Class, Politics, and the Working-Class
Experience   *Edited by Eric Arnesen, Julie Greene, and Bruce Laurie*
The Pullman Strike and the Crisis of the 1890s: Essays on Labor and
Politics   *Edited by Richard Schneirov, Shelton Stromquist, and*
Nick Salvatore
AlabamaNorth: African-American Migrants, Community, and Working-
Class Activism in Cleveland, 1914–45   *Kimberley L. Phillips*
Imagining Internationalism in American and British Labor,
1939–49   *Victor Silverman*
William Z. Foster and the Tragedy of American Radicalism
James R. Barrett
Colliers across the Sea: A Comparative Study of Class Formation in
Scotland and the American Midwest, 1830–1924   *John H. M. Laslett*
"Rights, Not Roses": Unions and the Rise of Working-Class Feminism,
1945–80   *Dennis A. Deslippe*

Typeset in 10.5/13 Adobe Garamond
with Garamond display
Designed by Dennis Roberts
Composed by Jim Proefrock
at the University of Illinois Press
Manufactured by Cushing-Malloy, Inc.

University of Illinois Press
1325 South Oak Street
Champaign, IL 61820–6903
www.press.uillinois.edu